EVENT PLANNING

Communicating Theory & Practice

Second Edition

Leeanne Bell McManus
Chip Rouse
Stephanie Verni

Kendall Hunt
publishing company

Book Team

Chairman and Chief Executive Officer   Mark C. Falb
President and Chief Operating Officer   Chad M. Chandlee
Vice President, Higher Education   David L. Tart
Director of Publishing Partnerships   Paul B. Carty
Senior Developmental Coordinator   Angela Willenbring
Vice President, Operations   Timothy J. Beitzel
Senior Production Editor   Sheri Hosek
Permissions Editor   Brianna Jentz Kirschbaum
Cover Designer   Heather Richman

Cover © Shutterstock.com

www.kendallhunt.com
Send all inquiries to:
4050 Westmark Drive
Dubuque, IA 52004-1840

Printed in the United States of America

BRIEF CONTENTS

CONTENTS

PREFACE

Event Planning: Communicating Theory & Practice, 2nd edition, offers a unique approach that connects concepts in communication to practical event planning ideas. Understanding the "why" behind successful events is fundamental to creating unique and successful experiences for companies, organizations, or clients. With a solid basis in communication theory, along with two new chapters that cover best practices in hospitality and event tourism, this text will enable students to manage each aspect of the planning cycle. Exemplary case studies from experts in the field, combined with thought-provoking activities and insightful text, will help students understand what it takes to succeed in a career as an event planner.

One case in point: in 2018, when the Eastern Communication Association held its annual convention in Pittsburgh, we were fortunate to be able to work with our students who helped us execute a very successful conference. The experience taught us that students could acquire the "how to" skills quickly, but often asked us why we wanted them to respond or behave in a certain way. Though they had taken many communication courses during their college years, they did not necessarily make the connection between the theories they studied and the practice of event planning. The idea for the first edition of the text came out of our experience working with the Eastern Communication Association, and has been reinforced in any number of on-campus events that students have helped to create and run since that convention. Since the first edition, we have worked with professionals in the hospitality field, and saw the need to bridge the gap between that field and event planning in this second edition. In addition, the explosion of tourism events around the world demanded that we inform students of the many opportunities in the tourism industry.

The event planning field has grown enormously in the last decade, and the United States Department of Labor has indicated that the number of meeting planner jobs will jump 11 percent in the next decade. The number of events—both corporate and private—continues to rise, and future event planners must be prepared for a variety of opportunities in the field. Event planning is a multi-billion dollar industry, one that will continue in the direction of rapid growth. The International Institute of Event Management notes that tens of millions of events take place each year across the world. Based upon these indicators, the need for competent communicators in the event planning industry warrants the publication of a book of this sort. While many companies talk about the need for "tools of the trade," it is rare to see them talk about communication theory as the basis of their success. Yet the intersection of communication theory and event planning helps specifically to explain the basis of human interactions that take place at every convention, every social event, and every corporate meeting.

Throughout the book, each chapter begins with a case study and offers various examples of events that will connect specific abilities to the field of communication, based on the fact that those in the industry must be able to send clear and persuasive messages. From brainstorming with clients on an event theme, to working out logistics with a sound system vendor, to conducting site feasibility studies, event planners depend upon their ability to send clear messages. Thus, communication is the most basic commonality among event planners. This book helps students understand how to communicate in each situation, and how to tailor their messages to those participating in each event.

ACKNOWLEDGMENTS

I, Leeanne M. Bell McManus, am deeply thankful to my co-authors, Chip Rouse and Stephanie Verni, who made this project an enjoyable learning experience. Additionally, my mentors, Ronald C. Arnett and Janie Harden Fritz, have shared their advice, knowledge, and support throughout my academic career, and I am forever grateful for their guidance and friendship. I dedicate this work to my family: Mark, Bella, and Elouise, and my parents, Gary and Darlene Bell, for their patience and persistent belief in me.

I, Chip Rouse, would like to thank my extraordinary colleagues, Leeanne M. Bell McManus and Stephanie Verni, for their unwavering commitment to this project and for their encouragement throughout the process. I have basked in the light of their creativity and knowledge and grown through the experience. I would also like to thank my son, Bryan Read, though he's no longer with us, for his encouragement and praise, and the rest of my family for their interest in and support for our work. Finally, I would like to thank our professional colleagues who offered us great inspiration along the way to completion.

I, Stephanie Verni, would like to express my gratitude to my exceptional colleagues, Leeanne M. Bell McManus and Chip Rouse, for their creativity, talents, and knowledge about the subject of event planning and dedication to this project. I would also like to thank my incredibly supportive family, including my husband, Anthony, and my children, Matt and Ellie, along with my parents, Leni and Doug Parrillo, for always encouraging me to tackle new endeavors. Finally, I would like to thank both my current and former colleagues, from whom I have learned much.

We would like to thank everyone who made this project possible. Paul Carty, Director of Publishing Partnerships; Angela Willenbring, Senior Developmental Coordinator; and Sheri Hosek, Senior Production Editor (Kendall Hunt Publishing) offered continual guidance and encouragement throughout this project.

We offer our gratitude to the Stevenson University community and to our colleagues in the Department of Communication for their support of this project and their enthusiasm for our work.

The research in the book is supported by the wonderful professionals in the field who shared their interesting and informative case studies with us. We thank the following contributors:

Candice Thomas-Maddox, Ed.D., Professor of Communication, Ohio University, Lancaster
Nancy J. Willets, Department Chair of Arts & Communication, Cape Cod Community College
Janie Harden Fritz, Ph.D., Professor of Communication & Rhetorical Studies, Duquesne University
Kristen Schultz, Director, Community Relations and Promotions, Baltimore Orioles

Linda Paris, Senior Sales Manager, Omni William Penn, Pittsburgh

Charles Steinberg, President, Pawtucket Red Sox

Corrin Harris, Lifestyle Manager, CCMC

Lynn H. Turner, Ph.D., Professor, Communication Studies, Marquette University

Stacey Haines, President, Earl Beckwith and Associates

Elle Ellinghaus, Owner, Elle Ellinghaus Designs

Morgan Cook, Senior Director of Women's Athletics, Corrigan Sports Enterprises

Jeanne M. Persuit, Ph.D., Associate Professor, Communication Studies, University of North Carolina, Wilmington

Angie Corbo, Ph.D., Chair and Associate Professor, Widener University

Rosalind Healy, Chief of Staff, Baltimore Office of Promotion & the Arts

Chris Daley, Principal and Founder, Whirlaway

Edie Brown, Principal, Edie Brown and Associates

Sandy Hillman, President, Sandy Hillman Communications

Matt Musgrove, CEO & President, Padonia Park Club

Julie Wagner, Vice President, Community Affairs, CareFirst BlueCross BlueShield

Paul Wolman, Principal, WolmanEdge

ABOUT THE AUTHORS

Leeanne M. Bell McManus, professor in the Business Communication department at Stevenson University, received her Ph.D. in Rhetoric from Duquesne University and her M.A. in Communication Studies from West Virginia University. She has co-authored three books, *Communication ethics literacy: Dialogue and difference* (1st & 2nd ed.) (Kendall Hunt, 2017/2018), *Conflict between persons: The origins of leadership* (1st & 2nd) (Kendall Hunt, 2014/2018) and *Event planning: Communicating theory and action* (Kendall Hunt, 2016/2019). She has also published excerpts in *Exploring communication ethics: Interviews with influential scholars in the field, The encyclopedia of social identity, The encyclopedia of communication ethics, and Integrated marketing communication: Creating space for engagement.* Dr. Bell McManus has published in *Atlantic Journal of Communication, Communication Education, Journal of Communication Administration, Review of Communication,* and *Communication Annual: Journal of the Pennsylvania Communication Association.* She is a member of the National Communication Association, the Eastern Communication Association and the Southern Communication Association. At the national level, she was the chair of the Communication Ethics Division, and at the regional level, she is the Past President. She was named Teacher of the Year (2014–2015) by the Public Relations Society of America, Maryland Chapter, and a Teaching Fellow (2019) by the Eastern Communication Association. She teaches and conducts research in event planning, public relations, conflict, leadership, communication ethics, and instructional communication.

Chip Rouse, associate professor in the Communication department at Stevenson University, has taught writing for over four decades and served as department chair of the Business Communication major for 15 years. She has been the faculty advisor to the student newspaper at the university for 25 years, during which time the news site went from paper to completely online. She has a decade of event planning and management experience as well at a private club in Maryland. She is a member of the College Media Association, the Associated Collegiate Press, the Journalism Education Association, and the Eastern Communication Association. She has Masters degrees from the University of Maryland and Loyola University of Maryland and has focused her current research in the fields of event planning and out-of-class communication.

Stephanie (Parrillo) Verni, professor in the Department of Communication at Stevenson University, instructs writing and communication courses. As part of Stevenson's new Center for Teaching and Learning, she was named a Teaching Fellow in 2019. She serves as the advisor to the communication club at the university, and was previously a member of two academic boards. Prior to working in academia, Stephanie spent 13 years with the Baltimore Orioles baseball team, where she worked in public relations, community relations, and then served as director of publishing. During her time working in baseball, Stephanie was a member of the events team and planned many large-scale events for the ballclub, including the closing of Memorial Stadium, the opening of Oriole Park at Camden Yards, All-Star Week, and Streak Week in celebration of Cal Ripken, Jr.'s consecutive games streak record, whereby he surpassed Lou Gehrig's long-standing record. After leaving the Orioles, Stephanie spent time at the *Baltimore Sun* as the creative services manager before managing her own consulting firm. On the side, Stephanie has authored five works of fiction, including the following: *Beneath the Mimosa Tree* (2012), *Baseball Girl* (2015), *Inn Significant* (2017), *The Postcard and Other Short Stories & Poetry* (2017), and *Little Milestones* (2019).

Chapter 1

COMMUNICATION: THE SECRET TO SUCCESS IN EVENT PLANNING

The ability to work with all involved in producing an event requires that the event planner have a keen ability to navigate all aspects of the job, including communicating ideas, concepts, and tactics. This chapter connects the art of event planning to the study of communication practices. The event planning business is a multi-billion-dollar industry that has grown tremendously over the last decade, and events such as fundraisers, receptions, and galas are becoming commonplace in today's society (Allen, 2009; Goldblatt, 2014; Jackson, Morgan, & Laws, 2018). As the field continues to grow and evolve, the responsibilities of the event planner broaden. Even though skills of the planner can range from designing an elaborate wedding to budgeting a corporate retreat in Las Vegas, one imperative skill is communication.

The best event planners realize how important communication skills are in their professional field, and they understand that a thorough and knowledgeable grasp of the characteristics of competent communication is not just a relevant skill but also an absolute necessity. Communication is a powerful tool that creates and shapes your social world (Pearce, 1994). Through communication, you create meaning with others and are able to understand the world in which you live. By studying communication, you will see the world from a different perspective and understand the reasons why communication is a needed skill in all aspects of your life (Littlejohn, 2002).

When you have finished reading this chapter, you will be able to

- define the term *event planning*;
- explain the job characteristics and responsibilities of the event planner;
- distinguish among the different types of events;
- describe the relationship between communication and event planning;
- outline the major components of dialogue in communication encounters.

Communication: The Key to Planning a Convention from a Distance

Candice Thomas-Maddox, Ed.D., Professor of Communication Studies, Ohio University, Lancaster

Whether you are planning a charity fundraiser, a concert, an athletic event, or a conference, a comprehensive communication plan is the key to your success. Most new event planners are excited by the prospect of utilizing their creativity to host an experience that attendees praise on social media. Creating a comprehensive communication plan will ensure that you are ready to manage whatever situations arise throughout the planning and hosting of your event. Consider this analogy: a coach would never dream of sending a team onto the field without having a game plan. The plan is carefully crafted, analyzed, and communicated so every player knows what is expected. Why devote countless hours to planning decor and arranging for entertainment without giving careful consideration to your event game plan, also known as your communication plan?

The need for a comprehensive communication plan was evident when planning the 100th anniversary convention of the Eastern Communication Association (ECA). While this historical event took place in Philadelphia in April 2009, preparations began years in advance. A unique challenge in planning this event was the geographical distance that separated those responsible for the preparations. Those who were charged with planning the events lived in different cities across the East Coast. To compensate for the hundreds of miles that separated them in the time leading up to the event, they utilized multiple communication channels to ensure effective communication.

During initial planning meetings, officers began brainstorming and sharing their visions for this historical occasion. The event coordinator created an online forum for sharing ideas. Discussions and deliberations for narrowing down the vast number of suggestions were carefully monitored on the discussion board to ensure that everyone's input was received, and processes for decision-making via email were created. The organization's historian was consulted to secure written records and archived photographs from the first convention, as well as from the 50th and 75th celebrations. As plans progressed, committees were formed to address specific aspects of the event. One group organized a competition in which students designed the convention logo, and another team was assigned the task of producing a video in which past officers shared their ECA memories. Additional committees focused their energy on coordinating the multiple events that would take place during the four-day celebration. A book-signing party, an awards luncheon, and a Presidents' Reception are just a few of the events that required committees to communicate with one another and with the convention coordinator. Event marketing utilized websites, email, print materials, and promotional giveaways in the year leading up to the convention to generate excitement.

Early in the process, email and phone rosters helped to ensure that planners had easy access to one another's contact information. Members of the event planning team received event manuals with checklists and deadlines a year prior to the convention to ensure that expectations were clearly outlined. Faculty and students from colleges in the Philadelphia area met with local florists, caterers, and photographers to finalize logistical details. Yet despite all of the careful coordination and communication efforts, details still "slipped through the cracks." Three weeks prior to the convention, the event coordinator received an email from one of the local venues selected for a reception, requiring a copy of the organization's liability insurance policy in order to host the event at the site. No such policy existed, and after many phone calls to the organization's officers, an attorney, and insurance agencies, the coordinator secured the required documentation. However, the confusion associated with the insurance issue threw other plans off track. On the morning of a pre-conference event, the coordinator discovered that she had neglected to place the luncheon order with hotel catering. Because she had established a good relationship with the hotel sales manager in the months leading up to the event, the hotel's sales team was able to resolve the issue quickly and coordinate the delivery of a Mexican buffet just in time for lunch. While the convention team probably has numerous stories of things that went wrong during the event, their dedication to effective communication ensured that attendees were unaware of these glitches.

Contributed by Candice Thomas-Maddox. Copyright © Kendall Hunt Publishing Company.

After reading this chapter, revisit the case study and respond to the following question:

Why is it important to have a communication plan for your event?

Event Planning

Events are common occurrences within various cultures and societies (Allen, O'Toole, Harris, & McDonnell, 2010; Getz, 1997, 2007; Jackson, Morgan, & Laws, 2018; Robson, 2011; Rogers, 2003), generating revenue and jobs in the economy (Higham & Ritchie, 2001; Lee, 2006; Weber & Ladkin, 2009), and producing some type of outcome (Goldblatt, 2014). The word *event* comes from the Latin word "e-venire," meaning outcome. Bladen, Kennell, Abson, and Wilde (2012) define an event as a "temporary and purposive gathering of people" (p. 3). Similarly, Dowson and Bassett (2015) define an event as a "planned gathering that is temporary and memorable" (p. 2), and Getz (2007) highlights the importance of an event being both noteworthy and unique. Events take place every day

Events: *Common occurrences within various cultures and societies generating revenue and jobs in the economy*

© bahri altay/Shutterstock.com

at all hours, and behind each event are the individuals who have created it, organized it, executed it, and then followed up afterwards. Occasions such as business meetings, fundraisers, black-tie galas, and sporting events all have someone behind the scenes who is making the decisions about every aspect of what happens. These individuals who work through all the details are often called **event planners**; however, they have many other titles.

Event planners: *Individuals who work through all the details of an event*

Diagram 01. *Alternate titles of event planners*

TIP

Keep in mind what sort of interaction you want to invite with your event. Send messages that invite work, conversation, private meetings, or serendipitous meetings with your arrangement of space.

— Janie Harden Fritz

As the popularity of events increases, the research in the field has continued to grow. In a demographic study of event planners, Robson (2011) found that event planners are "predominantly female, aged 35–44, with less than 15 years of experience, and who see the value of education" (p. 50). However, this does not mean that the field excludes men; many opportunities for men exist, including within the popular event fields of advertising, marketing, and sports. Men who enter the field have many opportunities to find a market niche and earn a lucrative salary (Goldblatt, 2014). Junek, Lockstone, and Mair (2009) discuss how the study of event planning is a growing discipline that creates skills associated with employability. Moreover, Grimaldi (2015) articulates the need for an increase in the number of event planners as companies are seeking help with "everything from site selection to turnkey event management" (para. 1). As more people employ event planners, it is important to recognize why someone would want to hire a planner.

Based on the research of Bailyn (2012) about why people make purchases, clients might hire an event planner for the following reasons: (1) anxiety—hiring an event planner helps relieve stress; (2) desire—hosting an event that a professional has organized makes the event more appealing; (3) ambition—striving to produce an effective event helps clients achieve their goals; (4) guilt—enlisting the help of a professional removes the responsibilities when clients cannot devote the time or energy to produce it effectively; (5) ego—working with an event planner adds an air of prestige to the event; and (6) simplicity—hiring an event planner allows clients the freedom to focus on the other tasks they want to tackle. In order to become a reputable and accomplished event planner whom clients will want to hire, you first need to understand the scope of event planning as a whole and then hone the communication skills needed to be a success in the field. Therefore, examining various definitions of event planning is the logical starting point for discussion.

Definitions of Event Planning

There are many ways to define **event planning**. A first source to consult might be the Cambridge Dictionary (event planning, n.d.), which defines event planning as "the task of planning large events such as conferences, trade shows, and parties." While this definition is true, it does not fully cover the scope and magnitude of what event planning entails. Another definition, created by the International Institute of Event Management (2014), cites the "industry" definition of event planning as follows:

> *Event planning is the process of managing a project such as a meeting, convention, tradeshow, ceremony, team building activity, party, or convention. Event planning includes budgeting, establishing timelines, selecting and reserving the event sites, acquiring permits, planning food, coordinating transportation, developing a theme, arranging for activities, selecting speakers and keynotes, arranging for equipment and facilities, managing risk, and developing contingency plans (para. 2).*

This definition offers an overview of event planning as a whole, and it explains the job more thoroughly and specifically. The International Institute of Event Management (2014) also states that the "official" definition, based on the U.S. Department of Labor, is the following:

© jurgenfr/Shutterstock.com

> *Event Planning consists of coordinating every detail of meetings and conventions, from the speakers and meeting location to arranging for printed materials and audio-visual equipment. Event planning begins with determining the objective that the sponsoring organization wants to achieve. Planners choose speakers, entertainment, and content, and arrange the program to present the organization's information in the most effective way. Meeting planners are responsible for selecting meeting sites, prospective attendees, and how to get them to the meeting (para. 3).*

Event planning: *A communicative process in which a person plans and coordinates the celebration of an occasion or forms a gathering at a specific location where attendees can learn, socialize, conduct business, and/or serve the community*

This definition offers an overview of the depth and breadth of event planning. The skills necessary to succeed as an event planner are incredibly diverse, as seen in an examination of the literature (Allen, 2009; Allen, 2010; Allen et al., 2010; Brown, 2015; Getz, 1997; 2007; Goldblatt, 2014; Rogers, 2003); it is a reminder that events are equally diverse—they are varied and unique, but what grounds all definitions of event planning is the need for a skilled communicator at the threshold (Arcodia & Barker, 2005). After examining various definitions, the authors have created a definition of event planning in which communication is central.

> *Event planning is a communicative process whereby a person creates and coordinates the celebration of an occasion or forms a gathering at a specific location where attendees can learn, socialize, conduct business, and/or serve the community. Those who attend the event typically have a specific purpose that coincides with the overall outcome or goal of the event.*

This definition highlights the purpose of an event planner with the overarching connection to communication. In addition to being strong communicators, event planners also have other responsibilities.

Responsibilities of an Event Planner

The job of an event planner is not a typical 9-to-5 career. According to Carmichael (2006), in a featured article on event planners in *The Wall Street Journal*, planners will typically "work at least 50 hours a week—often on weekends, with odd hours" (para. 2). Moreover, it could take up to 150 hours for an event planner and staff to produce a large-scale event (Carmichael, 2006). Event planning is a complex profession in which the responsibilities are constantly changing, even though it seems as if the main task of the job—planning events—stays the same (Rutherford Silvers, 2012). Each event will offer a unique experience that comes with various tasks, but a common theme that emerges is the event planner's desire to embrace lifelong learning. As an event planner, it is your responsibility to continually learn about the changing trends in the industry. Trends come and go, so it is important to be current regarding the latest techniques that might help make your event a success.

As you try to figure out if this is the career for you, it is important to understand some of the general job characteristics of an event planner. According to the Bureau of Labor Statistics (2017) and the Houston Work Chronicle (Brown, 2015), event planners will find themselves doing most, if not all, of the following tasks:

- Meeting with clients to understand the purpose of the event.
- Communicating the client's vision and reason for the event.
- Planning the scope of the event, including time, location, and cost.
- Organizing people to come together for a common purpose.

- Arranging details that lead up to the event.
- Coordinating displays, audio/visual equipment, and other event needs.
- Soliciting bids from venues and service providers.
- Inspecting venues to ensure that they meet the client's requirements.
- Coordinating event services such as rooms, transportation, and food service.
- Monitoring event activities to ensure the client and event attendees are satisfied.
- Reviewing event bills and approving payment.
- Obtaining various permits.
- Marketing the event as needed.
- Maintaining adequate records for future use.
- Conducting post-event evaluations.
- Reading trade publications.
- Attending educational trainings.

In addition to all of these responsibilities, Goldblatt (2014) states that in the postmodern world of diversity and difference, the event planner needs to be a "trained professional who researches, designs, plans, coordinates, and evaluates" (p. xiii). These tasks give you an overview of the vast array of an event planner's responsibilities. However, each task will vary depending on the type of event.

Types of Events

The event planner must understand the myriad of events that are conducted in today's society (See Table 1). People have been planning and staging events for centuries, both big and small, public and private, social and organizational. Take a look through history and consider examples such as the ancient Greeks and the staging of the Olympics; remember Samuel Adams and the dramatics of the Boston Tea Party. Recall the magnitude of the events that public relations leader Edward Bernays created when he organized the 50-year celebration of Edison's light bulb; and consider Susan G. Komen's numerous fundraising runs across America for breast cancer. All of these events were successful because of someone's ability to communicate a vision for a particular type of event.

TIP

Just because your plan is organized thoroughly on paper, know on "game day" there are many variables that affect your plan that are out of your control: people, weather, traffic, environmental or venue distractions.

— Kristen Schultz

TABLE 1. *Types of Events*		
Business events	**Social events**	**Other**
Board meetings	Anniversaries	Award ceremonies/meals
Business dinners	Baby showers	Banquets
Career fairs	Bachelor/Bachelorette parties	Charity gatherings
Conferences	Birthday parties	Community celebrations
Conventions	Bridal showers	Fashion shows
Corporate retreats	Cocktail parties	Festivals
Expos and exhibitions	Concerts	Fundraisers
Networking events	Dinners	Galas
Press conferences	Family reunions	Graduations
Product launches	Funerals	Opening ceremonies
Sales meetings	Holiday parties	Receptions
Seminars	Religious ceremonies	Retreats
Shareholder meetings	Theme parties	Sporting events/tournaments
Trade shows	Weddings	Workshops

© Brian A Jackson/Shutterstock.com

The number and variety of events have increased dramatically in the past decade. This is reflected in the phenomenal growth of the number of event planners during that time. In 2017, according to the Bureau of Labor Statistics, there were almost 117,000 event planners in the United States, with that number expected to grow by 11% in the next decade. Ten years ago, that number was significantly lower (Bureau of Labor Statistics, 2017).

Traditionally, events have included many different kinds of corporate meetings, conventions, conferences, and trade shows. These kinds of events have been the mainstay of the field for over 50 years (Bureau of Labor Statistics, 2017). However, as businesses have changed to become more social and often more internally focused, a wider range of events has opened up for planners. These include corporate retreats, training sessions, large fundraisers, travel conferences, and product launches. Sports events have grown to include media conferences, player introductions, sponsorship events, team meetings, facility tours, and grand openings. Bowdin et al (2012) categorized events by size and impact. The first category is local events, in which the main objective is to bring the community together. Businesses in a community might host a night out on Main Street or have Santa arrive on his sleigh during Small Business Saturday. The second category is major events. These events are usually larger in size and are likely to bring in visitors from outside the local region. Examples of these events might include a book festival or art show. The third type of event is a hallmark event, seen as a tradition within the particular location. For example, the Wimbledon tennis championships, the Kentucky Derby, and New York Fashion Week are all hallmark events that happen every year in the same city. The last category is mega events, considered large-scale productions that impact a national audience. Examples of mega events include the Super Bowl, the winter and summer Olympics, and music concerts such as Coachella. (More information about the variety of events is discussed in Chapter 11.) In addition, the area of hospitality (Chapter 5) has emerged as a factor in event planning, and events can include a variety of parties, milestone celebrations, reunions, weddings, religious ceremonies, and community events (Allen, 2009). Making guests feel welcome and included in any type of event is a vital characteristic of being hospitable. Not everyone will know each other at the event, and as you plan for different events, try to find ways to make people feel welcomed and included. Planning for this concern demands a knowledge of those who will be attending the event: how well do they know each other? How comfortable are they interacting with each other? Will there be a need to host some icebreakers at the start of the event in order to encourage communication? What level of interconnectedness will your client desire? The event planner must seek out this information in the planning stages and then work with the client to determine how to make every guest feel welcome. Even though there are many types of events, it is important to realize that replication of events, such as annual business meetings or retreats, will not work in an industry that demands a personal touch.

While event planners may rely on certain routines to accomplish tasks and plan events, a **trained incapacity** results when their routines remain static and lack innovation. According to Wais (2005), Thorstein Veblen (1914) coined the term "*trained incapacity*" (p. 1), whereas Kenneth Burke (1935) gave the term its popularity. In *Permanence and Change* (1984), Burke defined trained incapacity as "that state of affairs whereby one's very abilities can function as blindness" (p. 7). For example, as an event planner, it is easy to get into the routine of planning events that are remarkably alike. Past experiences working with a particular type of event can cause you to continue to create the same event for different audiences; however, this can be problematic. Take, for example, creating a mega event like the Super Bowl where the objective of playing football is the same each year, but the experience changes with the location, the teams playing, and the half-time show. No two events should be exactly the same. Each event offers a unique opportunity to create an exclusive experience for your client. Moreover, as you work with vendors, it may be simpler to fall back on the same caterers or florists; however, if you always use the same vendors, you might miss opportunities to experience something new and different. Planning events is about creating original experiences; as a result, having a trained incapacity is a detriment to your career.

Trained incapacity: *The state of affairs whereby one's own abilities can function as blindness*

One way to eliminate falling into the same old routine is to ask questions before you begin the planning process. The more questions you ask, the

better vision you will have for the event. Wolf, Wolf, and Levine (2005) believe that before you begin to plan each unique event, you need to ask yourself six fundamental questions: (1) Who are your guests? (2) What is your event? (3) When is your event? (4) Where do you want to have your event? (5) Why are you having this event? (6) How much is in your budget? (pp. 1–2). Wolf, Wolf, and Levine (2005) suggest that the framework of an event is found in the answers to the five *W* questions and the *how*, and will be further explored in Chapter 9. Once the structure is in place, it will guide the planning process; however, the foundation of each event is built upon the communication skills of the event planner.

All events are created for a particular audience, have a specific goal in mind, and most importantly, rely on communication as a crucial component of the event planning process.

Communication Connection

Communicating with others is at the crux of event planning. Joe Goldblatt (2014) and Julia Rutherford Silvers (2003), two premier scholars in the field of event planning, believe that coordinating events requires effective communication. Without this essential element, an event will not be a success. Communicating plans, forming strategies, and setting goals are at the forefront of the creation of events. Every aspect of event planning, from early inception to final delivery and follow-up, requires that competent communication take place. Communication scholars have articulated the importance of communication skills for success in any business enterprise (Lewis, 2019; Morreale, Osborn, & Pearson, 2000; Morreale & Pearson, 2008). The National Association of Colleges and Employers (2016) supports this rationale, stating that communication skills are a top-ranked requirement of employers, and the American Society for Training and Development (ASTD) (2009) also lists communication as one of the top-10 critical skills employers desire. Moreover, a survey conducted through the Pew Research Center's American Trends Panel, a nationally representative panel of 3,154 randomly selected U.S. adults, found that communication skills were singularly important if children are to get ahead in today's world. Ninety percent of individuals surveyed said communication is one of the most essential skills, followed by reading, math, teamwork, writing, and logic (Goo, 2015). Harvard Business School professors Kleinbaum, Stuart, and Tushman (2008) argue, "Communication is central to the very existence of organizations" (p. 1). Most people know communication is a vital skill, but successful individuals need to understand the philosophy (why) and the applied components (how) behind the field.

Scholars have articulated many different definitions and models of communication (Littlejohn, 2002). The early models of communication focused on a linear sequence in which communication was seen as something that a sender "does" to someone. These early models of communication were

TIP

Plan for internal as well as external communication.

— Jeanne Persuit

very simplistic and could be represented visually as a package on a conveyer belt.

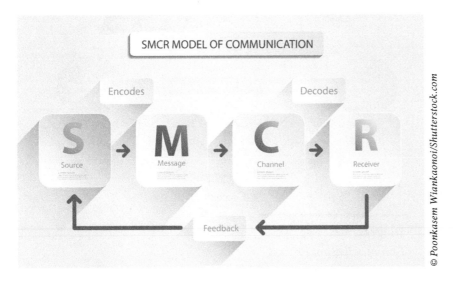

Today, communication is seen as a transactional model where success is dependent on interactions with others (Gergen, 1991) and can be visually represented as a dance between two people. Thus, **communication** is a complex process with many components (Berlo, 1960) and involves the creation of a message through which a receiver interprets the sender's meaning. Some of the components include the following:

1. **Sender**—the person who creates the message.
2. **Receiver**—the recipient of the message.
3. **Message**—verbal and nonverbal utterances used to convey meaning.
   a. **Encoding**—the cognitive process of creating a message.
   b. **Decoding**—the cognitive process of unpacking the meaning of a message.
4. **Channel**—the means by which a message is sent.
5. **Feedback Loop**—a verbal or nonverbal response to the message sent.
6. **Noise**—something that interferes with the message.
   a. **Internal Noise**—thoughts and feelings inside your head that distract you from the message.
   b. **External Noise**—stimuli in the environment that distract you from the message.
   c. **Semantic Noise**—meaning that is derived from certain symbols and behaviors that distract you from the message.
7. **Context**—the historical, physical, social, psychological, and cultural setting of the communication.

Communication: *A complex process with many components involving the creation of a message through which the receiver interprets the sender's meaning*

Sender: *The person who creates the message*

Receiver: *The recipient of the message*

Message: *Verbal and nonverbal utterances used to convey meaning*

Encoding: *The cognitive process of creating a message*

Decoding: *The cognitive process of unpacking the meaning of a message*

Channel: *The means by which a message is sent*

Feedback loop: *A verbal or nonverbal to the message sent*

Noise: *Anything that interferes with a message*

Internal noise: *Thoughts and feelings inside your head that distract you from the message*

External noise: *Stimuli in the environment that distract you from the message*

Semantic noise: *Meaning that is derived from certain symbols and behaviors that distract you from the message*

Context: *The historical, physical, social, psychological and cultural setting of the communication that helps people understand any distortions or miscommunications in the message*

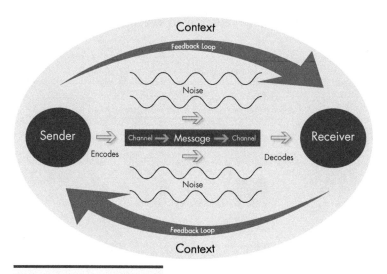

Diagram 02.
Communication Process

In addition to the model of communication, there are also different types of communication, including but not limited to the following:

- **Intrapersonal communication**—a form of communication within oneself (Barker & Wiseman, 1966).
- **Interpersonal communication**—communication with another (Knapp & Daly, 2011) that can range from close and intimate (Miller & Steinberg, 1975) to public interactions (Arnett, 2001).
- **Small group communication**—communication with at least three people who share a common purpose or goal (Beebe & Masterson, 2014).
- **Organizational communication**—communication that focuses on communicative understandings of business processes and practices (Putnam & Mumby, 2013).
- **Mass communication**—communication with a geographically dispersed, large, and diverse audience (Cathcart & Gumpert, 1983).
- **Public communication**—communication that shapes civic engagement with others (Arnett, Fritz, & Bell McManus, 2018).

In their historical overview of communication, Bryant and Pribanic-Smith (2010) articulate how communication is also a vital part of areas including debate, technology, family, health, instruction, intercultural, journalism, marketing, new media, nonverbal, political, public relations, rhetorical theory, and visual communication, among others. With all of these areas and sub-areas, it is easy to see how an event planner will need to develop a broad understanding of the field of communication. As an event planner, you will use all of the components found within the model of communication and engage in various types of communication.

Intrapersonal communication:
A form of communication within oneself

Interpersonal communication:
Communication that takes place between a few—typically two—people

Small group communication:
Communication with at least three people who share a common purpose or goal

Organizational communication:
The study of communicative understandings of business processes and practices

Mass communication:
Communication with a geographically dispersed, large, diverse audience

Public communication:
Communication that shapes civic engagement with others

Event planners are constantly communicating. The words you choose are very powerful and thus are essential for understanding interactions with others. Communication can cause both success and damage in different ways. For example, an event planner might be working with a color scheme that does not complement the venue's decor; however, the client loves the colors and is insistent on keeping them for her special day. If you express your concern insensitively about the colors, you might cause hurt feelings and the loss of future business. However, the ability to communicate positively and professionally can enhance your working relationships and may save the client from creating something that is not aesthetically pleasing. As you choose your words wisely and engage in competent communication, it is important to understand the power of speech and the various communication skills that make a successful event planner.

© michaeljung/Shutterstock.com

Communication Competence

Competent communicators are able to articulate messages in ways that help the self and others pursue goals (Wiemann, 1977). **Communication competence** is a dyadic process that includes one's self-perceptions of social/communication skills and is contingent upon the other's perception of one's social/communication skills (Arroyo & Segrin, 2011). Communication competence focuses on knowing the appropriate rules and behaviors in various communicative contexts and having the ability to understand the outcomes from both conforming to and violating the norms (Spitzberg & Cupach, 2002). Competent communicators are able to adapt a message to fit a particular person or context (Martin & Rubin, 1994; Spitzberg, Canary, & Cupach, 1994). A competent communicator can articulate a message to an audience who clearly understands the intended message. For example, an event planner might be working with a client who does not have enough money to realistically implement a vision; as a result, the event planner will have to communicate to the client other possibilities that are in line with the budget, without offending the client. Competent communicators must be able to alter the communicative strategies in response to varying situational factors and feedback from others (Kellermann, 1992). They must "not only 'know' and 'know how'"(Parks, 1985, p. 174), they must also act with intention. Individuals who are competent communicators generally possess accuracy, clarity, flexibility, success, affection, empathy, and effectiveness (Bell, 2010). Competent communicators are also more effective at working with others.

Communication competence: *A dyadic process that includes one's self-perceptions of social/ communication skills and is contingent upon the other's perception of one's social/ communication skills*

Intercultural and Interpersonal Interactions

Event planners should be strong communicators with the ability to interact with diverse clients, staff, vendors, and employees. This requires that event planners hone their interpersonal and intercultural skills. Interpersonal communication describes the verbal and nonverbal interactions that occur with others from a superficial level to an intimate level in both public and private locations (Arnett, 2001; Knapp & Daly, 2011; Miller & Steinberg, 1975). **Intercultural communication** examines communication across cultures (Spencer-Oatey & Kotthoff, 2007) and "understanding cross-cultural differences in behaviors is a prerequisite for understanding intercultural behavior" (Gudykunst, 2000 p. 314). Communication is often spontaneous, dynamic, and informal, and people rely on feedback from one another to determine how to change or adapt a message (Knapp & Daly, 2011). Communication for event planners evolves with each interaction they engage in during the stages of planning events. Building and sustaining relationships are integral components of an event planner's job. Working well with others and being able to communicate effectively with individuals such as bosses, clients, co-workers, vendors, and entertainers helps foster relationships and build trust. "Strong interpersonal relationships are not only the heart of a successful organization but they are also the foundation of our own business successes" (Hamilton, 2014, p. 82). Developing strong interpersonal and intercultural skills will enable event planners to conduct their business with more ease. The communication that takes place can be both verbal and nonverbal, and meaning must come from the interaction; however, the process should be continually adjusted, modified, and improved through understanding the diversity that exists not only in the task, but also in the interaction.

Intercultural Communication: *Examines communication across cultures*

© Andor Bujdoso/Shutterstock.com

Diversity

Diversity: *The ability to engage in various activities and work with various people*

In an age of diversity, this term can mean many different things (Makau & Arnett, 1997). **Diversity** has a twofold meaning when it comes to describing the work of an event planner. First, diversity relates to your ability to engage in various activities. As an event planner, you will be participating in diverse tasks; from a Bar Mitzvah to an opening for a new restaurant, each event will offer a unique experience. What makes an event planner great is the ability to be diverse in all facets of the job. The diversity in task helps to build a portfolio that allows clients to see your ability to meet their various needs. An example of a diverse portfolio might include the

Quinceañera, or Sweet Fifteen, a celebration of a Latina girl's 15th birthday. This event signifies the fact that she has left her childhood behind and begun the journey toward womanhood. The "quince" is an extravagant, ritualized fiesta tradition by those in Latin cultures with the birthday girl gathering around her a "court," similar to a bridal party, that includes as many as 14 girls, aged 1 to 14, signifying each year of her life. There are also escorts for many of the girls, particularly the older ones. A princess gown, the formal procession, a traditional dance (usually a waltz),

© Volt Collection/Shutterstock.com

the exchange of shoes from flats to heels, the giving of a last doll—these are all part of the customs that surround this milestone (Alvarez, 2007). However, the event can also be very simple in its celebration, without the sumptuous rituals, so it will be up to the event planner to listen carefully to the client's vision of what might occur. In any case, it celebrates a rite of passage that is culturally significant but also personally meaningful to the young girl. In a culture rich with many varied traditions, the Quinceañera offers a wealth of possibilities, but the event planner must be well-versed in the cultural traditions of the celebration before beginning the planning. Understanding the true meaning behind events, such as a Bar Mitzvah, baptism, Halloween, or Dia de los Muertos, helps plan a successful event that does not offend or misrepresent different cultural traditions. The more diversity event planners have in their portfolio, the more opportunities for diverse clients will exist.

The second feature of diversity focuses on working with people. Page (2011) states, "Diversity drives innovation and productivity" (p. 9). The common understanding of diversity relates to issues of demographics such as age, race, sex, gender, and religion, etc., but Rodriguez (2010) believes diversity goes beyond these factors by stating that "diversity is an ecological phenomenon that evolves between human beings rather than something that is possessed by us by merely being of a certain category or persuasion" (p. 32). As you engage different groups of people, you will need to learn how to work with others. Every client is unique, and the more you are able to adapt to the diversity of your audience, the easier it will be to work with others in an organized fashion. For example, not all clients will want loud music at a wedding reception. An older client who is having a second wedding might prefer to have jazz music and only light appetizers after a ceremony. Paying attention to the client's unique vision demands an understanding that goes beyond the expected. Moreover, understanding diversity in traditions will help you plan events that are inclusive and not exclusive of various cultures. Planning a business meeting in a foreign country brings with it the responsibility of understanding the dynamics of that particular culture. Doing your research before the planning begins will help eliminate the embarrassment that can occur if event planners are ignorant about how something is done in a particular culture. Remember that everyone views events differently; your job is to bring your clients' vision to fruition, and the best way to do this is to create a space for dialogue.

Dialogue

Dialogue: *The meaning made through words that implies more than a simple back-and-forth of messages in interaction; it points to a particular process and quality of communication in which the participants 'meet,' which allows for changing and being changed*

The word **dialogue** originated from the Greek work *dialogos*. The first part of the word, *dia*, does not represent the common notion of "two," but rather means "through." As a result, dialogue can occur with more than two people. The second part of the word, *logos*, has been translated into "language," "logic," "the word," or the most fundamental definition, "meaning" (Bohm, 1990; Garmston & Wellman, 1998; p. 32). The meaning made through words or dialogue occurs differently depending on the situation (e.g., social, political, educational, interpersonal, and philosophical) (Johannesen, Valde, & Whedbee, 2008), resulting in different implications and definitions of dialogue from scholar to scholar.

A definition that fits within the discipline of communication and applies to the field of event planning comes from Kenneth Cissna and Rob Anderson (1994), who state that "dialogue implies more than a simple back-and-forth of messages in interaction; it points to a particular process and quality of communication in which the participants 'meet,' which allows for changing and being changed" (p. 10). In addition, dialogue is a useful framework to understand how language and learning are enacted in various facets of life (Anderson, Baxter, & Cissna, 2004). Dialogue is a transformative endeavor in which participants discover new insights about each other; it is more than an exchange of words, for it allows for a greater understanding of the communicative exchange that exists in a particular context. Dialogue is a way to act, engage, prepare, listen, observe, and converse with others (Nixon, 2012). In event planning, understanding the importance of dialogue will help you engage and listen to clients with an open mind.

Richard Johannesen, Kathleen Valde, and Karen Whedbee (2008) discuss similarities that exist among dialogic scholars, all of which highlight the power of dialogue in communicative encounters.

Authenticity: *In the context of dialogue, being direct, honest and straightforward in communicating all information and feelings that are relevant and legitimate for the subject at hand*

Inclusion: *In the context of dialogue, the attempt to experience another perspective and see the other's perspective as an important part of the conversation*

1. **Authenticity**—"one is direct, honest and straightforward in communicating all information and feelings that are *relevant and legitimate* for the subject at hand" (p. 55). Authenticity allows you to be genuine without feeling the need to suppress information. This component focuses on the importance of all information that might be relevant in an event.

2. **Inclusion**—"one attempts to 'see the other,' to 'experience the other side,' to 'imagine the real,' the reality of the other's viewpoint" (p. 55). Inclusion allows you to see the other's perspective as an important part of the conversation. Through inclusion, event planners are better able to see what is needed at a particular event.

3. **Confirmation**—"a partner in dialogue is affirmed as a person, not merely tolerated, even though we oppose her or him on some specific matter" (p. 55). Confirmation opens up the possibility of learning from others. An event planner might not agree with all aspects of an event, but it is important to make sure you represent the client's vision, whether you like it or not.

4. **Presentness**—"participants in dialogue must give full concentration to bringing their total and authentic being to the encounter" (p. 55). Presentness allows individuals to show up for the conversation willing and able to learn from others without the everyday distractions that can impede a conversation. As you plan events, you will more than likely have multiple clients at once. Giving each client a sense of presentness means giving them your undivided attention without focusing on other events or tasks.

5. **Spirit of Mutual Equality**—"although society may rank participants in dialogue as of unequal status or accomplishment, and although the roles appropriate to each partner may differ, participants themselves view each other as persons rather than as objects, not as things, to be exploited or manipulated for selfish satisfaction" (p. 55). This component demands that you should treat your clients just as you would want to be treated. A client's budget, for instance, should not determine how hard you work on a project.

6. **Supportive Climate**—"one encourages the other to communicate" (p. 56). Individuals in dialogue need to allow each other to communicate with free expression, limiting prejudgment and assumptions that may cause harm to others. Supportive climates are necessary so that clients can feel free to express their wants and needs without being judged.

Confirmation: *In the context of dialogue, affirming and not merely tolerating a partner in dialogue, even though we oppose her or him on some specific matter*

Presentness: *In the context of dialogue, giving full concentration to bringing your total and authentic self to an encounter, willing and able to learn from others without the everyday distractions that can impede a conversation*

Spirit of Mutual Equality: *In the context of dialogue, treating each other as persons rather than as objects, not as things to be exploited or manipulated*

Supportive Climate: *In the context of dialogue, allowing each other to communicate with free expression, limiting prejudgment and assumptions that may cause harm to others*

These six components allow you to see the importance and power of dialogue, especially within an event planning setting where dialogue can produce great ideas for events. Through dialogue, event planners can gain a better understanding of the client's wants and needs. Arnett, Fritz, and Bell McManus (2018) articulate the need to understand dialogue and difference. As you engage clients, it is imperative to understand that many assumptions of common sense are no longer common. Wedding cakes, presents at birthday parties, or alcohol at a New Year's Eve party are not always common any more. Dialogue opens up the possibilities to listen and learn from different clients and different experiences. Most of the time, events that are planned will have an impact on someone's life. As you engage clients, remember the significance of the events you are planning. Great event planners take the time to get to know their clients and engage them in dialogic meetings. "Dialogue can identify the attitudes with which participants approach each other, the ways they talk and act, the consequences of their meeting, and the context within which they meet" (Cissna & Anderson, 1998, p. 64). Event planners need to treat each event as a unique and special occasion. As Cissna and Anderson (2002) state, "When a space somehow is cleared for dialogue and when sincere communicators expect and invite it, we glimpse futures that could not have been available or even imagined beforehand" (p. 11). For example, traditional convocations typically welcome first-year students to their new college or university. To make this event unique, consider offering students the opportunity to nominate their high school mentor for recognition. These faculty members are formally invited to attend the ceremony as evidence of the relationship between student and teacher that prompted the next step in education. Dialogue opens the door for an interpersonal connection that allows you to understand the other person's vision and create an event that leaves a lasting impression on your client.

Understanding the importance of communication and then developing strong communication skills will be the key to an event planner's growth and achievement, as indicated in Diagram 03. Communication is at the center of Diagram 03 because it is needed in all aspects of the event planning process. A vision is the starting point of the event, and allows both the client and the planner to 'see' what type of event needs to be executed. The second step, research, allows for information gathering to occur. Research fills in the gaps of what is missing and what needs to be done before the planning step begins. Once the planning stage starts, all of the details are set with the intention of the event running as smoothly as possible. Once the day of the event arrives, it is time to implement the vision by combining the vision, research and planning into a successful event. All of the hard work comes together in the implementation stage. Lastly, taking the time to evaluate an event allows for future successes.

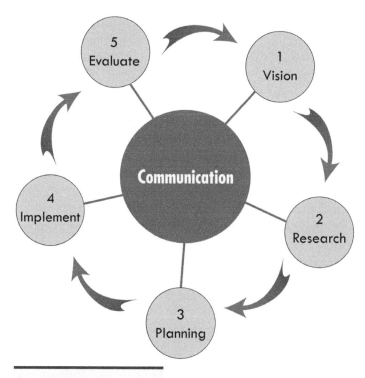

Diagram 03. *Event Planning Process*

Each event you plan offers a distinctive experience that will test your ability to adapt to various situations, but the key to success in every situation is rooted in the philosophy and application of communication. While there are many particular organizational skills that event planners must cultivate, developing a firm understanding of the essence of competent communication is crucial to success. Performing well is, of course, essential, but being a competent communicator will raise the event planner to new heights.

Key Terms

Events	Decoding	Interpersonal communication	Authenticity
Event planners	Channel	Small group communication	Inclusion
Event planning	Feedback loop	Organizational communication	Confirmation
Trained incapacity	Noise	Mass communication	Presentness
Communication	Internal noise	Public communication	Spirit of Mutual Equality
Sender	External noise	Communication competence	Supportive climate
Receiver	Semantic noise	Intercultural communication	
Message	Context	Diversity	
Encoding	Intrapersonal communication	Dialogue	

Discussion Questions

1. Describe an event you attended that went very well. What made the event a success? What made the event unique?
2. Describe an event you attended that did not go so well. What made the event feel chaotic or disorganized?
3. Explain a time when you experienced a breakdown in communication. How were the messages distorted? What was the outcome?

Communicative Competence Scale

Instructions: Complete the following questionnaire. Rank your interactions using the scale below.

(5) strongly agree, (4) agree, (3) undecided or neutral, (2) disagree, or (1) strongly disagree.

_____ 1. I find it easy to get along with others.

_____ 2. I can adapt to changing situations.

_____ 3. I treat people as individuals.

_____ 4. I interrupt others too much.

_____ 5. I am "rewarding" to talk to.

_____ 6. I can deal with others effectively.

_____ 7. I am a good listener.

_____ 8. My personal relations are cold and distant.

_____ 9. I am easy to talk to.

_____ 10. I won't argue with someone just to prove I am right.

_____ 11. My conversation behavior is not "smooth."

_____ 12. I ignore other people's feelings.

_____ 13. I generally know how others feel.

_____ 14. I let others know I understand them.

_____ 15. I understand other people.

_____ 16. I am relaxed and comfortable when speaking.

_____ 17. I listen to what people say to me.

_____ 18. I like to be close and personal with people.

_____ 19. I generally know what type of behavior is appropriate in any given situation.

_____ 20. I usually do not make unusual demands on my friends.

_____ 21. I am an effective conversationalist.

_____ 22. I am supportive of others.

_____ 23. I do not mind meeting strangers.

_____ 24. I can easily put myself in another person's shoes.

_____ 25. I pay attention to the conversation.

_____ 26. I am generally relaxed when conversing with a new acquaintance.

_____ 27. I am interested in what others have to say.

_____ 28. I do not follow the conversation very well.

_____ 29. I enjoy social gatherings where I can meet new people.

_____ 30. I am a likeable person.

_____ 31. I am flexible.

_____ 32. I am not afraid to speak with people in authority.

_____ 33. People can go to me with their problems.

_____ 34. I generally say the right thing at the right time.

_____ 35. I like to use my voice and body expressively.

_____ 36. I am sensitive to others' needs of the moment.

Note: Items 4, 8, 11, 12, and 28 are reverse-coded so that "strongly agree" would receive a 1, "agree" would receive a 2, undecided or neutral would receive a 3, "disagree" would receive a 4, and "strongly disagree" would receive a 5.

The median is 108; the best you can score is 180.

Where did you fall on the scale? _____

From "Explication and Test of a Model of Communicative Competence" by John M. Wiemann, published in _Human Communication Research._ Copyright © 2006 by John Wiley & Sons. Reprinted by permission.

References

Allen, J. (2009). _Event planning: The ultimate guide to successful meetings, corporate events, fundraising galas, conferences, conventions, incentives, and other special events._ Hoboken, NJ: John Wiley & Sons.

_____. (2010). _Event planning: Ethics and etiquette._ Hoboken, NJ: John Wiley & Sons.

Allen, J., O'Toole, W., Harris, R. & McDonnell, I. (2010). _Festival and special event management_ (5th ed.). Australia: John Wiley & Sons.

Alvarez, J. (2007). _Once upon a Quinceañera: Coming of age in the USA._ New York: Penguin.

American Society for Training and Development. (2009). _Bridging the skills gap: New factors compound the growing skills shortage._ Alexandria, VA: American Society for Training and Development.

Anderson, R., Baxter, L. A., & Cissna, K. N. (2004). _Dialogue: Theorizing difference in communication studies._ Thousand Oaks, CA: Sage.

Arcodia, C., & Barker, T. (2005). The employability prospects of graduates in event management: Using data from job advertisements. In J. Allen (Ed.), _Impacts of events: Proceeding of the international events research conference_ (pp. 175–202). Sydney, Australia: University of Technology Sydney.

Arnett, R. C. (2001). Dialogic civility as pragmatic ethical praxis: An interpersonal metaphor for the public domain. _Communication Theory, 11,_ 315–338.

Arnett, R. C., Fritz, J. H., & Bell McManus, L. M. (2018). _Communication ethics: Dialogue & difference_ (2nd ed.). Thousand Oaks, CA: Sage.

Arroyo, A., & Segrin, C. (2011). The relationship between self- and other-perceptions of communication competence and friendship quality. _Communication Studies, 62,_ 547–562.

Barker, L. L., & Wiseman, G. (1966). A model of intrapersonal communication. _Journal of Communication, 16,_ 172–179.

Bailyn, E. (2012). *Outsmarting social media: Profiting in the age of friendship marketing.* Fort Wayne, IN: Que Publishing.

Beebe, S. A., & Masterson, J. T. (2014). *Communication in small groups* (11ᵗʰ ed.). New York: Addison-Wesley Longman.

Bell, L. M. (2010). Communication competence. In R. L. Jackson II and M. A. Hogg (Eds.). *Encyclopedia of social identity.* (pp. 110–115). Thousand Oaks, CA: Sage.

Berlo, D. K. (1960). *The process of communication.* San Francisco: Rinehart.

Bladen, C., Kennell, J., Abson, E., & Wilde, N. (2012). *Events management: An introduction.* New York: Routledge.

Bohm, D. (1990). *On dialogue.* Ojai, CA: David Bohm Seminars.

Bowdin, G. Allen, J., Harris, R., McDonnell, I., & O' Toole, W. (2012). Events Management. (3ʳᵈ ed.). Elsevier Butterworth Heinemann, Oxford.

Brown, D. (2015). *Duties of an event planner.* Retrieved from http://work.chron.com/duties-event-planner-3092.html.

Bryant, J., & Pribanic-Smith, E. J. (2010). A historical overview of research in communication science. In C. R. Berger, M. E. Roloff, M. E., & D. R. Roskos-Ewoldsen (Eds.). *The handbook of communication science* (2ⁿᵈ ed., pp. 21–36). Thousand Oaks, CA: Sage.

Bureau of Labor Statistics, U.S. Department of Labor (2017). Meeting, Convention, and Event Planners. *In Occupational Outlook Handbook* (2016–17 ed.). Retrieved from https://www.bls.gov/ooh/business-and-financial/meeting-convention-and-event-planners.htm#tab-2.

Burke, K. (1984). *Permanence and change: An anatomy of a purpose.* (3ʳᵈ ed.). Berkeley: University of California Press. (Original work published in 1935)

Carmichael, A. (2006, July). *Backstage pass.* Retrieved from http://www.wsj.com/articles/SB115378527321215934

Cathcart, R., & Gumpert, G. (1983). Mediated interpersonal communication: Toward a new typology. *Quarterly Journal of Speech, 69,* 267–277.

Chaney, L. H., & Martin, J. S. (2007). *The essential guide to business etiquette.* Westport, CT: Praeger.

Cissna, K. N., & Anderson, R. (1994). Communication and the ground of dialogue. In R. Anderson, K. N. Cissna, & R. C. Arnett (Eds.). *The reach of dialogue: Confirmation, voice, and community* (pp. 9–30). Cresskill, New Jersey: Hampton Press.

Cissna, K. N. & Anderson, R. (1998). Theorizing about dialogic moments: The Buber-Rogers position and postmodern themes. *Communication Theory, 8,* 63–104.

Cissna, K. N. & Anderson, R. (2002). *Moments of meeting: Buber, Rogers, and the potential for public dialogue.* Albany: State University of New York Press.

Dowson, R., & Bassett, D. (2015). *Event planning and management: A practical handbook for PR and events professionals.* London: Kogan Page.

Event Planning [Def. 1]. (n.d.) Cambridge Dictionary. Retrieved from http://dictionary.cambridge. org/us/dictionary/business-english/event-planning

Garmston, R., & Wellman, B. (1998). Teacher talk that makes a difference. *Educational Leadership, 55,* 30–34.

Gergen, K. J. (1991). *The saturated self: Dilemmas of identity in contemporary life.* New York: Basic Books.

Getz, D. (1997). *Event management and event tourism.* New York: Cognizant Communication.

Getz, D. (2007). *Event studies: Theory, research, and policy for planned events.* New York: Elsevier.

Goldblatt, J. (2014). *Special events: Creating and sustaining a new world for celebration.* (7th ed.). Hoboken: New Jersey: John Wiley & Sons.

Goo, S. (Feb, 2015). *The skills Americans say kids need to succeed in life.* Retrieved from http://www.pewresearch.org/fact-tank/2015/02/19/skills-for-success/

Grimaldi, L. A. (2015). Third parties: Big, small or none at all? *Meetings and Conventions, 49,* Retrieved from http://www.meetings-conventions.com/News/Features/Third-Parties--Big, -Small-or-None-at-All-/

Gudykunst, W. B. (2000). Methodological issues in conducting theory-based cross cultural research. In Helen Spencer-Oatey (ed.). *Culturally Speaking: Managing Rapport through talk across cultures.* 293–315 London: Continuum.

Hamilton, C. (2014). *Communicating for results: A guide for business and the professions.* Boston, MA: Wadsworth, Cengage Learning.

Higham, J. E. S., & Ritchie, B. (2001). The evolution of festivals and other events in rural southern New Zealand. *Event Management, 7,* 39–49.

International Institute of Event Management (2014). *What is event planning?* Retrieved from https://institute-of-event-management.com/what-is-event-planning.

Jackson, C., Morgan, J., & Laws, C. (2018). Creativity in events: the untold story. *International Journal of Event & Festival Management, 9,* 2–19.

Johannesen, R. L., Valde, K. S., & Whedbee, K. E. (2008). *Ethics in human communication* (6th ed.). Long Grove, IL: Waveland Press.

Junek, O., Lockstone, L., & Mair, J. (2009). Two perspectives on event management employment: Student and employer insights into the skills required to get the job done! *Journal of Hospitality and Tourism Management, 16,* 120–129.

Kellermann, K. (1992). Communication: Inherently strategic and primarily automatic. *Communication Monographs, 59,* 288–300.

Kleinbaum, A. M., Stuart, T. E., & Tushman, M. L. (2008, July). *Communication (and coordination?) in a modern, complex organization.* Retrieved from http://hbswk.hbs.edu/item/5991.html

Knapp, M. L., & Daly, J. A. (Eds.). (2011). *The Sage handbook of interpersonal communication* (4th ed.). Thousand Oaks, CA: Sage.

Lee, M. J. (2006). Analytical reflections on the economic impact assessment of conventions and special events. *Journal of Convention & Event Tourism, 8,* 71–85.

Lewis, L. (2019). Organizational change: Creating change through strategic communication (2nd ed.). Hoboken, NJ: Wiley Blackwell.

Littlejohn, S. W. (2002). *Theories of human communication* (7th ed.). Belmont, CA: Wadsworth.

Makau, J. M., & Arnett, R. C. (Eds.) (1997). *Communication ethics in an age of diversity.* Chicago: University of Illinois Press.

Martin, M. M., & Rubin, R. B. (1994). Development of a communication flexibility measure. *Southern Communication Journal, 59,* 171–178.

Miller, G. R., & Steinberg, M. (1975). *Between people: A new analysis of interpersonal communication.* Chicago: Science Research Associates.

Morreale, S. O., Osborn, M. M., & Pearson, J. C. (2000). Why communication is important: A rationale for the centrality of the study of communication. *Journal of the Association for Communication Administration, 29,* 1–25.

Morreale, S. P., & Pearson, J. C. (2008). Why communication education is important: The centrality of the discipline in the 21st century. *Communication Education, 57,* 224–240.

National Association of Colleges and Employers. (2016, February). *Employers: Verbal communication most important candidate skill.* Retrieved from http://www.naceweb.org/career-readiness/competencies/employers-verbal-communication-most-important-candidate-skill/

Nixon, P. (2012). *Dialogue gap: Why communication isn't enough and what we can do about it, fast.* Singapore: John Wiley & Sons.

Page, S. E. (2011). *Diversity and complexity.* New Jersey: Princeton University Press.

Parks, M. R. (1985). Interpersonal communication and the quest for personal competence. In M. L. Knapp and G. R. Miller (Eds). *Handbook of interpersonal communication* (pp. 171–201). Beverly Hills, CA: Sage.

Pearce, W. B. (1994). *Interpersonal communication: Making social worlds.* New York: HarperCollins.

Putnam, L. L., & Mumby, D. K. (Eds.). (2013). *The SAGE handbook of organizational communication: Advances in theory, research and methods.* (3rd ed.). Thousand Oaks, CA: Sage.

Rogers, T. (2003). *Conferences and conventions: A global industry.* Boston, MA: Butterworth Heinemann.

Robson, L. M. (2011). A demographic study of event planners. *Journal of Convention & Event Tourism, 12,* 45–52.

Rodriguez, A. (2010). *Revisioning diversity in communication studies.* Kibworth, United Kingdom: Troubador.

Rutherford Silvers, J. (2012). *Professional event coordination.* (2nd ed.). Hoboken, NJ: John Wiley & Sons.

Spencer-Oatey, H., & Kotthoff, H. (2007). Introduction. In H. Spencer-Oatey & H. Kotthoff (Eds.). *Handbook of intercultural communication* (pp 1–8). Berlin: Walter de Gruyter GmbH & Co.

Spitzberg, B. H., Canary, D. J., & Cupach, W. R. (1994). A competence-based approach to conflict. In D. D. Cahn (Ed.), *Conflict in interpersonal relationships* (pp. 183–201). Hillsdale, NJ: Lawrence Erlbaum Associates.

Spitzberg, B. H., & Cupach, W. R. (2002). Interpersonal skills. In M. L. Knapp & J. A. Daly (Eds.), *Handbook of interpersonal communication* (pp. 564–611). Thousand Oaks, CA: Sage.

Veblen, T. (1914). *The instinct of workmanship and the state of the industrial arts.* New York: MacMillan.

Wais, E. (2005). "Trained incapacity": Thorstein Veblen and Kenneth Burke. *KB Journal, 2,* 1–8.

Weber, K., & Ladkin, A. (2009). Career anchors of convention and exhibition industry professionals in Asia. *Journal of Convention & Event Tourism, 10,* 243–255.

Wiemann, J. M. (1977). Explication and test of a model of communication competence. *Human Communication Research, 3,* 195–213.

Wolf, P., Wolf, J., & Levine, D. (2005). *Event planning made easy: 7 simple steps to making your business or private event a huge success.* New York: McGraw Hill.

Chapter 2

INTERPERSONAL ENGAGEMENT: THE IMPORTANCE OF LISTENING TO OTHERS

As you have seen in the previous chapter, event planners must be effective communicators. As such, competent communicators must interact with clients, staff, vendors, or employees on a daily basis, and to be successful, they must hone many of their communication skills. Most would agree that listening skills are essential for success in interpersonal, social, and business interactions, but many often dismiss this overlooked proficiency as too basic (Bunkers, 2010; 2015; Gentile, 2004; Kaufmann, 1993; Prager & Buhrmester, 1998; Pryor, Malshe, & Paradise, 2013; Purdy, 1997; Winsor, Curtis, & Stephens, 1997). Event planners create experiences by communicating prospective plans, coordinating event strategies, and supervising a wide range of tasks. Speaking effectively, listening, and responding to interpersonal interactions in a professional, proficient manner are crucial if event planners are to succeed in business (Smart & Featheringham, 2006). Knapp and Daly (2011) believe that the study of interpersonal communication is a process that takes place in an ongoing manner that constantly interacts and adapts as one listens and learns. As communication moves in a continuum, understanding its relevance and improving your interaction with others has the potential to elevate you in the event planning field. Additionally, as a communicator, you must be able to derive meaning and context from your interactions, which may require you to examine both verbal and nonverbal communication in your relationships.

© Jacob Lund/Shutterstock.com

When you have finished reading this chapter, you will be able to

- explain why strong interpersonal communication skills are important for fostering relationships in event planning;
- apply listening skills to build meaningful client relationships;
- describe how rhetorical sensitivity gives professional communicators an edge in their interactions;
- define several interpersonal theories in relation to their importance in professional interactions.

27

Campus events: Interpersonal skills, collaboration and the art of listening

Nancy J. Willets, Cape Cod Community College

At Cape Cod Community College, the Event Planning & Management class has an interdisciplinary focus, combining the Communication and Hospitality departments. This course brings together students from different disciplines with very different backgrounds. As the students work together to create, plan, and execute major events on campus, they are especially reliant on their interpersonal skills. Understanding the nuances of effective interpersonal communication takes practice, and it can be challenging for enthusiastic new event planners to integrate those skills effectively.

Having strong interpersonal communication skills is vital to working collaboratively while planning an event. Using class exercises that focus on practicing these skills, students learn more about one another, become more confident, and prepare to work together as they gear up to plan the class event. The process begins when they interview potential clients from various factions on campus in order to choose their event. Listening to what the client wants, asking the right questions, and reading between the lines all become crucial as these interviews help them choose the event they will work on for the semester. By listening carefully, they are able to anticipate situations that will allow them to be creative and those where the client is more likely to want things done in a traditional manner. Being sensitive to the client's needs is crucial, and finding ways to create a comfortable environment where the client can freely self-disclose their wish list and potential concerns lays the groundwork for a successful relationship and event. In addition, cooperative communication among team members is of the utmost importance. Creating a climate where all on the team feel valued is key.

One semester, while working with the college's educational foundation, students focused on the director's request that the guests "be treated as if they were the most important person in the room." Students who had listened carefully remembered certain words the client used and brought those words to the brainstorming session. Certain ideas rose to the top of the brainstorming session because students deemed them important to the client, and thus, a theme evolved. The result? A red-carpet theme, where guests were the stars and honored for their contributions to the foundation. Students collaborated on tasks, and, having learned more about one another's backgrounds and abilities, they were able to respect and trust each other's talents and expertise. However, they were clear that as a team, they all needed to pitch in cooperatively, self-disclose any concerns, and be transparent about progress being made or impeded for whatever reason. It was also important that feedback be exchanged.

But what happens when a member of the team goes off on his or her own and disregards the need for collaboration? One such student in the group decided to focus solely on his desire to create a signature drink for the event. Rather than work collaboratively with others, he worked on his own and did not consult the team about his ideas. He presented himself to others as an expert, but members of the team wanted to give input regarding his choices. They wanted to know what the drink would look like, how it would taste, and if it would be appealing to the average event attendee. Rather than consider his classmates' feedback, which included a reminder of the demographics of the guests, he chose not to listen, and the signature drink for the night was barely touched and considered an unsuccessful aspect of the event.

Having had both successful and unsuccessful moments over the years, the students have learned first-hand how effective communication skills can make or break the success of every event.

Contributed by Nancy J. Willets. Copyright © Kendall Hunt Publishing Company.

After reading this chapter, revisit the case study and respond to the following question:

As you engage in all types of interpersonal relationships, how do you manage and maintain these associations in times of tranquility and turmoil?

Interpersonal Communication

In the previous chapter, we learned that internpersonal communication is imperative to the success of an event planner and is at the heart of any event planner's job.

Fritz Heider (1958) states that **interpersonal communication** takes place between a few—typically two—people. Think about how imperative it is that event planners form relationships and then foster and massage them. At the crux of this notion, communicators—event planners—should feel connected to those with whom they have professional relationships, and therefore should experience a mutual understanding or commitment to one another, which in turn, helps secure each other's attention (Nardi, 2005). Interpersonal relationships seem to be more positive when skilled interaction takes place, often leading to more satisfying relationships (Montgomery, 1981; Noller, 1984). Therefore, refining how you talk, listen, write, and otherwise interact with clients, vendors, and employees will enable you to share ideas and commonalities, all of which can strengthen relationships. As an event planner, you know that competent interpersonal

Interpersonal communication: *Communication that takes place between a few—typically two—people*

TIP

Relationships are the most important aspect of what we do in the field. Listen to your client's needs. Their ideas represent their vision and values.

— Angela Corbo

© Yeexin Richelle/Shutterstock.com

communication is integral to the success of your company or department. Event planning requires you to work with and trust others on a daily basis. Whether you are selecting a proper venue for an event or scheduling entertainment for it, you must have several conversations about the decisions that you and the client will make. Additionally, when you begin to solicit clients, you are asking them to trust you and your services; therefore, in order to build that trust, a free exchange of ideas must take place in which interpersonal communication must flourish, and the client should feel comfortable with the idea of working with you on a project. For example, the exchange of communication might take place in an informal setting, such as over coffee, or in a more formal, corporate setting, such as in a conference room. Either way, event planners must understand how to guide and conduct their interpersonal communication, and what level—informal or formal—is most appropriate.

Fostering relationships in a professional setting demands that event planners continually polish and refine their interpersonal communication. Erozkan (2013) writes that the quality of communication that takes place between and among individuals can have a direct impact on the overall quality of the interpersonal relationships. Furthermore, these relationships can affect how individuals feel about themselves, which is why interpersonal communication is so vital in an event planner's role. Competency in event planning can help solidify the connection you find with the people with whom you must work regularly. Conversely, if a sent message is misinterpreted, misunderstood, or sent in error, it can end up causing harm to the relationship (Cupach & Spitzberg, 2010). Communication can be effective only when the message that is sent is the same as the message that is understood. When this happens, interpersonal relationships flourish.

© Konstantin Chagin/Shutterstock.com

The capacity to deliver strong, competent messages—verbal, nonverbal, and written—is at the core of communication; practicing strong interpersonal skills on a daily basis is essential for your success (Knapp & Daly, 2011). In order to succeed as an event planner, you must construct messages clearly so that the receiver will understand what you are communicating, and you must constantly adapt messages depending on your audience. Knowing how to engage and listen to clients will not only strengthen the client-planner relationship, but it will also make other interactions more fulfilling and consistent, opening up chances to embrace various opportunities. Relationship satisfaction depends not just on the ability to communicate, but also to listen with empathy, critical attentiveness, and an open mind.

The Importance of Listening

Event planners must recognize that listening is a continual work in progress, and they should develop and practice the skills needed to become strong and effective communicators. Both hearing and listening are important components of understanding a client's message. The major difference between hearing and listening is that the former is a passive activity—a physiological sense that focuses on sound waves entering the ear—while the latter is an active event that people consciously choose to do (Horowitz, 2012; Wolvin, 2010). Hearing and listening are essential pieces of communication, and by hearing and listening to a message, the event planner is in a stronger position to understand the client's wants and needs.

Listening is not easy, but it is a necessary task in today's society of constant communication. Listening is essential in everyday communicative interactions (Lipari, 2014; Purdy, 1991; 1997; Wolvin, 2010). Listening is more than recalling information (Todd & Levine, 1996); it is a process that involves understanding and paying attention to what others say and do (Razmjou & Ghazi, 2013; Thomas & Levine, 1994). The International Listening Association (ILA) (1996) defines listening as "the process of receiving, constructing meaning from and responding to spoken and/or nonverbal messages" (para. 1). Through listening, people can transform their thoughts, beliefs, and ideas by engaging others' words (McNaughton, Hamlin, McCarthy, Head-Reeves, & Schreiner, 2007). Listening is the most frequently used communication skill; unfortunately, schools spend only about one-sixth of the time focusing on it. Listening skills are rarely taught through the first 12 years of schooling, and when they do receive attention, the topic is hastily addressed and then abandoned. Other studies suggest that students spend between no time at all and six months in 12 years of formal schooling learning how to listen. Moreover, when listening is taught, it is not always taught effectively (Burley-Allen, 1982; Rankin, 1930; Szczepaniak, Pathan, & Soomro, 2013).

In the business world, executives spend about 60% of their communication time listening (Brown, 1982; Keefe, 1971; Steil, 1996). Additionally, research shows that listening is ranked as one of the most important skills in employees' job and career success (Hoppe, 2006; Landrum & Harrold, 2003; Rane, 2011; Sypher, Bostrom, & Seibert, 1989; Weinrach & Swanda,

1975; Wolvin & Coakley, 1991; Wolvin, Coakley, & Gwynn, 1999). However, bosses usually identify listening as a major communication problem that results in loss of time and money (Haas & Arnold, 1995). Sypher, Bostrom, and Seibert (1989) claim "An individual's listening ability has implications for the effectiveness of his/her work group, the overall organization, and perhaps for the individual's own success" (p. 295). When human resource executives were asked to identify skills of ideal managers, listening effectively was ranked at the top of the list (Winsor, Curtis, & Stephens, 1997). Listening was also identified over and over again by senior executives, students, and employers as one of the most important skills needed on the job. Listening trumped many skills including technical competence, computer knowledge, creativity, and administrative talent (Gabric & McFadden, 2001; Landrum & Harrold, 2003; Marchant, 1999). Those "who can keep their mouths shut and ears open have a better chance of being heard, believed, and followed" (Moore, 2005, p. 8). Research also shows that listening is not only vital for organizational success but also contributes to success in building relationships (Purdy, 1991; 1997; SmithBattle, Lorenz, & Leander, 2013).

As people engage others, listening is one of the main components of relationship satisfaction (Gentile, 2004; Prager & Buhrmester, 1998). Kaufmann (1993) believes that effective listening will build relationships, whereas poor listening has the potential to weaken or sometimes prevent relationships. As people listen, they move beyond the surface and improve their interpersonal relationships (Bunkers, 2010). Listening is a crucial skill for everyone, but especially for event planners; by understanding the various types of listening, they are able to create stronger relationships with clients.

Types of listening include discriminative, appreciative, empathic, comprehensive, and critical (Wolvin & Coakley, 1996).

Discriminative listening: *A type of listening that occurs when you distinguish among various sounds*

Appreciative listening: *A type of listening that occurs when people attend for pleasure or enjoyment*

Empathic listening: *A type of listening that demands looking at all conversations from the client's point of view, and which occurs when the goal is to provide emotional support for someone else*

Comprehensive listening: *A type of listening that occurs when people are focusing on understanding the message of a speaker*

1. **Discriminative listening** occurs when you distinguish among various sounds. For example, discriminative listening might cause you to stop and look around if you hear your name in a noisy and crowded room. This type of listening is more akin to hearing because you are not focusing on the details or the context of the message, but rather on something that captures your attention and makes you pause.

2. **Appreciative listening** occurs when you attend for pleasure or enjoyment. This type of listening fills the void of silence that may occur when, for instance, guests are arriving at an event where music would help to invite and welcome them into the room to mingle.

3. **Empathic listening** occurs when the goal is to provide emotional support for someone else. A client might need to discuss a close relative who passed away. Your role is to listen without judgment and be supportive.

4. **Comprehensive listening** occurs when you concentrate on understanding the message of a speaker. For example, this type of

listening is necessary if you are in a time crunch and someone is giving you directions to the nearest printing center to photocopy your event's program. Comprehensive listening focuses on understanding the details of the message.

5. **Critical listening** occurs when your goal is to evaluate a message for the purpose of accepting or rejecting an argument. For example, when inquiring about a price for a venue, you will need to listen critically in order to negotiate. This type of listening focuses not only on understanding the information but also assessing the content of the message.

In addition to these types of listening, people have a tendency to listen in a particular way. Barker and Watson's research (Barker, 1971; Barker & Watson, 2000; Watson & Barker, 1995) found that four preferences (people-oriented, action-oriented, content-oriented, and time-oriented) emerge while people listen.

1. **People-oriented listeners** focus on the relationship. These listeners are concerned with others' feelings and emotions while being non-judgmental, and are interested in building relationships. As an event planner, being a people-oriented listener will help build rapport with your clients and may result in repeated business.

2. **Action-oriented listeners** focus on the task. These listeners' primary goal is to keep the discourse on track. They are valuable in meetings when it would be easy to stray from the agenda. As an event planner, jumping from one detail to another without completing a task could result in a very disorganized and disastrous event.

3. **Content-oriented listeners** are more critical and evaluate what they hear. These listeners are able to listen for information and evaluate it from many different angles, and are helpful when it comes to detail-oriented tasks where the content of the message is essential. The success of an event may depend on your client's content-filled message.

4. **Time-oriented listeners** are concerned with efficiency and prefer information that is clear and concise. They have little patience for those who talk too much or wander off topic. Time-oriented listeners are needed on the day of the event since they are able to maintain the event's pace.

Listening is not an easy skill, but it is needed. Research shows that through education, instruction, and training, people can improve their listening skills (Lane, Balleweg, Suler, Fernald, & Goldstein, 2000; McGee & Cegala, 1998; Spinks & Wells, 1991; Steil, 1996). Focusing on methods of developing stronger listening skills gives event planners an advantage in their careers.

Critical listening: A type of listening that occurs when the goal is to evaluate a message for purposes of accepting or rejecting the argument

TIP

Provide forums where you can listen to what your constituents and potential attendees have to say. Involve as many stakeholders as possible. Communicate the fact that you are open, although it may not be possible to provide everything that each person wishes. Provide empathic responses showing that you care for members' and attendees' concerns.

— Lynn Turner

People-oriented listeners: Those who focus on the relationship during listening

Action-oriented listeners: Those who focus on the task during listening

Content-oriented listeners: Those who are more critical and evaluate what they hear during listening

Time-oriented listeners: Those who are concerned with efficiency and prefer information that is clear and concise

Improving Your Listening Skills

TIP

Brush up on your listening skills, and be prepared to have your own perceptions challenged. Think about these challenges as positive.

— Lynn Turner

Improving listening involves understanding and recognizing **thought speed**, or the rate at which an individual can process words during communication (Allen, 1977). Allen (1977) suggests that if you learn to use thought speed, you can improve comprehension. Generally, people have the capacity to hear between 400 and 500 words per minute—far more words per minute than the average speaker's rate of speech, which is approximately 125 words per minute. Because you have the ability to process spoken words at a quick pace, if the speaker is more methodical or slower in delivery, your mind can wander, and you can become lost in your own thoughts, filling in the blanks between words with your own internal noise. Not fully focusing on a client's words could cause event planners to miss out on important aspects of communication that the client is conveying. Paying attention to the messages, no matter the rate at which the client speaks, will prove to be valuable when listening to and comprehending messages.

Additionally, a fast rate of speech does not disturb reception of ideas, and, therefore, does not typically affect comprehension. Speakers who talk quickly are recognized as being highly credible people, and therefore, their believability levels rise, emphasizing that people who speak more quickly were found to be both trustworthy and credible (Miller, Maruyama, Beaber, & Valone, 1976). Despite the fact that people can speak quickly and still be considered credible, event planners should monitor their own rate of speech, being cognizant of their clients' listening abilities. Focusing on a client's message, and not allowing your thoughts to wander during important meetings and interactions, can enhance your listening skills, and thus improve your level of effectiveness as an event planner.

The National Communication Association (NCA) recognizes listening as an essential component of communication. According to a list of skills compiled in 1984 by members of the Speech Communication Association, now called NCA, and updated in 1998 by Morreale, Rubin, and Jones, there are two sets of skills essential to listening. The first is comprehension, which includes recognizing main ideas, identifying supporting details, recognizing explicit relationships among ideas, and recalling basic ideas and details. The second is evaluation, which includes attending with an open mind, perceiving the speaker's purpose and organization of ideas, discriminating between statements of fact and statements of opinion, distinguishing between emotional and logical arguments, detecting bias and prejudice, recognizing the speaker's attitude, synthesizing and evaluating by drawing logical inferences and conclusions, recalling implications and arguments, and recognizing discrepancies between the speaker's verbal and nonverbal messages.

© iQoncept/Shutterstock.com

Barriers to Listening

Event planners must recognize that listening is a continual work in progress, and they should develop and practice the skills needed to overcome any barriers to effective communication. Sharpening your listening skills will be vital to the success of each event you plan. Clients who believe you understand their vision and goals will trust in your services and recommend you to others. The best communicators do not just talk. They listen. Those who can listen well know that many factors can disrupt clear communication. The client's emotions, your own perceptions, as well as external factors in the environment, can all put up barricades to a successful conversation (Golen, 1990). You can work to overcome some of these obstacles easily enough, but others require more attention and thought.

By recognizing some of the barriers to listening, you can become a better listener. Golen (1990) offers some of the most common barriers to listening, which include being (1) lazy, (2) closed-minded, (3) opinionated, and (4) insincere. Moreover, many people will judge messages based on their pre-existing beliefs and thoughts, resulting in not listening to a message (O'Keefe, 2002) or listening only to what they want to believe (Ball & Zuckerman, 1992). All of these negative factors can prevent event planners from understanding the big picture. You can avoid barriers to effective listening if you continually practice your listening skills. You are not always going to agree with a client's ideas or vision; however, as an event planner, you must keep an open mind and allow the client to speak, while you take notes and try to comprehend the overall meaning of the vision. Listening genuinely and carefully can help ensure that an event goes off without a hitch and is an integral component to effective communication.

Effective listening is a skill that is vital in most social interactions. To be able to apply listening skills well is deliberate, conscious work that deserves practice and attention, for those who are poor listeners will find that they often fail to understand the message being communicated (Golen, 1990). Competent listeners know what to pay attention to in conversations, and proficient event planners use their listening skills to build relationships, strengthen connections to the public, and discover more about the world around them. Listening means being deliberate about evaluating all that you hear, and learning how to focus with a critical ear on those ideas that demand consideration and response. Event planners must apply this vital skill in every conversation if communication is to have meaning and to continue without confusion. Consistent and deliberate listening must thrive today in a world in which noise threatens to engulf every exchange.

Rhetorical Sensitivity

As event planners engage in listening and learning in their interpersonal interactions, understanding rhetorical sensitivity is important. A term

TIP

Consider how information will be exchanged between various persons or committees assigned to assist with event tasks. In addition to pre-event meetings to discuss planning and last-minute details, plan for post-event meetings with co-planners and event staff to solicit feedback for future events.

— Candice Thomas-Maddox

coined by Hart and Burks (1972), **rhetorical sensitivity** describes how individuals effectively analyze interpersonal situations (Dilbeck & McCroskey, 2009) through examining message transmission to develop effective communication behavior (Knutson, Komolsevin, Chatiketu, & Smith, 2003). In interpersonal relationships, individuals who are rhetorically sensitive will create messages that consider their own position, in addition to their partners' perspectives as well as the various constraints that the situation and the context present (Eadie & Paulson, 1984). Event planners will often face the challenge of communicating sensitive material; for example, a budget may not allow your clients to book their first-choice venue. How you phrase this dilemma to your clients is important.

In addition to developing the concept of rhetorical sensitivity, Hart and Burks (1972) advanced the term to describe five basic characteristics of rhetorically sensitive individuals:

1. Accepts role-taking as part of the human condition—You balance many roles in your life, and it is important to understand when a client is also trying to balance several different roles. For example, if clients are trying to be financially responsible because they are in the accounting department of an organization, but they are also in charge of the elaborate holiday party, these two roles might conflict.

2. Avoids stylized verbal behavior—Simplicity is the most direct way to communicate, and sometimes less is more in communication. The more you try to explain ideas in great detail, the more likely it is that your message will be misinterpreted. Keeping things simple, such as showing pictures of past events, rather than describing each event, might help alleviate misinterpretations.

3. Undertakes the strain of adaptation—Human beings are complex, and it is important to adapt your message based on others' communication. If clients are having difficulty understanding your vision of their event, it might be helpful to adapt your message to offer greater clarity.

4. Distinguishes between information acceptable and unacceptable for communicating—A simple rule is to think before you speak. Telling clients their theme is outdated might not be the best method of communicating your distaste.

5. Understands that ideas can be rendered in various ways—For example, people interpret death differently in various contexts. A funeral after the death of a good friend might include singing and dancing in one culture and silence and mourning in another. Someone's idea of a funeral might be completely opposite of your own. So as you plan an event, consider asking questions so that you plan what is appropriate.

By understanding these five basic characteristics of rhetorical sensitivity, you should have a greater understanding of how to interpret situations and react appropriately.

THiNK !
BEFORE
YOU SPEAK.

Darnell and Brockriede (1976) articulate two additional orientations to rhetorical sensitivity: the noble self and rhetorical reflection. The **noble self** focuses on individuals who are not sensitive to others and to contexts. Noble selves have a rigid form of communication limited to their own personal goals. In the United States, others may perceive these people as rude or insensitive. The second orientation, **rhetorical reflection**, focuses on those constantly willing to alter their personal goals in order to adapt to others. Rhetorical reflectors work so hard at taking the other person into consideration that they might forget to focus on their own wants and needs. Many brides, for example, are guilty of trying to please everyone else and are willing to give up a dream wedding to please a mother or mother-in-law. Placed on a continuum, rhetorical sensitivity resides in the middle between the noble self and rhetorical reflection.

Noble Self	Rhetorical Sensitivity	Rhetorical Reflection

Rhetorical sensitivity creates a balance between personal integrity and adaptation to situations and contexts. Those who engage in rhetorical sensitivity avoid rigid communication patterns—"my way is the right way" mentality—and are more likely to adapt to the situation and context, finding a balance between the self and others (Darnell & Brockriede, 1976). Rhetorical sensitivity demands that planners are able to see and analyze a situation from many perspectives besides their own. Balance, flexibility, and empathy characterize the person who understands the need for rhetorical sensitivity in professional interactions. Event planners must balance the call for simplicity and directness with tact and understanding in conversations. Thus, event planners must not only understand the importance of communication, but they must also be experts who understand what information to share and when to share it.

Self-disclosure

Self-disclosure is defined as any unknown information (Pearce & Sharp, 1973) individuals communicate verbally about themselves to others (Cozby, 1973). Psychologist Paul Cozby (1973) believed that a communication act is considered self-disclosure when (1) the message contains some type of personal information, (2) the message is communicated verbally, and (3) another person is the recipient of the message. Self-disclosure has three dimensions, which are breadth (Altman & Taylor, 1973), depth (Altman & Taylor, 1973), and duration (Cozby, 1973). **Breadth** is the amount of information disclosed (Altman & Taylor, 1973), **depth** is the intimacy of information disclosed (Altman & Taylor, 1973), and **duration** is the time spent by an individual describing each item of information (Cozby, 1973). In the communication field, Wheeless and Grotz (1976) conceptualized self-disclosure as consisting of five dimensions. These dimensions are amount, intent, honesty, valence, and depth. **Amount** is the frequency and the duration of the disclosure; **intent** is the willingness of the individual to disclose; **honesty** is the truth of those revelations; **valence** is positive and/or negative

Noble self: *The concept that focuses on individuals who are not sensitive to others and context*

Rhetorical reflection: *Analysis that focuses on those constantly willing to alter their personal goals in order to adapt to others*

> **TIP**
>
> Empathy is essential. See through the eyes, feel through the pores, of the person attending the event.
>
> — Charles Steinberg

Self-disclosure: *Any unknown information individuals communicate verbally about themselves to others*

Breadth: *In self-disclosure, the amount of information disclosed*

Depth: *In self-disclosure, the intimacy of information disclosed*

Duration: *In self-disclosure, the time spent by an individual describing each item of information*

Amount: *The frequency and the duration of the disclosure*

Intent: *The willingness of the individual to disclose*

Honesty: *The truth of the revelations disclosed*

Valence: *Positive and/or negative statements disclosed by the individual*

statements revealed by the individual; and depth is the self-perceived intimacy of the information topic revealed (Wheeless & Grotz, 1976). For example, an event planner who is meeting a client for the first time might self-disclose very little personal information. After several meetings discussing intimate planning details, the event planner might become more comfortable sharing personal information.

Regardless of how we conceptualize self-disclosure, five generalizations about it exist in interpersonal communication research (Pearce & Sharp, 1973). First, relatively few communication transactions involve high levels of disclosure, although individuals are always self-disclosing information. Second, self-disclosure usually occurs in dyads. Third, self-disclosure is usually symmetrical. Fourth, self-disclosure occurs in the context of a positive relationship. Fifth, self-disclosure usually occurs incrementally. All of these traits offer insights into the ways in which self-disclosure can unfold in various types of relationships. For example, the sales team for a cable sports network channel typically takes sponsors to Florida each spring on a spring training trip, a three-day event full of activities that the associates plan. This group of business clients enjoys a first-class trip—all expenses paid—as a thank you for their connection to the network. The weekend includes dinner parties, cocktail hours, golf excursions, transportation to and from the ballpark, game tickets, and other events. One of the perks includes a collection of thank you gifts that include Kindles, baseball jerseys, and other favors. As clients discover what is in their gift bag, each piece of merchandise becomes a point of conversation, and through this conversation, aspects of self-disclosure can occur. Clients may discuss personal stories, such as the first time they went to a game, sports jerseys they own, the influence of sports on their lives, or favorite books on the Kindle. As clients begin to share experiences and self-disclose, they may start to feel more connected with one another. Because

these clients may never have met or interacted before, a trip such as this—one that is interspersed with many social events that can lead to self-disclosure—may create new relationships, and these relationships often become an unexpected perk of the trip.

Self-disclosure is a gradual process; in relationships, closeness develops over time. When people first meet, they slowly start to share information if there is a sense of liking and trust (Van Lear, 1991). Self-disclosure is central to the development of interpersonal relationships. The closer the relationship becomes, the more individuals will self-disclose (Altman & Taylor, 1973). Interestingly, individuals who engage in personal disclosures tend to be liked more than individuals who disclose at lower levels. In addition, individuals are likely to disclose more to people they like (Collins & Miller, 1994). Personal and negative disclosures occur later in relationships, whereas positive disclosures usually occur earlier in relationships (Gilbert & Whiteneck, 1976). Self-disclosure is also dependent on the norms associated with sex and culture (Derlega, Metts, Petronio, & Margulis, 1993). Women and same-sex relational partners disclose more often than men and opposite-sex relational partners (Dindia & Allen, 1992). In North American and northern European cultures, self-disclosure is more common in social and professional settings with acquaintances, friends, and family members. In Middle Eastern and Asian cultures, individuals are less likely to share information with social and professional acquaintances. Most disclosures occur in private settings with close relationships (Triandis, 1989). Moreover, when someone self-discloses information, the norm of reciprocity usually occurs (Miller & Kenny, 1986), which supposes an even exchange.

In professional settings, self-disclosure is inevitable; however, what one chooses to self-disclose is a crucial characteristic of drawing the line between private and professional. Not all private information needs to be shared with clients, but if there is no self-disclosure, clients might feel less connected to the event planner. Some self-disclosure can be a useful tool in one's work practices (Murphy & Ord, 2013). As an event planner, your job is to develop and maintain professional relationships with your clients. There might be times when it is best to keep personal information to yourself, and other times when self-disclosing will make the client feel at ease. For example, an event planner might make a nervous bride feel at ease by sharing that the bride's colors are the same ones as the event planner chose for her own wedding.

Social psychologists Irwin Altman and Dalmas Taylor (1973) developed the theory of **social penetration** to describe how a person's self-disclosure moves from superficial topics to more intimate information. The model of self-disclosure appears visually like an onion. As one slices an onion, multiple layers are visible. Each layer of the onion is representative of how intimate a conversation can become. The first layer is the **orientation stage**. This stage is the peripheral layer where information includes small talk, and people might discuss topics such as age, hometown, and favorite books. The second layer is the **exploratory affective stage**. This intermediate layer reveals more information around your preferences; examples would include political beliefs, recreational activities, and future plans. The central layers, known as the **affective stage** and **stable stage**, are the most personal and explore ideas such as value systems, beliefs, deeply held fears/fantasies, and personal issues of the self. These stages are usually reserved for more intimate relationships. Understanding these levels of self-disclosure will give the event planner more insight into a client's communication.

Social penetration: *A theory that describes how a person's self-disclosure moves from superficial topics to more intimate information*

Orientation stage: *In Social Penetration Theory, the peripheral layer where information might be described as small talk*

Exploratory affective stage: *In Social Penetration Theory, an intermediate level in which people reveal more information around their preferences, such as political beliefs or recreational choices*

Affective stage: *In Social Penetration Theory, the inner core of social penetration that examines ideas such as value systems and beliefs*

Stable stage: *In Social Penetration Theory, the most personal stage of identity, in which information such as value systems is revealed*

Uncertainty Reduction Theory

You have a new client whom a friend of a friend has referred, and you have arranged a first meeting in person to listen to the client's ideas about an upcoming event and perhaps proceed with an event planning agreement. When you meet, there is almost certainly going to be some awkwardness and hesitation between you and the client. Why does this discomfort occur in initial interactions, and how can you manage this uncertainty?

One theory of interpersonal communication was formulated in the 1970s as an explanation for the behavior that can occur in this particular situation or one similar to it: the **uncertainty reduction theory** looks at initial interactions of an interpersonal nature (Berger, 1975, 1979; 1987; Berger & Calabrese, 1975). Because most people prefer to operate under conditions of confidence, when they face an unfamiliar situation, they tend to seek out information in order to reduce their uncertainty about what is going on. The axioms of the theory help to explain certain behaviors during which people try to find out more facts about those with whom they are interacting (Berger & Calabrese, 1975).

> Axiom 1—verbal communication: As the amount of verbal communication between strangers increases, the level of uncertainty decreases, and, as a result, verbal communication increases (pp. 101–103).
>
> Axiom 2—nonverbal warmth: As nonverbal affiliative expressiveness increases, uncertainty levels will decrease. Decreases in uncertainty level will cause increases in nonverbal affiliative expressiveness (p. 103).
>
> Axiom 3—information seeking: High levels of uncertainty cause increases in information-seeking behavior. As uncertainty levels decline, information-seeking behavior decreases (p. 103).
>
> Axiom 4—self-disclosure: High levels of uncertainty in a relationship cause decreases in the intimacy level of communication content. Low levels of uncertainty produce high levels of intimacy (pp. 103–105).
>
> Axiom 5—reciprocity: High levels of uncertainty produce high rates of reciprocity. Low levels of uncertainty produce low levels of reciprocity (pp. 105–106).

From "Some Exploration in Initial Interaction and Beyond: Toward a Developmental Theory of Interpersonal Communication" by C. R. Berger and R. J. Calabrese, published in *Human Communication Research*. Copyright © 1975 John Wiley & Sons.

Uncertainty Reduction Theory: *an interpersonal communication theory that looks at initial interactions of an interpersonal nature*

Axiom 6—similarity: Similarities between persons reduce uncer-tainty, while dissimilarities produce increases in uncertainty (pp. 106–107).

Axiom 7—liking: Increases in uncertainty level produce decreases in liking; decreases in uncertainty produce increases in liking (p. 107).

© Jeanette Dietl/ Shutterstock.com

These axioms continue to be developed as research into the uncertainty reduction theory grows (Berger & Gudykunst, 1991; Neuliep & Grohskopf, 2000). In today's society, uncertainty is inevitable: the government seeks to reduce uncertainty through intelligence-gathering; individuals spend billions annually relying on the financial advice of professionals; and even the field of meteorology has grown to the extent that the expectation of accuracy in forecasting is unrealistic (Kramer, 2014). Not surprisingly, a great amount of communication research focuses on theories of uncertainty; the desire to dispel uncertainty is so fundamental to human nature that management of the tentative facets of life is essential (Goldsmith, 2001; Gudykunst, 1995). Anxiety plays a major role in the desire to live in more certainty, so further development of the original uncertainty reduction theory occurred about a decade after the original ideas were posited (Gudykunst, 1995). While uncertainty surrounds every facet of life, individuals still seek to reduce it by relying on intuition as well as formal structures to help in coping.

Two kinds of uncertainty tend to increase anxiety: cognitive and behavioral (Berger, 1979). **Cognitive uncertainty**, insecurity about another's beliefs or attitudes, and **behavioral uncertainty**, in which individuals understand that the actions of others are often unpredictable, complicate the development of a relationship with the client. People can slowly reduce cognitive uncertainty over time as the relationship develops and as the event planner becomes more adept at probing for the kind of information that will be essential in order to carry out the client's vision. The best event planners are those who can formulate questions that reveal necessary information without making the client feel interrogated or uncomfortable. The event planner must also be aware that there is a degree of uncertainty on the part of the client as well, and so the more communicative event planners can be about their goals and talents, the easier it will be on the client. Behavioral uncertainty, on the other hand, is less predictable. Individuals understand behavior in terms of what they have seen in the past from others and from themselves, but behavioral predictability in times of conflict, crisis, or chaos rapidly decreases. A steady and foreseeable pattern of behavior will help calm a client's apprehension and reduce uncertainty. Development of a client's trust depends upon reduction of anxiety and uncertainty, since positive outcomes are expected whenever there is an interaction (Saee, 2006). Individuals' perceptions about the groups to which others belong may also influence the kind and depth of uncertainty and anxiety they feel, but the best event planners develop the habit of **mindfulness**, waiting to form judgments until their own intergroup attitudes can be set aside (Gudykunst, 1983). For example, a common stereotype might be the expectation at a business conference that the day begins always with a keynote

Cognitive uncertainty: *In Social Penetration Theory, insecurity about another's beliefs or attitudes*

Behavioral uncertainty: *In Social Penetration Theory, the belief that the actions of others is often unpredictable*

Mindfulness: *A mental state in which one waits to form judgments until information is completely collected*

© BlueSkyImage/Shutterstock.com

speaker, when in fact, closing with an inspirational message moving forward might be a more beneficial way to end the day.

Your desire (as well as the client's) is to be able to form educated predictions related to past experiences, verbal and nonverbal cues, and other predictable behaviors about someone else's attitudes and actions based upon what they learn early in an interaction (Berger, 1975). You have the ability to choose the proper behavior that a particular situation demands so that your own actions can help to reduce uncertainty in others. Consistency and clarity are needed if event planners are to be successful in building a client base. Your brand must be constant and reliable so that the client is able to predict future behavior. According to the theory, strangers will withhold a decision about someone else's likability until they reduce uncertainty. This suggests that any positive relationship that might develop between a client and the event planner must first seek to dispel any insecurity about what is known or not known (Kellerman & Reynolds, 1990).

Good communication habits and an easy flow of conversation upon an initial meeting can do a lot to dispel this uncertainty. Not only will communication help to establish the kind of relationship you have with a client, but it will also decrease the anxiety that comes from first-time meetings. The more uncertain a person is, the more important it will be to present information, to decrease uncertainty, and to offer consistent and predictable behavior in line with what the client may expect (Berger & Calabrese, 1975). For example, when meeting clients for the first time, the event planner might want to get a sense of who they are and what they want to achieve through the event. Once some basic information is shared, the event planner might feel more comfortable probing for additional details about the event's vision. This pattern of behavior will, in turn, increase communication in the future. While questions about the connection between levels of uncertainty and tolerance levels in a person have yet to be definitively answered (Kellerman & Reynolds, 1990), it is important to note that most people will seek to reduce uncertainty in relationships they care to pursue. You may exchange several kinds of information, overtly or subtly, in an initial meeting: the conventions and standards for the kind of relationship that will be developed; the mutual values and beliefs that may be shared; and perhaps the leadership roles that will be established (Berger & Calabrese, 1975). Understanding the client's vision by listening, questioning, and offering ideas will help to close the loop along each phase of the event's plan. Paying attention to the nonverbal cues, the client's word choices, the questions asked, and the seemingly random comments by a client can all give the event planner a clearer understanding of what is expected and reduce the client's uncertainty as well (Barker & Gower, 2009).

TIP

Avoid defensiveness when challenged, and frame unexpected issues that you will have to deal with in positive ways (as opportunities that will make your responses more creative, ultimately improving the event). Presume goodwill on the part of others and express goodwill yourself. Ask questions in a non-defensive manner to help you understand others' positions.

— Lynn Turner

Unfortunately, uncertainty also occurs through events that are completely unpredictable, such as the weather, crises, guests who neglect to R.S.V.P. or attend, and other unforeseen variables. Research in crisis management acknowledges that uncertainty and unpredictability are inherent in a crisis situation, and that as risk increases, so does the accompanying level of uncertainty (Seeger, 2006). Chapter 12 will further explore this topic. The job of the event planner is to continue to work to reduce this inherent uncertainty so that the relationship with the client remains strong. Acknowledging the uncertainty in any situation is often a good starting point, but this "strategic ambiguity" (Seeger, 2006, p. 242) should not shut down communication or obscure the truth. For instance, a corporate retreat has scheduled its closing barbecue for outdoors, when a sudden rainstorm forces the event to shift the final ceremonies from the waterfront location to back inside the venue. The event planner must rely on strategic ambiguity, knowing that the space indoors is still available even though it may not be as picturesque.

Event planners who are able to manage their own uncertainty as well as help to reduce the uncertainty and anxiety of their clients will find themselves developing a brand that is reliable, consistent, transparent, and professional as well as a personal reputation for being friendly and engaging. They also develop a habit of mindfulness, remaining unbiased with each client they meet and not presuming anything about ethnic, racial, and cultural choices. Though there have been challenges to the uncertainty reduction theory, it still offers answers to the basic human need for management of the world's vagaries (Berger, 1987; Brashers, 2001; Kellerman & Reynolds, 1990; Sunnafrank, 1986). Planners who understand and appreciate the human desire for constancy and preparedness will work to make sure they can answer their clients' questions without hesitation.

Perception

In his seminal work in psychology of interpersonal communication, Fritz Heider (1958) postulated that it is through **perception** that you can come to understand the world around you, including that which brings the environment together: people, things, and events. Heider divides perception into two main categories: (1) **nonsocial perception** (or thing perception) when speaking of inanimate objects, and (2) **social perception** (or person perception) when speaking of the perception of another person. When considering the two categories, it is important to note that nonsocial perception differs from social perception in many ways. For instance, you understand that things have shape, color, and smell, and are placed in positions that are functional and in real space. You can sit on a cozy chair in the lobby at an event; you can see white twinkle lights hanging from the beams in a barn at a wedding; and you can smell the Italian food wafting into the room from the chef's kitchen. All of these are examples of nonsocial perception. With social perception, it becomes more likely that you perceive things about

Perception: *Ways in which people come to understand the world around them*

Nonsocial perception (or "thing perception"): *Awareness of inanimate objects*

Social perception (or "person perception"): *An awareness that occurs when speaking of the perception of another person*

people, and not just information gleaned from the clothes they wear or the style of their hair. Heider (1958) writes that people are perceived as "action centers and as such can do something to us. They can benefit or harm us intentionally, and you can benefit or harm them. Persons have abilities, wishes, and sentiments; they can act purposefully, and can perceive or watch us" (p. 21). In other words, you often wonder about the internal makeup of a person, which requires that a deeper cognitive evaluation take place (Anant, 2010). For example, you are meeting with a bride and groom to plan their wedding. The groom is amenable and intent on giving his bride the perfect reception. However, at the event, he explodes over a minor detail. As an event planner, you must understand that his behavior at that moment might be a direct result of his nervousness.

Using Heider's (1958) theory as a guide, both nonsocial and social perception will take place as event planners organize, stage, and execute events. Guests will perceive nonsocial aspects of the event, such as the venue, the table settings, the signs, the flowers, and the theme colors, forming their own impressions. Additionally, those attending the event will develop specific perceptions regarding table size, proximity to their neighbor at the table, and stations at the cocktail hour. Social perceptions will take place when guests assess the people at their table as being friendly or unfriendly, and when determining whether the wait staff was helpful or unhelpful for the duration of the event. Both types of perception help people make sense of what is communicated around them.

There is a significant relationship between how people perceive their own skills as communicators and how effective they perceive others in an organization. Perception of how individuals see themselves is in some way a reflection of how they see others (Anant, 2010). For instance, when meeting a client for the first time, you both will perceive what each other's roles might be as the initial planning stages begin to progress, and as you get to know each other's work ethic. Throughout that first meeting and subsequent ones, the event planner and the client will discover things about each other that ultimately will guide their decisions and strategies.

Event planners should be conscious of the needs of those with whom they work, including vendors, entertainers, contractors, staff, and others, knowing that each one's identity is determined by the way in which they perceive each other. There can be confusion in meaning that affects perception, and a misjudgment on the part of either party can occur when communicating if they do not share thoughts and intentions. By sharing their objectives, intents, and goals, along with being patient listeners, event planners help confirm directions, as well as clear up any misconceptions about tasks. "The management function cannot exist without communication, an extremely vital part of any organizational system" (Minter, 1974, p. 40). Perception is integral to the communication process because it has the power to influence how you build internal data (Graham, Unruh, & Jennings, 1991). Event planners should keep in mind that clients and employees have different perceptions, see the world in different ways, and have dissimilar methods of solving problems (Epler, 2014). Clients may also have their own ideas with regard to how the event should run. While you will form your own perceptions, and clients will form their own perceptions, you must reserve passing judgment, find a common ground, and look for deeper meaning to help you creatively come to an agreement and continue planning the event.

Schnake, Dumler, Cochran and Barnett (1990) suggest that communication can benefit from an environment in which individuals share a mutual respect, concern, and trust among superiors and subordinates. This type of enterprise can help offset perceptual differences regarding superiors and subordinates when it comes to communication effectiveness. Think of how often you may have to inform clients that the way they want the event staged cannot happen due to technical issues. Your job is to help shape their perception and provide information as to why things need to change. Hopefully, they will trust your expertise and be open to a new approach. Even though the staging may not be as they originally envisioned it, the event can still be effective and entertaining. If the clients perceive you have their best interests at heart, they may be more likely to agree.

Heider (1959) studied the work of novelist and essayist Marcel Proust as an example of someone who was able to interpret how individuals perceive reality and how the subjective impressions they gain can be different from the objective world. What resulted in Proust's brilliant writings was his remarkable ability to describe and comment on what French society was like at the time. Through those keen observations, Proust recorded perceptions of the time that may not have been widely known, or indeed, years later, remembered. His writing captures the essence of the period. Likewise, as an event planner, your perceptions will guide how you interact with people interpersonally through social perception. Understanding the role of nonsocial perception will advise you as to how physical aspects of the event will influence people and help them form their own perceptions of what you planned.

TIP

Remember, you are the event planner and were hired for a reason, so take charge and be sure everyone knows you are running the day and all decisions must be made by you. This also lets everyone know they can depend on you for any questions and/or needs.

— Elle Ellinghaus

Attribution Theory

The study of attribution theory can be credited initially to the work of Heider (1958), then to Kelley (1973) and Weiner (1972, 1974, 1986), who

Attribution Theory: *A theory that seeks to explain why people do the things they do*

Attributions: *Perceived causes that individuals select or construct for events in their lives*

derived much of their work from Heider's initial framework. **Attribution theory** is a way to explain why people do the things they do. **Attributions** are perceived causes that individuals select or construct for events in their lives. People want to understand the causes of important happenings, and they want to know if their particular attributions have the potential to influence their responses to these outcomes (Heider, 1958). Heider assumed that people want to draw their own conclusions, and that the significance or meaning of a happening—including the cause of it—can be attributed either to a person or to the environment. Knowing how successes and failures affect you can ultimately influence how you behave, as well as influence expectations, emotions, and behaviors (Martinko, Harvey, & Douglas, 2007). Overall, people seek attributions because everyone wants to understand behavior.

Event planners may attribute certain behaviors by clients or guests at an event because they want to understand why people behave in a certain way. If a client storms out of a meeting, event planners will want to understand the reasons for this type of behavior. Was it because she was not happy with the plans? Did she feel like she was being let down? Did someone say something that she interpreted incorrectly? Likewise, event planners may assess their own behaviors when a crisis happens or when something surprising hinders or enhances an event. By searching for the underlying meaning as to why people behave the way they do, event planners can better understand themselves as well as their clients and/or guests.

Martinko, Harvey, and Dasborough (2010), in their study of organizations, suggest that behavior is determined through a system of rewards and punishments, and that attributions can affect exactly how people behave. Individuals typically have an interest in understanding what makes someone behave a certain way, whether these reasons connect to a specific incident, or whether they simply relate to behaviors that occur often and over time. Moreover, attribution styles can have an impact on interpersonal relationships, and as these relationships change and grow and adjust over time, the effects of attributions can be even more profound. Think about a recent

© *sirtravelalot/Shutterstock.com*

situation you have encountered at school or at work with an individual who seemed to be a team player, but then betrayed your trust and allowed something to fall through the cracks, causing you to earn a bad grade or receive reduced hours at work. At the crux of this situation is your curiosity: how could it have come to this? Individuals act as psychologists because they want to know why people behave the way they do (Heider, 1958). While it is common to ask why certain behavior occurs, event planners must be careful not to overanalyze and form unwarranted perceptions.

Weiner's (1972, 1974, 1986, 1989) attribution theory focuses mostly on achievement, and explains that it is based on four notions including ability, effort, task difficulty, and luck. Weiner developed a model that related attributions to achievement behaviors. The theory stated that one's attributions for either success or failure could be classified in two ways: (1) the locus of control, which was determined to be either within or outside the person, or (2) stability, which was determined by how consistent or inconsistent the characteristics were. However, before assessing which classification it could be, internal and external causes must be identified. Effort and ability would be seen as internal causes; aspects like luck and how difficult a task is would be perceived as external causes (Dubinsky, Skinner, & Whittler, 1989). Imagine that you are supposed to book a venue for a corporate event, and the number one choice frequently used is booked. At this point, you have to choose the number two venue. Your clients are disappointed at first, but then, after seeing the venue that is available, they become extremely excited about the new space. Their emotional state is due to external causes—simply that the venue was not available. However, once they saw the alternative space, they were pleased, and their behavior reflected their satisfaction. Now, imagine that by a stroke of luck, they learn venue one is available. How will the clients' behavior change? Will they want you to secure their original choice?

Kelley's model (1973) expanded Heider's (1958, 1959) notion that people want to know what causes certain behaviors or outcomes. Kelley suggests that people want to know if their behavior is derived from their own motives or traits (which is called a **person attribution**), because of the task or situation (which is called an **entity attribution**), or a combination of the two of them (which is called a **context attribution**). These different attributions require you to examine yourself first. Do you behave a certain way because of your own motives and traits? When you are with clients in a business setting, do you behave in a professional manner? Are you courteous? Do you listen well? Do you allow others to speak? Your behavior is guided by person attribution because it is coming from within you. Now imagine that you are at an outdoor festival, under a canopy in which the tent flaps keep blowing, and it is clear they are not properly anchored into the ground. This disturbance reflects on your professionalism and leadership of the event. In this case, the tent problem is the entity attribution—an outside task or situation. Based on this difficulty, the event planner might decide never to use a tent again or blame the company for the malfunction. Finally, context attribution would include a blend of intrinsic motives combined with the actual task or situation, which then causes you to examine your behavior accordingly. For example, your client is speaking at a corporate event, and you have already booked the room. However, upon entering the venue for the presentation, he is dissatisfied with the small space. Trying to accommodate his desire for a larger venue, you must determine how to proceed. Both the motives for success of the task and the personal behaviors of each of you will establish a means of negotiating the space.

Person attribution: *The belief that behavior is derived from one's own motives or traits*

Entity attribution: *The belief that behavior is derived from a task or situation*

Context Attribution: *The belief that behavior is derived from a combination of one's own motives or behaviors combined with a task or situation*

An event planner's interpersonal skills are vital. Understanding the importance of listening, and improving your listening skills, will help you succeed in the industry. Fostering an understanding of how relationships are developed and nurtured through interpersonal communication means cultivating the most basic characteristics of professional relationships: clarity, credibility, and competency. Event planners rely on these enviable characteristics to win clients, build a brand, and expand their business. Many different areas of interpersonal communication help form the event planner's strengths.

Each meeting of the minds between planner and client can be fraught with misconceptions, confusion, and misunderstanding. The event planner's authenticity and desire to communicate on a professional level offers the opportunity to see and accept another's point of view that could be inconsistent or even contradictory at times. Patience and empathy are two very significant qualities in these cases. Drawing the line between the professional and the private takes balance, practice, and confidence. Because most people have an innate desire to learn as much as they can about others, event planners can build assurance in their expertise by revealing information honestly and openly from the start. A balanced and predictable pattern of behavior, language choices, and emotion can encourage clients to set aside their uncertainties and rely on the skills of their event planner. By developing listening skills and interpersonal relationships, event planners can better understand themselves as well as their clients.

Key Terms

Interpersonal communication	Time-oriented listeners	Honesty	Perception
Hearing	Thought speed	Valence	Nonsocial perception
Listening	Rhetorical sensitivity	Social penetration	Social perception
Discriminative listening	Noble self	Orientation stage	Attribution Theory
Appreciative listening	Rhetorical reflection	Exploratory affective stage	Attributions
Empathic listening	Self-disclosure	Affective stage	Person attribution
Comprehensive listening	Breadth	Stable stage	Entity attribution
Critical listening	Depth	Uncertainty Reduction Theory	Context attribution
People-oriented listeners	Duration	Cognitive uncertainty	
Action-oriented listeners	Amount	Behavioral uncertainty	
Content-oriented listeners	Intent	Mindfulness	

Discussion Questions

1. What type of listening (discriminative, appreciative, empathic, comprehensive, or critical) do you find yourself engaging in the most? Offer an example.
2. What kind of listening (people-oriented, action-oriented, content-oriented, or time-oriented) do you find yourself engaging in the most? Why?

3. Give an example of when you or someone else self-disclosed too much information. How did you respond?
4. How do you personally reduce uncertainty when meeting new people? How do these strategies ease the conversation?
5. Explain a time when your perception was inaccurate. What caused you to change your perception? How did you come to this conclusion?

Activity

Working with your classmates, create an informal networking event where you have the opportunity to meet others and learn about others' likes and dislikes. Each member of the class should bring a guest (friend, family member, colleague, and faculty member, etc.) to the classroom event. This activity will allow you to plan your first event and practice your interpersonal skills.

References

Allen, T. (1977). How good a listener are you? *Management Review, 66,* 37–39.

Altman, I., & Taylor, D. A. (1973). *Social penetration: The development of interpersonal relationships.* New York: Holt, Rinehart, & Winston.

Anant, H. (2010). Interpersonal perceptions within organizations: An exploratory study. *The IUP Journal of Soft Skills, 4,* 34–47.

Ball, S. A., & Zuckerman, M. (1992). Sensation seeking and selective attention: Focused and divided attention on a dichotic listening task. *Journal of Personality and Social Psychology, 63,* 825–831.

Barker, L. L., & Watson, K. W. (2000). *Listen up: How to improve relationships, reduce stress, and be more productive by using the power of listening.* New York: St. Martin's Press.

Barker, L. L. (1971). *Listening Behavior.* Englewood Cliffs, New Jersey: Prentice Hall.

Barker, R. T., & Gower, K. (2009). Use of uncertainty reduction and narrative paradigm theories in management consulting and teaching: Lessons learned. *Business Communication Quarterly, 72,* 338–341.

Berger, C. R. (1975). Proactive and retroactive attribution processes in interpersonal communications. *Human Communication Research, 2,* 33–50.

_____. (1979). Beyond initial interaction: Uncertainty, understanding, and the development of interpersonal relationships. In H. Giles and R. St. Clair (Eds.), *Language and social psychology* (pp. 122–144). Baltimore, MD: University Park Press.

_____. (1987). Communicating under uncertainty. In M. E. Roloff & G. R. Miller (Eds.), *Interpersonal processes: New directions in communication research* (pp. 39–62). Newbury Park, CA: Sage.

Berger, C. R., & Calabrese, R. J. (1975). Some exploration in initial interaction and beyond: Toward a developmental theory of interpersonal communication. *Human Communication Research, 1,* 99–112.

Berger, C. R., & Gudykunst, W. B. (1991). Uncertainty and communication. In B. Dervin & M. J. Voight (Eds.), *Progress in Communication Sciences,* (pp. 21–66). Norwood, NJ: Ablex.

Brashers, D. (2001). Communication and uncertainty management. *Journal of Communication, 51,* 477–497.

Brown, L. (1982). *Communicating facts and ideas in business.* Englewood Cliffs, NJ: Prentice Hall.

Bunkers, S. S. (2010). The power and possibility in listening. *Nursing Science Quarterly, 23,* 22–27.

————. (2015). Listening: Important to the stuff of a life. *Nursing Science Quarterly, 28,* 103–106.

Burley-Allen, M. (1982). *Listening: The forgotten skill.* New York: Wiley.

Collins, N. L., & Miller, L. C. (1994). Self-disclosure and liking: A meta-analytic review. *Psychological Bulletin, 116,* 457–475.

Cozby, P. C. (1973). Self-disclosure: A literature review. *Psychological Bulletin, 79,* 73–91.

Cupach, W. R., & Spitzberg, B. H. (2010). *The dark side of close relationships II.* New York: Routledge.

Darnell, D., & Brockriede, W. (1976). *Persons communicating.* Englewood Cliffs, NJ: Prentice Hall.

Derlega, V. J., Metts, S., Petronio, S., & Margulis, S. T. (1993). *Self-disclosure.* Newbury Park, CA: Sage.

Dilbeck, K. E., & McCroskey, J. C. (2009). Socio-Communicative orientation, communication competence, and rhetorical sensitivity. *Human Communication, 12,* 255–266.

Dindia, K., & Allen, M. (1992). Sex differences in self-disclosure: A meta-analysis. *Psychological Bulletin, 112,* 106–124.

Dubinsky, A. J., Skinner, S. J., & Whittler, T. E. (1989). Evaluating sales personnel: An attribution theory perspective. *Journal of Personal Selling & Sales Management, 9,* 9–21.

Eadie, W. F., & Paulson, J. W. (1984). Communicator attitudes, communicator style, and communication competence. *The Western Journal of Speech Communication, 48,* 390–407.

Epler, D. (2014). The habits of communication. *Strategic Finance, 96,* 15–61.

Erozkan, A. (2013). The effect of communication skills and interpersonal problem solving skills on social self-efficacy. *Educational Sciences: Theory & Practice,13,* 739–745.

Gabric, D., & McFadden, K. L. (2001). Student and employer perceptions of desirable entry-level operations management skills. *Mid-American Journal of Business, 16,* 51–59.

Gentile, J. S. (2004). Telling the untold tales: Memory's care-taker. *Text and Performance Quarterly, 24,* 201–204.

Gilbert, S. J., & Whiteneck, G. G. (1976). Toward a multidimensional approach to the study of self-disclosure. *Human Communication Research, 2*, 347–355.

Goldsmith, D. J. (2001). A normative approach to the study of uncertainty and communication. *Journal of Communication, 51*, 514–533.

Golen, S. (1990). A factor analysis of barriers to effective listening. *Journal of Business Communication, 27*, 25–36.

Graham, G., Unruh, J., & Jennings, P. (1991). The impact of nonverbal communication in organizations: a survey of perceptions. *Nonverbal Communication, 28*, 45–62.

Gudykunst, W. W. (1983). Theorizing in intercultural communication. In R. L. Wiseman (Ed.), *Intercultural communication theory* (pp. 1–20). Beverly Hills, CA: Sage Publications.

_____. (1995). The uncertainty reduction and anxiety-uncertainty reduction theories of Berger, Gudykunst and associates. In D. P. Cushman & B. Kovacic (Eds.), *Watershed research traditions in human communication theory* (pp. 67–100). New York: SUNY Press.

Haas, J. W., & Arnold, C. L. (1995). An examination of the role of listening in co-workers. *Journal of Business Communication, 35*, 123–139

Hamilton, C. (2014). *Communicating for results: A guide for business and the professions.* Boston, MA: Wadsworth, Cengage Learning.

Hart, R. P., & Burks, D. M. (1972). Rhetorical sensitivity and social interaction. *Speech Monographs, 39*, 75–91.

Heider, F. (1958). *The psychology of interpersonal relations.* New York, NY: John Wiley & Sons, Inc.

_____. (1959). *Psychological issues on perception, event, structure, and psychological environment.* New York: International Universities Press.

Hoppe, M. (2006). *Active listening: Improve your ability to listen and lead.* Greensboro, NC: Center for Creative Leadership.

Horowitz, S. S. (2012). *The universal senses: How hearing shapes the mind.* Fairfield, PA: Westchester Book Group.

International Language Association (ILA). (1996). *Listening definition.* Retrieved from http://www.listen.org.

Kaufmann, P. J. (1993). *Sensible listening: The key to responsive instruction* (2nd ed.). Dubuque, IA: Kendall Hut.

Keefe, W. F. (1971). *Listening management.* New York: McGraw Hill.

Kellerman, K., & Reynolds, R. (1990). When ignorance is bliss: the role of motivation to reduce uncertainty in uncertainty reduction theory. *Human Communication Research, 17*, 5–75.

Kelley, H. H. (1973). The process of causal attributions. *American Psychologist, 28*, 107–128.

Knapp, M. L., & Daly, J.A. (Eds.). (2011). *The Sage handbook of interpersonal communication* (4th ed.). Thousand Oaks, CA: Sage.

Knutson, T. J., Komolsevin, R., Chatiketu, P., & Smith, V. R. (2003). A cross-cultural comparison of Thai and U.S. American rhetorical sensitivity: Implications for intercultural communication effectiveness. *International Journal of Intercultural Relations, 27*, 63–78.

Kramer, M. W. (2014). *Managing uncertainty in organizational communication.* New York: Routledge.

Landrum, R. E., & Harrold, R. (2003). What employers want from psychology graduates. *Teaching of Psychology, 30*, 131–133.

Lane, K., Balleweg, B. J., Suler, J. R., Fernald, P. S., & Goldstein, G. S. (2000). Acquiring skills—Undergraduate students. In M. E. Ware & D. E. Johnson (Eds.), *Handbook of demonstrations and activities in the teaching of psychology: Personality, abnormal, clinical-counseling, and social* (Vol 3., 2nd ed., pp. 109–124). Mahwah, NJ: Erlbaum.

Lipari, L. (2014). *Listening, thinking, being: Towards an ethics of attunement.* University Park, PA: The Pennsylvania State University Press.

Marchant, V. (1999). Listen up! *Time, 153*, 74.

Martinko, M. J., Harvey, P., & Dasborough, M. (2010). Attribution theory in the organizational sciences: A case study of unrealized potential. *Journal of Organizational Behavior, 32*, 144–149.

Martinko, M. J., Harvey, P., & Douglas, S. C. (2007). The role, function, and contribution of attribution theory to leadership: A review. *The Leadership Quarterly, 18*, 561–585.

McGee, D. S., & Cegala, D. J. (1998). Patient communication skills training for improved competence in the primary care medical consultation. *Journal of Applied Communication Research, 26*, 412–430.

McNaughton, D., Hamlin, D., McCarthy, J. Head-Reeves, D., & Schreiner, M. (2007). Learning to listen: Teaching an active listening strategy to preservice educational professional. *Topics in Early Childhood Education, 27*, 223–231.

Miller, L. C., & Kenny, D. A. (1986). Reciprocity of self-disclosure at the individual and dyadic levels: A social relations analysis. *Journal of Personality and Social Psychology, 50*, 713–719.

Miller, N., Maruyama, G., Beaber, R. J., & Valone, K. (1976). Speed of speech and persuasion. *Journal of Personality and Social Psychology, 34*, 615–624.

Minter, R. L. (1974). Interpersonal dynamics of organizational communication: An Overview. *Journal of Business Communication, 11*, 40–52.

Montgomery, B. M. (1981). The form and function of quality communication in marriage. *Family Relations, 30*, 21–30.

Moore, K. (2005). Become a better communicator by keeping your mouth shut. *Journal for Quality & Participation, 28*, 8–10.

Morreale, S., Rubin, R., & Jones, E. (1998). *Speaking and listening competencies for college students.* Washington, DC: National Communication Association.

Murphy, C., & Ord, J. (2013). Youth work, self-disclosure and professionalism. *Ethics & Social Welfare*, 7, 326–341.

Nardi, B. (2005). Beyond bandwidth: Dimensions of connection in interpersonal communication. *Computer Supported Cooperative Work: The Journal of Collaborative Computing*, 14, 91–130.

Noller, P. (1984). *Nonverbal communication and marital interaction*. Oxford: Pergamon.

Neuliep, J. W., & Grohskopf, E. L. (2000). Uncertainty reduction and communication satisfaction during initial interaction: An initial test and replication of a new axiom. *Communication Reports*, 13, 67–77.

O'Keefe, D. J. (2002). *Persuasion: Theory and research* (2nd ed.). Newbury Park, CA: Sage.

Pearce, W. B., & Sharp, S. M. (1973). Self-disclosing communication. *Journal of Communication*, 23, 409–425.

Prager, K. J., & Buhrmester, D. (1998). Intimacy and need fulfillment in couple relationships. *Journal of Personal and Social Relationships*, 15, 435–469.

Pryor, S., Malshe, A., & Paradise, K. (2013). Salesperson listening in the extended sales relationship: An exploration of cognitive, affective, and temporal dimensions. *Journal of Personal Selling & Sales Management*, 33, 185–196.

Purdy, M. (1991). Listening and community: The role of listening in community formation. *International Journal of Listening*, 5, 51–67.

_____. (1997). What is listening? In M. Purdy, and D. Borisoff (Eds.). *Listening in everyday life* (pp. 1–20). Lanham, MD: University Press of America.

Rane, D. B. (2011). Good listening skills make efficient business sense. *IUP Journal of Soft Skills* 5, 43–51.

Rankin, P. T. (1930). Listening ability. *Chicago Schools Journal*, 12, 177–179.

Razmjou, L., & Ghazi, J. (2013). Listening practice influence on the use of communication strategies in oral translation. *Theory & Practice in Language Studies*, 3, 1645–1650.

Saee, J. (2006). *Managerial competence within the tourism and hospitality service industries: Global cultural contextual analysis*. New York: Routledge.

Schnake, M. E., Dumler, M. P., Cochran Jr., D. S., & Barnett, T. R. (1990). Effects of differences in superior and subordinate perceptions of superiors' communication practices. *Journal of Business Communication*, 27, 37–50.

Seeger, M. W. (2006). Best practices in crisis communication: An expert panel process. *Journal of Applied Communication Research*, 34, 232–244.

Smart, K. L., & Featheringham, R. (2006). Developing effective interpersonal communication and discussion skills. *Business Communication Quarterly*, 69, 276–283.

SmithBattle, L., Lorenz, R., & Leander, S. (2013). Listening with care: using narrative methods to cultivate nurses' responsive relationships in a home visiting intervention with teen mothers. *Nursing Inquiry*, 20, 188–198.

Spinks, N., & Wells, B. (1991). Improving listening power: The payoff. *Bulletin of the Association for Business Communication, 54,* 75–77.

Steil, L. K. (1996). Listening training: The key to success in today's organization. In M. Purdy & D. Borisoff (Eds.), *Listening in everyday life: A personal and professional approach* (2nd ed., pp. 213–237). Lanham, MD: University Press of America.

Sunnafrank, M. (1986). Predicted outcome value during initial interactions: A reformulation of uncertainty reduction theory. *Human Communication Research, 13,* 3–33.

Sypher, B., Bostrom, R. N., & Seibert, J. (1989). Listening, communication abilities, and success at work. *Journal of Business Communication, 26,* 293–303.

Szczepaniak, M., Pathan, H., & Soomro, N. (2013). A study of teaching listening to intermediate learners. *International Journal of Academic Research, 5,* 207–212.

Thomas, L. T., & Levine, T. R. (1994). Disentangling listening and verbal recall: Related but separate constructs? *Human Communication Research, 21,* 103–127.

Todd, T. L., & Levine, T. R. (1996). Further thoughts on recall, memory, and the measurement of listening: A rejoinder to Bostrom. *Human Communication Research, 23,* 306–308.

Triandis, H. C. (1989). The self and the social behavior in differing cultural contexts. *Psychological Review, 96,* 506–520.

Van Lear, C. A. (1991). Testing a cyclical model of communicative openness in relationship development: Two longitudinal studies. *Communication Monographs, 58,* 337–361.

Watson, K. W., & Barker, L. L. (1995). *Listening styles profile.* Amsterdam: Pfeiffer & Company.

Weiner, B. (1972). *Theories of motivation: From mechanism to cognition.* Chicago: Markham.

_____. (1974). *Achievement motivation and attribution theory.* Morristown, N.J.: General Learning Press.

_____. (1986). *An attributional theory of motivation and emotion.* New York: Springer-Verlag.

_____. (1989). *Human Motivation.* New Jersey: Lawrence Erlbaum Associates, Inc. (Original work published in 1980)

Weinrach, J., & Swanda Jr., J. R. (1975). Examining the significance of listening: An exploratory study of contemporary management. *Journal of Business Communication, 13,* 25–32.

Wheeless, L. R., & Grotz, J. (1976). Conceptualization and measurement of reported self-disclosure. *Human Communication Research, 2,* 338–346.

Winsor, J. L., Curtis, D. B., & Stephens, R. D. (1997). National preferences in business and communication education: An update. *Journal of the Association for Communication Administration, 3,* 170–179.

Wolvin, A. D. (Ed.). (2010). *Listening and human communication in the 21st century.* Malden, MA: Blackwell.

Wolvin, A. D., & Coakley, C. G. (1991). A survey of the status of listening training in some Fortune 500 companies. *Communication Education, 40,* 152–164.

_____. (1996). *Listening.* (5th ed.). Columbus, OH: McGraw-Hill.

Wolvin, A. D., Coakley, C. G., & Gwynn, C. (1999). *Listening* (6th ed.). Boston McGraw-Hill.

Chapter 3

NONVERBAL COMMUNICATION: THE UNSPOKEN WORDS OF EVENT PLANNING

© pcruciatti/Shutterstock.com

In a world increasingly filled with multi-taskers who are not always attuned to the world around them, it is essential that competent communicators pay attention to the signals that others may be sending nonverbally. Specifically, in the world of event planning, to be aware of and deliberate about communication style means to act consciously and intentionally, considering what may happen as a result of the signals being sent and received (Berlo, 1960). Yet so often, people fail to contemplate the consequences of their own nonverbal cues or miss the feedback others are sending. This lack of attentiveness in the world of event planning can have disastrous effects, for entire environments are filled with nonverbal cues that demand focus in order to make any event successful. Most communicators would acknowledge that deliberate nonverbal skills are necessary for success in the majority of interactions (Birdwhistell, 1970; Hogan & Stubbs, 2003; Mehrabian, 1972). Sundaram and Webster (2000) argue that service fields should focus on nonverbal proficiencies because there is a direct link to credibility, friendliness, competence, empathy, courtesy, and trustworthiness. Moreover, Behesti (2018) discusses the power behind mindful nonverbal communication that deliberately reinforces a message. However, people take this nonverbal proficiency for granted all too often. This chapter will discuss significant areas of nonverbal communication: kinesics, facial displays, oculesics, olfactics, haptics, physical appearance, artifacts, paralanguage, proxemics, and chronemics in relation to event planning. Event planners must recognize and adapt to nonverbal behaviors, as nonverbal communication can be instrumental as planners become competent at deciphering and improving the exchange of messages with clients.

When you have finished reading this chapter, you will be able to

- explain the social importance of nonverbal communication;
- identify the significant areas of nonverbal communication;
- choose the proper area of nonverbal communication to help explain a particular client behavior.

Nonverbal Communication and Event Planning: Messages Everywhere!

Janie Harden Fritz, Ph.D., Professor of Communication & Rhetorical Studies, Duquesne University

To plan an event that rocks, think about the way it is set up as an exercise in nonverbal communication competence. We do not always think about space until it gets in our way (or gets away from us)—when we find ourselves crowded against other people, tripping over tables, or unable to get to snacks, drinks, or restrooms without a GPS.

Elements of space and event structure send powerful nonverbal messages not only to guests of an event, but also to those who are helping to host or sponsor it. As vice-president and planner of the 101st convention of the Eastern Communication Association (ECA), I was concerned about giving our textbook publishers' representatives a space with lots of traffic. If vendors cannot get their books under the eyes of instructors or scholars who might want to adopt or buy those books, vendors are less likely to see the event as a good investment of resources. I wanted to tell them, through where they were positioned, that we wanted and appreciated their sponsorship, and I wanted to announce to convention goers that attention to our sponsors was important.

My second vice-president, Leeanne M. Bell (now Leeanne M. Bell McManus and one of the authors of this book), suggested that we locate the vendors in the main thoroughfare of the convention area, in a sunny, open space near the coffee café, rather than in an isolated room. The message this placement sent delighted the representatives and also invited convention-goers to browse through the books regularly. This nonverbal message of welcome generated much gratitude and future business for the association.

Food showcased at an event—both featured selections and the way they are served and designed to be consumed—is a message as well. For this Baltimore convention, crab cakes were a must for the elaborate President's Reception. For the Welcome Reception, more casual fare of veggies, cheese and crackers, and fruit worked well. The key in each case, however, was to make sure there was plenty of food available to communicate hospitality. Another key nonverbal message of hospitality is honoring diversity in the dietary needs of guests, whether those needs are based on health issues or religious observation. For example, featuring gluten-free selections, vegetarian and vegan options, and Kosher items sends a welcoming message of inclusion.

For serving food at a main meal, what nonverbal messages does a planner send with a buffet line, a sit-down dinner, or stations scattered throughout the space dedicated to particular categories of food, such as vegetables, desserts, or main dishes? A sit-down, plated dinner speaks of a more formal atmosphere, but offers fewer choices for guests, who may want different quantities or types of food. However, remaining seated invites guests to concentrate on conversation without significant interruption.

For receptions, having some food items passed around by serving staff slows down consumption and sends a message of grace, opulence, and indulgence to guests who are being served, while including some buffet items says that food is easily available for those whose appetites are more vigorous. Paying attention to the nonverbal message communicated can help ensure that your event has a rhythm that satisfies guests.

Contributed by Janie Harden Fritz. Copyright © Kendall Hunt Publishing Company.

After reading this chapter, revisit the case study and respond to the following question:

In what other ways could you focus on nonverbal communication to enhance your event?

Nonverbal Communication

Clearly and deliberately communicating through nonverbals in the field of event planning will help you become successful. Adapting your unspoken cues in exchanges with clients will not only strengthen the client-planner relationship, but it will also make other interactions more fulfilling and consistent. Developing heightened awareness of nonverbal signals lets others know how well you are listening, how truthful you are, and how much trust they can put in you (Ekman, 1999; Patterson & Manusov, 2006; Sundaram & Webster, 2000). Event planners need to build rapport through the consistent and competent use of nonverbal communication.

Communication scholars Judy Burgoon and Aaron Bacue (2003) state that "upward of 60% of meaning in any social situation is communicated nonverbally" (p. 179). Anthropologist Ray Birdwhistell (1970) believes that generally 65% of meaning comes from nonverbal interactions while 35% comes from verbal interactions. Psychologist Albert Mehrabian (1972) claimed that 93% of the emotional impact behind a message comes from nonverbal cues. No matter what discipline you study, the message is the same: nonverbal interactions are important.

Nonverbal communication describes all communication interactions that transcend the written and/or spoken word (Knapp, Hall, & Horgan, 2014). Nonverbal communication has an im pact in everyday interactions with others (Giles & Le Poire, 2006). Nonverbals are a central part of the communication process (Burgoon, 1994), meaning acquisition (Birdwhistell, 1970), and impression management (Xin, 2004). When event planners fail to use the right nonverbal cues in their interactions, others perceive them as being dull, withdrawn, uneasy, aloof, and deceptive (DePaulo, 1992). What makes nonverbal communication essential is the significant role it plays in interpreting a message (Mehrabian, 1972); however, one encodes nonverbal behavior with various degrees of control, accuracy, and awareness (Lakin,

TIP

The type, amount, and availability of food all send messages. Be aware of food needs of varied guests. Responsiveness to allergies, religious observances, and personal convictions sends a nonverbal message of welcome.

— Janie Harden Fritz

Nonverbal communication: *All communication interactions that transcend the written and/or spoken word*

TIP

In addition to your verbal responses to others, consider the messages conveyed by your non-verbals. Murphy's Law states that something WILL go wrong. Maintain your composure—after all, you're probably the only one aware of the glitches that occur.

— Candice
Thomas-Maddox

2006). As an event planner, you not only want your verbal and nonverbal cues to match, but you also want to be able to read others' nonverbal language.

Nonverbal and verbal behaviors are intertwined during human interaction. Paul Ekman (1965) states that working together, verbals and non-verbals can repeat, conflict with, complement, substitute for, and accent/moderate each other, and they also regulate interaction. For example, an event planner giving directions to the nearest coffee shop might repeat a message by pointing to the left and saying, 'Go left at the light.' Conflicting messages would occur when someone states, 'I am not nervous at all,' but you can see trembling hands and beads of perspiration. Nonverbal behavior complements verbal behavior when a client smiles when looking at a venue and says, 'This is the perfect place for the event.' A substitution could be a facial reaction of disgust as you try various foods that could be served at an event—no words are needed as you politely remove the dish from the menu. You might accent (emphasize) an interaction by throwing your hands up in the air and saying, 'That is the PERFECT arrangement' or moderate (downplay) an interaction by clenching your fists instead of getting angry and yelling about the height of a floral arrangement. Finally, an event planner might glance occasionally at a watch to regulate time. In response, the staff should be able to pick up on the nonverbal cues and move on to the next segment. Research also shows that nonverbals have many different components and forms (Hostetter, 2011; Knapp, Hall, & Horgan, 2014).

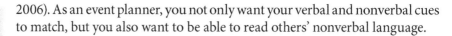

© Rido/Shutterstock.com

Kinesics

Kinesics: *The study of body language as it relates to communication and is patterned by both social and cultural experiences*

Kinesics, or the study of body language as it relates to communication, is patterned by both social and cultural experiences (Birdwhistell, 1970). Being aware of kinesics can help event planners understand and interpret nonverbal behavior, and further assist in deciphering messages exchanged with clients and colleagues. Kinesics includes gestures and body movement, and is broken down into five particular areas of study. These include the following: (1) emblems, (2) illustrators, (3) manipulators, (4) regulators, and (5) emotional expressions (or affect displays) (Ekman, 1999). All of these nonverbal behaviors help people convey messages; however, if event planners do not understand the different areas of kinesics, confusion can occur if they misinterpret or misunderstand what these particular kinetic movements actually mean. Event planners can glean meaning from a client from gestures. For instance, if a client is meeting with you and has his arms folded across his chest when he speaks, you may become concerned that the client is closed off, unhappy, or unapproachable. Reading these cues may help you ask a follow-up question, such as, 'Are you happy with the direction of the event?' or "Would you like to alter anything with the plan?'

Emblems are movements that have meaning and are understood by all members of a particular culture or subculture (Ekman, 1999). Knapp (1980) notes that emblems represent nonverbal actions that have shared meaning within a culture. In American culture, giving a 'thumbs up' means everything is good, and giving 'the finger' connotes a very strong dislike. Event planners have to be attuned to emblems in order to decipher nonverbal, unspoken communication. Think about receiving nonverbal communication in an event setting. A client may give you the 'okay' sign from across the room at an event. Receiving this communication helps you understand that the client is pleased and that everything is going well. A 'thumbs down' emblem would indicate that something may not be going as planned or that something is wrong.

© Africa Studio/Shutterstock.com

Emblems: *Movements that have meaning and can be understood by all members of a particular culture or subculture*

Illustrators are movements that help explain speech, usually augmenting it, but sometimes contradicting it (Ekman, 1999). Illustrators are nonverbal cues connected to speech (Knapp, 1980). What illustrators can ultimately do is help explain and enhance verbal communication while prompting interest in, and keeping people engaged in, what you are saying (Ekman, 1999). Knapp (1980) states, "Movements are not produced randomly during the stream of speech; speech behavior and movement behavior are inextricably linked—they are part and parcel of the same system" (p. 126). Event planners should always be conscious of these verbal enhancers as they communicate with clients, especially when clarity is of the utmost importance. For instance, an event planner in an exhibit hall might point to the left and hold up the index finger, saying, 'First, people will enter through this door.' Then the event planner might point to the center aisle, and, holding up two fingers, say, 'Second, people will move into this space.' The pointing of fingers and use of arm movements are illustrators that clarify and enhance verbal communication.

Illustrators: *Movements that help explain speech, usually augmenting it, but sometimes contradicting it*

Manipulators are movements whereby "one part of the body or face manipulates in some fashion—stroking, pressing, scratching, licking, biting, sucking, etc.—another part of the body or face" (Ekman, 1999, p. 43). Once you notice clients using these self-imposed manipulators, such as cracking their knuckles, biting their fingernails, or playing with their hair, you will barely be able to focus on anything else. Those who use a lot of manipulators when communicating were found to be less trustworthy— and often led to mistrust in relationships—because manipulators can be perceived as indicators of a tendency to lie. Self-focused touch can manifest itself unconsciously, such as wiggling your foot or wringing your hands (Ekman, 1999).

Manipulators: *Movements whereby one part of the body or face manipulates in some fashion—stroking, pressing, scratching, licking, biting, sucking, etc.—another part of the body or face*

Regulators are "actions which maintain and regulate the back-and-forth nature of speaking and listening between two or more interactants. They tell the speaker to continue, repeat, elaborate, hurry up, become more interesting, less salacious, give the other a chance to talk, etc." (Ekman & Friesen, 1969, p. 82). In an exchange of communication, regulators indicate when

Regulators: *Actions that maintain and regulate the back-and-forth nature of speaking and listening between two or more interactants*

to talk and when to listen. If your client goes to open his mouth, leans in to hear what you are saying, or nods and holds up a hand in agreement, you may interpret these regulators as signals that it is your turn to stop speaking and to listen. Conversations take place between and among people, and regulators help communicators know when it is their turn to speak.

Emotional expressions (or affect displays), as defined by Paul Ekman (1999), are "involuntary signals which provide important information to

Emotional expressions (or affect displays):
Involuntary signals that provide important information to others

© Golden Pixels LLC/Shutterstock.com

others" (p. 44). He further elaborates that words themselves are not emotions, but that, instead, they represent emotions. Stone, Markham, and Wilhelm (2013) assert that feelings are nonverbal in nature; therefore, nonverbal communication can directly relay expression more aptly than can verbal communication. Argyle (1992) writes that human infants respond to emotional faces and voices in the early stages of their lives, and joy is the first and easiest emotion for them to recognize, demonstrating that nonverbal communication is partly or mostly innate.

Whatever emotion is expressed, event planners must be able to assess and adjust communication behaviors to change perception or help clarify messages if needed. Being acquainted with the realm of emotional expressions, and understanding that they can represent many different feelings such as anger, fear, concern, disgust, happiness, contentment, or bliss, among others, can help event planners dissect complex nonverbal behavior. Conversely, event planners should be cognizant of how they display their own emotions, being careful not to react too excitedly in business and professional settings.

TIP

Never let anyone know anything is wrong. The flowers might be dying, the cake might be missing, the ring bearer may have swallowed the ring, but the only emotion you should be showing on your face is happiness. A huge part of a successful event is to always keep a smile on your face and portray an attitude of how wonderful everything is progressing.

— Elle Ellinghaus

While facial expressions can clearly help to gauge emotions, App, McIntosh, Reed, and Hertenstein (2011) tested for more than just facial expressions in conveying emotion; they tested a wide range of emotions through the channels of body, face, and touch, and found that some emotions can be displayed primarily through nonverbal channels. "Emotions are not merely subjective, internal experiences; rather, they arise from the individual's interactions with the social and physical environment and serve valuable functions" (App et al., 2011, p. 613). By paying attention to kinesics during interactions with clients, event planners can gain insight into how people are feeling and better assess the emotions they are conveying: a curl of the lip can express displeasure, a smile can communicate pure happiness, and a frown can indicate dissatisfaction or disgust.

Facial Displays

The face is an important visual cue that people use to identify one another (Ellis & Young, 1989). In western culture, you usually observe the other's face only 50% of the time out of politeness during a conversation (Ekman

& Friesen, 1975). Paul Ekman and Wallace Friesen (1975) in their seminal work, *Unmasking the face*, discuss six basic emotions that are expressed universally by the face—surprise, fear, disgust, anger, happiness, and sadness. In 1986, Ekman and Friesen added contempt as a universal expression by the face, and further research continues to expand in the nonverbal field (Behesti, 2018; Ekman, 1992; 2003; Izard & Haynes, 1988). People universally recognize these facial expressions because of biological heritage; as a result, these expressions are communicated spontaneously by facial muscles and are very difficult to control (Buck, 1984). Facial expressions are usually shown momentarily. A person will hardly ever hold a look of surprise for longer than a few seconds.

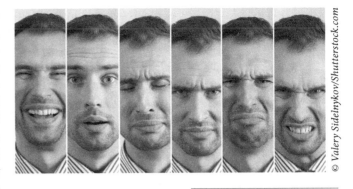

© Valery Sidelnykov/Shutterstock.com

Ekman and Friesen (1975) separate the face into three different muscle regions that show expressions: (1) the brow and forehead, (2) the eyes, eyelids, and root of the nose, and (3) the cheeks, mouth, most of the nose, and chin. Ekman and Friesen also identify eight different styles of facial expressions in their research: (1) **Withholders** show very little expressiveness, (2) **Revealers** show all expressions with the face, (3) **Unwitting Expressors** do not realize they express emotions with the face, (4) **Blanked Expressors** believe they are expressing emotions; however, they show very little expression, (5) **Frozen-Affect Expressors** constantly show one emotion even if they are not feeling that particular way (e.g., the person always looks happy), (6) **Substitute Expressors** feel an emotion but do not necessarily express that emotion to others (e.g., the person is angry but looks sad), (7) **Ever-Ready Expressors** display the same emotion as a first response to various situations (e.g., the person instinctively smiles and looks happy even if bad news is given), and (8) **Flooded-Affect Expressors** frequently show more than one emotion. These eight styles help event planners remember that clients are unique when it comes to how they use their face to express emotions. As an event planner, it might be difficult to read your clients exclusively through the face, but other nonverbal cues can help interpret their likes and dislikes.

Oculesics

Oculesics refers to the study of eye contact and pupil dilation in nonverbal communication (Ellsworth, Carlsmith, & Henson, 1985; Masin, 2010; Ting-Toomey, 1999). Eye movement, directness of gaze (how one looks at another), eye contact, and glances all are connected to emotion, relationships, and the level of involvement with others. Understanding how people look at others—including the client—may determine the ongoing development of the relationship. Beebe (1974) found that higher levels of eye

Withholders: *In facial displays, those who show very little expressiveness*

Revealers: *In facial displays, those who show all expressions with the face*

Unwitting Expressors: *In facial displays, those who do not realize they express emotions with the face*

Blanked Expressors: *In facial displays, those who believe they are expressing emotions but actually show very little expression*

Frozen-Affect Expressors: *In facial displays, those who constantly show one emotion even if they are not feeling that particular way*

Substitute Expressors: *In facial displays, those who feel an emotion but do not necessarily express that emotion to others*

Ever-Ready Expressors: *In facial displays, those who display the same emotion as a first response to various situations*

Flooded-Affect Expressors: *In facial displays, those who frequently show more than one emotion*

Oculesics: *The study of eye contact and pupil dilation in nonverbal communication*

contact were associated with greater perceived enthusiasm, likability, and trust. Thus, the amount of eye contact a person makes is an invitation to communicate, or to defer communication, with others. An understanding of the many variations of eye contact and gaze is essential for anyone who makes a living in face-to-face communication.

Studies have looked at the relationship of gaze with correlated verbal ratings. Some researchers posit that the correlation between these two factors is low because people might not be cognizant of their gaze in an interpersonal meeting (Breed & Porter, 1972; Kleinke, 1977; Kleinke & Walton, 1982). In other words, many people are not very self-aware of their gazing behaviors and the associated messages they may be sending. Thus, it would be easy to misinterpret someone's gaze as meaning something different from what it was meant to be. Those in contact with clients must be aware not just of how they look at others, but also how others might interpret or misinterpret their gaze.

Pressmaster/Shutterstock.com

Research has indicated that those who maintain a steady gaze at their audience are rated as more skillful, sincere, knowledgeable, qualified, and welcoming (Wyland & Forgas, 2010), as well as more attentive (Norton & Pettegrew, 1979). These are qualities that any event planner would wish to convey, so effort in focusing on proper gaze characteristics is important. Gaze can also make a difference in assessment of competence, attraction, likability, and mental health, among others (Abele, 1981; Shrout & Fiske, 1981). Of course, the gaze may turn into a stare, which is usually intimidating and perceived as negative (Goffman, 1964), but implied and generally understood rules of social interaction establish how close strangers and friends can be when they make and break eye contact. In social settings, as in events, the gaze is often directed at a particular person to convey a specific message that may not be perceived by others. Gaze can also indicate when it is the other's turn to speak, so attention to the client's eye contact patterns may help the event planner keep the conversation lively.

Culture plays a significant role in how eye contact is perceived, as does gender. Cook (1979) found that men are less likely than women to be comfortable with mutual gaze, so the gender of the event planner's client may help to determine the kind of eye contact that is established. In general, there are higher levels of direct gaze when there are feelings of affection and fondness between two people (Patterson, 1982). Thus, understanding what others' gaze may mean can amplify confidence in the event planner and even provide cues as to how the client relationship is developing.

Ultimately, eye contact will demonstrate to clients that you are paying attention to them (Kendon, 1967), but remember that eye contact can be accompanied by other kinds of verbal communication that may subtly change or subvert its meaning. More eye contact increases the chances for communication to occur, and though there are sometimes subtle and unperceived variations in what the gaze suggests, eye contact in general can provide a key to a more fully developed relationship. An understanding of oculesics is important in any social profession, just as a sense of smell may be helpful in communication.

Olfactics

Olfactics, or the study of communication through the sense of smell, can affect one's perceptions (Dawes, 1996). "Our bodies associate certain smells with emotions and feelings. Some smells can be powerful triggers for memories of and emotions toward people, events, or things" (Hadnagy, 2014, pp. 16–17). Imagine a bride walking down the aisle with a bouquet of fragrant flowers, a football kick-off party with the smell of hot wings permeating the room, or the smell of your boyfriend's cologne still fragrant at the end of the day. The sense of smell can bring you back in time—to a specific place you remember being when you first smelled that scent.

Olfactics: *The study of communication through the sense of smell*

© wavebreakmedia/Shutterstock.com

There is a reason event planners must pay close attention to smells, as event attendees may come away with a lasting impression based not just on how a venue looked, but also how it smelled. "Smells, scents, whiffs and stinks are incredibly important in our experience and understanding of the surrounding world" (Henshaw, 2014, p. 28). A study conducted at Rockefeller University and the Howard Hughes Institute found that humans with a solid sense of smell have the ability to decipher a minimum of one trillion odors; it was previously thought that humans could detect only a mere 10,000 odors (Henshaw, 2014). Therefore, the reality is that people have a very keen sense of smell.

Event planners should consider olfactory detection and use it to their advantage. Think of real estate agents who are attempting to sell a property; often they will suggest that sellers bake brownies shortly before prospective buyers come to see the home. According to a report by MediaRadar (2013), advertisers employ scented pages in magazines to grow sales, and advertisements for fragrances that ran over a four-month period increased by 3% that year. Likewise, event planners can incorporate the same techniques in creating an overall appeal; the sense of smell will last, and it will also help attendees remember the particulars of the event. A movie night on campus would not be the same without the scent of popcorn in the air.

Additionally, olfactics can refer to the smells that the body produces. In some cultures, people who are freshly showered and perhaps use powder, deodorant, cologne, or perfume afterwards are considered clean and

© c12/Shutterstock.com

fragrant. Conversely, if they are unkempt and have not showered for days at a time, their body odor may become offensive to some. Reeves (2006) states that employers have the right to request that employees meet the needs of the organization's standards for personal hygiene. While event planners certainly cannot control each staff member's personal hygiene, they also would not want to offend guests with improper personal care. Lycan (2014) argues that smells can also create a misrepresentation of something. For example, a client who insists on lilies at her wedding may want the flowers to represent happiness; however, many guests may associate the scent of that flower with death, since lilies are often found at funerals. Thus, olfaction can play a part in the enjoyment and memory of an event.

Haptics

Haptics: *The study of touch*

Another important nonverbal cue in communication is touch. **Haptics** is the study of touch, which is associated with a wide range of meanings (Jones & Yarbrough, 1985) and has been categorized in various ways (Argyle, 1975; Heslin & Alper, 1983; Morris, 1977). Touch can also communicate a variety of emotions including anger, fear, disgust, love, gratitude, and sympathy (Hertenstein et al, 2006). For some individuals, touch is a very comfortable activity. Research on the positive effects of touch shows that it can result in happy clients and employees. For example, Hornik (1991; 1992) found that shoppers who were touched by greeters were more likely to give a favorable rating of their shopping experience. Guéguen and Jacob (2006) found that consumers are more likely to purchase products if a sales associate engages in some type of touch. In addition, servers received greater monetary tips when some type of favorable touch happened (Crusco & Wetzel, 1984). In the medical field, patients who viewed touch as a sign of

© EDHAR/Shutterstock.com

interpersonal warmth had more verbal interactions, greater medical compliance, and better attitudes (Aguilera, 1967; Pattison, 1973). Additionally, when touch is initiated, people are more likely to help others in various situations (Goldman, Kiyohara, & Pfannensteil, 1985; Guéguen & Fischer-Lokou, 2002; 2003; Nannberg & Hansen, 1994). The negative effects of touch are usually associated with expressing anger or frustration and can include slapping, pinching, or mocking someone (Jones & Yarbrough, 1985; Morris, 1977).

Heslin and Alper (1983) discuss the most common forms of touch, which include the following: (1) functional/professional, in which the purpose of touch is impersonal and businesslike; for example, the event planner might move people to create a line for a book signing; (2) social/polite, in which touch is used as a common courtesy; for example, a handshake in the United States symbolizes acknowledging the other person; (3) friendship/warmth, in which touch conveys a unique connection based on liking; for example, a hug at the end of an important event might convey a personal thank you. Overall, the study of haptics can enlighten you as to how to make your event more successful.

Physical Appearance

When people are introduced, they immediately form perceptions of others. In a matter of seconds, people assess each other with little substantiation except for analyzing what they look like. Research conducted at Harvard Medical School and Massachusetts General Hospital found that people assess others, including their competence and trustworthiness, in a matter of seconds—a quarter of a second, to be exact (Goudreau, 2012). "Our culture places a lot of emphasis on physical attractiveness; however, that may be defined from year to year and from fashion style to fashion style. Physical appearance is one of the major determinants in first impressions" (Myers & Myers, 1992, p. 225). People attempt to gauge the intrinsic makeup of others (how nice, intelligent, or competent they are) merely by critiquing their physical appearance. Considerations such as build, height, weight, and clothing choices are examples of **physical appearance**. Tsai, Huang, and Yu (2012) found that in jobs requiring personal interaction with customers, employers preferred more attractive applicants over less attractive applicants.

Physical appearance: *The qualities that characterize someone's outward form such as build, height, weight, and clothing*

Karl, Hall, and Peluchette (2013) recognized that another important determinant in evaluating physical appearance is connected to an organization's mission, goals, or types of clients it may serve; these notions could also play a role in critically assessing the physical appearance of others. In fact, research shows that employers believe that public opinion of their company as a whole can be decided by how the public views just one or a few employees (McAdams, Moussavi, & Klassen, 1992). Keep in mind that those who work an event represent not only the organization for whom the event has been planned, but also the event planning company as well. People working the event can make or break its success, as attendees may judge both their appearance and behavior.

© bikeriderlondon/Shutterstock.com

Judging a person's physical appearance negatively happens in business and can vary in cases of race, sex, age, or national origin. Cases can also include discriminating against someone with a temporary condition, such as pregnancy or a stroke, or those with more long-term disabilities that are unlikely to change (McAdams, Moussavi, & Klassen, 1992). People with disabilities now have protected rights. Congress passed the **Americans with Disabilities Act** to help combat discrimination, and it states the following:

> *The Americans with Disabilities Act of 1990 (ADA) prohibits discrimination and ensures equal opportunity for persons with disabilities in employment, state and local government services, public accommodations, commercial facilities, and transportation (http://www.ada.gov/2010_regs.htm, para. 1).*

Even before the Americans with Disabilities Act, there was a conscious effort to eliminate appearance bias in the workplace. In fact, Michigan and Washington, D.C. were early adopters of prohibitions against personal appearance discrimination, including height and weight (Gomez, 2012).

Americans with Disabilities Act (ADA): *The federal law that prohibits discrimination and ensures equal opportunity for persons with disabilities in employment, state and local government services, public accommodations, commercial facilities, and transportation*

© Anthony Correia/Shutterstock.com

Planning events requires that you consider all people who may attend your event; putting plans into action for those who may have a disability should be at the forefront of your thinking. According to the State of New York Department of Health (2008) event guide, there are many things to consider in planning an event for those with disabilities. From specifics concerning handicapped seating to parking accommodations, event planners must acknowledge and recognize the need to plan for those with disabilities. When you take these ideas into consideration, your event becomes more welcoming. For example, at a graduation ceremony or other public event, having someone use sign language to communicate for the hearing-impaired shows that the organization has considered its attendees. Similarly, making signs in Braille or including a handicapped-accessible ramp will help welcome and facilitate the movement of guests.

Realizing that physical appearance means that people come in all shapes and sizes requires that event planners ask the right questions and plan accordingly; taller and heavier guests should not have to sit on chairs that may be too small or flimsy for them. Additionally, people who are shorter should not have to sit on chairs that are too high for them, causing their feet to dangle. Putting a bridal party on a riser or platform so that they are clearly visible to all guests might be something to consider for an event. Being cognizant of contingency plans is helpful, as making guests feel comfortable should be a top priority for any event planner who recognizes that physical appearances vary widely and should all be respected.

TIP

When listening to the client, focus on the language that gets repeated. If you hear "I just want it to be bright" multiple times, make sure to include that in your suggested ambiance.

— Nancy Willets

Artifacts

Artifacts include all of those pieces of your outward physical appearance, including clothing and other accessories, and most obviously one's facial features, hair and hair style, posture, and body type (Schein, 2010). They are uniquely and visibly connected to how you consider and display personal or professional identity, and they can communicate a great deal about relationships, profession, culture, ethnicity, religion, and more. While most of these identifiers have no real innate meaning in and of themselves, they still communicate much about people. Some of that identity lies in how the messages are communicated, and some of it lies in the ways in which you try to make sense of, or decode, the message you think is being sent. That meaning may vary, depending on the culture in which it rests (Masin, 2010).

A person's dress, for instance, may convey an unintentional message that others read as suggestive; piercings, tattoos, and other mutations to the human body convey such a variety of messages that many corporate offices have banned such body art. The 6th District Circuit Court of Appeals ruled in *Robert v. Ward* that dress code policies can be enforced when it comes to tattoos as long as these policies are handled equitably. Even as tattoos enter mainstream America, those with tattoos are still unprotected within the courts (Weiss, 2008). Clothing may also convey a message about ethnic identity, and in an increasingly diverse world, event planners must become familiar with those identities. The ways in which people adapt and personalize their environments also include the artifacts used to define the setting (Prown & Haltman, 2000). Consider, for example, an office in a university that someone has personalized with photographs of family and loved ones, or with plants, certificates, framed diplomas, or memorabilia. All of these artifacts—or the lack of them—convey a specific message about the person and the organization. In short, artifacts serve to communicate a cultural belief held by an individual or a group (Prown & Haltman, 2000).

Clients may be extremely concerned about the artifact elements over which they have control, since they may believe that these elements convey a certain message. Event planners need to practice sensitivity to the ways that artifacts impact communication patterns. This practice demands careful observation of clients to see how they interact with their environment and with their belongings. Sentimental photographs of absent loved ones, for instance, may be placed prominently at a wedding reception, and the event planner should take the lead from the client as to how these pieces are handled. Artifacts help to mark one's territory (Wood & Duck, 2006), and research indicates their importance in relationships and family (Lohmann, Arriaga, & Goodfriend, 2003). Heirloom jewelry passed down through

> **Artifacts:** *All of those pieces of the outward physical appearance, including clothing and other accessories, and most obviously one's facial features, hair and hair style, posture, and body type*

generations of a family may carry more meaning than economic value. Understanding and respecting the message of the artifact is essential if you want to appreciate identity, culture, and relationships. Artifacts thus personalize space and make connections with familial, professional, and social worlds (Wood, 2006).

In the corporate world, artifacts include a company's technology, art, style, myths, stories, and values (Schein, 2010). Clearly, this definition includes some concrete and tangible items but also some intangible elements as well. Often, these artifacts are not part of the conscious definition of the culture but rather are intuitively perceived (Geertz, 1973). This means that misperception of meaning can be common among those in the culture and may result in miscommunication among others as well. Knowledge of the context of the artifacts, then, becomes vital (Geertz, 1983). Think of the unspoken and unwritten traditions that accompany life in a corporate setting. Perhaps 'Casual Friday' in some settings is not really as casual as its name suggests, and the intern who takes the day at its name value the first time learns a lesson about the tacit yet very real belief in proper corporate wear.

High-context cultures: *Cultures in which the message is communicated indirectly*

Low-context culture: *A culture's communication in which the message is directly stated, often through facts and personal reports*

Hall (1989) explains that understanding context is important when dealing with details embedded in the culture. He makes a distinction between high-context cultures and low-context cultures, and the need for clear definitions when people from these two kinds of cultures interact. In **high-context cultures**, the message is communicated indirectly. Age and status, for instance, offer indirect clues for how to "read" what is unsaid. In **low-context cultures**, someone directly states the message, often through facts and personal reports. The higher the context of the culture, the greater the amount of context is necessary for understanding. Thus, information drawn from a culture's artifacts must be read in terms of the context in which they are situated (Anderson, Hecht, Hoobler, & Smallwood, 2002; Ting-Toomey, 1991). Event planners must know and appreciate cultural distinctions in order to build relationships; knowing when to bow or offer a handshake, for instance, can make a difference in how the client perceives the event planner.

Context: *The historical, physical, social, psychological and cultural setting of the communication that helps people understand any distortions or miscommunications in the message*

What does this mean to the event planner? **Context** helps explain any distortions or miscommunications in the message, and so in order to 'read' the message correctly, event planners must comprehend both implied and direct communication (Anderson et al., 2002). Perception of artifacts is often deeply embedded in the human power of observation. Using interpersonal and observational skills to discern artifact importance and meaning is central to professional success.

Paralanguage

Paralanguage: *The nonverbal vocal qualities and sounds that are produced by the throat, nasal cavity, tongue, lips, mouth and jaw*

Paralanguage refers to the nonverbal vocal qualities and sounds produced by the throat, nasal cavity, tongue, lips, mouth, and jaw (Juslin & Scherer, 2005). Various techniques and methods have been used to study the role paralanguage has on the communication process (Scherer, 2003).

Paralanguage focuses on the idea that it is not what you say, but how you say it. An individual's voice is capable of producing a variety of sounds (Poyatos, 1993). Some of these nonverbal cues common in speech behavior are **voice qualities** (e.g., pitch, range, and tempo) and **vocalizations**, which are made up of vocal characterizers (e.g., laughing, crying, and yawning), vocal qualifiers (e.g., overly loud or soft), and vocal segregates (e.g., 'um,' 'ah,' and 'uh') (Trager, 1958).

Voice qualities: *A subset of paralanguage that includes specific nonverbal cues in speech including pitch, range, and tempo*

Vocalizations: *A subset of paralanguage that includes specific nonverbal cues in speech, made up of vocal characterizers, vocal qualifiers and vocal segregates*

Paralinguistic cues have a major impact on listeners. Burns and Beier (1973) found that listeners focus more on paralanguage than on the actual content of a message when asked to determine the speaker's attitude. Moreover, when one's paralanguage contradicts the actual message, the listener tends to focus on the nonverbal language cues instead of the words (Mehrabian & Weiner, 1967). Hearing the client say, 'I like it,' with the sounds of trepidation echoing each syllable might trigger event planners to offer other options. One's paralanguage also influences the way others perceive a speaker (Castelan-Cargile & Bradac, 2001). Mulac's (1976) research illustrates that people perceive speech through socio-intellectual status (e.g., high or low social status, blue or white collar, rich or poor, and literate or illiterate), aesthetic quality (e.g., pleasing or displeasing, nice or awful, beautiful or ugly), and dynamism (e.g., aggressive or unaggressive, active or passive). Another study by

© racom/Shutterstock.com

Tusing and Dillard (2000) found that those who spoke louder than others are perceived as being more dominant. Voices play a major role in the communication process, and as event planners, it is necessary to understand what your voice and other voices are communicating.

Proxemics

Proxemics, introduced by anthropologist Edward T. Hall (1963), refers to the study of messages sent in a spatial environment. This area of nonverbal communication examines measurable distances between people as they interact as well as the kinds of public closeness that characterize relationships. Proxemics includes several subsets, including territoriality, public spaces, and private space, to name a few. An understanding of spatial relationships is vital for those working in public domains where space is shared. Ideas of closeness and distance help to define this domain (Hall, 1963).

Proxemics: *The study of messages sent in a spatial environment*

Territoriality refers to the space people claim and preserve as their own (Knapp, Hall, & Hogan 2014). This could be as personal as one's own house, or as public as a seat in a classroom or a bench in the park. Since spaces also have proxemic standards, and though these are rarely clearly defined, most

Territoriality: *The space people claim and preserve as their own*

TIP

Work within the limits of the space provided. Be creative as you consider how best to make use of what you have, not what you wish had been available to you, and make the space send a constructive, positive message.

— Janie Harden Fritz

people have a sense if the public space has been compromised. The space markers for territoriality in the United States are very generous; under most conditions, if possible, people prefer not to be seated with strangers or sit too closely to those they do not know (Guerrero & Floyd, 2006).

Customs dictate the kind of markers people use to define their territories, and politeness demands that others respect these markers, whether they are legitimate or not (Guerrero & Floyd, 2006). Hence the use of placecards at many formal social functions—these not only assure that tensions at any table will be minor, but also that no one has the chance to pre-empt anyone else's space. Consider also the first day of classes in which students in a room choose their seats and subsequently expect to be able to sit in the same seat on following days, having claimed them as their own. Though they made no overt or explicit arrangements to request the space, the expectation is that by virtue of sitting in that seat once, students have a right to it for the duration of the course (Guyot, Byrd, & Caudle, 1980).

Hall (1973) theorized that there are three types of distance: intimate, social, and public, and that cultures define these distances. Politeness demands that people follow a particular culture's proxemic values, so understanding physical proximity will keep an event planner from offending a client whose personal space might feel invaded. Event planners also must understand how to coordinate public space for an event, how to read an event by noticing the body orientations and barriers that people exhibit, and how to successfully navigate physical contact (Roman, 2006).

There is a relationship between liking someone and physical closeness, which Mehrabian (1967) posited as the immediacy hypothesis. In other words, in conversation, the distance between a speaker and the addressee decreases as the warmth of the relationship increases. The degree of openness with which speakers position their bodies in relation to listeners can also communicate a specific degree of friendliness (Machotka, 1965). Thus, arms folded over the chest might serve as a barrier to closeness and communication, while an open-armed greeting might indicate acceptance and welcome. Similarly, at a wedding, the guests who are closest to the bride and groom typically sit nearest to the head table. Thus, the head table itself connotes much more than just its location in a room; it suggests a power relationship that is visibly depicted socially and publicly (Ben-Peretz & Shifra Schonmann, 2000).

Close observation about how the use of space might indicate relationship status helps event planners understand vital information about the client's leadership and interactional style. Does an open door necessarily indicate availability? If someone places a handbag on a chair prior to a dinner event, is it permissible to move it? What are the rules governing the proxemics in each of these cases? Often people need more cues before they can make assumptions about what the space is indicating. Proxemics, combined with other nonverbal and visual cues, can offer a lot of valuable information about space and its meaning.

Chronemics

Chronemics is the study of time and focuses on the concepts and processes of how people manage their formal and informal obligations in relation to time (Bruneau, 2009). Social psychologist Robert Levine (1988) says that time communicates, and culture plays, a large role in one's perception of time. For example, geographic areas that value time (United States, Canada, and northern Europe) perceive waiting as an indicator of status. Some people who perceive their time as more valuable may demand an appointment well in advance. In some cultures punctuality is critical, while in other cultures being on time is barely considered essential (Levine & Norenzayan, 1999).

© Photographee.eu/Shutterstock.com

There are two distinguishing components of time—monochronic and polychronic. **Monochronic time** is viewed as linear space where time is tangible, compartmentalized, and planned. Time can be wasted, saved, gained, and lost. Moreover, time is usually referred to as sacred or compared to money as in the phrase 'time is money.' Monochronic perceptions of time value the importance of deadlines and sticking to one task. **Polychronic time** is viewed spatially where people are more important than planning (Hall, 1973).

Time is not tangible or controlled by a clock. Polychronic perceptions of time value the importance of conversations and multitasking (Hall, 1973). As you interact with clients and prepare events, understanding the concepts of monochronic and polychronic time is key.

Time can also be associated with task time or event time. Task and event time focus on how much time is given to accomplish a goal versus how much time is used to socialize. In the United States, people spend about 80% of time on task and 20% on socializing, whereas in Latin America there is usually a 50/50 split on time spent on task and socialization (Martin & Chaney, 2006). Knowing your audience's goal of staying on task or engaging in social activities will help you plan client-specific events.

The areas of nonverbal communication (kinesics, facial displays, oculesics, olfactics, haptics, physical appearance, artifacts, paralanguage, proxemics, and chronemics) are vital indicators for all event planners to recognize. Being aware of nonverbal behavior assists with the many tasks used to make an event run successfully. As you decipher nonverbal cues exchanged, keeping the lines of communication open will help alleviate any misinterpretations. Consistency in communication patterns forms the basis of trust in a relationship (Van Servellen, 2009), and thus it is important that the event planner conveys the same message through both verbal and nonverbal cues. If either the client or the event planner sends contradictory messages, then a breach

Chronemics: *The study of time, focusing on the concepts and process of how people manage their formal and informal obligations in relation to time*

Monochronic time: *Time that is viewed as linear and is tangible, compartmentalized, and planned*

Polychronic time: *Time that is viewed spatially where people are more important than planning*

in the communication bridge can lead to mistrust and confusion. Being able to read the nonverbal cues while listening to what is being said is vital, but just as important is the event planner's own message's reliability. One study reported that 91% of all Americans lie on a regular basis, and this fact demonstrates how essential it is to be able to read the nonverbals that often betray us (Patterson & Kim, 1991). Pay attention to nonverbal signals that may indicate a particularly important detail or trigger, making a note of them. Being mindful of these nonverbal skills and being deliberate in using them needs to be at the forefront of any event planner's professional inventory.

Key Terms

Nonverbal communication	Revealers	Haptics	Voice qualities
Kinesics	Unwitting Expressors	Physical appearance	Vocalizations
Emblems	Blanked Expressors	Americans with Disabilities	Proxemics
Illustrators	Frozen-Affect Expressors	Act (ADA)	Territoriality
Manipulators	Substitute Expressors	Artifacts	Chronemics
Regulators	Ever-Ready Expressors	High-context cultures	Monochronic time
Emotional expressions (or affect displays)	Flooded-Affect Expressors	Low-context culture	Polychronic time
Withholders	Oculesics	Context	
	Olfactics	Paralanguage	

Discussion Questions

1. Explain a time when you perceived someone's nonverbals incorrectly. What caused you to make the assumptions that you did? What were the consequences of being inaccurate?

2. What area of nonverbal communication (kinesics, facial displays, oculesics, olfactics, haptics, physical appearance, artifacts, paralanguage, proxemics, and chronemics) do you believe is the easiest to interpret? What area is the most difficult? Explain.

3. You are in an initial meeting with a client discussing an upcoming event. What nonverbal cues will you pay attention to as the exchange of information about ideas for the event occurs?

Activities

Olfactics Activity

Smell can cause many different perceptions. For the next class, in a non-see-through bag, bring in something that has a potent scent. Each class member will have the opportunity to smell each bag and guess what is in it. (Hint: cotton swabs can be soaked with various perfumes or oils, and spices should be placed in the bag for at least 24 hours to give a strong smell.)

Proxemics Activity

For the first 15 minutes of class, push all of the desks to the back of the room and move all chairs right next to each other. Describe how you felt as you tried to take notes.

Facial Displays

Using notecards, write down each of these emotions—surprise, fear, disgust, anger, happiness, and sadness—and see if your partner can accurately guess which expression you are showing.

References

Abele, A. (1981). Acquaintance and visual behavior between two interactants. Their communicative function for the impression formation of an observer. *European Journal of Social Psychology, 11,* 409–425.

Aguilera, D. C. (1967). Relationships between physical contact and verbal interaction between nurses and patients. *Journal of Psychiatric Nursing, 5,* 5–21.

Americans with Disabilities Act of 1990 (ADA). *Information and technical assistance on the Americans with Disabilities Act.* Retrieved from http://www.ada.gov/2010_regs.htm.

Anderson, P. A., Hecht, M. L., Hoobler, G. D., & Smallwood, M. (2002). Nonverbal communication across cultures. In W. B. Gudykunst, & B. Mody (Eds), *Handbook of international and intercultural communication* (pp. 89–106). Thousand Oaks, Calif.: Sage.

App, B., McIntosh, D. N., Reed, C. L., & Hertenstein, M. J. (2011). Nonverbal channel use in communication of emotion: How may depend on why. *Emotion, 11,* 603–617.

Argyle, M. (1975). *Bodily communication.* New York: International University Press.

_____. (1992). Does nonverbal communication cause happiness? In F. Poyatos (Ed.), *Advances in non-verbal communication: Sociocultural, clinical, esthetic, and literary perspectives* (pp. 99–112). Philadelphia, PA: John Benjamins Publishing Company.

Beebe, S. A. (1974). A nonverbal determinant of speaker credibility. *The Speech Teacher, 23,* 21–25.

Beheshti, N, (2018). The power of mindful nonverbal communication. Retrieved from https://www.forbes.com/sites/nazbeheshti/2018/09/20/beyond-language-the-power-of-mindful-nonverbal-communication/

Ben-Peretz, M., & Shifra Schonmann, M. (2000). Behind closed doors: *Teachers and the role of the teachers' lounge.* New York: SUNY Press.

Berlo, D. K. (1960). *The process of communication.* San Francisco: Rinehart.

Birdwhistell, R. L. (1970). *Kinesics and context.* Philadelphia: University of Pennsylvania Press.

Breed, G., & Porter, M. (1972). Eye contact, attitudes, and attitude changing among males. *Journal of Social Psychology, 120,* 211–217.

Bruneau, T. (2009). Chronemics. In S. W. Littlejohn & K. A. Foss (Eds.), *Encyclopedia of communication theory* (pp. 96–101). Thousand Oaks, CA: Sage

Buck, R. (1984). *The communication of emotion.* New York: Guilford Press.

Burgoon , J. K., & Bacue, A. E. (2003). Nonverbal communication skills. In J. O. Greene & B. R. Burleson (Eds.), *Handbook of communication and social interaction skills* (pp. 179–220). Mahwah, NJ: Erlbaum.

Burgoon, J. K. (1994). Nonverbal signals. In M. L. Knapp & G. R. Miller (Eds.), *Handbook of interpersonal communication* (2nd ed., pp. 229–285). Thousand Oaks, CA: Sage.

Burns, K. L., & Beier, E. G. (1973). Significance of vocal and visual channels for the decoding of emotional meaning. *Journal of Communication, 23,* 118–130.

Castelan-Cargile, A., & Bradac, J. J. (2001). Attitudes towards language: A review of speaker-evaluation research a general process model. In W. B. Gudykunst (Ed.), *Communication Yearbook, 25* (pp. 347–382). Thousand Oaks, CA: Sage.

Cook, M. (1979). Gaze and mutual gaze in social encounters. *American Scientist, 65,* 328–333.

Crusco, A. H., & Wetzel, C. G. (1984). The Midas touch: The effects of interpersonal touch on restaurant tipping. *Personality and Social Psychological Bulletin, 10,* 512–517.

Dawes, P. (1996, Nov.). *"Scent" story Perception.* Paper presented at the annual meeting of the Speech Communication Association, San Diego, CA.

DePaulo, B. M. (1992). Nonverbal behavior and self-presentation. *Psychological Bulletin, 3,* 203–243.

Ekman, P. (1965). Communication through nonverbal behavior: A source of information about an interpersonal relationship. In S. S. Tomkins & C. E. Izard (Eds.), *Affect, cognition and personality* (pp. 390–442). New York: Springer.

_____. (1992). Facial expressions of emotions: New findings, new questions. *Psychological Science, 3,* 34–38.

_____. (1999). Emotional and conversational nonverbal signals. In L. S. Messing, & R. Campbell, (Eds.), *Gesture, speech, and sign* (pp. 45–55). New York, NY: Oxford University Press.

_____. (2003). *Emotions revealed.* New York: Times Books.

Ekman, P., & Friesen, W. V. (1969). The repertoire or nonverbal behavior: categories, origins, usage, and coding. *Semiotica, 1,* 49–98.

_____. (1975). *Unmasking the face: A guide to recognizing emotions from facial expression.* Englewood Cliff, NJ: Prentice Hall.

_____. (1986). A new pan-cultural facial expression of emotion. *Motivation & Emotion, 10,* 159–168.

Ellis, H. D., & Young, A. W. (1989). Are faces special? In A. W. Young & H. D. Ellis (Eds.), *Handbook of research on face processing* (pp. 1–26). Amsterdam: North-Holland.

Ellsworth, P. C., Carlsmith, J. F., & Henson, A. (1985). The stare as a stimulus to flight in human subjects. *Journal of Personality and Social Psychology, 21,* 302–311.

Geertz, C. (1973). *The interpretation of cultures.* New York: Basic Books.

————. (1983). *Local knowledge: Further essays in interpretive anthropology.* New York: Basic Books.

Giles, H., & Le Poire, B. A. (2006). Introduction: The ubiquity and social meaningfulness of nonverbal communication. In V. Manusov & M. L. Patterson (Eds.), *The Sage handbook of nonverbal communication* (pp. xv–xxvii). Thousand Oaks, CA: Sage.

Goffman, E. (1964). *Behavior in public places.* New York: Free Press.

Goldman, M., Kiyohara, O., & Pfannensteil, D. (1985). Interpersonal touch, social labeling, and the foot-in-the-door effect. *The Journal of Social Psychology, 121,* 125–129.

Gomez, E. (2012). *Should businesses worry about appearance-based discrimination in the workplace?* Retrieved from http://www.forbes.com/sites/evangelinegomez/2012/01/31/should-businesses-worry-about-appearance-based-discrimination-in-the-workplace/

Goudreau, J. (2012). *The seven ways your boss is judging your appearance.* Retrieved from http://www.forbes.com/sites/jennagoudreau/2012/11/30/the-seven-ways-your-boss-is-judging-your-appearance/

Guéguen, N., & Fischer-Lokou, J. (2002). An evaluation of touch on a large request: A field setting. *Psychological Reports, 90,* 267–269.

————. (2003). Tactile contact and spontaneous help: An evaluation in a natural setting. *Journal of Social Psychology, 143,* 785–787.

Guéguen, N., & Jacob, C. (2006). The effect of tactile stimulation on the purchasing behavior of consumers: An experimental study in a natural setting. *International Journal of Management, 23,* 24–33.

Guerrero, L. K., & Floyd, K. (2006). *Nonverbal communication in relationships.* Mahweh, NJ: Lawrence Erlbaum.

Guyot, G.W., Byrd, G. R., & Caudle, R. (1980). Classroom seating: An expression of situational territoriality in humans. *Small Group Behavior 11,* (1), 120–128.

Hadnagy, C. (2014). *Unmasking the social engineer: The human element of security.* Indianapolis, IN: John Wiley & Sons, Inc.

Hall, E. T. (1963). *Proxemics: The study of man's spatial relations and boundaries: Man's image in medicine and anthropology.* New York: International Universities Press.

————. (1973). *The silent language.* New York: Anchor Books. (Original work published 1959)

————. (1989). *Beyond culture.* New York: Anchor Books.

Henshaw, V. (2014). Welcome to the smellscape. *New Scientist, 222,* 28–29.

Hertenstein, M. J., Keltner, D., App, B., Bulleit, B. A., & Jaskolka, A. R. (2006). Touch communicates distinct emotions. *Emotion, 6,* 528–533.

Heslin, R., & Alper, T. (1983). Touch: A bonding gesture. In J. M. Wiemann & R. P. Harrison (Eds.), *Nonverbal interaction.* (pp. 47–76). Beverly Hills, CA: Sage.

Hogan, K., & Stubbs, R. (2003). *Can't get through: Eight barriers to communication.* Grenta, LA: Pelican Publishing Company.

Hornik, J. (1991). Shopping time and purchasing behavior as a result of in-store tactile stimulation. *Perceptual and Motor Skills, 73,* 969–970.

_____. (1992). Tactile stimulation and consumer response. *Journal of Consumer Research, 19,* 449–458.

Hostetter, A. B. (2011). When do gestures communicate? A meta-analysis. *Psychological Bulletin, 137,* 297–315.

Izard, C. E., & Haynes, O. M. (1988). On the form and universality of the contempt expression: A challenge to Ekman and Friesen's claim of discovery. *Motivation and emotion, 12,* 1–16.

Jones, S. E., & Yarbrough, A. E., (1985). A naturalistic study of the meaning of touch. *Communication Monographs, 52,* 19–56.

Juslin, P. N., & Scherer, K. R. (2005). Vocal expression of affect. In J. A. Harrigan, R. Rosenthal, & K. R. Scherer (Eds.), *The new handbook of methods in nonverbal behavior research* (pp. 65–135). Oxford, UK: Oxford University Press.

Karl, K. A., Hall, L., & Peluchette, J. V. (2013). City employee perceptions of the impact of dress and appearance: You are what you wear. *Public Personnel Management, 42,* 452–470.

Kendon, A. (1967). Some functions of gaze direction in social interaction. *Acta psychological, 26,* 22–63.

Kleinke, C. L. (1977). Compliance to requests made by gazing and touching experimenters in field settings. *Journal of Experimental Social Psychology, 13,* 218–223.

Kleinke, C. L., & Walton, J. H. (1982). Influence of reinforced smiling on affective responses in an interview. *Journal of Personality and Social Psychology, 42,* 557–565.

Knapp, M. L. (1980). *Essentials of nonverbal communication.* New York: Holt, Rinehart and Winston.

Knapp, M., Hall, J. A., & Horgan, T.G. (2014). *Nonverbal communication in human interaction* (8th ed.). Boston, MA: Wadsworth, Cengage Learning.

Lakin, J. L. (2006). Automatic cognitive processes and nonverbal communication. In V. Manusov & M. L. Patterson (Eds.), *The Sage handbook of nonverbal communication* (pp. 59–78). Thousand Oaks, CA: Sage.

Levine, R. V. (1988). The pace of life across cultures. In J. E. McGrath (Ed.), *The social psychology of time* (pp. 39–60). Newbury Park, CA: Sage.

Levine, R. V., & Norenzayan, A. (1999). The pace of life in 31 countries. *Journal of Cross-Cultural Psychology, 30,* 178–205.

Lohmann, A., Arriaga, X. B., & Goodfriend, W. (2003). Close relationships and placemaking: Do objects in a couple's home reflect couplehood? *Personal Relationships, 10,* 437–450.

Lycan, W. (2014). The intentionality of smell. *Frontiers in Psychology, 5,* 1–8.

Machotka, P. (1965). Body movements as communication. *Dialogues: Behavioral Science Research, 2,* 33–66.

Martin, J. A., & Chaney, L. H. (2006). *Global business etiquette: A guide to international communication and customs.* Westport, CT: Praeger.

Masin, H. M. (2010). Cross Cultural Communication. In R. Leavitt (Ed.). *Cultural competence: A lifelong journey to cultural proficiency* (pp. 159–186). Thorofare, NJ: Slack, Inc.

McAdams, T., Moussavi, F., & Klassen, M. (1992). Employee appearance and the Americans with Disabilities Act: An emerging issue? *Employee Responsibility & Rights Journal, 5,* 323–338.

MediaRadar (2013). Spring and summer ads bloom bright. *Media Industry Newsletter, 66,* 5.

Mehrabian, A. (1967). Orientation behaviors and nonverbal attitude communication. *Journal of Communication, 17,* 324–332.

_____. (1972). *Nonverbal communication.* Chicago: Aldine-Artherton.

Mehrabian, A., & Weiner, M. (1967). Decoding of inconsistent communications. *Journal of personality and social psychology, 6,* 109–114.

Morris, D. (1977). *Manwatching: A field guide to human behavior.* New York: Abrams.

Mulac, A. (1976). Assessment and application of the revised speech dialect attitudinal scale. *Communication Monographs, 43,* 238–245.

Myers, G. E., & Myers, M. T. (1992). *The dynamics of human communication: A laboratory approach* (6th ed.). New York: McGraw-Hill.

Nannberg, J. C., & Hansen, C. H. (1994). Post-compliance touch: An incentive for task performance. *Journal of Psychology, 134,* 301–307.

Norton, R.W., & Pettegrew, L. S. (1979). Attentiveness as a style of communication: A structural analysis. *Communication Monographs, 46,* 13–26.

Patterson, J., & Kim, P. (1991). *The day America told the truth: What people really believe about everything that really matters.* Upper Saddle River, New Jersey: Prentice Hall.

Patterson, M. L. (1982). A sequential functional model of nonverbal exchange. *Psychological Review, 89,* 231–249.

Patterson, M. L., & Manusov, V. L. (2006). *The Sage handbook of nonverbal communication.* Thousand Oaks: Sage.

Pattison, J. E. (1973). Effects of touch on self-exploration and the therapeutic relationship. *Journal of Consulting and Clinical Psychology, 40,* 170–175.

Prown, J. D., & Haltman, K. (2000). *American artifacts: Essays in material culture.* East Lansing: Michigan State University Press.

Poyatos, F. (1993). *Paralanguage: A linguistic and interdisciplinary approach to interactive speech and sound.* Amsterdam, NL: Benjamins.

Reeves, S. (2006). *Smell ya later.* Retrieved from http://www.forbes.com/2006/03/15/employment-work-management-cx_0316bizbasics.html.

Roman, J. D. (2006). *The communication man.* Buenos Aires: LibrosEnRed.

Schein, E. H. (2010). *Organizational culture and leadership.* New York: Wiley & Sons.

Scherer, K. R. (2003). Vocal communication of emotion: A review of research paradigms. *Speech Communication, 40,* 227–256.

Shrout, P. E., & Fiske, D. W. (1981). Nonverbal behaviors and social evaluation. *Journal of Personality, 49,* 115–128.

State of New York Department of Health (2008). *People first: How to plan events everyone can attend.* Retrieved from https://www.health.ny.gov/publications/0956.pdf

Stone, B., Markham, R., & Wilhelm, K. (2013). When words are not enough: A validated nonverbal vocabulary of feelings. *Australian Psychologist, 48,* 311–320.

Sundaram, D. S., & Wester, C. (2000). The role of nonverbal communication in service encounters. *Journal of Service Marketing, 14,* 378–391.

Ting-Toomey, S. (1991). Intimacy expression in three cultures: France, Japan, and the United States. *International Journal of Intercultural Relations, 15,* 29–46.

————. (1999). *Communicating across cultures.* New York: Guilford Press.

Trager, G. L. (1958). Paralanguage: A first approximation. *Studies in linguistics, 12,* 1–12.

Tusing, K. J., & Dillard, J. P. (2000). The sounds of dominance: Vocal precursors of perceived dominance during interpersonal influences. *Human Communication Research, 26,* 148–171.

Tsai, W., Huang, T., & Yu, H. (2012). Investigating the unique predictability and boundary conditions of applicant physical attractiveness and non-verbal behaviours on interviewer evaluations in job interviews. *Journal of Occupational & Organizational Psychology, 85,* 60–79.

Van Servellen, G. M. (2009). *Communication skills for the health care professional: Concepts practice and evidence.* (2nd ed.). New York: Jones and Bartlett.

Weiss, D. C. (2008). As tattoos enter mainstream, courts uphold employers' right to ban them. ABA Journal. Retrieved from http://www.abajournal.com/news/article/as_tattoos_enter_mainstream_courts_uphold_employers_right_to_ban_them/

Wood, J. T. (2006). Chopping the carrots: Creating intimacy moment by moment. In J. T Wood and S. W. Duck (Eds.) *Composing relationships: Communication in everyday life.* (pp. 15–23) Belmont, CA: Thompson/Wadsworth.

Wood, J. T., & Duck, S.W. (Eds.) (2006). *Composing relationships: Communication in everyday life.* Belmont, CA: Thompson/Wadsworth.

Wyland, C. L., & Forgas, J. P. (2010). Here's looking at you, kid: Mood effects on processing eye gaze as a heuristic cue. *Social Cognition, 28,* 133–144.

Xin, K. R. (2004). Asian American managers: An impression gap?: An investigation of impression management and supervisor-subordinate relationships. *Journal of Applied Behavioral Science, 40,* 160–181.

Chapter 4

SKILLS OF THE EVENT PLANNER: YOUR ROAD MAP TO SUCCESS

Event planners must both understand and utilize a host of skills in order to become effective and successful within the field. This chapter considers some of those skills that are imperative for an event planning career. While communication is central in event planning, the skills listed in this chapter will help you under-

© Joseph Sohm/Shutterstock.com

stand the multifaceted discipline. Event planners must regularly and competently practice these skills—all vital in communication—to develop the muscle memory that will help incorporate them into part of the planning regimen. In addition, besides strong communication skills, there are a host of other abilities that event planners must develop, such as ingenuity, flexibility, and thoughtfulness (Camenson, 2002; Sanders, 2016). Professional event planners can use their knowledge and experience to take the worry out of an event, and thus need strong communication skills to convey to the client that they can create and develop an event that will fulfill the client's vision (Greenwell, Danzey-Bussell, & Shonk, 2014). While one or two other professions might occasionally demand clairvoyance and superhuman skills, event planners must constantly be attuned to what *might* occur and know immediately how to address unforeseen challenges.

When you have finished reading this chapter, you will be able to

- identify the particular skills that event planners should include as part of their expertise;
- suggest practical ways to manage time and balance commitments;
- express a client's vision clearly in terms of business and design.

Planning an Anniversary Celebration

Kristen Schultz, Director, Community Relations and Promotions, Baltimore Orioles

Type A personalities are defined as ambitious, well-organized, and concerned with time management. They are often high-achieving, multitasking workaholics who are driven by deadlines. In contrast, Type B personalities are defined as creative and visionary risk takers. Event directors must carefully balance each of these conflicting personality traits to produce successful events.

As the Director of Special Events for the Baltimore Orioles, I produced a commemorative event recognizing the Orioles 60th Anniversary in 2014. In doing so, I had to resist my conservative Type A personality traits of practicality and common sense in favor of creative vision. I used this vision to produce a magical ceremony that was filled with huge risk but high reward.

Event professionals are often faced with obstacles that go beyond their control. In this case, my challenge was to produce an outdoor post-game event that captivated 40,000 fans while facing the risk of thunderstorms, extra innings, or a devastating loss. The event demanded a first-class showcase, honoring the largest number of Orioles Hall of Famers ever assembled at Oriole Park. The event also needed to surpass previous celebrations and become a unique historical milestone in its own right.

My vision was to create a Disney-like event that combined themed music and special effects with historic game footage and live player introductions. To bring vision to reality, I collaborated with our internal events staff and an outside special effects company to capture 60 years of Orioles baseball within a 30-minute show. We started with a storyboard and a timeline, two essential elements that kept the project on task. The storyboard helped to communicate my vision onto paper while the timeline kept us organized and on schedule. The storyboard outlined the conceptual elements of the show. The three-month timeline detailed when we would send pictures, logos, audio, and video to the production company. It also provided approval deadlines and a final completion date for the project. During production, the event team coordinated player travel, provided hospitality, and promoted the event. One week prior to the event, I scheduled a dress rehearsal to identify unforeseen issues and allow for last-minute changes.

On game day, the risk paid off with clear weather, a sold-out crowd, and a decisive Orioles victory. The atmosphere was electric, setting the stage for an iconic celebration. The event was flawless, as 23 members of the Orioles Hall of Fame appeared from the shadows of the dugout into the spotlight at home plate as lasers and fireworks illuminated the sky. Music and video prompted fans to cheer, cry, and applaud throughout the show. The celebration garnered rave reviews from players, media, and Orioles ownership.

Planning and executing this event left me with a profound understanding of how to utilize my predominant Type A personality traits in harmony with my less instinctive Type B traits to produce a balanced outcome. High risk produced high reward but demanded clear communication, effective time management, creative vision, and an eye for design, all skills necessary to produce an event of this magnitude.

After reading this chapter, revisit the case study and respond to the following question:

Do some research on Type A and Type B personalities. Based upon your type, what challenges would you face in planning a large-scale public event?

Skills for Successful Event Planning

A wide variety of skills are necessary for success in the field of event planning. This chapter focuses on several characteristics of event planners: responsibility and self-control; availability; flexibility; organization; time management and multi-tasking skills; detail orientation; business savvy; an eye for design; vision and intuition; and passion. Much of the literature reiterates some of the specific abilities this chapter covers, but sometimes these lists of skills are focused on the management aspect of event planning, while other inventories are more attuned to client interaction (Camenson, 2012; Getz, 2012; Sanders, 2016; Silvers & Goldblatt 2012; Van der Wagen, 2010). Any event demands strong communication and social abilities, including interpersonal and presentation skills, as well as the ability to remain calm in chaos (Camenson, 2012; Silvers & Goldblatt, 2012). A solid organizational sense seems to be a commonality as well, which can include administrative, strategic, human resource management, budget planning, risk analysis, and marketing abilities (Getz, 2012; Van der Wagen, 2010). In addition, event planners generally need a strong technical or technological side (Silvers & Goldblatt, 2012), and lastly, there are several personality characteristics that are prominent in the literature, including flexibility, optimism, creativity, leadership, accountability, and passion (Epler, 2014; Getz, 2012; Smart & Featheringham, 2006). While these are some of the important skills of the event planner, communication remains central.

© Polarpx/Shutterstock.com

© Kendall Hunt Publishing Co.

Diagram 04. *Skills of the Event Planner*

© FashionStock/Shutterstock.com

In each instance, the explanatory approach concentrates on why these particular characteristics are essential, how they are connected to communication, and where and when they can be utilized. This list is by no means exhaustive, but it covers many of the optimal attributes of event planners. Think of all the skills needed to plan an event such as New York Fashion Week. This event brings together fashion lovers from all over the world as designers exhibit their latest creations on elaborate runways underneath tents at various locales. Sponsors line the inside of the tents, giving away items that guests can place in a branded goodie bag. In the past, Mercedes-Benz was the primary sponsor of New York Fashion Week, but as of 2019, major sponsors include BMW, Maybelline New York, TRESemmé, Intel, DHL, and E! Entertainment. This elaborate event takes place generally over two weeks in both February and September when the fall and spring lines are showcased. Tickets are distributed to lists of celebrities, fashion writers, buyers, and industry specialists all over the world. Photographers set up at the end of the catwalk in tiers ready to snap a photo as models pause and pose walking the runway. This large-scale city event captures the attention of the world for many days as celebrities sitting in the front row grab headlines in the Style section of newspapers and in magazines online. Planning and preparation for this event is multilayered and creative. Designers organize their fashion shows, but a planning team

86   **Chapter 4**

orchestrates the overall implementation of Fashion Week. This team is responsible for scheduling and coordinating the shows that happen inside the tents as well as in various locations throughout the city.

Responsibility and Self-Control

For the event planner, **responsibility** means authenticity of design, consistency of delivery, and commitment to excellence for the client. These qualities demand **self-control**, or restraint regarding one's own actions in order to achieve a goal. Emotional events occur in the field of planning and management, but the very best event planners depend upon their self-control to keep them from indulging in negative actions when something goes awry (Brown, Westbrook, & Challagalla, 2005). In a society where a public brand depends on its image, most people want to associate with a brand that stands for integrity and responsibility (Doyle, 2012). The current trend is to connect corporate responsibility to social change (Jakobson, 2013), but individual responsibility can also be demonstrated in a variety of ways. Since more and more levels of management are encouraging employees to exercise self-discipline in what they are charged to do, rather than relying on top-down controls (Hamel, 2009), developing this responsibility early in a career will ready the event planner for any worst-case scenario.

Responsibility: *The ability to perform a duty that is demanded of someone*

Self-control: *Restraint regarding one's own actions in order to achieve a goal*

If the event planner does not have effective coping skills and cannot maintain self-control when a cool head is called for, it is likely that **goal-directed behavior**, a way of acting that is motivated by the desire to achieve an outcome, will be disrupted (Weiss & Cropanzano, 1996). As a result, performance levels decline, and the event may not be as successful as was planned. Emotions that arise as a response to a negative event keep the event planner from focusing on the goal and instead indulge in too much self-analysis (Brown, Westbrook, & Challagalla, 2005). Often, such self-analysis will mean that the event planner 'gets stuck' at a certain juncture and cannot move forward toward the goal. Those who can stay focused on reaching the goal without letting the emotions of the moment influence their performance will not be affected as overwhelmingly by any emotional occurrence (Brown, Westbrook, & Challagalla, 2005). For example, an event planner who has to arrange a charity event for a sick child cannot get caught up in the sadness of the situation, but needs to focus instead on the celebration of life. This task is easier said than done, but emotions cannot trump the creation of a successful event.

Goal-directed behavior: *A way of acting that is motivated by the desire to achieve an outcome*

GOLD RIBBON
children's cancer
month awareness

© *Little Unicorn/Shutterstock.com*

A good practice for the event planner is to develop a **problem-focused approach** to ideas of self-control and responsibility. This approach is a rational way of responding to a challenge that involves taking control, seeking information, and evaluating choices. Bandura (1997) notes that those who are action-oriented and task-focused tend to be able to avoid getting stuck and wallowing in self-doubt. Emotion-focused drama queens

Problem-focused approach: *A rational way of responding to a challenge that involves taking control, seeking information, and evaluating choices*

who love heightened levels of negative excitement are not generally cut out for a career in event planning, for the ability to manage negative occurrences at events will necessarily affect long-term performance (Brown, Westbrook, & Challagalla, 2005). Event planners must develop a level of self-monitoring coping tactics that will help improve their individual performance. Event planning is a stressful job, and with so much emotion riding on every little detail, it is important to stay focused on the task at hand (Bean-Mellinger, 2018). If event planners learn how to assess a situation calmly and realistically, and then stabilize it by reducing any possible negative outcomes, the level of emotion will subside and all parties can move on. Venting or storming out only serves to aggravate the negative outcomes (Brown, Westbrook, & Challagalla, 2005) and demonstrate a lack of self-discipline that should not be a part of any event planner's brand. Having self-control, knowing when to say yes and no, being responsible for your clients, and having their best interest at heart are all attributes of the self-disciplined event planner.

Availability

Knowing how to handle details and be a problem solver means being available through the duration of the event creation, affair, and debriefing. Clients and vendors alike depend on the event planner to provide service, advice, organization, decision-making, eloquence, and negotiation whenever these qualities are demanded; thus, the need for immediate availability becomes crucial. You can manage this skill by developing a fine balance between your own **availability** to clients and over-commitment to the point of burnout. The days leading up to an event can be very stressful, and planners need to realize the importance of being available at key times of the day (Bean-Mellinger, 2018). Juggling both the creative and the business aspects of any corporate work means understanding time management and developing a willingness to cut back on personal time during periods of high activity. Clients may believe that they can contact you at any time of the day, but it is your job to let them know clearly and directly what your professional boundaries are. Conflict arises when demands from the workplace impinge upon non-work life in ways that cause frustration and imbalance (Sturges & Guest, 2004). For example, a demanding bride might feel that it is appropriate to call, text, or email her planner at 10 p.m. because that is the only time the bride is available. Frantic messages might help ease the client's nerves, but continuous communication late at night might cross the lines of acceptable employee/client boundaries.

Event planners should examine certain facets of their personal and professional life that impact their availability and prevent them from being able to balance their time. This process could involve several steps. Kahle (2004) writes about the unpredictable kaleidoscope of the life of a salesperson, much like that of an event planner. Unforeseen events are the norm, and while they may offer an adrenaline rush for the moment, they sap time and energy and eat into a schedule that has no extra time in it. Because many

Availability: *Accessibility for service or help*

TIP

The event planning profession is not a 9–5 job.

— Kristen Schultz

event planners prefer the personal aspect of their work (as opposed to the financial side), they may simply prefer to go 'off the grid' for a more enjoyable two hours shopping with a client rather than spending that time with the finances or budget work at the office. Sticking to the plan may afford a less hectic workday, offering a bit of free time at day's end. Tracking your daily/weekly time expenditures through careful logging (Allen, 2005) will ensure there are no time bandits in your professional life. Face-to-face meetings, for instance, might offer personal advantages but internet voice communication or telephone conversations could save time within a busy schedule. Building and keeping a strong relationship with clients often means making clear your availability from the start. Being an advocate for both the client and yourself helps you better negotiate your working schedules.

© oliveromg/Shutterstock.com

Flexibility

Many times in the field of event planning, scheduling an event down to the very minute will give you a sense of how the event is going to run. Staying on task is a desirable attribute of a great event planner, but being flexible is also crucial. The Event Planning Association (2017) states that being able to stay flexible and being able to adapt to various situations is the key to success in event planning. While planning and **flexibility** might seem to be extreme opposites, that is not always the case. In the event planning industry, something will always go differently than planned, and you need to be flexible enough to adapt to the situation at hand (Peters, 2007). An adaptable event planner will know how to make an event a success when the caterer is stuck in traffic and the delay completely throws the schedule off.

Flexibility: *Willingness to yield in a certain circumstance; adaptability*

Ermenegildo Zegna (2014), the CEO of a luxury menswear brand, believes that for individuals to succeed in any business, "flexibility is key" (p. 10). Individuals rarely can foresee what events can occur that will cause a major disruption to a well-planned schedule. Without a schedule, chaos is bound to happen, but more commotion might arise when an individual refuses to be flexible and meet the needs of that particular moment. In his book *Drive: The surprising truth about what motivates us*, Daniel H. Pink (2009) states, "Flexibility simply widens the fences and occasionally opens the gates" (p. 90). When event planners are flexible, the options for creating new ideas can become endless. Take, for example, the caterer who is running late due to traffic. Instead of panicking, a great event planner might have a discussion with the client who agrees to leave the bar open an hour longer for an impromptu meet and greet until the caterer is ready. Being flexible will allow you to adjust a schedule to make an event work. Moreover, flexibility

© totallyPic.com/Shutterstock.com

will create a space that is fluid and can ebb and flow instead of becoming rigid and stagnant.

Flexibility is a skill that can be used in various aspects of the event planning job. In examining organizations, John Atkinson (1984) notes three types of flexibility that make an organization productive: (1) **numerical flexibility**—finding the number of people needed to complete a task; (2) **functional flexibility**—being able to perform and move among a range of jobs; and (3) **financial flexibility**—understanding how to move and shift numbers depending on the budget. Sparrow and Marchington (1998) then added four more types of flexibility to create seven overall categories; (4) **temporal flexibility**—examining the time patterns of when things get done at work; (5) **geographical flexibility**—comprehending the increased mobility of working groups; (6) **organizational flexibility**—allowing for changes in the structure and system of how the company operates; and (7) **cognitive flexibility**—creating a mindset of continual change. By understanding these categories, you will be able to create flexibility in all facets of your job. As an event planner, you need to understand how flexibility will not only benefit your overall success in the industry, but also how it can lead to greater success for the event planning company. Clients will like working with planners who are flexible.

Organization

The difference between working efficiently and inefficiently lies in your ability to develop strong organizational skills (Worth, 2004). Woodward (2019) believes that event planners need to be extremely organized to succeed in the industry. **Organization** is a skill that requires you to classify things into various categories (Issa, 2009). White (1978) states, "The beginning of all understanding is classification" (p. 22). By breaking down the components of an event, you are able to understand what needs to get done and when it needs to get done. If you are lacking organizational skills, your life and many of the events you plan will feel very chaotic. Worth (2004) believes that when you have organizational skills, you will have "more control of your life, a greater sense of accomplishment, and a higher level of success" (p. 4). Learning to be an organized person is a process that has many different characteristics (Goldberg, 2005). As an event planner, some guidelines to keep you organized are as follows:

1. Create a great filing system—label all of your documents in a way that helps you remember the best vendors, for instance. There is no need to recreate each event. Keep your favorites on file with detailed notes as a point of referral should you ever have to execute that event—or a similar one—again. An organized and functional filing system will also help you remove clutter from your desk.

2. Invest in paper and electronic planners—both will keep you on task. Looking at a calendar is a helpful reminder of what needs to

be completed by an exact date. Develop a system that integrates the best of both schedulers and that works for you.

3. Develop to-do lists—these types of lists keep you on task. If you write a to-do list every day, you are less likely to miss important deadlines. Checking off what you have accomplished will also keep you on point as you move through the project. Keeping daily, weekly, and long-term lists is helpful.

4. Prioritize and do not procrastinate—all event planners need to know what must be handled immediately and what details you can save for later. Great venues fill up quickly, and the best caterers are usually booked a year in advance. If something does not need to be tackled right away, save it for a day when you are less busy. However, do not procrastinate and wait until the day of the event because you need time to plan for the unexpected.

5. Write everything down—you might think you can remember the details of every client's wish list, but that is not always the case. Carry a pen and notebook with you at all times. Keep detailed notes as a reference so that you can always go back to them and find answers.

6. Track notes, contacts, and vendors in spreadsheets—these records will help you build a comprehensive database of information. This list is a continual work in progress and will make your job easier as it continues to grow.

Events run more smoothly when both you and your event are organized. As Edmund Burke (1790/2008) wrote, "Good order is the foundation of all good things" (p. 248). If you are able to stay organized, you will be able to keep yourself and your event on track.

to do list

i.
ii.
iii.
iv.
v.
vi.
vii.
viii.
ix.
x.

© underverse/Shutterstock.com

Time Management and Multi-Tasking Skills

In today's society of constant communication, it is easy to say there is not enough time in the day, but effective time managers are able to prioritize their schedule so that time is on their side. Woodward (2019) believes that successful planners must have the skills to prioritize and focus on multiple tasks while not becoming distracted by the overwhelming number of tasks that need to be completed in a short amount of time. This skill, **time management**, is defined as "behaviors that aim at achieving an effective use of time while performing goal-directed activities" (Claessens, van Eerde, Rutte, & Roe, 2007, p. 262). The literature on time management discusses skilled time managers as being able to set and prioritize goals, monitor goal progress, and manage productivity (Britton & Tesser, 1991; Jex & Elacqua, 1999; Orpen, 1994; Peeters & Rutte, 2005). Skilled time managers are more selective in prioritizing their time and are more likely

Time management: *The ability to create behaviors that achieve an effective use of time while performing goal-directed activities* to focus on high-priority tasks (Hall & Hursch, 1982). They consider the time required for each activity and systematically account for the time it will take to achieve a designated outcome (Claessens, van Eerde, Rutte, & Roe, 2004; Tripoli, 1998). Effective time managers are less likely to over-commit, resulting in a better sense of the time needed to complete tasks (Burt & Kemp, 1994). With effective time management skills, event planners are able to multitask. Greenwell, Danzey-Bussell, and Shonk (2014) state that those who are great managers of time should also have an easier time multitasking.

Multitasking has become an integral skill in today's society and occurs when you work on several tasks simultaneously (Shao & Shao, 2012). Individuals multitask to accomplish numerous demands of the various roles event planners play (Kaufman, Lane, & Lindquist, 1991). Imagine working as an event planner on two separate events that occur during the same weekend. As you try to manage two different venues, it is essential to keep the details of each event separate but simultaneously complete all the particulars of the events before the big days arrive. Multitasking allows event planners, for instance, to prepare for a 50th anniversary party on a Friday night and an engagement party on Saturday morning. The details for each event should remain separate, but an effective multitasker might meet with a favorite florist and receive a discount for a double booking that uses the same centerpieces for both parties. A busy event planner must develop strong time management and multi-tasking skills in order to succeed in the business.

Multitasking: *The act of performing several tasks simultaneously*

Detail-Oriented Skills

Detail-oriented: *The ability to see the big picture and also have an eye for the particulars*

There's a fine line between being **detail-oriented** and letting yourself get mired in endless trivia (Benton, 2000). Event planners need to be able to see the big picture while they also must have an eye for the particulars; this means a constant shifting of focus and an alertness for what may be different from the scripted plan. Peters (2007) states, "Planners must think of, and keep track of, an amazing number of details" (p. 7). Paying attention to details can also be a time-saver, since it eliminates repetition, carries out the plan, and helps to prevent mistakes. However, many who are detail-oriented are also perfectionists, and may have to teach themselves not to let these perfectionist tendencies prevent them from moving on to the next task (Basco, 2000). Training yourself to use your proclivity for details to your advantage will be instrumental in the life of an event planner. For example, imagine that you have created a program for a convention in which you have left out a name of a prominent sponsor. Reprinting 1,200 programs is not an option because of the cost. You must consider alternatives, such as creating an embossed gold sticker that could be affixed to the front of every program and which highlights the sponsor. While this may be labor intensive and require additional cost, it demonstrates your ability to prioritize details. However, if you have slightly misspelled the name of

TIP

Good planning and forethought are at the core of the best events. I don't like process, but when it comes to event planning and execution I know that the devil is in the details.

— Sandy Hillman

a breakout session room on one page, would you endure the cost and the labor time to fix it?

Developing an event fact sheet that you can distribute to others helps the planner keep all the event details aligned and focused (Diggs-Brown, 2011). Knowing that you must convey the details of the event to others will force you into a regular review of the occasion's elements. This insistence on attention to details often becomes the hallmark of the successful event planner (Wendroff, 2004). As Steeves (2015) states, "When planning an event, regardless of the size, the key to success is in the details" (para 1). Being detail-oriented means more than just making hundreds of decisions during the planning stages; it means knowing what those details are without having to check and recheck the plan and your progress.

Critical path: The sequence of stages that indicate the minimum time needed for an event's duration

Event planners often call this detailed plan the **critical path**, which had its origins in project management in the 1950s (Tracy, 2002; Wong, 1964). The **critical path method**, or CPM, helps to determine the progress of a project at any interval. Each assignment in a project has a space on a path, generally using a bar chart, according to the order in which the tasks must

Critical Path Method: A plan in which all the connected jobs of a project are laid out in paths according to the order they must be performed, with a time listed for completion

be completed. The project manager, in conjunction with all the project's players, determines the time required for each job, and the chart clearly demonstrates all the interrelationships of the pieces of the project. The manager records every change in deadline and each person's responsibility. The longest path, known as the critical path, shows the project duration (Wong, 1964). While the Critical Path Method is extremely useful for its ability to display the plan and thus afford collaboration and agreement among those working on the project, often its parts, including terms, definitions, methods, and functions, are not standardized within the industries that use it. Project managers define processes and use the critical path differently, so a lack of consensus in the use of the Critical Path Method has created a wide variety of exemplars and many variations (Galloway, 2006). The method remains, however, a very useful tool in the event planner's toolbox, especially when connected to a long-term plan or assignments for the day of an event.

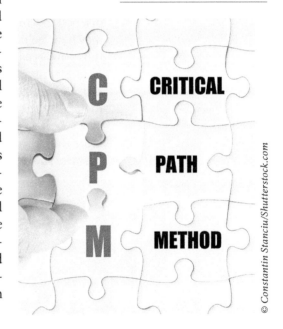

© Constantin Stanciu/Shutterstock.com

Business Savvy

Event planners must have a strong sense of the industry and be business savvy in order to be successful. Many event planners do not succeed because they do not realize the importance of the business side of the industry (Givner, 2013). According to Brown (1983), "**Business savvy** is the ability to comprehend the social and economic systems and realities that affect one's success in the marketplace: it is being able to harness these forces to facilitate achievement of goals and use them to stimulate further growth

Business savvy: The ability to comprehend the social and economical systems and realities that affect one's success in the marketplace

and achievement in oneself and others" (p. 53). As event planners create and manage events, they must understand all facets of business, including budgeting, sales, negotiation, marketing, advertising, and promotions, among others; additionally, they should be able to work well with people.

Successful, shrewd businesspeople aim to build win-win situations, whether it is with their customers, clients, employees, business alliances, or vendors (Stephenson & Thurman, 2007). Building relationships will help foster the business side of event planning and will make the execution of the event run that much more smoothly. In order to succeed in the industry, event planners should implement responsible business practices. Browne (2006) states, "Our commitment to responsibility has to be expressed not in words, but in the actions of the business, day-in and day-out, in every piece of activity, and every aspect of behavior" (p. 55). Clients rely on event planners for everything from determining costs to selecting a location for an event, so having a mind for business is an absolute necessity. For example, depending on local chambers of commerce for networking events can provide event planners with opportunities both to meet other business professionals and rely on them for referrals. An article titled "Savvy advice is nice, but cash is even nicer" (2006) in *Adweek* reported findings of a poll in which owners of small businesses were asked to cite things that may have helped them during their start-up phase. Forty-nine percent of those surveyed stated that it would have been helpful to reach out to more business folks for advice; 39% said they wished they understood financial management better; 32% said they needed more legal and accounting assistance; and 32% said they needed to spend less on non-essential expenditures. Furthermore, participants recognized that it typically took more than three years for their businesses to begin to flourish. Becoming business savvy requires event planners to take time to learn all the different aspects of how their company will conduct business—and help it to thrive.

© dizain/Shutterstock.com

Understanding the business world and your company's goals will help guide you as you grow and shape your business. Miller (2006) suggests that businesses typically have three common goals: (1) to increase revenues through differentiated products or services, (2) to decrease costs, usually via better execution, and (3) to provide better customer experience to improve loyalty (p. 17). Vass (2007) notes that savvy business people will understand that adding value to an existing product or improving on one already in existence can help guide their company's success. Vass also advises looking into your products or services to see where there may be gaps that need solutions. Through a careful study of the event planning industry, you will be able to see if your offerings match those of your competitors, and if there is any room for you to expand.

Another way to become business savvy is to trust your most talented people (Allen, 2005). When you trust those with whom you work, they will not only live up to your expectations, but also to their own. "When you want people to produce at their peak levels, empowerment and communication are vital" (Allen, 2005, p. 48). The event planning field is one based on relationships—both building and sustaining them—and only the most adept professionals will understand the importance of the relational and business sides.

An Eye for Design

Event planners must constantly **design** events to make them interesting, intriguing, entertaining, or beautiful. Being able to envision how an event could be staged and executed means developing exceptional creativity and designing the event for maximum impact. But what is design? And how can design thinking help motivate an event planner? Tim Brown (2009) states that **design thinking** offers "an approach to innovation that is powerful, effective, and broadly accessible, that can be integrated into all aspects of business and society, and that individuals and teams can use to generate breakthrough ideas that are implemented and that therefore have an impact" (p. 3). Inspiration for design thinking can come from people, places, or things, and it asks you to trust your intuition and feelings, even though event planners tend to rely primarily on their rational and analytical selves in the business world.

Design: *The ability to envision how an event could be staged and executed with exceptional creativity*

Design thinking: *An approach to innovation that is powerful, effective, and broadly accessible, that can be integrated into all aspects of business and society, and that individuals and teams can use to generate breakthrough ideas*

While Tim Brown discusses design thinking, the founder of IDEO, David Kelly (2006), suggests another strategy you can incorporate that might help you design many aspects of an event. He uses a technique called mind mapping that begins with an initial idea and allows for visual brainstorming with both words and pictures. **Mind maps** depend upon free association, showing relationships among ideas. Imagine a tree with many branches emanating from it. The tree is the central idea, and the branches are supporting ideas and details. Mind maps can help anyone expand ideas and build upon them using association. Some great ideas might come from this exercise, but it requires you to allow yourself time to sit, create, and design. The net goal is to come up with ideas that work for the client and for the good of the event.

Mind map: *A trademarked system of representing ideas, with related concepts arranged around a core concept*

As you begin to plan events, the spaces in which the events will take place, for instance, will challenge you, and it will be your job to bring design thinking into the venue or location. Event planners must think in pictures—visually—to bring events to life. This can mean you have to visualize the decorations and flowers, the placement of the DJ, or the candlelit walkway. You will have to decide how to get the best flow in the room by placing the food stations strategically. Getz (2012) states that events do require aesthetic design,

© Andrey_Popov/Shutterstock.com

© Bill Florence/Shutterstock.com

because it is the event planner's job not only to create atmosphere, but also to be a problem solver. Will the chairs work where you have placed them? Is the entrance to the event constricting or welcoming? At what time will the program begin? These are all questions that will need answers, but they must be answered in conjunction with each other and with your design in mind. All the elements must work together well so that they function as a whole rather than individually. As you design your event, keep in mind the creative and practical elements that will make it a success.

Vision and Intuition

Vision: *The ability to see what the future may hold and plan accordingly*

An event planner's responsibility is to create a **vision**, and the process begins with asking three questions: (1) What is the significant purpose of the business? (2) What is the picture of the business' future? and (3) What are the clear values upon which you base your decisions? (Blanchard, 2007). An event planner's job is to understand all three of these questions in order to execute each event. Planning daily for each event and those scheduled for the future is at the forefront of an event planner's tasks. Being able to see what the future may hold helps an event planner make educated decisions. Kramer (2002) discusses the former chairman and CEO of General Electric Jack Welch's lexicons. Jack Welch believed that it was important for leaders in business to create a vision and then to step aside. Event planners will have to trust those with whom they work—from vendors to colleagues—to do their jobs. This requires that the event planner communicate details of the event's overall vision so that there is clear understanding among all involved.

© Rawpixel/Shutterstock.com

In their seminal work, Daft and Weick (1984) found that top leaders must interpret the environment in order to develop a comprehensive strategic vision; the vision must be shared by, reduce uncertainty for, and generate meaning for, stakeholders. Westley and Mintzberg (1989) believe that a strategic vision should be a priority for improved performance within the organization. Event planners should be able to identify what their goals are and how they will achieve them, but they should also be able to articulate goals to all who will work with them on events. Understanding and then communicating a client's vision can help you guide others through all the steps necessary for the event to come to fruition.

Event planners also rely on **intuition**. Intuition is a non-linear process that bolsters innovation and creates results (Glaser, 1995), and the Oxford Dictionary defines intuition as "the ability to understand something immediately, without the need for conscious reasoning"—to let you know if something is right or wrong and/or working or not working. Bacon (2013) states, "Intuition can reveal some aspects of your situation which your ability to reason cannot. In fact, your internal radar works perfectly. It is the operator who is in question. There are things your gut knows long before your intellect catches on" (p. 29). In event planning, there will be times when you will have to rely on your intuition to make decisions. In fact, Keen (1996) reported that 89% of marketing professionals used intuition to guide some part of their decision-making.

Sadler-Smith and Shefy (2004) recommend asking yourself some questions to see just how much intuition tends to guide your own decision-making. Can you trust your intuition in times of stress? Are you comfortable relying on your intuition when meeting new people? Do you rely on feelings rather than logic and reasoning in decision-making? Questions like these can help you form decisions when you must rely on your intuition. Understanding how your intuition works and what guides you can be helpful in discerning how you make decisions as an event planner. Your instincts bring together many facets of knowledge and emotion. Williams (2012) links intuition to awareness, and believes that those with good intuition usually have a high degree of empathy; being able to master your own sense of truth or understanding can lead you to become a more intuitive manager. Knowing when to listen to your gut and when to adhere to rational thought is not always a black-and-white endeavor, and should be rooted in your experience and practice. However, respecting your intuition and understanding it as a necessary skill for event planners may help you trust and hone it in order to serve clients in the best manner.

> Intuition: *The ability to understand something immediately, without the need for conscious reasoning*

Passion

To be an effective event planner, you must have a **passion** for the field. But how do you know if you do? Being excited about a career is wonderful; however, it is passion, a fervor or enthusiasm for an idea or a plan, that will sustain you over time. This passion is easily perceived by others. In *Start with Why*, Simon Sinek (2011) wrote, "People don't buy what you do, they buy why you do it" (p. 41). Boverie and Kroth (2001) identified five keys to passion (pp. 97–178), and suggested ways to find it and maintain it.

> Passion: *A fervor or enthusiasm for an idea or plan*

Key #1—The Discovering Process: This idea asks you to discover work that excites you. Sometimes people know what they want to do at a very young age; for others, the discovery comes later in life or through a process of soul-searching.

Key #2—The Designing Process: This is where you find a way to implement your passion. Once you learn what will make you happy, you design plans to make it work, whether it means taking additional classes, becoming an apprentice to someone, or deciding to be an entrepreneur.

Key #3—Risking: Most people who have taken the plunge into the world of making their passion a reality have taken some sort of risk, whether it is a financial risk, a personal risk, or an educational risk.

Key #4—Learning: Passionate people have a desire to grow. They are constantly learning, evolving, and investigating new ways to make things happen.

Key #5—Building Self-Efficacy: Albert Bandura (1982) created the term **self-efficacy**, which states that people believe in their own abilities to accomplish something. The concept relies heavily on ideas about what people believe they are capable and not capable of doing; for example, those who believe they have the skills and talent that merit a promotion may very likely receive a promotion. Those who desire to do so have the power to build their self-efficacy.

Self-efficacy: *The idea that people believe in their own ability to accomplish something*

By understanding these five keys to passion, and applying them to your future as an event planner, you will develop a clear direction and impetus for this career.

© Rawpixel/Shutterstock.com

There is no denying that being an event planner is a somewhat unconventional occupation. From dealing with design elements to being detail-oriented, event planners must be multi-faceted professionals. Those in the field are required to work long days as well as nights and weekends, or whenever events are scheduled to occur. If you do not have a passion for the work, you may experience disillusionment with your career. Understanding the time commitment will be necessary for you to execute your role in the organization of events. Therefore, it is important to enter the field fully aware of the benefits and drawbacks. The benefits of the job and the happiness you can bring to others through your work should leave you feeling passionate about your chosen career path. Good event planners know how and when to make themselves available, juggling their personal and professional lives with expertise and organization. Event planners must also understand the many ways to interact in a diverse society, and to do so, they must develop business acumen and be able to use their skills effectively to create events with passion and vision.

TIP

Balance your creativity with your organizational skills so that your event is unique and successful. This way, it's a win-win for everyone.

— Corrin Harris

Key Terms

Responsibility
Self-control
Goal-directed behavior
Problem-focused approach
Availability
Flexibility
Numerical flexibility

Functional flexibility
Financial flexibility
Temporal flexibility
Geographic flexibility
Organizational flexibility
Cognitive flexibility
Organization

Time management
Multitasking
Detail-oriented
Critical path
Critical Path Method (CPM)
Business savvy
Design

Design thinking
Mind map
Vision
Intuition
Passion
Self-efficacy

Discussion Questions

1. Good intuition is needed in event planning. Name a time when you followed your gut, and your intuition did not lead you astray. Then name a time when your intuition betrayed you.
2. Are you an organized person? Did you have to learn to become more organized? Discuss your organizational behaviors and why organization is one of the keys to success in event planning.
3. Event planning requires a great deal of innovation. Discuss an event that you have attended where the event planner's eye for design was omnipresent and helped create a unique atmosphere.

Activity

Using the Likert scale below, be honest and rank the strengths of each of your skills, with 5 being the highest possible score and 0 being the lowest. After you have scored yourself, write a summary in paragraph form indicating where you can improve and why you think there is room for improvement. Use this record as a guide and reminder when you are planning events so that you can focus on areas that need improvement. Sometimes event planners strengths are so great, they carry them through events, whereas their weaknesses can hold them back from success. Being conscious of where you need to improve will help you become an all-around better event planner.

Skill	Strong		Average		Weak
Responsibility & Self-Control	5	4	3	2	1
Availability	5	4	3	2	1
Flexibility	5	4	3	2	1
Organization	5	4	3	2	1
Time Management and Multi-Tasking Skills	5	4	3	2	1
Detail Oriented	5	4	3	2	1
Business Savvy	5	4	3	2	1
An Eye for Design	5	4	3	2	1
Vision and Intuition	5	4	3	2	1
Passion	5	4	3	2	1

References

Allen, E. K. (2005). Creativity on demand. *Harvard Business Review, 83,* 46–48.

Allen, J. (2005). *Time management for event planners: Expert techniques and time-saving tips for organizing your workload, prioritizing your day, and taking control of your schedule.* New York: Wiley.

Atkinson, J. (1984). Manpower strategies for flexible organizations. *Personal Management, 16,* 28–31.

Bacon, B. (2013). Intuitive intelligence in leadership. *Management Services, 57,* 26–29.

Bandura, A. (1997). *Self-efficacy: The exercise of control.* San Francisco: Freeman.

_____. (1982). Self-efficacy mechanism in human agency. *American Psychologist, 37,* 122–147.

Basco, M. R. (2000). *Never good enough: How to use perfectionism to your advantage without letting it ruin your life.* New York: Touchstone.

Bean-Mellinger, B.. (2018, March). Duties of an event planner. *Work-Chron.com.* Retrieved from http://work.chron.com/duties-event-planner-3092.html

Benton, D. A. (2000). *How to think like a CEO.* New York: Warner Brooks.

Blanchard, K. (2007). *Leading at a higher level.* Upper Saddle River, NJ: Prentice Hall.

Boverie, P. E., & Kroth, M. (2001). *Transforming work: The five keys to achieving trust, commitment, and passion in the workplace.* Cambridge, MA: Perseus Books.

Britton, B. K., & Tesser, A. (1991). Effects of time-management practices on college grades. *Journal of Educational Psychology, 83,* 405–410.

Brown, B. S. (1983). What is business savvy? *Nursing Economics, 1,* 52–72.

Brown, S. P., Westbrook, R. A., & Challagalla, G. (2005). Good cope, bad cope: Adaptive and maladaptive coping strategies following a critical negative work event. *Journal of Applied Psychology, 90,* 792–798.

Brown, T. (2009). *Change by design.* New York, NY: Harper-Collins.

Browne, J. (2006). Making sense of big business. *Business Strategy Review, 17,* 52–56.

Burke, E. (2008). *Reflections on the revolution in France.* New York: Cosimo. (Original work published in 1790)

Burt, C. D. B., & Kemp, S. (1994). Construction of activity duration and time management potential. *Applied Cognitive Psychology, 8,* 155–168.

Camenson, B. (2002). *Opportunities in event planning careers.* New York: McGraw Hill Professional.

Claessens, B. J. C., van Eerde, W., Rutte, C. G., & Roe, R. A. (2004). Planning behavior and perceived control of time at work. *Journal of Organizational Behavior, 25,* 937–950.

_____. (2007). A review of the time management literature. *Personnel Review, 36,* 255–276.

Daft, R. L., & Weick, K. E. (1984). Toward a model of organizations as interpretation systems. *Academy of Management Review, 9,* 284–295.

Diggs-Brown, B. (2011). *Strategic public relations: An audience-focused approach.* Stamford, CT: Cengage Learning.

Dolliver, M. (2006). Savvy advice is nice, but cash is even nicer. (2006). *Adweek, 47,* 25.

Doyle, A. (2012). Responsible and profitable. *Successful Meetings, 61,* 18–22.

Epler, D. (2014). The habits of communication. *Strategic Finance, 96,* 15–61.

Event Planners Association (2017, April). Stay flexible & adaptable. Retrieved from https://event-plannersassociation.com/stay-flexible-adaptable/

Galloway, P. (2006). Comparative study of university courses on Critical-Path Method scheduling. *Journal of Construction Engineering and Management, 132,* 712–722.

Getz, D. (2012). *Event studies: Theory, research, and policy for planned events.* New York: Routledge.

Givner, H. (2013, July). Why event planning businesses fail. Retrieved from https://www.eventleadershipinstitute.com/why-event-planning-businesses-fail/

Glaser, M. (1995). Measuring intuition. *Research Technology Management, 38,* 43.

Epler, D. (2014). The habits of communication. *Strategic Finance, 96,* 15–61.

Goldberg, D. (2005). *The organized student: Teaching children the skills for success in school and beyond.* New York: Fireside.

Greenwell, T. C., Danzey-Bussell, L. A., & Shonk, D. (2014). *Managing sport events.* Human Champaign, IL: Kinetics.

Hall, B. L., & Hursch, D. E. (1982). An evaluation of the effects of a time management training program on work efficacy. *Journal of Organizational Behavior Management, 3,* 73–96.

Hamel, G. (2009, February). *Moon shots for management.* Retrieved from https://hbr.org/2009/02/moon-shots-for-management

Intuition [Def. 1]. (n.d.). *Oxford Dictionary.* Retrieved from http://www.oxforddictionaries.com/us/definition/american_english/intuition

Issa, S. (2009). An approach to teaching organizational skills to adults. *English Teaching Forum, 47,* 8–17.

Jakobson, L. (2013). Corporate social responsibility. *Successful meetings, 62,* 22–23.

Jex, S. M., & Elacqua, T. C. (1999). Time management as a moderator of relations between stressors and employee strain. *Work & Stress, 13,* 182–191.

Kahle, D. (2004). *10 Secrets of time management for salespeople: Gain the competitive edge and make every second count.* New Jersey: Career Press.

Kaufman, C.F., Lane, P. M., & Lindquist, J. D. (1991). Exploring more than 24 hours a day: A preliminary investigation of polychromic time use. *Journal of Advertising Research, 18,* 392–401.

Keen, T. (1996, October). What's your intuitive decision-maker quotient? *Marketing Perspective, 6.*

Kelley, D. (2006). In mind. *BusinessWeek,* 4002, 16.

Kramer, J. A. (2002). *The Jack Welch lexicon of leadership.* New York: McGraw-Hill.

Miller, B. (2006). How much do companies need to know about their customers? *Baylor Business Review, 24,* 16–19.

Orpen, C. (1994). The effect of time-management training on employee attitudes and behavior: A field experiment. *Journal of Psychology: Interdisciplinary and Applied, 128,* 393–396.

Peters, J. (2007). *Start your own even planning business: Your step-by-step guide to success.* Irvine, CA: Entrepreneur Press.

Peeters, M. A. G., & Rutte, C. G. (2005). Time management behavior as a moderator for the job demand–control interaction. *Journal of Occupational Health Psychology, 10,* 64–75.

Pink, D. H. (2009). *Drive: The surprising truth about what motivates us.* New York: Riverhead Books.

Sanders, K. (2016). 33 skills needed to become an event planner. Retrieved from https://planyour-meetings.com/the-33-skills-you-need-to-pay-the-bills/

Sadler-Smith, E., & Shefy, E. (2004). The intuitive executive: Understanding and applying "gut feel" in decision-making. *The Academy of Management Executive, 18,* 76–91.

Shao, D. H., & Shao, L. P. (2012). The effects of multitasking on individual's task performance. *Journal of International Business Strategy, 12,* 75–80.

Silvers, J. R., & Goldblatt, J. (2012). *Professional event coordination.* New York: John Wiley and Sons.

Sinek, S. (2011). *Start with Why.* New York: Penguin.

Smart, K. L., & Featheringham, R. (2006). Developing effective interpersonal communication and discussion skills. *Business Communication Quarterly, 69,* 276–283.

Sparrow, P. R., & Marchington, M. (Eds.). (1998). *Human resource management: The new agenda.* London: Financial Times Pitman Publication.

Steeves, G. (2015, February). Get detailed-oriented with your event planning. Retrieved from https://smallbusinessbc.ca/article/get-detail-oriented-your-event-planning/

Stephenson, J., & Thurman, C. (2007). *Entrepreneur magazine's ultimate small business marketing guide: 1500 great marketing tricks that will drive your business through the roof.* Irvine, CA: Entrepreneur Press.

Sturges, J., & Guest, D. (2004). Working to live or living to work? Work/life balance early in the career. *Human Resource Management Journal, 14,* 5–20.

Tracy, B. (2002). *The 100 absolutely unbreakable laws of business success.* San Francisco, CA: Berrett-Koehler Publishers.

Tripoli, A. M. (1998). Planning and allocation: Strategies for managing priorities in complex jobs. *European Journal of Work and Organizational Psychology, 7,* 455–476.

Van der Wagen, L. (2010). *Events management.* London: Pearson.

Vass, K. (2007). Savvy marketers learn to think like entrepreneurs. *Textile World, 157,* 22–23.

Weiss, H. M., & Cropanzano, R. (1996). Affective events theory: A theoretical discussion of the structure, causes and consequences of affective experiences at work. In B. M. Staw & L. L. Cummings (Eds.), *Research in organizational behavior* (Vol. 18, pp. 1–74). Greenwich, CT: JAI Press.

Wendroff, Alan L. (2004). *Special events: Proven strategies for nonprofit fundraising.* Hoboken, NJ: John Wiley & Sons.

Westley, F., & Mintzberg, H. (1989). Visionary leadership and strategic management. *Strategic Management Journal, 10,* 17–32.

White, H. (1978). *Tropics of discourse: Essays in cultural criticism.* Baltimore: Johns Hopkins University Press.

Williams, K. C. (2012). Business intuition: The mortar among the bricks of analysis. *Journal of Management Policy & Practice, 13,* 48–65.

Wong, Y. (1964). Critical path analysis for new product planning. *Journal of Marketing, 28,* 53–59.

Woodward, M. (2019). 5 event planning skills you need for success: Skills you must have to be an event planner. Retrieved from https://www.thebalancesmb.com/successful-event-planning-skills-4051976

Worth, R. (2004). *Career skills library: Organization skills* (2nd ed.). New York: Ferguson.

Zegna, E. (2014). Flexibility is key. *IESE Insight, 20,* 10.

Chapter 5

HOSPITALITY: INVALUABLE LESSONS FROM AN ESTABLISHED INDUSTRY

The hospitality industry in the United States has grown exponentially since the start of the 20th century, when the Statler Hotels set the standards for travelers by offering comfortable, affordable accommodations and good service. As the hospitality market expanded, middle class and business travelers began to look for high quality, efficient, and moderately priced rooms at chains like Conrad Hilton's Hilton brand and Ernest Henderson's Sheraton, as meetings, conventions, events, and expositions drew business travelers and then vacationers (Hudson & Young, 2017). These activities now generate almost $1 trillion in yearly spending in the United States (Glion Institute of Higher Education, 2018), and the Bureau of Labor Statistics (2016) indicates that employment of meeting, convention, and event planners is projected to grow 11 percent from 2016 to 2026, as the industry continues to expand. Research from Deloitte (2018) notes that industry growth in 2018 alone was expected to top 6 percent. Social, military, education, religious, and fraternal (SMERF) meetings continue to figure prominently in the hospitality industry. For instance, that market as a whole has increased for Benchmark Hospitality International, a leading United States hospitality management company, by 5 percent yearly (Welly, 2011). From businesses that have been successfully established in the United States for over 150 years, event planners can learn much about hospitality and service, gaining knowledge from the lessons of an industry that must constantly reinvent itself in order to succeed in a changing world. The industry's ever-increasing annual revenues have altered the ways in which businesses, hospitality organizations and resorts function (Claver-Cortes, Molina-Azorin, & Pereira-Moliner, 2007; Glion Institute of Higher Education, 2018). A brief examination of the ways in which hospitality services lead to success can certainly leave event planners with a great deal of additional insights.

© Andrey_Popov/Shutterstock.com

SMERF: *Acronym for social, military, educational, religious, and fraternal*

When you have finished reading this chapter, you will be able to

- identify the commonalities between the hospitality industry and event planning;
- explain how event planners can benefit from an understanding of the hospitality industry;
- describe trends in the hospitality industry that could affect event planners.

CASE STUDY

Hotel Magic: Impress and Delight

Linda Paris, Senior Sales Manager, Omni William Penn Hotel, Pittsburgh

© Tupungato/Shutterstock.com

One of the most important steps in the sales process is showing your product to the potential client. In my position as Senior Sales Manager at the Omni William Penn Hotel/Pittsburgh, showcasing our city is as important as showing our hotel. Getting clients into the city averages a 70% chance of a successful outcome (sale) for our town.

PCMA, the Professional Convention Management Association, is the world's largest network of Business Event Strategists (association and hospitality industry members with a large student section). Convening Leaders is their annual gathering, drawing more than 4,200 professionals for three days of high-level education and networking. Pittsburgh was honored to be the host for this event in January 2019. Imagine having thousands of current and potential clients coming to see you, all at the same time!

What is your goal and how will you get there? In this case, our goal was to 'Impress and Delight' every attendee with the further goal of becoming a destination for their association conferences. To achieve this goal, we focused on three main steps: Prepare, Execute, and Follow Up.

Prepare. It is never too early to start the preparation steps with, of course, many meetings with various individuals. First, you must determine the overall goal you want to achieve—in this instance, 'Impress and Delight' every guest who stays with us. This is Omni Hotels & Resort's motto, with the goal to offer local flavor during the stay, show the magic in the details and make every guest want to return. There were many areas to consider, including assigning specific guest rooms to VIPs, lobby food and beverage stations during peak arrival and departure times, daily amenities delivered to guest rooms, staff schedules, restaurant hours, and more. My main focus was reviewing the guest list for my clients, sending a personal email to welcome/request arrival information and ask what we could do for them in advance of their stay. All of this information was entered into a spreadsheet to allow key staff members to view and update the information as needed. We reviewed this sheet numerous times and assigned our best rooms to the top potential clients. All important factors such as room type, allergies, arrival times, etc., were added to each reservation for all hotel staff to see. I also included an invitation in my emails to set up a time for a personal tour or meet in the main lobby or at the convention center for coffee. We wanted to reach out to as many attendees as possible in advance to say welcome to our hotel and our city.

Execute. Not only did I attend this conference, I also worked it, being in the lobby every morning at 6:30 to greet and assist all of the hotel guests. Taking care of a full house took the coordination and assistance from our entire hotel: guest alerts, adjusting staffing in our outlets, coordinating multiple volunteers to assist in the lobby for directions and help room service deliver 500 nightly amenities. We had a food and beverage station twice daily in the lobby during peak travel times to and from the convention center. Each item represented a taste of what Omni could do for larger parties and conferences. At the convention center, I met with many attendees and always asked if I could help them with anything in Pittsburgh. They were genuinely grateful just for the asking. When the meetings concluded, I headed back to our hotel lobby to once again be the greeter for several hours until the next of the evening events. One tip to remember during a multiple-day conference: comfortable footwear!

Follow up. This step is just as important as the preparation. Working in the lobby during heavy departure times, it was critical to have a face-to-face 'farewell, thank you, come back again.' Every person, whether guest or vendor, leaves with a final impression, and we wanted it to be a positive one. Within one week of the conclusion of the conference, I sent a personal email to each client, thanking them for staying with us, asking them to complete a survey and send feedback, including things we can do better next time. Asking for honest feedback— good and not so good—shows guests how we truly value their opinion. This is also the gateway to future correspondence with guests since a personal connection has been established

Overall, the conference was a huge success for the city and our hotel. It took hard work, long hours and our entire team to ensure we achieved our goal: to 'Impress and Delight' every guest. The feedback was overwhelming, with the guests thanking us for giving them an amazing experience, and commenting that they can't wait to return to stay at our hotel or see other parts of the city, things they did not get to do during the conference. We are a friendly town, greeting everyone with a smile, and a come-back-and-see-us-again attitude. As we like to say in Pittsburgh: Pull up a chair, you are always welcome here. Hospitality is the name of our game, and we thrive on the gratification of a successful day.

Contributed by Linda Paris. Copyright © Kendall Hunt Publishing Company.

Hospitality: *The inherent value of making guests feel welcome away from their homes*

Service: *The action of handling a welcoming task*

After reading this chapter, revisit the case study and respond to the following question:

What special touches have you noticed during your stay at a hotel?

The Hospitality Industry

There is a difference between **hospitality** and **service**, and many in the industry agree that hospitality is an important value today across the world, implying "prompt, proper, expedient, and professionally delivered service" (Pezzotti, 2013, p.6). Hospitality is based on the idea that people can be made to feel comfortable by how they are treated and by what others do for them. Hospitality implies that complete strangers can be welcomed in a way that makes them feel like family, while the company providing the hospitality can still conduct business and make a profit (Bagdan, 2013; Solomon, 2016; Woodruff, 2017). Service, the act of handling welcoming tasks, implies a delivery at touchpoints by paying attention to details, providing personal attention, and offering extra value, attentive caring, and anticipation of the needs of guests. These are attributes within a person, often innate, though service can be taught, scripted, and customized to the setting where it is needed. Thus, it is quantitative, while hospitality is often qualitative (Pezzotti, 2013). Guests may examine the service they have received in order to distinguish among hospitality providers. For instance, the food in a hotel restaurant or the bed in a hotel room might seem similar to others, but the service will set one provider apart from the rest (Bagdan, 2013; Woodruff, 2017). The hospitality exhibited throughout the experience enhances the provider's reputation even more. When a front-desk clerk answers a call for and promptly delivers more towels to a guest's hotel room, that's service. The follow-up call later that morning from the hotel manager, asking if the guests would like anything else to make their stay more pleasant, that's hospitality.

© Monkey Business Images/Shutterstock.com

According to hospitality scholar John R. Walker (2016), the industry is marked by several characteristics that help to define its nature, and which are shared by many event functions as well:

- Shift work and longer working hours
- Emphasis on guest satisfaction and intangible services
- Inseparability of production and consumption of the service product
- Perishability of the product (p.7)

An examination of these characteristics can provide some insight into the industry. Because hospitality services operate 365 days a year, 24 hours a day, those who provide guest services must be available whenever there are guests to be served. This means that entry-level hospitality workers and often their supervisors work in shifts to make certain that guests are accommodated at all times of the day (Solomon, 2016; Walker, 2017). Next, the industry focuses on providing a product that cannot be personally evaluated prior to use, and once it has been provided, it disappears, such as a hotel room. Unlike the purchase of an automobile, for instance, which can be taken for a test drive, the hospitality industry is more perishable. Success is uniquely tied into both the service provided and the guest's response to that service (Bagdan, 2013; Kotler, Bowen, Makens, & Baloglu, 2017; Walker, 2017). These same traits apply to event planning as well, particularly the emphasis on the intangible services an event planner supplies. Take, for instance, the distraught bride with wedding-day anxieties. After the special day is concluded, she and her bridal party may not remember exactly what kind of flowers were in the bouquets or what was served as appetizers at the reception, but they will remember the calm, soothing demeanor of the planner whose ability to diffuse nervousness was exceptional. The impalpable characteristics of service will encourage guests to endorse the planner, the hotel, or the restaurant far more than they will make a recommendation based on the size of the room, for example.

Thus, event planners would do well to examine and learn from the focuses and best practices of the hospitality industry. Specifically, these include the following:

- The pre-eminence of customer service
- The necessity of knowing the guest
- The importance of the planning process
- The need for a wide range of skills
- The usefulness of understanding industry trends

Each of these demands deserves a deeper examination so that event planners can begin to see the importance and impact of the hospitality industry.

TIP

Be a part of the event! Walk around. Talk to participants. Talk to spectators. Talk to your sponsors. It's very easy to take a break once an event is up and running, however, it's so important to be involved and have a feel for how things are going. As an event director, I prefer to be seen at an event as opposed to running the show from behind the scenes. This also helps in establishing long term relationships.

— Morgan Cook

The Pre-eminence of Customer Service

Good service actually begins within the organization and then reaches out to guests (Brownell, 2013; Pont, 2014). Developing a team mentality among hospitality workers demands that they are taught what good service means and are willing to do what it takes to make guests comfortable and welcome (Berry, 1984; Ford, Sturman, & Heaton, 2012; Walker, 2016). Hiring managers can seek out those who can intuitively work well with others; new employees can learn the skill set necessary, but it's nearly impossible to craft a good-hearted person (Solomon, 2016). Thus, good service starts with consistent and deliberate hiring, clear internal training for employees, and modeling by management. Committed employees are key to service success, and performance and reward systems can help to focus workers on their service strengths (Berry, 1984; Ford, Sturman, & Heaton, 2012; Smith & Kemmis, 2010). Every encounter that a guest has with an employee, every "**touch point**" (Bagdan, 2013, p.135) or "moment of truth" (Woodruff, 2017, p. 45) demands proper attention and an understanding that guest expectations, expressed or implicit, can make or break an event. For example, in the harried rush of guests pouring into a convention hall as breakout sessions end and lunch service begins, an employee unfortunately gives a curt answer to a guest's question about vegetarian options. That sour touch point may easily color the guest's recollection of her time at the event, far outweighing every other positive experience. Additionally, it is worth considering that the guest/employee interchange about vegetarian options may have been overheard by others, and so the effects of the encounter continue to grow. What happened cannot be undone, nor can it be made less public (Bagdan, 2013). The better option is to train employees to see that their responses and reactions to guests must be carefully and thoughtfully constructed (Pont, 2014; Tracey & Tews, 1995; Woods & King, 2010). As employees learn that each touch point is precious, they can help to make the guest experience superior.

Good guest service does not change with the number of customers (Ford, Sturman, & Heaton, 2012; Kotler, Bowen, Makens, & Baloglu, 2017; Solomon, 2016). Despite the size of the hotel, restaurant, or event, each guest still must be treated as unique and individual. Event planners can profit from this lesson as well. "Guests assume that your world revolves around them and that you are theirs for the duration. Create and maintain the illusion that you are always ready and waiting to serve your guests" (Solomon, 2016, p.13). How, then, to make this happen? Those in the hospitality industry know to focus on one guest at a time and to listen carefully for the subtext of what the guest is asking (Noe, 2005; Solomon, 2016; Walker, 2017), especially in response to an unpleasant experience. The larger hotel chains have developed acronyms for their approaches to improving service: Marriott's **LEARN**—Listen, Empathize, Apologize, Respond, Notify is quite similar to the Broadmoor's **HEART**— Hear, Empathize, Apologize, Respond, Take Action and Follow Up, and another popular acronym is **ARFD**— Apologize, Review, Fix and follow up, Document (Solomon,

2016, p. 32). In any event, when service recovery is needed, those working with guests must learn how to offer a sincere apology and listen carefully to recover from the gaffe (Baum, 2002; Ford, Sturman, & Heaton, 2012). Failure to do so quickly and earnestly could indicate that the service system is broken or nonresponsive. Take, for instance, the angry guest, who, left alone, can do substantial damage to reputation. During the anger experience, guests may not be rational or even coherent. Bagdan (2013) suggests that hospitality workers refrain from responding personally and try instead to understand what has caused the outburst. Though the temptation may be strong to respond angrily as well, the better choice is to refrain from getting defensive. Ask yourself what the customer actually wants, besides the desire to vent. If all else fails, call for a colleague to join you for assistance. Remain under control, with a lowered voice and increased eye contact, and then try to work with the guest on a 'we' solution: what can we do to eliminate this problem? (Solomon, 2016). Offer some options, while continuing to address the guest's emotions.

© Iakov Filimonov/Shutterstock.com

Anticipation of the guests' needs is essential in developing service that stands out. Walker (2017) notes that a system of error detection as opposed to error prevention will help develop guest loyalty and perhaps reduce the number of negative touch points throughout the day. Though it is impossible to foresee every expected consequence or to predict what will occur, those in the hospitality industry make it a point to plan for a variety of outcomes, including negative ones. With options, the risks can be diminished, and, in time, perhaps eliminated. Knowing what guests expect, within reason, is a beginning for exemplary service (Bagdan, 2013; Gill & Mathur, 2007). Albrecht (1992) has developed what he calls the "**Seven Deadly Sins**" of service: "apathy, brush-off, coldness, condescension, robotics, rule book, and runaround" (p. 13). All of these 'sins' can be reduced to just a few basic premises: focusing empathetically on the guest's point of view, understanding the role of the service provider, paying attention to every detail, remembering what guests have already told you, and using language that demonstrates a commitment to the guest (Brownell, 2013; Woodruff, 2017). Remembering and using guests' or clients' names is a good start, but it means practice in the art of mnemonics, and beyond that, those in the world of hospitality must be able to recognize cultural differences as well as understand a variety of nonverbal messages without being distracted by the setting (Pont, 2014; Walker, 2016). The industry is well aware of the rule of 10-1 (Woodruff, 2017), which notes that guests will tell 10 people about a bad experience but only one person about a good one, and that most unhappy guests never lodge an official complaint, despite being dissatisfied (Evenson, 2007). With the rise of social media, it is important to delegate responsiveness to negative public reviews to an alert and empathetic employee, who will handle each criticism personally. Service providers need to make sure guests feel that their experiences are positive ones. This goal can be accomplished by guiding them to concentrate on all of the

Seven Deadly Sins: *Service errors including apathy, brush-off, coldness, condescension, robotics, rule book, and runaround.*

TIP

See your event through your clients' eyes and use your training to allow them to experience the joy of their event. This is true success.

— Angela Corbo

enjoyable aspects of the event or stay, and helping them to see through all five senses that the experience is worth repeating in some form (Brownell, 2013; Michelli, 2008). A simple thing like assisting guests to take photographs of themselves enjoying part of the experience can create a lovely memory of the event. In short, service excellence demands that all who are involved in providing the experience work together to build a 'culture of yes' so that effortless hospitality becomes a brand. The charge, then, is to increase guest loyalty through incomparable service, turning guests into "brand ambassadors" (Solomon, 2016, p. 76) who use their voice to communicate the message of hospitality they have received. From the hospitality industry, event planners can learn the preeminence of customer service and attentiveness to event details.

© AYA images/Shutterstock.com

The Necessity of Knowing the Guest

Hospitality means finding answers to questions the guest has not yet asked, and this can be a difficult challenge. Those in guest services must be attentive to a variety of clues surrounding the event, the guests, or the locale in order to anticipate the needs of visitors. While the expectations of many customers are explicit, many remain unspoken (Bagdan, 2013), and it is these implicit expectations that cause difficulties. Take, for instance, adjusting to the rather new experiential demands of millennials. According to legendary chef Eric Ripert, this generation is looking for something beyond a price tag: an experience (Ripert, 2016, as cited in Solomon, 2016). This "differentiated hospitality" (Solomon, 2016, p.16) means that each experience can be separately created for each guest, depending on guest preferences. Of course, if these preferences are not communicated, it will be up to the service team to ascertain just what is desired. Event planners as well as those directly involved in hospitality fields need to adjust approaches, proposals, and offerings based upon the guest or client. For instance, a Baby Boomer couple planning a 50th anniversary party with friends might want to select from a very different menu than a 20-something couple organizing an engagement party: deviled eggs, pork crown roast, and chocolate mousse as opposed to mini tacos, uramaki, and boozy popsicles. Listen carefully to what the guests are asking for (or not asking for) in terms of food, decor, staging and comfort. Decisions like these are made not just by managers, but with input from **front-of-house** workers, those who interact directly with guests, such as concierge and guest registration, as well as line level, **back-of-house** workers, including housekeepers, stewards, and valets, who can all keep a watchful eye on guests' behaviors and demands (Bagdan, 2013; Walker, 2016; Woodruff, 2017). Teaching employees to look beyond their reporting area can help managers understand more precisely what guests' needs are (Solomon, 2016).

TIP

Pay attention to details. As easy as it is to get swept away by the big picture, it's the details that bring an entire event together.

— Corrin Harris

Front-of-house workers: *Hospitality workers who interact directly with guests on a regular basis*

Back-of-house workers: *Those in hospitality who deal with housekeeping, food, and engineering, and whom guests seldom see*

Guest demands have changed within the last two decades, and many younger guests are focused on speedier service and increased technology (Bagdan, 2013; Kim & Park, 2009; Pont, 2014; Solomon, 2016; Walker, 2016), as well as fitness centers, organic choices, and holistic lifestyle experiences (Ford, Sturman & Heaton, 2012). Marketing for **Gen X** (b. 1965–1976), **Gen Y (Millennials)** (b. 1977–1997) and **Gen Z** (b. after 1997) continues to be developed. These digital generations can access information quickly and fluently, and expect the same from those from whom they are buying services. They have grown up spending their time differently, and the changes in technology within their lives have influenced the ways in which they interact and communicate. Smartphones have provided rapid and instant answers, and the cloud technology has allowed for collaboration across space. These generations' influence through social media is vast, and although they may not make as much as **Baby Boomers** did, research has shown that they are willing to spend money on a wide range of experiential activities (Oshins, 2017). These changes, however, may mean that event planners and those in other fields of hospitality will need to develop a vision of the next trend as well as maintain an even higher degree of personal contact to improve the guest experience. Some guests will want to use technology, for instance, to check in to a hotel or conference; others will not. To respond to this generational penchant for technology, some hotels have already partnered with companies like ITI Marketing and QuickMobile to help them with registration processes for those guests who find mobile technology appealing ("Can you text me now? Good!" 2008). The industry must not only be ready to address both kinds of guests, but also know each guest's preferences (Beck & Wade, 2006; Claver-Cortes, Molina-Azorin, & Pereira-Moliner, 2007; Ford, Sturman & Heaton, 2012).

Gen X: *Those born approximately between 1965 and 1976*

Millennials (Gen Y): *Those born approximately between 1977 and 1997*

Gen Z: *Those born after 1977*

Baby Boomers: *Those born approximately between 1946 and 1964*

On the other hand, those in the field of hospitality cannot afford to assume that all guests can work with technology as well as many millennials (Solomon, 2016). Knowing what the social expectations are despite rapid changes in society is essential. Hosting guests with disabilities, for instance, demands that hospitality managers understand current policies and laws, and know how and where to access ports of entry for these guests (Pont, 2014). Every guest will want to be treated with patience and empathy, but particularly guests with special needs and their companions may need more deliberate attention.

© *Tekkol/Shutterstock.com*

TIP

Be on the floor early and triple check everything.

— Linda Paris

High- and low-context cultures also can present challenges for those in the industry who have not done their intercultural homework and prepared for the globalization that is impacting the industry (Beer, 2013; Bureau of Labor Statistics, 2016). Understanding the guest's message, despite barriers in language, vocabulary, focus, and interest, is nonetheless crucial to the industry (Brownell, 2013). Additionally, many guests are now asking for authentic experiences to be gained by being able to enjoy local customs

and foods (Brymer, R. A., Brymer, R.A., & Cain, 2017). In order to provide these experiences, hospitality service managers must become familiar with more than just the farmers' market around the corner or the best local restaurant for crab cakes. Indeed, an entirely new range of experiences, from gaming contests to virtual reality facilities to LGBTQ+ events must be within the wheelhouse of those in the industry. Those who plan events must be similarly cognizant of the variety of needs that guests may require.

The Importance of the Planning Process

The title "event planner" was first introduced by hotels and convention centers (Walker, 2017, p. 559), and planning continues to be an essential element of the hospitality industry. Organizations must understand the value of planning so that they can successfully implement their mission and vision (Ivanović, Galičić, & Mikinac, 2010). The planning process includes several pieces that event planners and others in the hospitality industry must consider. Planning must include methods of managing time, including delegation, record keeping, and conducting meetings according to an agenda. It also includes managing finances and keeping track of the budget. Good managers also can use technology in their planning through programs that help develop Gantt charts, for instance. Finally, planning goes into the management of personnel. Employees must be hired, coached and encouraged to offer the best possible service in line with the organization's mission (Crook, Ketchen, & Snow, 2003; Kim & Oh, 2003; Walker, 2017). Additionally, strategic planning can help the industry identify and resolve problems and reduce uncertainty. As event planners have come to understand, all within the industry must learn how to plan, communicate, and monitor progress, which requires discipline and flexibility (Evenson, 2007; Ivanović, Galičić, & Mikinac, 2010). Problems with the planning process can include the following:

- over-planning and becoming obsessed with detail as opposed to overall strategic considerations
- viewing plans as one-off exercises rather than active documents to be regularly consulted and adapted
- seeing plans as conclusive rather than directional in nature (Ivanović, Galičić, & Mikinac, 2010, p. 926).

In summary, the real challenge is to see planning as an ongoing process rather than a final destination. When planning for a new event or product, a **feasibility study** can uncover or examine ideas that may not have occurred to planners or hospitality managers. Such a study can, for instance, look at the budget, location, and other support, as well as the success of similar events or products (Walker, 2017; Evenson, 2007; Ivanović, Galičić, & Mikinac, 2010).

Feasibility study: *a research project that examines new or untested ideas through best practices in research, design, budget planning, coordination, and evaluation*

Planning for an event, a change, a new product, or a rebranding, for example, involves best practices in research, design, budgeting, coordination, and evaluation with each step. The process can be cyclical, and the steps often overlap (Walker, 2017; Woodruff, 2017; Woods & King, 2010).

Action plans that are successful involve every department, and all players are involved since many in the organization have varying areas of expertise. Those in human resources, legal, and management must be aware of changes within the economy as well as in governmental laws, and the marketing team must always be aware of the competition, both from traditional players and those new to the business (Ford, Sturman, & Heaton, 2012). Event planner and managers must monitor variables such as the environment, the weather, news of the world, and the stock market. Planning can be based on what are called "strategic premises" (Ford, Sturman, & Heaton, 2012, p. 55), educated guesses about what may be upcoming in the industry.

Good planners rely on many forecasting tools including trend analyses, focus groups, brainstorming sessions, scenario building, and methods such as the Delphi Technique (Ford, Sturman, & Heaton, 2012). **Trend analyses** are based on the idea that what has happened in the past can give investigators an idea of what will happen in the future. These analyses attempt to find patterns in data that has been collected (Murphy, 2009). **Focus groups** include a small number of carefully chosen volunteers who participate in discussions for research about a new product or any other topic so that the group's results can be applied to a larger population. A moderator usually runs the focus group so that the discussion remains unbiased (Greenbaum, 2015; Kotler, Bowen, Makens, & Baloglu, 2017). **Brainstorming** is a well-known practice in which all participants in the brainstorming group either formally or informally offer a variety of ideas that are creative, free-flowing, and often useful in planning (Formica & Kothari, 2008). **Scenario building** has gained recent popularity and involves envisioning a future situation and then assessing its future organizational repercussions based on the analysis of historic trends. This technique can be useful if change needs to happen quickly (Ford, Sturman, & Heaton, 2012; Van der Heijden, 2005). The **Delphi Technique** is a process conducted by industry experts who are asked the same question about the future, after which their answers are collated and averaged. This process offers the results of this first round to the experts once again, who give another round of responses, usually quantitative. Several repetitions of this cycle can offer a legitimate estimation of the future (Ford, Sturman, & Heaton, 2012; Linstone & Turoff, 1975). These techniques and more can offer planners a variety of strategies for developing a road map of future plans. Though no one can predict with certainty what will happen even during the next day, those in the hospitality industry and event planners still need ways to develop a vision of what lies ahead.

Trend analysis: *A study that attempts to find patterns in data that has been collected*

Focus group: *A small group of carefully chosen volunteers who participate in discussions for research about a new product*

Brainstorming: *The practice of developing ideas through creative, free-flowing discussion*

Scenario building: *A practice that involves envisioning a future situation and then assessing its organizational repercussions based on the analysis of historic trends*

Delphi Technique: *A business process in which several cycles of questions are asked and re-asked in order to look at future possibilities*

© Pressmaster/Shutterstock.com

The Need for a Wide Range of Skills

© farland2456/Shutterstock.com

There is a great deal of similarity between the skills that event planners need (see Chapter 4) and the skills demanded in the hospitality industry. In addition, some event planners straddle both career fields and thus need a wide range of abilities. For instance, event planners begin their work at conventions and hotels once the sales team has a signed contract and a selected space. They work with the client from the beginning to the end of the event, serving as the main point of contact between the site and the guest. From their own experience and from their wide range of contacts, managers in the hospitality field work with vendors and subcontractors who know the site, and as the event planning progresses, they create a plan, perhaps a Gantt chart, and a list of assigned duties. **WAG** (week-at-a-glance) meetings held just before the event can help circumvent oncoming problems since the event manager is the central figure who is in communication with every player in the event (Claver-Cortes, Molina-Azorin, & Pereira-Moliner, 2007; Evenson, 2007; Walker, 2017). Event planners must be good at marketing, sales, organization, finance, and human resources (Walker, 2016), and additional skills associated with managing events in the hospitality industry include leadership, the ability to delegate and negotiate, budget management, the ability to multitask, and a wide set of social skills that require positivity, charm, enthusiasm, and cool-headedness (Ford, Sturman, & Heaton, 2012; Noe, 2005; Walker, 2016, 2017). Event planners, like hospitality managers, must observe and appraise employee progress, make decisions in order to meet objectives, and motivate fellow staffers so that they perform in outstanding ways (Ivanović, Galičić, & Mikinac, 2010). Guests have an emotional investment in their stay—whether at a hotel or at a standalone event—so another necessary skill is **empathy** (Bagdan, 2013), the ability to understand others, acting in ways that demonstrate you know what others are experiencing. Empathy is a necessity for a well-run business, for it can result in stronger teamwork, greater leadership and heightened creativity (Krznaric, 2014). For instance, imagine a first-time event planner who has worked with you, the convention hotel's event manager, for a year, making sure every last detail of the three-day event is perfect, from breakfast biscuits to valet parking to welcome gifts. On the second evening of the conference, you are surprised to find out that a lavish wedding has been booked at the last minute into one of the rooms that had been reserved by you for an evening conference session. The event planner is more than distraught to find this out and becomes frantic with worry. You have spent the last hours frazzled, looking for a solution with your own co-workers, but more important first is addressing your collaborator's anxiety. Your empathy helps you imagine the stress she is experiencing: worried about a solution, upset that the contract was broken, fearful that the change would reflect negatively on her, and troubled that the attendees would not learn about any locale changes. Speaking and acting with

WAG: *Acronym for "Week-at-a-glance" meetings that occur before an event (week-at-a-glance)*

Empathy: *The ability to understand others*

empathy can lessen the strain and help communicate a compromise solution that will be heard and accepted.

In the world of hospitality, choices always exist. A particular hotel may brand itself to fill a special niche in the market, and job of the planner is to execute events that speak to that niche (Ford, Sturman, & Heaton, 2012; Solomon, 2016). For instance, a millennials' reception is scheduled for a hotel that specifically markets itself to that generation. Not only must the hotel's staff adhere to and support the hotel's mission, but the planner must also know exactly how to execute the brand within the guests' wishes. Making suggestions that support the niche brand as well as please the customer is no small feat. Choices in menu, music, decor, and staging must all be cohesive and consistent—quite a task. Helping guests to see that their choices might be better made requires tact and earnestness. In addition, knowing how to respond in the most extreme circumstances gives those in the hospitality industry an edge when dealing with guests who require additional pampering (Woodruff, 2017). Guests may not always be right, but they are still guests, and to that end, every interaction with each guest must convey the mission of the organization.

When your day has begun at 5 a.m. and it's now 2 a.m. the next morning, and you must handle some rowdy partiers, the easy choice would be to quickly dispense with them, but the better plan of action might be to summon up as much humor as you have left, and escort them to their rooms with coffee, croissants, and some jam. The influence that those in the hospitality industry have over each guest experience demands the right touch in empathy, listening, and communication (Bagdan, 2013; Solomon, 2016; Walker, 2017; Woodruff, 2017).

© Edvard Nalbantjan/Shutterstock.com

The Bureau of Labor Statistics (2016) compiled its own list of skills needed for success in the hospitality field. These include the following:

- Active listening
- Speaking
- Reading comprehension
- Time management
- Critical thinking

From this list, it is clear that the hospitality field demands many of the same skills that are asked of event planners. Beyond this list of personal skills, there are a few more essential abilities that those in the industry might need. One of these proficiencies is to be able to identify future opportunities for expansion or development. This demands an understanding of the organization's mission as well as a vision of the 'big picture' (Glion, 2016). Other simple demands include a knowledge of email technology and protocol, basic business writing skills, and phone etiquette, as well as the ability to make small talk with strangers (Albrecht, 1992; Pont, 2014). In short, the most proficient workers in the hospitality industry will be able to make every guest encounter a success.

The Usefulness of Understanding Industry Trends

Those who work in the hospitality industry must be aware of upcoming trends long before any changes are instituted within the organization. Here, too, event planners can take a lesson from the steady exploration in hospitality of what is trending in the economy, in social life, and in the field itself. Last year's specialty drink is old news today, and can badly brand a planner who does not stay on top of the latest development. Recent trends in the industry have become increasingly more complex (Walker, 2016) and have demanded expert planning, an ever-widening set of skills, and a deep understanding of the service field. In the past, the hospitality trade has been influenced by developments in transportation and the building of roads as well as by a shift in the distribution of wealth (Hudson & Young, 2017). These major changes in society set the stage for ways in which the hospitality industry has responded through the years to economic development. Today, trends in the industry are wide-ranging and powerful. Indications point to an advancing state of technology that impacts many areas of the hospitality field ("Can You Text Me Now? Good!" 2008; Ford, Sturman & Heaton, 2012; Ivanović, Galičić, & Mikinac, 2010; Walker, 2016, 2017; Welly, 2011). Shifts in technology can be seen in several areas. The demographic of travelers has shown that they can be more technology-savvy and self-sufficient. Reputations of hotels or resorts, for instance, are often influenced by information that guests have shared online during their experience, and it will be essential for the hospitality industry to learn how to manage reputation based upon these public postings. The internet has made finding places to visit quite easy, and guests have shown themselves to be more independent in choosing a destination through distribution companies like Priceline, Expedia, and Trivago. Planners will have to increase their scope of recommendations based upon this trend (Ford, Sturman & Heaton, 2012; Oshins, 2017; Walker, 2017). Event planners and hospitality managers must also understand the usefulness of services like

© ymgerman/Shutterstock.com

mobile polling, which "enables presenters to customize and ask questions in real time. Attendees are prompted to participate using their mobile phones, and polls can be projected onto large screens" ("Can You Text Me Now? Good!" 2008, p. 24). Technology can also be used to register guests and convention-goers, improve communication with conference attendees, and develop sponsorship opportunities (Kotler, Bowen, Makens, & Baloglu, 2017; Walker, 2016). Hotels are seeing a stronger blend of work and relaxation during guest stays, and to that end, guests anticipate that hotels, for example, can provide iPads or tablets, or at the very least, free WiFi access (Bagdan, 2013; Pinsker, 2017). However, these in-room technologies should be more than just available upon request; they should be uncomplicated, modern, and simple to use. It would be a mistake to assume that every guest knows how to access technology of any kind (Solomon, 2016). Restaurants use technology to observe customer preferences; theme parks can track guest wait time in lines; hotels can monitor guest favorites from the in-room minibar and be prepared when the guest arrives for another visit. Being aware of the vast number of uses for technology can only help those in the service industry meet with success.

Trending as well is the desire for **sustainability** and a **green economy** (Ford, Sturman & Eaton, 2012; Oshins, 2012; Walker, 2016, 2017). The holistic approach of an organization that focuses on sustainability—taking into account the process, not just the green product—has provided the industry with some definite advantages. Some members of the hospitality industry have become leaders in environmentally conscious planning, and conducted initiatives that focus on water and energy conservation, for instance, as well as recycling material and supplies that are better for the environment. The Green Resource Center, which was originally established through the American Hotel and Lodging Association (AH&LA), examines best practices through its comprehensive Green Guidelines (Ford, Sturman & Heaton, 2012). Hotels can now proudly display their accreditation seals in green certification programs, and a public list of these hotels is available for all to see online. Of course, the desire for a green certification must be balanced against the budget, so organizations would profit from getting input from those who understand the trend and know how to make it work economically. An article in *Entrepreneur* magazine notes that

Sustainability: *Avoiding the exhaustion of natural resources to maintain an ecological balance*

Green economy: *A system that tries to reduce environmental risks and that promotes sustainable development without harming the environment*

millennials will choose hotels that are environmentally or community responsible over those that simply provide personalized service (Chitre, 2018). In its desire for increased levels of environmental awareness, the industry will continue to search for ways to address developments in global warming and climate change, which ultimately affect the weather and thus the guest experience (Oshins, 2012). Event planners traditionally try to balance the client's desire for sustainability against the budget, using green, organic, or local natural products when possible.

© petrmalinak/Shutterstock.com

Another trend in the hospitality industry focuses on increased client health and well-being ("Eight Wellness Trends for 2018," 2018; Ford, Sturman & Heaton, 2012; Oshins, 2012; Walker, 2016, 2017). Baby boomers and millennials alike are interested in healthier living through many aspects from food choices to sleep lighting. The concept of the healthy kitchen has made its way into the hospitality industry with the growth in organic, vegetarian, and vegan offerings, as well as simpler fare. Fresh fruits and vegetables, rather than processed foods, are now being showcased, and interested guests may want to know where their food is sourced. Low-fat and low-carb

© Yulia Grigoryeva /Shutterstock.com

offerings have become more plentiful, and menu items may also reflect a guest interest in less salt and sugar ("Eight Wellness Trends for 2018," 2018; Walker, 2017). Those who work in event planning must be aware of these developments since they impact clients as well. For example, it is up to the event planner to know which venues are green certified if clients consider that a priority.

Attentiveness to new food trends can give event planners an edge when suggesting menus to potential customers. This boom in a desire for a healthier lifestyle has influenced the hospitality industry in other ways as well. Hotels and resorts are responding to the fitness trend by building better fitness spaces and updating equipment; some even offer running shoes for rent, and many hotel vending machines are stocked with healthier snacks for guests (Oshins, 2017). A fitness-themed hotel brand addresses the fact that people want to look as healthy as they feel, and be pampered in doing so. Thus, comfort is essential as they spend more time in a larger, more luxurious bathroom (Pinsker, 2017). In short, societal developments in health and wellness are reflected in the hospitality industry, and can offer event planners extra insights when working with clients.

Sharing economy: *An economic system in which individuals share services, sometimes free, usually through the Internet*

A final development of importance that could also influence event planners is the growth of the **sharing economy** (Oshins, 2017), an economic system in which individuals share services, sometimes free, usually through the Internet. With the increase in shared services and spaces for hospitality, including VRBO, Airbnb, HomeAway, FlipKey, HomeToGo, Flipping.com, and other similar peer-to-peer networks, the industry is rethinking what services can be provided and by whom. These shared homestays are working to keep hotel rates lower and increase the number of available rooms, so the competition they offer for larger hotels has made the hospitality industry reimagine ways in which service can be uniquely provided. How can event planners use this knowledge for their clients? Clearly, overnight booking processes have been expanded beyond the typical large hotel chains, and planners who understand the sharing economy can provide their clients with a larger range of choices, many of which may be less expensive than traditional selections. The days of convention-goers who choose to book into a pricey room block or hope to catch the hotel's shuttle from the airport are waning (Alonzo, 2015). Airbnb, for example, lists over 4 million properties in 191 countries, and continues to expand (Divine, 2016; Gerdeman, 2018). Knowing how to access these and other similar listings makes the event planner's job more complex, but ultimately more successful. Another factor in the shared economy has developed in the area of transportation. Lyft and Uber, for instance, have become forces that cannot be ignored, and they have disrupted the ways in which travelers think about getting from one place to another, though concerns about vetting sites and drivers, as well as safety issues, have continued to surface (MacMillon & Karmin, 2014).

Hilton has recently partnered with Uber in coordinating apps that work together in terms of ride service, hotel registration, room entry, and ride reminders throughout guests' visits (Samuely, 2019). Additionally, Uber and its competitor Lyft have begun to ease into and sometimes supplant the hotel shuttle operation, since guests who are traveling to and from airports or train depots, for instance, don't want to wait for a shuttle. Stepping into this niche, a company called Twenty Four Seven Hotels has partnered with Uber and several hotels including Marriott, Hyatt, and Hilton to make travel more responsive for guests. Using this connection, hotel staffers can quickly and easily summon rides for guests without relying upon a hotel shuttle ("Twenty Four Seven Hotels + Uber: Rethinking the hotel shuttle," 2018). Hotels have become more responsive to guests' needs and wants through relying to a greater extent on these shared platforms. Event planners, too, can benefit from the knowledge of what these rideshares can provide for their clients in terms of savings and ease of use.

© Jonathan Weiss/Shutterstock.com

Trends that move the hospitality industry also affect many segments of the event planner's world, and the knowledge gleaned from a study of the hospitality industry can offer event planners many additional opportunities for success. As event planning expands into new sites, and as the world of events changes with the times, learning as much as possible about the hospitality industry can only enhance the event planner's expertise.

Key Terms

SMERF
Hospitality
Service
Touch point
LEARN
HEART
ARFD

Seven Deadly Sins
Front of House
Back of House
Gen X
Millennials (Gen Y)
Gen Z
Baby Boomer

Feasibility study
Trend analysis
Focus group
Brainstorming
Scenario building
Delphi Technique
WAG

Empathy
Sustainability
Green economy
Sharing economy

Discussion Questions

1. You have been hired as an event planning assistant at a major and very large hotel in your city's urban center. You enjoy your job after two weeks there, but notice that you are notified of team meetings only at the last minute, which makes your attendance difficult and you feel unprepared. What kind of dysfunctionalities in the big picture of hospitality does this suggest? How can it be remedied without complaining?

2. What are some of the most important elements in your own "Professional Code of Conduct"?

3. What qualities make a hotel stand out in the field of hospitality? How can you apply those standards to any event that you are planning?

Activity

You have noticed that the food and the ambience in the dining hall could be improved. You want to plan an event there, but prior to executing that event, you need more information. Keeping the Delphi Technique in mind, create a survey for your event to be held in the dining hall.

References

Albrecht, K. (1992). *At America's service: How your company can join the customer service revolution*. New York, NY: Warner Books.

Alonzo, V. (2015, November). Room at the inn. *Successful Meetings*, 6.

Bagdan, P. (2013). *Guest Service in the Hospitality Industry*. Hoboken, NJ: Wiley.

Baum, T. (2002). Skills and training for the hospitality sector: A review of issues. *Journal of Vocational Education and Training*, 54, 343–364.

Beck, J.C. and Wade, M. (2006). *The kids are alright: How the gamer generation is changing the workplace*. Boston, Mass: Harvard Business School Publishing.

Beer, J. L. (2013). "Communicating across cultures: High and low context." Culture at Work. Retrieved from http://www.culture-at-work.com/highlow.html

Berry, L. (1984). The employee as customer, in Lovelock, C.H. (Ed.) *Services marketing* (pp. 65–68). Englewood Cliffs, NJ: Prentice Hall.

Brownell, J. (2013). The listening fast track. In M. C. Sturman, J. B. Corgel, & R.Verma (Eds.) *The Cornell School of hotel administration on hospitality: Cutting edge thinking and practice* (pp. 37–51). Hoboken, NJ: Wiley.

Brymer, R. A., Brymer, R. A., & Cain, L. N. (2017). *Hospitality: An introduction*. 16th ed. Dubuque, IA: Kendall Hunt.

Bureau of Labor Statistics, U.S. Department of Labor (2016). Meeting, Convention, and Event Planners. In Occupational Outlook Handbook. Retrieved from https://www.bls.gov/ooh/business-and-financial/meeting-convention-and-event-planners.htm

Can you text me now? Good! (2008, September). *Meeting News*, 32(16), 24.

Chitre, S. (2018, October). Exploring three major trends driving the hospitality industry. *Entrepreneur*. Retrieved from www.entrepreneur.com/article/321723.

Claver-Cortes, E., Molina-Azorin, J.F., & Pereira-Moliner, J. (2007). The impact of strategic behaviors on hotel performance. *International Journal of Contemporary Hotel Management, 19*(1), 6–20.

Crook, T. R., Ketchen, D.J., & Snow, C.C. (2003). Competitive edge: A strategic management model. *Cornell Hotel and Restaurant Administration Quarterly, 44*(3), 44–53.

Divine, J. (2016, November). Is Airbnb a threat to the hotel industry? *U.S. News and World Report.* Retrieved from https://money.usnews.com/investing/articles/2016-11-02/is-airbnb-a-threat-to-the-hotel-industry

"Eight Wellness Trends for 2018, from Global Wellness Summit." *2018 Global Wellness Trends Report.* Retrieved from https://www.globalwellnesssummit.com/2018-global-wellness-trends.

Evenson, R. (2007). *Award-winning customer service: 101 ways to guarantee great performance.* New York: AMACON.

Ford, R. C., Sturman, M. C., & Heaton, C. P. (2012). *Managing quality service in hospitality: How organizations achieve excellence in the guest experience.* Clifton Park, NY: Delmar.

Formica, S., & Kothari, T.H. (2008, January). Strategic destination planning: Analyzing the future of tourism. *Journal of Travel Research, 46*(4), 355–367.

Gerdeman, D. (2018, February). The Airbnb effect: Cheaper rooms for travelers, less revenue for hotels. *Forbes.* Retrieved from https://www.forbes.com/sites/hbsworkingknowledge/2018/02/27/the-airbnb-effect-cheaper-rooms-for-travelers-less-revenue-for-hotels/#355e4731d672

Gill, A., & Mathur, N. (2007). Improving employee dedication and pro-social behavior. *International Journal of Contemporary Hospitality Management, 19*, 328–334.

Glion Institute of Higher Education (2016). "Forget about luxury trends!"- Insights from the Innovation in Luxury Conference. Sept. 26, 2016. Retrieved from https://www.glion.edu/blog/insights-from-innovation-in-luxury-conference/

Glion Institute of Higher Education (2018). "Why events are so important to the hospitality industry," Feb. 19, 2018. Retrieved from https://www.glion.edu/blog/events-important-hospitality-industry/

Greenbaum, T. L. (2015). *The handbook for focus group research.* 1st ed. Thousand Oaks, CA: Sage.

Hudson, B. T., & Young, M.E. (2017). History. in R. A. Brymer, R. A. Brymer, and L. N. Cain (Eds.) *Hospitality: An introduction* (pp. 15–26). 16th ed. Dubuque, IA: Kendall Hunt.

Ivanović, S., Galičić, V., & Mikinac, K. (2010, May). "Event planning as a function in the hospitality industry." *Conference Proceedings, Tourism & Hospitality Management* 2010, 925–930. Retrieved from https://www.researchgate.net/publication/305721675_event_planning_as_a_function_in_the_hospitality_industry

Kim, B.Y., & Oh, H. (2008, October). An integrated approach to strategic management for the lodging industry. *International Journal of Hospitality & Tourism Administration* 4(2), 1–16.

Kim, D.Y., & Park, O. (2009, July). A study on American meeting planners' attitudes toward and adoption of technology in the workplace. *Tourism and Hospitality Research* 9(3), 209–223.

Kotler, P., Bowen, J. T., Makens, J. C. & Blaoglu, S., eds. (2017). *Marketing for hospitality and tourism*. 7th ed. London: Pearson Education Ltd.

Krznaric, R. (2014). *Empathy: Why it matters, and how to get it*. New York: TarcherPerigee.

Linstone, H.A., & Turoff, M. (1975). *The Delphi Method: Techniques and applications*. Glenview, IL: Addison-Wesley Educational Publishers Inc.

MacMillan, D., & Karmin, C. (2014, July). Uber, Airbnb woo business travelers. *Wall Street Journal*, Eastern edition. July 29, 2014: B4.

Michelli, J. (2008). *The new gold standard: 5 leadership principles for creating a legendary customer experience courtesy of the Ritz-Carlton Hotel Company*. New York: McGraw Hill.

Murphy, J. (2009). *The visual investor: How to spot market trends*. 2nd ed. Hoboken, NJ: Wiley.

Noe, R.A. (2005). *Employee training and development*. 3rd ed. New York: McGraw Hill.

Oshins, M. (2017). Emerging trends. In R. A. Brymer, R. A. Brymer, and L. N. Cain, *Hospitality: An introduction* (pp. 27–40). 16th ed. Dubuque, IA: Kendall Hunt.

Pezzotti, G. (2013). The essence of hospitality and service. (2013). In M. C. Sturman, J. B. Corgel, & R.Verma, (Eds.) *The Cornell School of Hotel Administration on hospitality: Cutting edge thinking and practice* (pp. 5–20). Hoboken, NJ: Wiley.

Pinsker, J. (2017, September). How the hotel industry views its future (and Airbnb). *The Atlantic*. Retrieved from https://www.theatlantic.com/business/archive/2017/09/hotels-magazine-industry-airbnb/540525/

Pont, L. (2014). *Hospitality management: People skills and manners on and off the job*. Bloomington, IN: Manners Press.

Ripert, E. (as cited in Solomon, 2016). *The heart of hospitality: Great hotel and restaurant leaders share their secrets*. New York: SelectBooks.

Samuely, A. (2019, January). Hilton unrolls expanded Uber integration as hospitality partnerships thrive. *Retail Dive: Mobile Commerce*. Retrieved from https://www.retaildive.com/ex/mobilecommercedaily/hilton-unrolls-expanded-in-app-uber-integration-as-hospitality-partnerships-thrive.

Smith, E., & Kemmis, R.B. (2010). What industry wants: Employers' preferences for training. *Education and Training 52*(3), 214–225.

Solomon, M. (2016). *The heart of hospitality: Great hotel and restaurant leaders share their secrets*. New York: SelectBooks.

Sturman, M. C., Corgel, J. B., & Verma, R. (Eds.). (2013). *The Cornell School of Hotel Administration on hospitality: Cutting edge thinking and practice*. Hoboken, NJ: Wiley.

Tracey, J.B. & Tews, M.J. (1995). Training effectiveness: Accounting for individual characteristics and the work environment. *Cornell Hotel and Restaurant Administration Quarterly 36*(6), 35–42.

Twenty-Four seven hotels + Uber: Rethinking the hotel shuttle. (2018, July). Retrieved from https://www.uber.com/blog/twenty-four-seven-case-study/

Van der Heijden, K. (2005). *Scenarios: The art of strategic conversation.* 2nd ed. Hoboken, NJ: Wiley.

Walker, J. R. (2016). *Exploring the hospitality industry.* 3rd ed. Boston, MA: Pearson.

Walker, J. R. (2017). *Introduction to hospitality.* 7th ed. London: Pearson Education Ltd.

Welly, K. (2011, March). There goes the neighborhood? *Successful Meetings 60*(3), pp. 20–22.

"Where the science of fitness meets the art of travel." (2019, January). Retrieved from https://equi-nox-hotels.com.

Woodruff, C. (2017). Hospitality service excellence. In R. A. Brymer, R. A. Brymer, & L. N. Cain (Eds.) *Hospitality: An introduction.* 16th ed. Dubuque, IA: Kendall Hunt.

Woods, R. H. & King, J. Z. (2010). *Leadership and management in the hospitality industry.* 3rd ed. Lansing, MI: American Hotel and Lodging Educational Institute.

Chapter 6

CREATIVITY: EVENT PLANNING WITH PANACHE

Incorporating innovative and interesting ideas that motivate people in different ways is a vital ingredient of creativity. Tim Brown (2009), the CEO and president of IDEO, a creative company focused on human-centered design, states, "The creative process generates ideas and concepts that have not existed before" (p. 41). Creativity is something that should be fostered continually within yourself and as you work with others on events. Allen (2005) believes that you can learn a great deal from creative people and that they have the potential to surprise you with ideas. While creativity in business includes many different definitions, Fillis and Rentschler's (2010) research offers a view of creativity that states the following:

© Longkau D/Shutterstock.com

> There is no universally accepted definition of creativity, although there are a number of overlaps in its interpretation. A preliminary analysis identifies creativity as showing imagination and originality of thought in moving beyond everyday thinking. It can be characterized by stretching or even breaking the rules of convention, with even the smallest departure from the norm being deemed creative (p. 51).

Creativity comes in many forms and is a key component of an event planner's overall perspective and originality regarding each event that must be envisioned, planned, and executed. Allowing room for creativity—and applying it to the events you create—is vital to your continued success.

When you have finished reading this chapter, you will be able to

- explain the necessity of being creative in every professional or social event planning setting;
- model creative brainstorming techniques to aid in project development;
- apply best practices in creativity for specific projects.

127

CASE STUDY — How Long Does it Take to Plan an Event?
100 Years. . .or 5 Days

Charles Steinberg, President, Pawtucket Red Sox

April 20 has always been an important date on the Fenway Park calendar. Even the distance to centerfield at Major League Baseball's smallest ballpark suggests the date: 420.

Amid grief, shock and sorrow, fans filled the Fens in Boston on April 20, 1912. The unsinkable *Titanic* had sunk just days before. It was still the lead story the day the ballpark opened. With strength and resilience, Boston Mayor John F. Fitzgerald threw the Ceremonial First Pitch, his daughter Rose by his side. The hometown team, playing in its big new ballpark (it was considered big at the time), became a source of spring and summer joy—extending the warmth of baseball right into autumn as they won a World Series in that inaugural season.

How easy it was, then, for generations of Red Sox event planners to plan future celebrations. They could envision a 25th anniversary of both the ballpark and the world championship in the distant year of 1937. They could start imagining a 50th in 1962, or a 75th in 1987. And one thing is for sure—they had 100 years to plan an event on April 20, 2012. They just did not know in 1912 who would be the creators of that grand event. As it turned out, that job was mine, and it was a grand celebration that took place post-game.

Almost a year later, Boston was enjoying another splendid and beautiful afternoon. The worldwide attraction of the Boston Marathon is a holiday in this history-rich town. It is Patriots Day, and the weather was gorgeous. The Red Sox won their traditional 11 a.m. game (concurrent with the Marathon) with a sudden-death win in the bottom of the ninth. Delirious fans continued the annual tradition of walking from Fenway Park just a couple of blocks to Boylston Street to cheer on the laboring runners headed for the finish line.

Some were still on their way when they heard the explosion.

Seconds later, they heard another.

Two brothers had terrorized and terrified a jubilant and boisterous city. They had killed a child. They had killed a student. They had killed a young woman. And they would still kill a police officer. They had maimed hundreds. They had traumatized thousands.

Our team was already aboard its bus and proceeding to fly to Cleveland as the news unfolded. When they reached Cleveland, they went to dinner together as one—a rarity. They asked the clubhouse manager to make a jersey with Boston's area code on it instead of a uniform number. Young Red Sox third baseman Will Middlebrooks tweeted a message of sympathy to Boston, and a phrase took off: #BostonStrong. By nighttime, the Twitter hashtag was circulating. The jersey embroidered *Boston Strong* with 617 in between the words hung in the dugout every game thereafter.

© Joyce Vincent/Shutterstock.com

The morning after the tragedy, in our staff meeting, our team president Larry Lucchino charged us with thinking about what we might do charitably when he was interrupted by a call. It was Mayor Thomas M. Menino; he and Governor Deval Patrick would create the One Fund, and all monies would be centralized and distributed.

I began doodling. I drew our Boston "B" with the word "STRONG" beneath it. I mentioned to the staff that if we took this red B, and wrote STRONG in white beneath it, and put it on a bed of our navy blue, it would be a double entendre, Boston Strong and Be Strong, and a triple entendre, because the Red Sox' B would connote that the Red Sox are saying to Be Strong. We all liked it, and several hours later, six months of red tape was shredded, and Major League Baseball had approved the logo for charitable uses. It would generate more than $2 million for the One Fund.

Later, standing at the elevator, a colleague offered the idea of wearing "Boston" on the jerseys as opposed to "Red Sox," as they did in 1912. While some colleagues plummeted into the pit of negativity that so often prevails, saying it would not work, our president made a call to the Commissioner and got approval. It was a good idea. (We are in the "Yes" business.)

The city was full of sorrow and sadness, but it also felt resolve and resilience. There was an emerging attitude of, "Oh yeah? You messed with the wrong city. We will show you." It is that Boston Strong attitude.

The upcoming on-field ceremony we were planning needed to be solemn and dignified, not showy or glitzy. It was more of a community gathering.

When the police caught the bombers, we were awash in other emotions: resolve, resilience, and triumph. These sentiments were scripted into the ceremony. A key to event planning is empathy. You have to imagine how you will be feeling at that moment in the event. It would be a jarring disconnect to go from a solemn ceremony to suddenly playing ball.

We needed an elbow. A pivot. A change in feeling.

David Ortiz, the Red Sox future Hall of Famer, whose nickname is Big Papi, was our choice. After the previous season's injury, the next day would be his first game back with us, and the crowd would be excited to see him. However, it is not easy for the most accomplished of public speakers to handle a microphone on the field in front of a packed park. It is even harder when it is a baseball player speaking in his second language.

Reading from a script might lose sincerity; it had to be spontaneous and sincere. We could offer him a line or two, but not more than that. *"You see this jersey? Today it doesn't say Red Sox; it says Boston."*

We selected appropriate music and secured an emcee with a rich, baritone voice, who reads well and speaks well. We rehearsed every word, every phrase, every accent point, and every pause. At 12:30 p.m., just a half hour before the ceremony, we were ready.

Amid grief, shock, and sorrow, fans filled the Fens in Boston once again. Everyone was in position, and our scripts were in hand. You could feel the emotion in the ballpark. And then it was Papi's turn.

"This jersey that we wear today, it does not say Red Sox. It says Boston. We want to thank you, Mayor Menino, Governor Patrick, the whole police department for the great job that they did this past week. This is our f---ing city! And nobody's going to dictate our freedom! Stay strong!"

The ad lib was shocking, but we were not surprised. I was actually shocked by the last clause. "And nobody's going to dictate our freedom!" Wow, where did that come from? (His heart.) He brought down the house, eased the tension, and converted the emotions into raucous pride.

Our job was done, until singer Neil Diamond showed up at the ballpark, having flown from Los Angeles to Boston to show his support. His song, "Sweet Caroline," is the Red Sox anthem. In an impromptu moment, he took the hot mic and led the fans in a moving rendition of the song. Another rule of event planning: unexpected moments can be some of the most memorable.

And then outfielder Daniel Nava hit a three-run home run, and we won the game.

And like their brethren of 101 years ago, with strength and resilience, the hometown team, playing in its little old ballpark, became a source of spring and summer joy—extending the warmth of baseball right into autumn as they won a World Series in that unforgettable season.

Contributed by Charles Steinberg. Copyright © Kendall Hunt Publishing Company.

When you have finished reading this chapter, revisit the case study and respond to the following question:

What elements of this case study are examples of fostering creativity?

Creativity

Event planners are required to be creative thinkers in order to produce events that people can remember and enjoy. Creativity is imperative to an event planner's success; it requires you to wear your inventive and

TIP

Don't become a captive of your own ideas. Sometimes even the best idea should not be executed if it does not satisfy strategic aims.

— Sandy Hillman

resourceful hat as you generate ideas for your clients. These ideas do not all have to be ingenious, but they do have to take into account what the client or company needs and wants to achieve from the event. Event planners are responsible for coming up with exciting, inventive ideas that suit the client's needs and leave a lasting impression on those who attend the event.

But what is creativity, and where does it come from? How can event planners foster and nurture creativity in order to spawn ideas that will work to their benefit and to the benefit of their clients? **Creativity** is the development of ideas explained by new combinations or by the regrouping and restructuring of concepts that involve thinking (Lewin, 1935; Vygotsky, 1962). Several years ago, one of the authors of this textbook worked for the Baltimore Orioles on an event that the team was sponsoring to raise money for the American Cancer Society. At the time, the film *Men in Black* with Will Smith and Tommy Lee Jones had recently been released. As the planning group brainstormed ideas for the event, they kept coming back to a theme that played upon the *Men in Black* title. They decided to give the idea a creative twist and call it *Men with Bats*. Because the ballplayers were going to be hosting the event to raise money for the non-profit organization, they wanted something enticing to draw people to the event. Posters replicated the *Men in Black* movie poster in which the ballplayers were photographed holding bats and wearing sunglasses, similar to the poster of Smith and Jones. The theme was hugely successful. Members of the front office who volunteered to work the event wore the players' jerseys and dark sunglasses to help set the mood; attendees received a pair of dark sunglasses as they entered the venue; and the entire site was decorated so that guests could play games against the ballplayers, eat food, drink beverages, and bid on silent auction items. The event raised funds for a great cause, and those who attended enjoyed a unique and creative experience that they would not soon forget. This example shows how tapping into the pulse of current pop culture can help distinguish an event by tying into trends that are timely and relevant.

© Rawpixel/Shutterstock.com

Runco (2004) believes that people have the potential to be creative because they can transform the physical world through their own interpretations of ideas. Unfortunately, many people often overlook the power of creativity. The Human Resource Institute (1997), a training institute that works with federal agencies to increase employee value, conducted a survey that found 80% of 750 top managers from 150 corporations said creativity is important to their organizations, but reported that a mere 4% of them do a good job at fostering creativity and innovation. Amabile and Khaire (2008) state that creativity has always been at the heart of business endeavors, and that the ability to create something new and innovative is what starts and sustains businesses.

Not surprisingly, creativity is a "basic resource" that is needed for ideas to flourish in the business world (Crosby, 1968, p. xii). Goodwin and Sommervold (2012) state that "creativity drives economies and cultures and makes people think in different ways. People who have the ability to think creatively come up with novel solutions, make connections in new and exciting ways, and brainstorm ideas that are in high demand" (p. 9). Organizations can see creativity as a way of life for the business because it is an ongoing process (Ray, 1987). As an event planner, you must embrace the idea that creativity is a continuum; as each event comes along, you must always be considering what can be done to make the event distinctive, as well as what you can alter if you plan any future events for the same company or client. Lotts (2015) writes about developing a culture or climate of creativity in the area of **maker spaces**, a designated location where creativity can occur, but notes that such cultures take time and effort to develop. Those who participate in any experience, she notes, will get more out of the event if it draws upon a fun and creative encounter.

Maker space: *a designated location where creativity can occur*

Creativity is a term event planners often use, but it should not be taken for granted. Gregoire (2014) states, "Creativity works in mysterious and often paradoxical ways" (para 1). Traditional views of creativity primarily focus on right brain (creative and emotional)—left brain (rational and logical) thinking; however, neuroscientists now believe that creativity is more complex than this (Kaufman, 2013). Research illustrates the complexity of creativity by offering five alternative views on the subject (Kaufman & Sternberg, 2010):

1. Creativity as a trait—people have innate characteristics (e.g., humor, courage, independence, resourcefulness, intuition, expressiveness) that predispose them to being creative (Wycoff, 1991).
2. Creativity as cognitive skills and abilities—creativity is a function of conceptual skills related to divergent and abstract thinking (Barron & Harrington, 1981).
3. Creativity as a behavior—creativity is a result of establishing new ideas or solutions (Amabile, 1997).
4. Creativity as a process—creativity is generated through testing and ideas (Torrance, 1988).
5. Integrated view of creativity—creativity is a result of interactions among people, tasks, and environment (Woodman, Sawyer, & Griffin, 1993).

TIP

Design from the ideal. Silence naysayers during the creative process. The devil deserves no advocate. Dream and imagine the ultimate event. Then see how close you come.

— Charles Steinberg

All of these views have produced prolific research, and all have a position in the conversation on creativity. However, this chapter focuses on a view consistent with Robert Sternberg and Todd Lubart (1995) who state,

> *We believe that creativity, like intelligence, is something that everyone possesses in some amount. Moreover, creativity is not a fixed attribute: a person's level of creativity is not carved in stone at birth, and like any talent, it is something virtually anyone can develop in varying degrees (p. vii).*

Developing your creativity is not an easy task, but it is an important undertaking if you want to succeed in the field of event planning. Do not let past concerns about creativity dampen your enthusiasm to cultivate it now.

Fostering Creativity

Karwowski et al (2017) notes that creativity naturally occurs in everyday actions and behaviors, though people may not be aware of the occurrence. However, through creative training, a method that allows people to think in various ways about multiple problems, people can learn to be more creative thinkers. In fact, the most effective creativity training allows participants to generate ideas that they can apply to various problems (Baruah & Paulus, 2008; Dow & Mayer, 2004; Scott, Leritz, & Mumford, 2004). Much the same way that a writer may experience writer's block, an event planner may have trouble developing new ideas for a client. However, there are ways you can combat this. Young (2003) suggests a process that can help your individual creativity. The first step is to gather information from sources— as many as possible. The second step requires you to order and organize the information in a way that allows you to play with it. This could involve putting ideas on notecards or scribbling random ideas and thoughts on paper. The third step asks you to then walk away from everything you have come up with and let the ideas sit for a while; this way when you come back to them, new ideas may emerge.

© Kachergina/Shutterstock.com

As an event planner, you should never turn off your imagination. Create events that have their own personality and flavor. Jacobson (2014) states, "Hosting events in a creative way not only demonstrates an organization's appreciation for its attendees, but helps make the event or meeting a worthwhile investment for the company or organization" (p. 12). Jacobson also suggests crafting a unique element that will make your meeting or event stand out; think about adding something unexpected that will create memories. For example, intimate bridal showers boasting innovative themes are currently the rage. Varying degrees of creativity are involved to execute the shower and make the bride-to-be happy, so incorporating the things she likes and appreciates into the theme is important. Perhaps she and the groom are headed to Paris for their honeymoon; in that case, a Parisian-themed party may be well-suited for her. Incorporating chandeliers and a French color scheme with stripes and femininity into the decorations, along with cultural food choices into the menu for the shower, would certainly please her. Another bride-to-be may have chosen a rustic wedding in a barn; perhaps for her shower, the event planner could coordinate an outdoor space such as a winery or picnic area as a locale, replete with flowers and decorations that enhance the already picturesque setting.

Additionally, in a corporate setting, meetings held in destination cities are popular. Consider providing a small welcome basket for attendees upon check-in that reflects that city's personality, culture, or food. All of these ideas can offer a creative touch to your event. There is a lot you can do to develop your inventiveness. Creativity is not just about playing with ideas; it also includes focusing and analyzing ideas to make critical judgments about what is best in a particular circumstance (Robinson, 2011). Adair (2007) believes you need to develop a creative attitude in which you are continually listening, reading, and looking at situations creatively. As you think about ways to create unique events, The Human Resource Institute (1997) suggests that creativity can be encouraged in different ways. These include developing analogies, suggesting alternative solutions, encouraging new approaches, and challenging the event design from beginning to end. Developing these habits or practices will help event planners make creativity a part of their everyday regimen. As a result, creativity becomes intuitive rather than systematic. As you develop an imaginative muscle memory, creativity will ultimately become who you are rather than what you do. By cultivating and using prompts, the event planner will be able to keep the creative juices flowing, even after planning years of events. To avoid becoming complacent in their practice, event planners can utilize these tips and reinvent innovative ways to satisfy their clients.

Creativity in the Environment

The most successful corporations are those that encourage creativity and imagination among employees in an effort to innovate. When companies remove emotional anxiety from the workplace and replace it with

an emphasis on creativity, innovation can occur more easily. Event planners must find a way to encourage creativity among those with whom they work closely and should be sure to involve employees, event staff, or vendors in the process. Encouraging creativity is a way to boost ideas and is imperative for developing new, valuable products and services, as well as solving challenging business problems (Amabile, 1996). As Amabile (1996) states, "The hallmark of outstanding creative achievement is a passionate motivation to create" (p. 1). Therefore, if event planners foster their team's passion and allow them to become involved in the process of brainstorming, creating, and implementing events, motivation levels are likely to rise, and their team may become more committed to and vested in the tasks at hand.

Kelley and Littman (2005) suggest that in today's business world, promoting a sense of innovation in the workplace is vital to success, and it is individuals and teams who help ignite creativity. "People make it happen through their imagination, willpower, and perseverance. And whether you are a team member, a group leader, or an executive, your only real path to innovation is through people. You can't do it alone" (Kelley & Littman, 2005, p. 6). Being able to invent and produce effective, worthwhile, and memorable events will require you to listen to the input of others and encourage a welcome exchange of ideas within your work setting. You will inspire those with whom you work by the sincerity of the atmosphere you have established, and they will be more apt to become participatory members during all stages of innovation. Fred Mandell, who teaches leadership at MIT, subscribes to the idea that all the great artists from history were great because they pushed themselves to take risks and to put themselves out there, thereby stepping into the space where creativity takes hold and happens (Schulaka, 2015). Event planners should be prepared to do the same.

A creative environment might also include elements of humor. While humor can certainly lighten the mood and stimulate creativity, it is also a way to motivate the work environment. In business, humor often fosters a culture of risk taking, flexibility, and openness (Lang & Lee, 2010). In a stuffy corporate culture, or one in which creativity is not encouraged, humor inspires people to leap past the voice of judgment and break out of the bounds of conformity. Some of the more creative concepts come from what might have begun as a nutty idea that was not stifled or negated. Thus, people with a better sense of humor seem to be

© Kachergina/Shutterstock.com

more able and ready to consider new ideas and approaches (Yi, Nguyen, & Zeng, 2013). Managers can use humor to reduce anxiety and boost leadership, group cohesiveness, communication, creativity, and organizational culture (Cody, 2012). Understanding appropriate humor styles and selecting the kind of humor that will work in a particular group or situation can enable managers to address the needs of the employees when anxiety rises (Romero & Cruthirds, 2006). Humor serves many purposes, emotionally distancing individuals from the problem and giving those involved a chance to relax from the stress (Lang & Lee, 2010). Often, it can change your mental perspective, since it offers an opportunity to stretch your thinking and make sense out of something that might not typically make sense (Yi, Nguyen, & Zeng, 2013). Humor also reduces tension that might get in the way of trying something new and energizes people to think in outrageous ways (Holmes, 2007). However, not all organizations view humor as positive. Morreall's (1991) research indicates that some employers see humor at work as an interruption from the real task of achieving corporate objectives. Thus, the amount of humor depends on the work culture and the extent of encouragement from the management team. Event planners often find themselves in situations when a little humor might indeed lessen the

© BooHoo/Shutterstock.com

tension, but of course, they must moderate their humor based on their knowledge of the client.

Management also plays a major role in promoting and stimulating creativity in the work environment. Creative management shows employees that it is acceptable to do things differently, allowing for innovation and motivation (Fariborizi, 2015). Glăveanu and Lubart (2014) found that creativity comes not only from exchanges with peers and colleagues, but also from client and sponsor contributions. While these collaborators can offer insightful ideas, they can also hinder creativity because sometimes clients simply want what they want in an event, no matter what creative concepts your team offers. Nevertheless, staying open to this type of communication exchange will nurture the relationships you have built and perhaps embolden greater participation in the creative, supportive environment you have established. Event planners can also generate creativity in the workplace. For example, an event planner is helping to organize a corporate picnic in which the main attractions are barbecued ribs and corn on the cob, not known for their elegance. Because the event is scheduled for the afternoon of a workday, most of the attendees will be dressed in their business attire and may not want to dress down for the picnic. Instead of the usual 'Hi! My name is ____' name tags, the event planner came up with the idea of handing out barbecue aprons to forestall the messiness, simple aprons upon which attendees could write their names in permanent marker and take them home as a favor. In a brainstorming session during which the planners were worried about the untidiness that could have resulted from an afternoon of finger-lickin' ribs, the group was able to laugh about the problem as they came up with a humorous solution that served many purposes: socialization, branding, and practicality. This kind of creative brainstorming occurs when a group of employees are not afraid to share every idea, silly or not, in order to address a problem.

The Creative Process

Brockling (2006) believes that creativity is tied to human potential and asks individuals to bring something new to the table. First, you should not discount the power of your imagination and its ability to make the absent present; and, second, fantasy has the power to make something that is nonexistent existent. Remember that what was old can be new simply by building upon it, modifying it, and distancing yourself from it. After you examine your ideas for a while—and then, after taking a break from them— you may see things from a different angle. Does this mean you can control every idea that pops into your brain? Not exactly. As Max Weber (1946) said, "Ideas occur to us when they please, not when it pleases us" (p. 136). Often, the more relaxed you are, the better flow of ideas. Event planners are in the unique position of having to come up with ideas constantly. Sometimes these ideas may come to you unexpectedly, such as when you are driving or in the shower. Keeping a notepad or voice recorder nearby so that you can jot down or record your ideas as they come—even if they come at inconvenient times—can allow you to better examine and improve upon them at a more expedient time. For example, cookie tables are a Pittsburgh wedding tradition (Lieber, 2009). In 2018 when planners were organizing the Eastern Communication Association convention in Pittsburgh, the traditional cookie table became the social center of the event and the talk of the convention. Pizzelles, chocolate chip cookies, and lemon bars, among others, became the iconic trademarks of the 2018 convention.

As an event planner, you are required to create events of distinction. Clients do not want the same event as those who have come before them. In order to deliver something unique, event planners should draw upon interesting characteristics or attributes of the client or company. This may require you to 'get your hands dirty,' or involve yourself in a human-centered approach (McCorvey, 2013). If you are working for an organization, spend time at your client's business; immerse yourself in the company's surroundings; meet business constituents and talk to them. You can also bring in a fresh pair of eyes. Getting another's input may help you see the event's overall possibilities and expand upon what already exists. Understanding your client's business is paramount to the type of event you will plan, which will then relate directly to how pleasurable the attendees find the event. You cannot deliver something spectacular if you have not learned about the client. Allowing yourself the time to investigate and understand the scope of the client's expectations of the event can better prepare you to offer the most dynamic suggestions.

© Chip Rouse

The creative process involves brainstorming the event's big idea and is key to its creation, theme, or special nature. Sunwolf (2002) looks at creativity in groups and examines how they generate new ideas. An example of creativity training used in groups is the art of **brainstorming**, an idea coined by advertising executive Alex F. Osborn (1953) to stimulate creativity; the notion is over 60 years old and is still used today. Osborn's concept of brainstorming was relatively simple: place 10–12 people in a room, a mix of novices and experts, and see what kinds of ideas they can generate in response to a problem (Gobble, 2014). Osborn (1953) states that to participate in a brainstorming activity, a group must follow four basic rules:

1. Do not evaluate ideas during this session. Judging ideas will suppress creativity.
2. The more ideas generated, the better the outcome. The goal of brainstorming is quantity over quality.
3. Group members should feel free to say anything that might seem out of the ordinary or eccentric.
4. Broadening ideas or adding to others' ideas is an important component to creating better ideas.

The best brainstorming sessions typically involve generating many creative ideas with the goal of being able to select the viable options at a later date.

Tim Brown (2009) asserts that "brainstorming is as essential to creativity as exercise is to a healthy heart" (p. 78). IDEO also has rules for brainstorming, including holding brainstorming sessions in dedicated rooms. These rooms have slogans on the walls that state the following: *Defer Judgment*; *Encourage Wild Ideas*; *Stay Focused on the Topic*; and *Build on the Ideas of Others* (Brown, 2009, p. 78). When you need to generate a wide variety of ideas and concepts, brainstorming has tremendous value. "Good idea generation requires a process, in which brainstorming may be one productive step" (Gobble, 2014, p. 65). There are viable reasons why event planners need to brainstorm. For example, they must come up with several different ideas to present to a client; they are taking on an established event that needs reworking or rebranding; or they are moving into a field for which they have not yet created an event. Brown (2009) states that there are other ways to draw conclusions about making choices, but brainstorming is the best way. Duggan (2012) suggests cultivating curiosity about things and creating a "presence of mind" (p. 10) where you can deal with problems in a calm fashion, letting your mind wander freely instead of looking for answers because you feel stressed.

Brainstorming allows ideas to flow before they are developed, and event planners must remember that there are no bad ideas when it comes to brainstorming. Event planners will need to study these ideas later, taking into consideration how they will play out with regard to the event. "Creative thinking is taking it from a lot of different sources and putting it together in a way that ladders up to something bigger, so you need a mix of people who are specialists and generalists to drive diverse thinking" (Wyner, 2013, p.17). Innovative, compelling ideas come from everywhere, and encouraging creativity will benefit each event you plan and execute.

TIP

Make time to brainstorm new and creative ideas without limitations or budget constraints. Engaging your event team to tap into their imaginations can result in great ideas. When empowered to bring their ideas to fruition—the team is more invested and excited about working on the project. Getting the team motivated by asking them to come up with event themes or new twists on annual events results in a positive and entertaining atmosphere. Also, it gives you a chance to market what is new and different about your event to the media.

— Rosalind Healy

Deuja, Kohn, Paulus, and Korde (2014) found that it is useful for individual and group brainstorming to begin with a series of abstract categories of ideas. When abstract categories are formed prior to brainstorming, more ideas were generated (Coskun, Paulus, Brown, & Sherwood, 2000). Ward (2008) found that broader categories typically generate a larger scope of ideas, and perhaps even more original ones. For example, if you were going to brainstorm ideas for a fundraising event, group members would begin to think of overarching ideas for it, and perhaps even come up with a theme. Conversely, if you selected a more defined focus, such as ideas for a circus-themed fundraising event, you have already narrowed the focus. Additionally, research has found that groups generate more ideas when they brainstorm one idea at a time than when trying to brainstorm all categories simultaneously (Coskun et al., 2000).

© wavebreakmedia/Shutterstock.com

The goal of brainstorming is to create more ideas working in a group than individuals might produce on their own (Scheidel, 1986). The key to brainstorming lies in the execution of the idea; successful brainstorming sessions require balance and structure, through which the best ideas come from sessions that offer freedom to express ideas without deviating too far from the discussion at hand (Phillips, 2012). The resulting idea for the event may come from the initial brainstorming session. For example, members of the Baltimore Orioles front office brainstormed ideas for a ballpark celebration of Hall-of-Famer Cal Ripken, Jr. when he surpassed Lou Gehrig's consecutive games record. The event committee, which consisted of various members of the Orioles staff, including those who worked in public relations, marketing, publications, community relations, grounds crew, ballpark operations, and sales, among others, met several times and collected ideas generated by all members of the group. The committee recorded and valued every idea. At the end of the brainstorming session, the group critically evaluated the ideas, and the committee later developed the best of these. Banners hung from the warehouse at Oriole Park at Camden Yards as the team counted down the streak, ceremonies were planned for pre-game entertainment, and a parade in the city of Baltimore celebrated Ripken's accomplishment. All of these ideas came from multiple committee brainstorming sessions.

© James R. Martin/Shutterstock.com

Another way to promote creativity in groups is through de Bono's (1985) **Six Thinking Hats**. This process of stimulating creativity examines the aspects of emotion, logic, wishful thinking, and both the negative and positive consequences of making a particular decision. The hats, which

Six Thinking Hats: *The process of stimulating creativity by examining the aspects of emotion, logic, wishful thinking, and both the negative and positive consequences of making a particular decision*

are color-coded, represent different roles people assume in the decision-making process.

1. **White hat**—analyzes information, facts, and figures that are known and needed. This person's goal is to approach a decision in a neutral and objective manner.
2. **Red hat**—examines emotions and feelings. This person's goal is to figure out how people are feeling about a particular situation.
3. **Green hat**—focuses on creativity by exploring alternatives or imagining new possibilities for ideas. This person's goal is to create ingenious ideas.
4. **Yellow hat**—explores the positive aspects that can encompass one's values and beliefs about the potentially strong components of a decision. This person's goal is to act as a cheerleader for idea generation.
5. **Black hat**—evaluates the negative aspects and plays devil's advocate toward decisions. This person's goal is to identify problems or flaws that could occur.
6. **Blue hat**—creates summaries, conclusions, and overviews of the decision-making process. This person's goal is to bring closure to the idea-generating session.

Even though there appears to be a sequence to this process, there is no particular order to follow when engaging in this creative endeavor. Used together, but viewed separately, these six hats focus on creative thinking that turns ideas on all sides to agree upon the most creative decision.

After brainstorming has taken place, someone must form conclusions regarding the ideas presented. Whereas idea generation is expected to produce new concepts, idea evaluation is expected to improve the quality of these concepts (Paletz & Schunn, 2010). Runco and Smith (1992) suggest that the evaluation of these ideas can come from several different sources. **Intrapersonal evaluation** occurs when you evaluate your own ideas. **Interpersonal evaluation** occurs when others evaluate your ideas and you evaluate the ideas of others. **Criticism** requires the party providing the critique to add a new or innovative idea into the mix (Mumford & Gustasfson, 2007). The result of criticism means more creative thinking is required. New ideas that are presented may come with additional information. This knowledge can help those who are criticizing interpret the information more clearly (Ericsson & Charness, 1994). Criticism of this nature—especially when it is worthy and inquisitive—can serve to further stimulate creative thought and problem solving. Gibson and Mumford (2013) found that criticizing the ideas of others can be a stimulus for creative thinking. However, sometimes criticism can inhibit creative thinking and creative problem solving, but when the criticisms are specific and highlight key issues, creative thought becomes easier to facilitate.

Creativity is different from **creative problem solving**. Creativity involves generating new ideas that can become useful. Creative problem solving, however, requires individuals to identify, construct, search, and acquire information, generate ideas, and then select, evaluate, and implement them (Carmeli, Gilbert, & Reiter-Palmon, 2013). In the case of event planning, you can generate ideas that are creative for your client, but as you begin to plan and organize the event, you will see that creative problem solving will help you begin to implement what you have envisioned. Recognizing that creativity is a continual process, and that you should not turn off your creativity once the event has been planned, is crucial to the execution, and, later, to the success of the event. Your creativity will have to evolve as the event comes to fruition.

Creative problem solving: *A method of discovery that requires individuals to identify, construct, search, and acquire information, generate ideas, and then select, evaluate, and implement them*

With the arrival of shared online creativity platforms like Pinterest and PearlTrees, event planners have a new tool at their disposal that can enable them to help clients visually construct their ideas for an event. These tools are often called **vision boards**. "Pinterest may be viewed as a scrapbooking platform with appeal to users with specific interests, but it can be a valuable tool in infusing creativity in programming" (Alston, 2015, p. 25). Besides providing a wide perspective for theme generation, these social media web and mobile application companies can offer inexpensive, flexible, and efficient advertising concepts as well as ideas for interactive experiences. While event planners may use Pinterest to begin their own research and to build inspiration regarding an upcoming event, Pinterest boards pinned and shared by clients with the event planner can offer a glimpse into their personal taste and style, thus helping the event planner create the best event possible for the client (Phillips, Miller, & McQuarrie, 2015). When communicating an idea to a client, it can sometimes be difficult to explain verbally exactly what the vision is. However, with online platforms like Pinterest, event planners can easily share their concepts through pictures and examples.

Vision board: *A tool that helps clients visually construct their ideas for an event*

Barriers to Creativity

Event planners should respect, value, and embrace the creative aspects of their job. If you embrace creativity, unique ideas may flourish. Event planners should enable those who work for them and with them to engage in the creation of the event, encouraging innovation during which a free exchange of ideas is possible; the creative team can generate, discuss, and sustain these ideas. Sadly, however, there are many reasons people do not act creatively, but one of the main reasons is that people believe they are just not creative.

© wavebreakmedia/Shutterstock.com

Two kinds of barriers to creativity exist in the corporate world: habits and blocks (Evans, 1993). Habits confine event planners to paths they have taken in problem solving in the past, simply because such choices may be easier. However, when creative people follow the same path, they arrive at the same conclusion. For instance, event planners may develop the habit of working with the same vendors who create one type of product again and again. Habits make event planning easy, comfortable, familiar and undemanding. But they do not inspire event planners to reach beyond what has been done in the past.

Blocks operate differently. They can keep the event planner from perceiving the problem that exists or understanding what information is necessary to solve the problem. They can also be emotional, such as when an event planner freezes for fear of making a mistake, or when a risk might be perceived as too emotionally challenging. Often, event planners find themselves unable to relax and generate spontaneously new ideas, which is a kind of emotional block as well. Blocks can also come from the cultural environment around the event or the event planner (Evans, 1993). These barriers can exhibit themselves in a lack of understanding of how to proceed in an unfamiliar setting, or they can exist when an event planner has a great new idea but does not have the support necessary to make it a reality. Perhaps an event planner has a vision for a new corporate holiday fete, but the company sponsors are apprehensive about creating such an unusually innovative event.

© Alex Andrei/Shutterstock.com

Event planners should also be confident about challenging the presuppositions of their clients in a tactful and diplomatic way. Just because something has occurred a certain way in the past does not mean that same path must be followed in the future. Conscious decision-making and a fearless approach to risk-taking by the event planner may yield a multitude of creative approaches to timeworn events. The importance of developing a workplace environment where creativity is encouraged cannot be overlooked, either (Evans, 1993). Though creativity may be less predictable, removing the barriers to creative thinking can open up new pathways to event planning success. Event planners must try to resist believing they are not creative, or that their creativity has been stifled, as the profession relies so heavily upon it. Telling yourself you are not creative, that you do not know how to formulate innovative ideas, that you do not like taking risks, or that you do not have time for creativity, could prove harmful to the success of the events you plan (Shinton, 2008). Negative beliefs regarding your own creativity will not help achieve the client's goals or the goals of the event itself.

Event planners should be willing to take risks without fear of criticism; additionally, they must make time to convey ideas to their clients and present them in a way that encourages feedback. This is particularly true if you are running your own event planning company; you must rely on the input of others in order to garner advice and commentary. When you are solely responsible for offering creative ideas to your clients, it can become burdensome at times, so you will need to find people you trust to listen to your ideas and offer you feedback. Someone who works in a similar field would be a good source with whom to share information, but it also could be someone who knows very little about your business, because when you have to explain something in detail, it may stimulate creative thinking and perhaps even offer a creative solution (Shinton, 2008). Finding a mentor in your field or a similar one would certainly offer significant help as you develop your creativity.

Robinson (2011) states, "The more complex the world becomes, the more creative we need to be to meet its challenges" (p. xiii). In the world of event planning, there will be innumerable events with varying degrees of complexity, each of which will demand different levels of creativity. From a simple luncheon to an extravagant gala to a professional trade show, events will require your innovative talent in order to be successful. Event planners should remember that every client—not just the ones who express a desire for a truly creative event—should be offered a range of creative experiences. "The term business-to-business should not be used as an excuse to lack imagination, excitement or energy. Whoever makes up the audience, whatever their job title is, they are still humans and want to be treated like consumers" (DiLieto, 2018, p. 4). Creativity is a desirable component in the field of event planning, and you should see it as something that can be cultivated in many different ways. Your job as an event planner is to generate new and innovative events and avoid the barriers that can stifle your creativity.

TIP

There's strength in teams. Until you have the capital to build a permanent one, consider other ways to leverage yourself. Virtual assistants, interns, freelancers and prospective alliance partners can provide great support as you begin and grow.

— Paul Wolman

Key Terms

Creativity	White hat	Black hat	Criticism
Maker space	Red hat	Blue hat	Creative problem solving
Brainstorming	Green hat	Intrapersonal evaluation	Vision board
Six Thinking Hats	Yellow hat	Interpersonal evaluation	

Discussion Questions

1. Has there ever been a time when you felt as if you were unable to be creative or generate new ideas? How did you work through that? What tactics did you use to unlock your creativity?

2. Describe a time when brainstorming worked very well within a work or school group. Describe a time when brainstorming did not go very well within a work or school group.

3. The idea of creativity with regard to event planning as an evolving and ever-changing continuum is an interesting notion. Discuss why you, as an event planner, must always wear your creativity hat and continue to develop your creativity.

Activity

The Science Center in your city is about to hold its 50th Anniversary celebration during the month of August. The locale is a landmark in the city and draws people from within your region, as well as tourists from out of state who come to visit. The Science Center is known for its dinosaur exhibit, its living butterfly greenhouse, and its technology area. There is also an IMAX Theatre where people can watch films related to science, nature, travel, and adventure.

Using de Bono's Six Thinking Hats, and discussing each exhibit, brainstorm ideas for this 50th Anniversary celebration.

1. **White hat:**

2. **Red hat:**

3. **Green hat:**

4. **Yellow hat:**

5. **Black hat:**

6. **Blue hat:**

References

Adair, J. E. (2007). *The art of creative thinking: How to be innovative and develop great ideas.* Philadelphia, PA: Kogan.

Allen, E. K. (2005). Creativity on demand. *Harvard Business Review, 83,* 46–48.

Alston, D. J. (2015). Pinterest: Three ways it gives a bump to programming creativity. *Campus Activities Programming, 48* (5), 24–26.

Amabile, T. M. (1996). *The motivation for creativity in organizations.* Harvard Business School.

_____. (1997). Motivating creativity in organizations: On doing what you love and loving what you do. *California Management Review, 40,* 39–58

Amabile, T. M., & Khaire, M. (2008). Creativity and the role of the leader. *Harvard Business Review, 86,* 100–109.

Barron, F. B., & Harrington, D. M. (1981). Creativity, intelligence, and personality. *Annual Review of Psychology, 32,* 439–476.

Baruah, J., & Paulus, P. B. (2008). Effects of training on idea generation in groups. *Small Group Research, 39,* 523–541.

Brockling, U. (2006). On creativity: A brainstorming session. *Educational Philosophy & Theory, 38,* 513–521.

Brown, T. (2009). *Change by design*. New York: Harper Collins.

Carmeli, A., Gelbard, R., & Reiter-Palmon, R. (2013). Leadership, creative problem-solving capacity, and creative performance: The importance of knowledge sharing. *Human Resource Management, 52*, 95–121.

Cody, S. (2012). How humor can make you a better leader. *Public Relations Strategist, 18*, 14–16.

Coskun, H., Paulus, P. B., Brown, V., & Sherwood, J. J. (2000). Cognitive stimulation and problem presentation in idea-generation groups. *Group Dynamics: Theory, Research, and Practice, 4*, 307–329.

Crosby, A. (1968). *Creativity and performance in industrial organizations*. London: Tavistock.

deBono, E. L. (1985). *Six thinking hats*. Boston: Little Brown and Company.

Deuja, A., Kohn, N. W., Paulus, P. B., & Korde, R. M. (2014). Taking a broad perspectivebefore brainstorming. *Group Dynamics: Theory, Research, and Practice, 18*, 222–236.

DiLieto, C. (2018). Every event should be experiential. *Conference & Incentive Travel*. Summer 2018, 4.

Dow, G. T., & Mayer, R. E. (2004). Teaching students to solve insight problems: Evidence for domain specificity in creativity training. *Creative Research Journal, 16*, 389–402.

Duggan, W. (2012). *Creative strategy: A guide for innovation*. New York: Columbia UniversityPress.

Ericsson, K. A., & Charness, W. (1994). Expert performance: Its structure and acquisition. *American Psychologist, 49*, 725–747.

Evans, J. R. (1993). Creativity in MS/OR: Overcoming barriers to creativity. *Interfaces* 23 (6), pp. 101–106.

Fariborzi, E. (2015). Increasing creativity in virtual learning space for developing creative cities. *Journal of Academic Research, 7*, 99–108.

Fillis, I., & Rentschler, R. (2010). The role of creativity in entrepreneurship. *Journal of Enterprising Culture, 18*, 49–81.

Gibson, C., & Mumford, M. D. (2013). Evaluation, criticism, and creativity: Criticism content and effects on creative problem solving. *Psychology of Aesthetics, Creativity, and the Arts, 7*, 314–331.

Glăveanu, V. P., & Lubart, T. (2014). Decentring the creative self: How others make creativity possible in creative professional fields. *Creativity & Innovation Management, 23*, 29–43.

Gobble, M. M. (2014). The persistence of brainstorming. *Research Technology Management, 57*, 64–66.

Goodwin, M., & Sommervold, C. (2012). *Creativity, critical thinking, and communication: Strategies to increase students' skills*. Lanham, MD: Rowan & Littlefield Education.

Gregoire, C. (2014). *18 things highly creative people do differently*. Retrieved from http://www.huffingtonpost.com/2014/03/04/creativity-habits_n_4859769.html

Holmes, J. (2007). Making humor work: Creativity on the job. *Applied Linguistics*, *28*, 518–537.

Human Resource Institute (1997). Stimulating creativity and innovation. *Research Technology Management*, *40*, 57.

Jacobson, L. (2014). Creativity counts. *Successful Meetings*, *63*, 12–13.

Karwowski, M; Lebuda, I; Szumski, G., & Firkowska-Mankiewicz, A. (2017). From moment-to-moment to day-to-day: Experience sampling and diary investigations in adults' everyday creativity. *Psychology of Aesthetics, Creativity, and the Arts, Special Issue: Aesthetics, Creativity, and the Arts in Everyday Environments 11*(3), 309–324.

Kaufman, S. B. (2013). *The real neuroscience of creativity*. Retrieved from http://blogs.scientificamerican.com/beautiful-minds/the-real-neuroscience-of-creativity/

Kaufman, J. C., & Sternberg, R. J. (Eds). (2010). *The Cambridge handbook of creativity*. Cambridge, UK: Cambridge University Press.

Kelley, T., & Littman, J. (2006). *The ten faces of innovation: IDEO's strategies for defeating the devil's advocate and driving creativity throughout your organization*. New York: Crown Business.

Lang, J., & Lee, C. (2010). Workplace humor and organizational creativity. *The International Journal of Human Resource Management*, *21*, 46–60.

Lewin, K. (1935). *A dynamic theory of personality*. New York: McGraw-Hill.

Lieber, R. (2009, Dec.). The wedding? I'm here for the cookies. *The New York Times*, Retrieved from https://www.nytimes.com/2009/12/16/dining/16cookies.html

Lotts, M. (2015). Implementing a culture of creativity: Pop-up making spaces and participating events in academic libraries. *College & Research Libraries News*, *76*, 72–75. Retrieved from doi:10.7282/T3D2208V

McCorvey, J. J. (2013). Lessons learned at IDEO. *Fast Company*, *172*, 54.

Morreall, J. (1991). Humor and work. *Humor*, *4*, 359–374.

Mumford, M. D., & Gustafson, S. B. (2007). Creative thought: Cognition and problem-solving in a dynamic system. In M. A. Runco (Ed.), *Creativity Research Handbook* (Vol. II, pp. 33–77). Cresskill, NJ: Hampton.

Osborn, A. F. (1953). *Applied imagination*. New York: Scribner.

Paletz, S., & Schunn, C. (2010). A social-cognitive framework of multidisciplinary team innovation. *Topics in Cognitive Science*, *2*, 73–95.

Phillips, J. (2012). *Relentless innovation*. New York: McGraw-Hill.

Phillips, B., Miller, J. & McQuarrie, E. (2014) Dreaming out loud on Pinterest, *International Journal of Advertising*, *33*, 633–655.

Ray, M. L. (1987). Strategies for stimulating personal creativity. *Human Resource Planning*, *10*, 185–193.

Robinson, K. (2011). *Out of our minds: Learning to be creative*. West Sussex: United Kingdom: Capstone Publishing.

Romero, E. J., & Cruthirds, K. W. (2006). The use of humor in the workplace. *Academy of Management Perspectives, 20*, 58–69.

Runco, M. A. (2004). Everyone has creative potential. In R. J. Sternberg, E. L. Grigorenko, & J. L. Singer (Eds), *Creativity: From Potential to realization* (pp. 21–30). Washington, DC: American Psychological Association.

Runco, M. A., & Smith, W. R. (1992). Interpersonal and intrapersonal evaluations of creativeideas. *Personality and Individual Differences, 13*, 295–302.

Scheidel, T. M. (1986). Divergent and convergent thinking in group decision-making. In R. Y. Hirokawa & M. S. Poole (Eds.), *Communication and group decision-making* (pp. 113–130). Beverly Hills, CA: Sage.

Schulaka, C. (2015). Fred Mandell on embracing creativity, finding inspiration, and reinventing yourself. *Journal of Financial Planning, 28*, 13–17. Retrieved from https://ezproxy.stevenson.edu/login?url=https://search.ebscohost.com/login.aspx?direct=true&db=bth&AN=100778211&site=eds-live&scope=site

Scott, G., Leritz, L. E., & Mumford, M. D. (2004). The effectiveness of creative training: A quantitative review. *Creativity research journal, 16*, 361–388.

Shinton, S. (2008). Switching on light bulbs—Stimulating your creativity. *Analytical & Bioanalytical Chemistry, 392*, 561–563.

Sternberg, R. J., & Lubart, T. I. (1995). *Defying the crowd: Cultivating creativity in a culture of conformity*. New York: The Free Press.

Sunwolf (2002). Getting to "groupaha!": Provoking creative processes in task groups. In L. R. Frey (Ed.), *New directions in group communication* (pp. 203–217). Thousand Oaks, CA: Sage.

Torrance, E. P. (1988). The nature of creativity as manifest in its testing. In R. J. Sternberg (Ed.), *The nature of creativity: Contemporary psychological views* (pp. 43–75). Cambridge, UK: Cambridge University Press.

Vygotsky, L. S. (1962). *Thought and language*. Cambridge, MA: MIT Press.

Ward, T. B. (2008). The role of domain knowledge in creative generation. *Learning and Individual Differences, 18*, 363–366.

Weber, M. (1946). Science as vocation. In H. H. Gerth & C. W. Mills (Eds.), *Max Weber: Essays in sociology* (pp. 129–156). New York: Oxford Press.

Woodman, R., Sawyer, J., & Griffin, R. (1993). Toward a theory of organizational creativity. *Academy of Management Review, 18*, 293–321.

Wycoff, J. (1991). *Mindmapping: Your personal guide to exploring creativity and problem solving*. New York: Berkeley Books.

Wyner, G. (2013). Help wanted: Business-savvy marketers. *Marketing News, 47*, 16–17.

Yi, H., Nguyen, T., & Zeng, Y. (2013). Humour and creative design: Twins or partners? *Journal of Integrated Design and Process Science, 17*, 81–92.

Young, J. W. (2003). *A technique for producing ideas*. New York: McGraw-Hill.

Chapter 7

BUDGETING: THE FINANCIAL SIDE OF EVENT PLANNING

Perhaps the thorniest part of the event planner's experience is budget creation and management. Many event planners would say that while their interpersonal, time management, and coping skills are well-developed, budgetary strengths are not necessarily part of the package. In fact, not much about budget knowledge is inherent in most people. "People may be born with an aptitude for numbers, but budgeting requires more than that" (McCaffery, 2003, p. 60). Budgets are more than just numbers on a page, displayed correctly.

They are living documents that reflect the humans in charge (Van der Wagen & White, 2018). Successful budgeters have to know how the human factor is going to respond to those numbers. Thus, event planners must be able to calculate, commiserate, and negotiate when it comes to their client's budget. New budget data from over 400 companies in 2018 indicates that many of the most effective businesses are spending 1.7 times the average marketing budget on live events, believing that the return on their investment is worth the expense. In addition, 63% of those polled intend to grow their total event budgets by 22% in the next year, on average. (Event Marketing 2019: Benchmarks and Trends Report, 2019). Additionally, with the rise of mega-events such as the World Cup and the Super Bowl, those budgets have routinely reached more than $10 billion in capital investment (Muller, 2015). All of this data shows that event planners must fully understand the significance and the weight of the budget in future event planning.

Successful budget control demands more than an understanding of the spreadsheet. Often it means that clients will have to seek out sponsorships to balance their event budgets, and the event planner will need strong communication skills to convince potential sponsors that their investment in an event can offer unique branding opportunities and philosophical and philanthropic positioning, as well as partnership prospects with a wide variety of like-minded organizations (Kilkenny, 2011). In addition, the event's vision and purpose are inextricably linked to the budget, so the event planner must establish those key points as the budget is being considered. Ultimately, the budget will measure performance against a calculable figure, but it also must reflect the human factors that influence the numbers (Masterman, 2014). At each stage throughout the event planning process, the budget must serve as both a guide and a forecaster, and the event planner should learn to balance the budget's constraints against the client's vision at every step of the process.

When you have finished reading this chapter, you will be able to

- explain what a budget is and what it conveys;
- discuss ways in which event planners can help clients address budget issues;
- describe the stressors to proper budget implementation, as well as their solutions.

CASE STUDY

No Budget, No Event . . . Not True!

Corrin Harris, Lifestyle Manager, CCMC

You may have heard it said that without a budget, there is no event. What if I told you it was possible to take an empty wallet and turn it into a successful event? Event planners of all experience levels have the ability to get creative with budgeting. Creative budgeting requires out-of-the-box thinking.

Celebration is a master-planned community in central Florida with a little over 12,000 residents. The community was brought to life by the Walt Disney Company and continues to live by the five cornerstones set forth: health, sense of place, technology, education, and community. As a member of the lifestyle team, our main focus is community. Our events are designed to be interactive and social, allowing neighbors to be the focus of the community. A majority of our larger-scale events are complimentary for our residents and provide a wide variety of entertainment, from movie nights and concerts on the Great Lawn to large-scale events such as Fourth of July spectaculars complete with fireworks.

Most events in Celebration are already budgeted for and approved by the Board of Directors; however, some events start with a budget of zero, and the lifestyle team builds an event from scratch through creative budgeting tactics.

A creative budgeting tactic that is commonly used in Celebration is 'pay-to-play.' This design allows planners to coordinate events without a budget. A popular 'pay-to-play' event we host is 'Kids Night Out.' The lifestyle team sets a fee, and the fees paid by participants go directly to the budget for the event. There is a registration deadline, so the department has enough time to create a proper working budget and order supplies. This tactic allows the lifestyle team to schedule several more events throughout the year that are not in the budget.

Celebration holds many events throughout the year with a wide range of budgets. In-house marketing eases costs when it comes to promotion. Celebration's main promotion outlets are flyers, social media posts and the monthly Celebration magazine. Most flyers are created in-house, which eliminates the cost of hiring outside vendors. There are many websites and applications that allow users to create flyers for little to no cost.

Each aspect of planning provides its own set of challenges and curveballs. As odd as it sounds, event planners want to make sure they 'budget' the budget. It is not uncommon to have to cut items from a budget; eliminating components should not be seen as a sign of defeat. Beginning a working budget with the necessities, followed by add-ons, is the best way to ensure all the basics are covered and the budget stays on track. Another option to sustain costs is to utilize existing resources. For example, Celebration movie nights are very low-cost events that only require an annual public performance license and a movie screen and movies, which are usually already purchased. Combining events is another creative budgeting tactic. Hosting a movie night during a Food Truck Friday provides residents with the option to purchase snacks and food while enjoying a movie on the lawn. This event combination provides residents extra options and absorbs the cost of bringing in vendors for two separate events.

The phrase 'event planning' typically brings the word 'budget' to mind. It is important to learn different approaches to budgeting and figure out which style works best with your event and budget. All events encounter slight speed bumps when it comes to finances, and event planners must remember that there are always solutions to concerns; it may just require creative thinking. Events of all scales are feasible with creative budgeting techniques. When it comes to event planning, remember this part of the Disney philosophy: "If you can dream it, you can do it!"

After reading this chapter, revisit the case study and respond to the following question:

What are some other cost-effective strategies you might consider as you plan events?

Budgeting

Budgets emerge from a variety of standpoints, both mathematical and human. From a simple, personal event such as a wedding anniversary, to a large corporate extravaganza, the budget deserves consideration and examination. Understanding what the budget is and what it conveys is essential. Hanson (1966) says that "a **budget** is a formal statement by management of its plans for a given time period which will be used as a guide

Budget: *A formal statement by management of its plans for a given time period which will be used as a guide during that period*

during that period" (p. 239). Though this statement seems to address budgeting in the corporate world, it is still important that event planners see the budget as a blueprint for action, a manual that keeps the event as close as possible to the plans. Thus, budgets signify a desired state and can act as guides designed to provide direction (Hanson, 1966). See **Appendix A** for a sample event budget.

While there may be corrections to the guide as the event takes shape, the budget is always present, never to be disregarded in an effort to make the client happy. Bates (2014) suggests that the best way to approach the process is to encourage the client to offer you a starting point in terms of budget and then begin to design the event. Because so many elements affect the budget, such as the audience and the purpose of the event, it is vital that the event planner take control of budgetary discussions when possible. Clients must know from the beginning what their priorities are since every element of the event will affect the budget (Polansky, 2016; Waters, 2006). Each detail emanates from the mission or goal statement, and that includes the particulars of the budget (Kwiatoski, 2008). Budgets impose financial discipline and allow others to impact the allocation of financial resources (Bowden, Allen, O'Toole, Harris, & McDonnell, 2011). This means that transparency, honesty, and good communication skills will be indispensable as the budget is developed.

© Kemal Taner/Shutterstock.com

A budget is "a device for control, coordination, communication, performance evaluation, and motivation" (Kenis, 1979, p. 707). While budgets can accomplish each of these tasks, not all of those efforts go into each budget's construction. Through ways that money is delegated, budgets communicate norms, values, and rules for behavior (Collins, 1978). In times of corporate belt-tightening, for instance, extravagant jaunts to island paradises for weekend workshops are cut in lieu of less excessive destinations. How people spend their money says a lot about what they esteem, and thus the budget, which may initially appear as just a mathematical equation that needs some manipulation, is actually a living part of the event. The budget does, in fact, indicate a nexus of control, and thus demands communication among all parties if it is to satisfy the event's outcomes. Budgets are not just about the bottom line in terms of money spent (Kenis, 1979); they must also be about how funds are delegated, who has been satisfied, and what will happen as a result of the money spent. Budgets are about people, even more than they are about money, so as the budget is built, consider the importance of building relationships with the people involved in the event (Freeman, 2011; Van de Wagen & White, 2018).

When determining your budget, you will have to consider basing your numbers on fixed costs and variable costs. Marquis (2014) states that fixed costs are those that do not change during the fiscal year and are not affected by changes that occur in production, revenue, or expenses. Fixed costs can be the easiest expenses to determine because they typically remain the same from month to month. Some examples of fixed costs for an event may include costs for the venue or room rental, advertising costs, postage, stationery, electronics costs, salaries, and decorations. All of these are fixed costs because they do not rely on how many people actually attend the event; the event planner will still have to plan for these things no matter what the attendance may ultimately be. **Variable costs** are those that can change and can include anything from materials to electrical costs to labor and distribution costs. Examples of variable costs might include food and beverages, gift bags or favors, and perhaps even printing costs for programs or other collaterals. Controlling these costs through vendor negotiation and wholesale licensing is an asset to any event planner (Bowens, 2016).

Fixed costs: *Costs that do not rely on the number of people attending an event*

Variable costs: *Costs of those items dependent on the number of people attending an event*

Direct costs are those expenses incurred because of a consequence of producing a good or service and are not related to overhead or indirect costs (Harvard Business Essentials, 2002). Direct costs are all related to producing a certain product. Examples of direct costs for event planners may be anything that needs to be developed or staged for a particular event; these costs will be incurred to produce an event for a client. Building a stage will require lumber, labor, and tools that you may have to purchase. Direct costs can be both fixed and variable. In addition, **indirect costs** are expenses that pertain to the company doing business and not to the product that one is selling or producing. Indirect costs often refer to the real costs of doing business, and can include line items such as overhead, allocations, taxes, or burden (Harvard Business Essentials, 2002). As with direct costs, indirect costs can be both fixed and variable. For instance, the environment in which you work may be important to you and to running a successful business. Having an office space that is roomy with airy conference rooms and offices that feature an abundance of natural light would be an indirect cost you believe is worth supporting. Being able to meet with your clients in a space that is inviting may secure and keep clients; it can also be a place to showcase aspects of your work, and, therefore, is an indirect cost that is beneficial to your company.

Direct costs: *Expenses incurred because of a consequence of producing a good or service and are not related to overhead or indirect costs*

Indirect costs: *Expenses that pertain to the company doing business and not to the product that one is selling or producing*

© Rawpixel.com/Shutterstock.com

Hidden costs are those that occur every day in organizations and thus are typically accepted as normal; they are usually expenses that do not include the purchase price of goods (Idhammar, 2014). Hidden costs can include items such as transportation to an event for which a limousine must be rented; however, some companies do not rent limousines by the hour, but rather have three- or four-hour minimums. Furthermore, while a bride may have a budget for a dress, tailoring for her gown may not be a cost she initially thought to include in a budget. Alterations for some gowns can cost more than anticipated and may not have been allocated in the budget.

Hidden costs: *Costs that occur every day in organizations and are usually expenses that do not normally include the purchase price of goods*

Likewise, charges such as postage for invitations would be a hidden cost when the client chooses a heavier paper stock that warrants more postage.

Revenue is "the amount of money that results from selling products or services to customers" (Harvard Business Essentials, p. 12). Some events, such as a 5K race to raise money for a cause, will require a registration fee for participants; dollars raised from the registration fee will benefit the planning and organization of the event, as well as pay those planning the event and contribute to the cause. Revenue comes from selling tickets or a table to a benefit, or requiring registration fees. These are examples in which revenue can help pay for the event itself. Similarly, event planners earn revenue through the services they offer. When a company decides to hire you to plan an event, you will negotiate and agree upon fees, and your client will know exactly what it will cost to hire you for that function. In that case, the revenue produced goes directly into the cost of doing business and pays your other expenses and the salaries necessary for you to continue operating. Additionally, sometimes revenue comes from other sources: a corporate or private sponsorship, a donation of money, or a partnership with another organization.

If you are working as an entrepreneurial event planner, different fee structures exist for the social and the corporate worlds. Kimball (2015) notes that in the social events industry, most event planners and managers generally charge a fee for what they do, plus a percentage of the vendor fees. Looking at this from an hourly scale, event planners organizing social events can earn up to $75 per hour, along with commissions from vendors. In the corporate planning world, event planners still charge a fee for their services, but on top of that they usually add a 'handling charge' for each item they contract. If, for instance, an event planner purchases giveaways for the client, those items would be marked up by about 15% on the event planning invoice. Some event planners may instead charge a flat fee when the event is large. Generally, those who work in the corporate event planning world bill at a higher rate than social event planners, perhaps up to $150 per hour, plus vendor commissions (Kimball, 2015). To sum up, there are a variety of fee structures that event planners should examine:

TIP

Good clients expect to pay fairly for good value; pay yourself first. Put a realistic hourly rate (fair market value based on your experience, education, preparation, talent, etc.) on your time. This will force you to be conscious about if not disciplined with your time.

— Paul Wolman

1. Flat fee—this is a good choice for packaged events and offers the client a bottom-line price for the full service of the event planner.

2. Hourly rate—this demands that event planners carefully monitor their hours spent on a project, and let the client know their rate per hour, usually about $50.

3. Percentage of expenses—some event planners will charge about 15% of the total cost of an event.

4. Percentage of budget plus expenses—some practiced event planners charge between 15% and 25% of the event budget as a service fee and then add in all their expenses to that total.

Event planners also know that these fee structures are significantly influenced by geographic location, seasonality, and the event planner's own reputation (Kimball, 2015).

All budgets must have goals, and only the client can reveal what those objectives are. Thus, as soon as the budget is determined, the event planner must probe a little more deeply about the event's purpose. The problem is that once the budget is established, most clients will want to move immediately to logistics: venue, dates, guests, for instance (Freeman, 2011). However, your job is to help the client look first at the big picture and set clear goals with no ambiguity. This means asking many deliberate and incisive questions of the client, not just at the initial meeting, but ongoing throughout the process. Does the client hope to conserve money for the event or put on an extravagant affair? Where is the bulk of the money to be dedicated? (Kenis, 1979; Kwiatoski, 2008). In order to best serve your client, you must ask if the budget goals are attainable based upon the amount of money allocated. If they are not, research shows that frustration, inefficiency, and shortcutting may be the results (Carter, 2014; Dunbar, 1971; Hanson, 1966; Kenis, 1979; Polansky, 2016). Budgetary goals should be realistic (Polansky, 2016) yet challenging, or as most corporations have found, a "tight but attainable" (Kenis, 1979, p. 716) budget seems to provide the greatest amount of satisfaction. Most clients will not know how to allocate budget monies specifically, so that is your job: to help the client determine the event's focus and purpose as you plan strategically. Yes, a client might express one goal as just to have fun, but most companies simply cannot afford to do that anymore (Carter, 2014). Your job is to help offer focus to the event.

You might consider beginning with a **preliminary budget**, composed during the stage in which you are gathering information, prices, and vendor bids, knowing that you will make modifications when the information gathering is nearing completion. This budget is a work in progress and represents your initial investigation into a response to the client's vision. Eventually, this preliminary work becomes a **working budget**, which serves as a guide during the remainder of the planning process. The working budget tracks revenues and expenses, and then ultimately tracks net income or losses so that the client can see where the money has been allocated (Greenwell, Danzey-Bussell, & Shonk, 2013). Of course, events have different goals, and these goals will drive the financial philosophy. For instance, if the event is expected to generate a profit, the budget will look different from a break-even event, in which revenues are balanced with profits, or a hosted event, which typically loses money. Event planners must develop a clear understanding of the differences between **net profits** (the actual profit after working expenses not included in the calculation of gross profit have been paid) and **gross profits** (revenue minus the cost of goods sold,

Preliminary budget: *A financial tool composed during the initial planning stage of an event that will be emended as the project gets underway*

Working budget: *A financial tool that grows from the preliminary budget for an event and that becomes more specific and detailed as the project develops*

Net Profits: *The actual profit after working expenses not included in the calculation of gross profit have been paid*

Gross profits: *Revenue minus the cost of goods sold, shown on the income statement*

shown on the income statement) (Goldblatt, 2010). With a profit-driven budget, those involved will want to see a **return on investment (ROI)**—the benefit to the investor resulting from an investment of some resource—and it will be the event planner's job to demonstrate to investors or clients how that can happen.

Everyone has a perception of what is important, whether in the event vision or in determining how much money should be allocated for certain details of an event. Many disagreements can occur over what is determined 'worthy' of one's time, effort, energy, and money. Two clients with the same budget might arrange the budgets differently. For example, one set of clients might spend $5,000 on flowers because they believe exotic arrangements will offer a unique touch, whereas another client might spend $50 on flowers, believing they will die in a couple of days. Thus, event planners must look at the human factors that impact the event's budget, as well as economic influences, financial goals, past events of a similar nature, and the origin of the financial resources (Bowens, 2016; Goldblatt, 2010). In developing a sense of the budget, social exchange theory can help explain the interpersonal aspects of economics.

Social Exchange Theory

Social exchange theory examines human relationships in economic terms. Berger (1985) defines social exchange as a variety of theories that seek to explain the development, maintenance, and decay of social relationships in terms of the balance between the rewards that people can achieve and the costs that they acquire through various social situations. **Rewards** are positive aspects of relationships, whereas **costs** are negative aspects of relationships. To determine if a relationship is worth having, people will subtract its costs from its rewards; therefore, rewards minus costs equals the worth of the relationship (rewards-costs = worth). Relationships that have more rewards than costs are presumed to last, whereas relationships that have greater costs are presumed to cease. Social exchange is a form of social interaction in which participants trade something of importance. What they exchange can range from specific goods or services to information, love, or approval. If a person has control over a resource that another person wants, then that person has power over the other, unless there is an alternative means for obtaining the resource. The resources exchanged offer insight into what is valued (Berger, 1985). For example, you are contracted to arrange a keynote speaker for a large trade show. In brainstorming sessions with the client, several names are suggested, including a local celebrity. Your job is to determine if the cost of securing the celebrity is worth the overall expense. Is the reward of inviting this celebrity worth the added components that come with hiring a high-profile speaker (e.g., security, media, travel, accommodations, and special requests)?

Michael Roloff (1981) states that there are five social exchange approaches that relate to the structure of social exchange theory. These five approaches are as follows: (1) Homans' Operant Psychology Approach (1958); (2) Blau's Economic Approach (1964); (3) Thibaut and Kelly's Theory of Interdependence (1959); (4) Foa and Foa's Resource Theory (1974); and (5) Walster, Berscheid, and Walster's Equity Theory (1973). Each approach offers a perspective on how exchanges promote or devalue rela-

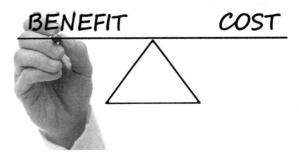

tionships (Roloff, 1981). All five approaches are important to understanding the breadth and depth of the theory; however, this chapter will focus only on Blau's Economic Approach. (For a comprehensive review of each approach, see Roloff, 1981.)

Blau's Economic Approach (1960; 1964; 1968) uses economics as an underlying theoretical base in which people's expectations determine their behavior. This approach focuses on emergent properties of the exchange and also applies principles from the field of economics. Blau describes three types of expectations that will influence a person's decision. The first, general expectations, are rewards that people think are available in various aspects of life. For example, in a marriage a young couple might celebrate their fifth anniversary with a relaxing vacation. The second type, particular expectations, are rewards received from another person. For example, one person might expect an extravagant, rewarding vacation for every anniversary, whereas another couple might celebrate only milestone years. The person from whom the reward was received determines the importance of these rewards. For instance, a handwritten thank-you note from a long-standing client would be more meaningful than a generic thank-you postcard from a vendor. The third, comparative expectations, are rewards received from a relationship and are determined by subtracting the costs of the relationship; thus, the more profitable the rewards, the more committed a person will be to that relationship. For example, a couple who argue about wedding finances (cost) might realize that being with each other (reward) is worth a small argument over the bills. The economic approach posits that social exchange is influenced by the nature of the relationship between people, and that the relationship will develop with various social exchanges between the individuals. The theory also holds that social context influences the exchange and encompasses concepts such as norms and power differences. Blau (1968) believes that the "most important benefits involved in social exchange do not have any material value on which an exact price can be put at all, as exemplified by social approval and respect" (p. 455). In summary, people base their behaviors on the anticipation of rewards however the recipient defines those rewards (Roloff, 1981).

Social exchange theory is a useful framework with wide application to many types of human interactions including interpersonal and organizational exchanges (Huston & Burgess, 1979; Lambe, Wittmann, & Spekman,

© Arina P Habich/Shutterstock.com

2001; Myers, Knox, Palowski, & Ropog, 1999). Even though social exchange theory is concise and economical, there are limitations when it comes to actually testing hypotheses derived from the framework of the theory. One of the major problems is measurement, because it is very difficult to measure rewards, costs, equity, and other important exchange concepts. These terms lack a concrete definition, and researchers must weigh the relative advantages and disadvantages of a global measure, such as how rewarding something is overall. Furthermore, the value of certain resources might change over time, and what people value in relationships differs (Sprecher, 1998). For example, what is rewarding for one person might not be rewarding for another. While planning events, many people will disagree on what is important in terms of actual costs and rewards. A band will usually cost about double the price of a DJ, for instance. Balloons deflate after a day at an outdoor festival and would need to be replaced on day two. A buffet can cut down on food costs, but a seated dinner has a more elegant feel with a higher price tag. Handmade favors can cost less and mean more to your guests, but buying favors takes less time. Is the gift worth spending the extra effort, time, or money? These are the questions you will need to ask your client when determining a budget, but be aware that these budgetary details do not transfer from client to client. Getting to know what is rewarding for your clients will help determine what elements are worth spending extra on to make their event a success.

Client Collaboration

Goal clarity is essential; goals become clear through consistent questions and feedback, all of which have positive effects on managing a budget (Kenis, 1979). To ensure that budget goals remain clear, event planners should encourage clients to connect each budgetary line item with a stated goal (Daks, 2018), so that all of their choices make sense, and money is being appropriated in the right places. Event planners also must establish who has the authority to handle the budget and create budgetary goals (Hanson, 1966). If a budgetary cut or shift is needed, who will make that decision? Is there a team, or is an individual in charge? Because line items in the budget reflect someone's personal choices, the event planner should not presume what decision to make if a cut is needed. "Conscious goals regulate behavior" (Kenis, 1979, p. 709), and thus the client's goals are the foundation for how the budget will operate. Ask clients what their objectives are, and what they want to be the takeaway. Once you know these answers, your task is to meet those goals in the brightest and most thoughtful way (Carter, 2014; Daks, 2018). But it is also important to count in your own value and fees, which can be a tricky proposition. Many novice event planners are hesitant to discuss their fees for fear of offending the client or damaging the beginning of a relationship. However, neglecting this conversation directly impacts the budget, the honesty with which you manage the event, and the relationship you are hoping to develop (Herman & Risser, 2009).

Because budgets are often linked to people's behavior (Milani, 1975), the more people who are involved in the budget construction, the stronger the budget will be. According to Kenis (1979), budgetary participation leads to a better client attitude. Event planners should develop a way to work sensitively with their clients, since talking about money often makes people uncomfortable. People are hesitant to bring up unwelcome news, so establishing specific times to talk about the budget should be a priority. Whether there is a single client or an event team, involving them in decision-making whenever possible

© CandyBox Images/Shutterstock.com

is a good idea. Participation in monetary decision-making improves client attitudes (Milani, 1975), but the event planner needs to establish how much participation is reasonable from the start. Event planners must balance their time getting input with the degree of participation they desire. Efficiency in operation is just as important as budget collaboration, so the level of budgetary detail the event planner asks for is counterbalanced by getting the job done. For instance, if an event planner has a clear concept of an event's food budget as well as the goal of the meal, then the level of decision-making detail is flexible, depending on the client's needs. Hofstede (1967) found that participation in the budget has an enormous effect on client buy-in, so offering clients budget choices whenever possible will help them feel more connected to the event's outcomes. Brownell (1981) also argued for participation in the budget process, for he found that those who had some personal control over the budget were more eager to accept personal responsibility for the outcome of the event.

Clear communication on a regular basis with the client concerning expenditures will lead to a successful relationship and an effective event. Establish from the start who can sign for budgetary expenditures, and limit that number (Waters, 2006). Seek feedback after every budgetary change (Kenis, 1979) and get everything in writing—from the client, from vendors, and from sub-contractors, from anyone who impacts the budget. Thus, the event planner should become familiar with the kind of guest who will actually attend the event (Waters, 2006). The attendees' likes and dislikes, their demographics, as well as their needs, will affect the budget. Communication directly impacts the delegation of the budget and how it must be individually tailored to each client. Communication will also help to avoid budgetary stress and its effects on the client's expectations and flexibility (Collins, 1978). These effects may include negative attitudes, sacrifices in quality, or a budget shortfall, among other things. Consider, for instance, the event planner working with a small company, planning a 25-year anniversary celebration. The planning committee, who expressed a desire to be included in every aspect of the decision-making, established the budget from the start. However, the event planner must make sure that the committee has selected one person to be in charge of all final budgetary decisions. Even though that choice may leave some members of the team feeling dissatisfied, decisions take longer when too many people are involved in the budgetary decisions.

Zero-based budgeting: *A kind of budgeting plan that begins each event with a clean slate*

A certain amount of budget flexibility on your client's part will ease the moments when money becomes an issue. Using **zero-based budgeting**, which requires you to begin each plan with a clean slate, seems to be smarter than using a previous year's budget, since costs change, and the last thing you want to do is make presumptions about any expenses to be incurred (Eisenstodt, 2014). Collins (1978) found that an accurate budget and careful estimates help keep a client flexible. In other words, the less disruption there is to the original plan, the more accommodating clients will be when changes are necessitated. As the action plan is developed, the event planner must align each budgetary item to some particular piece of the plan for expenditures to make sense (Kwiatoski, 2008). When drawing up a budget, it is probably better to err on the side of overestimating what costs will be, since coming in under budget is much more preferable than exceeding the limit (Lawson, 2009). In a much-cited classic study by Simon, Guetzkow, Kometzky, and Tyndall (1954), support for budgets was stronger when the budget was thought to be relatively more accurate, more reasonably attainable, and more controllable. These qualities are well within the domain of the event planner who pays attention to detail, communicates clearly, and looks at the budget daily (Waters, 2006).

TIP

When budgeting, be conservative. It is always tough to ask for more money. It is better to be a hero and spend less than budgeted.

— Sandy Hillman

Clients manage budgeting differently, so no single approach to developing a fiscal relationship with a client will work (Fisher, Frederickson, & Peffer, 2000). Some clients will hold fast to their original conception, while others will find more flexibility in the process. The event planner must understand this aspect of the relationship and find ways to help the client adjust to changing expenses. When cuts in a budget threaten a key element of the plan, people tend to be very careful to look at alternatives (McCaffery, 2003), depending on the importance of that element. Clients may be willing to compromise on smaller issues like linen rentals but want to retain control when it comes to a menu or the guest list. Knowing which items are inflexibly linked to the budget means that the event planner must have thoroughly inventoried each line of the budget and marked its importance.

Asking the client the right questions at different times will also help clarify choices that can be made when the budget needs trimming.

Budget Stress

When times of budget stress arise, the event planner needs to be creative in conserving funds so that the outcomes of the event are affected as little as possible. Of course, being prepared for unexpected expenses is a given, so it is important to keep a spreadsheet that reflects possible overage with a 10% contingency. This spreadsheet tracks incomes and expenditures, and is meticulously accurate and updated daily (Waters, 2006). Remember to use filing terms that are consistent so that nothing is repeated and all terms are searchable. Of course, budgetary technology will not actually solve any budget woes, since decision making still depends on humans making choices (McCaffery, 2003), and there is always room for error in human choice. However, the event planner's job is to minimize those possibilities. Check every invoice that comes in; a surprising number of them are inaccurate or wrong and can be corrected in your favor. A good idea is to look at notes you have taken from past, perhaps similar, events, to find out where costs were conserved. Read your post-event summaries to minimize repeating the same mistakes, and ask for help from all those you consider knowledgeable in the field. Negotiate with every vendor you utilize, asking for discounts, for you will not get them unless you ask (Waters, 2006). There are lots of other ways to save on costs as well: consider sponsorships, when appropriate, as a possible revenue source; use local speakers to save on expensive transportation costs; investigate vendor relationships that might offer you volume discounts. Exercising efforts like these can alleviate some of the stress. Suppose an historic movie theatre is scheduled to host a Hollywood-style movie premiere at its location because the film was shot in the city. Your client expects a red carpet, stanchions, spotlights, and neon signs to showcase the movie event properly, but they are very expensive and exceed the budget. Additionally, tickets to the premiere have sold out, as dignitaries, key actors, producers, the director, and other film aficionados are scheduled to be in attendance. While some members of the general public have obtained tickets to the premiere, others have been told the event is sold out. The owner of the historic theatre has agreed to sell **standing room only** (SRO) tickets to the event to accommodate as many people as the theatre's fire code will allow. In this case, the idea of SRO tickets helps increase profit and makes the event even more desirable, as people may want to attend the event even if they have to stand. SRO tickets have become popular in the world of entertainment and sports because so many people want to be there and not miss out on a big event. Selling SRO tickets offsets the costs of the event and alleviates some of the stress associated with the budget.

© pedrosek/Shutterstock.com

Standing room only (SRO):
A reference to an event where space is at a premium but such popularity will help increase profit and make the event even more desirable

Budgetary risk prevention plan: *A strategy that looks ahead of an event in order to reduce the likelihood or severity of a possible loss*

Another stressor in budget management is risk oversight. Fiscal stress will take its toll on the budget, especially as the number of risks involved escalates (Hildreth & Miller, 1983). These might include costs that are associated with liability, facilities damage, weather conditions, legal compliance, insurance, injury prevention and response, vendor cancellations, sanitation, food hygiene, and a myriad of other unexpected concerns. Just as there should be a plan to manage the entire event, there should also be a plan in place that addresses the risks and risk management associated with the event. Until the first outdoor event has to be quickly moved inside when hail is forecasted, event planners may not realize the importance of planning for every contingency. For larger events, consider creating a team to help manage budgetary risk. Additionally, create objectives that address any possibility for a threat to the event; doing so will bring to your consciousness the possibilities of what may occur as well as associated costs and impact on the budget. A **budgetary risk prevention plan**, a strategy that looks ahead of an event in order to reduce the likelihood or severity of a possible loss, will also reduce anxiety in both the clients and event planners. A contingency fund embedded in the budget for unexpected emergencies is an absolute necessity (Herman & Risser, 2009). There are varieties of budgeting software available that have built-in variables for risks associated with the particular kind of event. Event planners should consult with an accountant in choosing appropriate software for their budget needs.

© Lisa S./Shutterstock.com

Consider some tips for preserving the budget: for example, choose meeting times around lunch rather than dinner when possible, and conserve snacks before and after the meal is served; perhaps present an informal theme for the affair, for such a casual event (like a beach picnic or a western hoedown) will suggest a simpler style of food. And setting up water stations, for instance, rather than serving bottled water, is a cost-cutting measure that might work in your favor as a green choice ("Frugal but classy event planning," 2011), since people perceive friendly environmental options at an event with goodwill (Allen, 2009). Added to this might be a complimentary water bottle with the company logo on it to serve as a favor or takeaway at the event. More and more event planners are re-examining the concept of the open bar, opting for a shorter period or two complimentary coupons for drinks instead, and a premium bar might be replaced by standard beverages. Another idea is to reduce time spent at lunch, and serve dessert not directly after the meal but rather at the afternoon coffee break (Eagle, 2009). Professional trade magazines are replete with cost-conserving measures such as these that might help you think outside the box if the budget needs to be tightened.

Similarly, there are hundreds of free online resources such as meeting space calculators, room planners, free worksheets, timelines, and budget templates that can be accessed and downloaded to help make the responsibility of managing a budget easier. Last-minute budget surprises can wreak havoc with a perfectly planned spreadsheet: entertainment vendors may add in projection costs; menu prices may have risen since you first chose the items; and hotels may charge as much as a 23% catering service fee that covers overhead, gratuities, labor, accounting, and setup. The solution? Lock in catering prices at the first moment decisions are made about the menu (Freeman, 2011), and realize that very few initial statements actually include the tax total, so be prepared when the final invoice arrives with additional charges. Finally, remember that there are numerous miscellaneous costs that often escape notice until they begin to add up: signage, office supplies, paper goods, prizes, gas, postage, and complimentary tickets are some of the forgotten expenses that can make an unforeseen dent in the budget. Adding an extra 20% into the budget for unexpected expenses, including food cost increases and other emergencies, will help balance your projection (Devney, 2001).

As businesses are tightening corporate budgets and cutting back on extras, it would be easy to see how holiday parties, company dinners, or anniversary celebrations might fall under the domain of frivolous spending. However, when companies cut out events, they are eliminating an easy way to thank their employees who actually look forward to getting together for celebratory occasions. People like to feel appreciated, and events that are occasional offer the chance for employees to unwind and see the company's brand more clearly (Huff, 2013). Though the budget may appear to be a rigid and formal document, it actually can be a living, breathing chronicle that can build company morale despite its size and limitations. Thus, the event planner who is working with a tight budget that might be eliminated altogether in the future must be especially cost-conscious while still taking into account the necessity to communicate a sincere and thoughtful message to employees and guests. This balancing act gets easier with practice for event planners who understand the connection between the budget, the brand, and the event's mission.

TIP

When pricing out vendors, ask for a full estimate with the total final price. Venues, caterers and other vendors tend to price things differently, including service charges, delivery charges, etc. You want to know the final price.

— Matt Musgrove

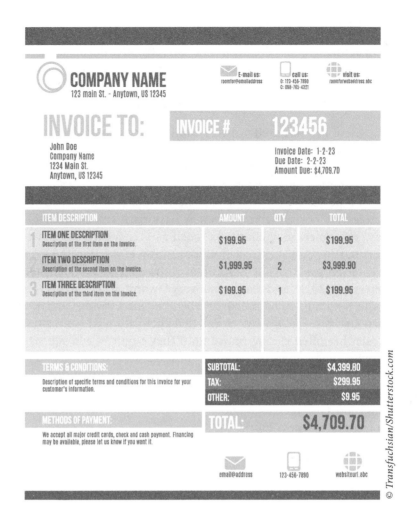

Soliciting feedback—both along the way and at the event's conclusion—is absolutely integral to the event planner's future success. Event planners must ultimately re-evaluate how they could have changed or worked the budget more effectively (Kenis, 1979), and the only way to ascertain this is by asking for evaluation from all those involved. In every phase of event planning and management, you will need to ask questions of those involved and listen carefully to their responses in order to make sure you are meeting their expectations. Do not leave this feedback request until it is too late to do any good. One problem is that guests are sometimes reluctant to give feedback in person or in writing, so you must find another way to encourage them to evaluate the event. An anonymous electronic survey might be the answer, with a response tied to a gift voucher of some sort.

Prepare an assessment checklist that is tagged to the budget-line items for your own use, and at the conclusion of the event, you will want to establish how the actual expenses matched your projected costs for each part of the event. If the numbers are widely disparate, you will need to pinpoint any atypical factors that may help explain the differences. Update the bottom line of the spreadsheet to account for all of your expenses. Next, develop a separate assessment tool for the client's use. Since in the best of all possible worlds, the client has developed a mission statement or a set of goals for the event, the assessment tool can be tied into evaluation of each of these goals. Review the commitments you made to the client at the outset of event planning (Lawson, 2009). How closely did you meet those goals? If not, what prevented you from attaining this commitment? Faulkner (2003) notes that long-term goals (as opposed to an immediate event appraisal) demand a different kind of evaluation. This type of instrument looks at a farther-reaching impact and requires some projection.

© PTstock/Shutterstock.com

Working with a corporate team might make this kind of assessment easier. Once any type of evaluation is completed, the event planner must analyze all the data; in other words, it is not enough to collect and collate it. Depending on the amount of evaluative data gathered, you might consider writing a summary of what you have learned from the information. Events evaluation is still a developing field of research, especially when connected to budget assessment, and more attention will undoubtedly help the event planner focus on improved methods of gathering and analyzing feedback.

The budget is one of the most important communication tools of the event plan. Budgets demand constant oversight, for they reflect not just the client's vision, but also the daily changes in plans that occur as event goals evolve. Clarity in communication will help the client understand the budget process and will enable event planners to deal effectively with all those who impact the budget as well as the additional unexpected variables the event planner may face. Development of an event budget does not need to be an overwhelming challenge if it is approached with organization, deliberation, and creativity. Event planners who are attentive to detail, scrupulous in monitoring their costs, and creative thinkers, as well as those who encourage flexibility in their clients, will be able to find success in budget management.

Key Terms

Budget	Hidden costs	Gross profits	Zero-based budgeting
Fixed costs	Revenue	Return on investment (ROI)	Standing room only (SRO)
Variable costs	Preliminary budget	Social Exchange Theory	Budgetary risk prevention plan
Direct costs	Working budget	Rewards	
Indirect costs	Net profits	Costs	

Discussion Questions

1. Why do you think the budget for an event is often such a point of contention? What is there about the finances of an event that can pit parties against each other? What is the role of the event planner in the battle?

2. Often a key factor in the budget crunch are the hidden costs that arise as the event planning begins. These hidden charges can be a real blow to the budget. How might some of these unknown charges crop up? Brainstorm with a small group and create a plan to avoid having these costs mount up.

3. Why might zero-based budgeting be a good idea? On the other hand, what disadvantages might arise from this kind of budget planning?

Activity

A budget is actually a simple (or more complex) spending plan. In a group, construct a budget for the following scenario.

a. You want to buy a used car within a year, paid for out of your own (not your parents') funds, to take you to events and help transport items needed for the event. The car will cost $3200. Your parents will pay for your automobile insurance for the first year as long as there are no accidents or traffic tickets.

b. Out of your part-time job as an event planning assistant (which pays $12/hour and you work 12 hours a week), you must also pay for your entertainment expenses—dates, for instance. If you continue to work at this rate for a year, how much should you budget for your own weekly spending in order to buy the car a year from now?

c. What might sabotage this plan? What other choices do you have? What else should you plan for?

References

Allen, J. (2009). *Event planning: The ultimate guide to successful meetings, corporate events, fundraising galas, conferences, conventions, incentives and other special events.* Hoboken, NJ: John Wiley & Sons.

Bates, B. N. (2014). An affair to remember: Corporate event planning tips from a taste of Excellence. *Smart Business Akron, 24,* 22–25.

Berger, C. R. (1985). Social power and interpersonal communication. In M. L. Knapp & G. R. Miller (Eds.), *Handbook of interpersonal communication* (pp.439–499). Beverly Hills, CA: Sage.

Blau, P. (1960). A theory of social integration. *The American Journal of Sociology, 65,* 545–556.

————. (1964). *Exchange and power in social life.* New York: Wiley.

————. (1968). Interaction: Social exchange. *International Encyclopedia of the Social Sciences, 7,* 452–458.

Bowden, G., Allen, J., O'Toole, W., Harris, R., & McDonnell, I. (2011). *Events management* (3rd ed.). Oxford: Elsevier Butterworth-Heinemann.

Bowens, B. (2016). 6 Event planning myths. *Successful Meetings, 12*, 14.

Brownell, P. (1981). Participation in budgeting, locus of control and organizational effectiveness. *The Accounting Review, 1,* 844–860.

Carter, J. (2014). Event must prove its worth. *Conference and Incentive Travel, 9,* 18–19.

Collins, F. (1978). The interaction of budget characteristics and personality variables with budgetary response attitudes. *The Accounting Review, 53,* 324–335.

Daks, M. (2018). Big ideas, small budget: Marketing on a shoestring. *njbiz* 7/23/2018, (31) 30, 20–21.

Devney, D. C. (2001). *Organizing special events and conferences: A practical guide for busy volunteers and staff.* Sarasota, FL: Pineapple Press.

Dunbar, R. L. M. (1971). Budgeting for control. *Administrative Science Quarterly, 16,* 88–96.

Eagle, S. (2009). Twenty ways to save money on your next event. *Canadian Business, 82,* 5–7.

Eisenstodt, J. (2014). Planning your first big event? Here's what you need to know. *Administrative Professional Today, 40,* 3.

Event Marketing 2019: Benchmarks and trends report, 2019. New York: Bizzabo.

Faulkner, H. W. (2003). Evaluating the tourism impact of hallmark events. In L. Fredline, L. Jago, & C. Cooper (Eds.). *Progressing tourism research.* (pp. 93–113). Tonawanda, NY: Channel View.

Fisher, J. G., Frederickson, J. R., & Peffer, S. A. (2000). Budgeting: An experimental investigation of the effects of negotiation. *The Accounting Review, 75,* 93–114.

Foa, U. G., & Foa, E. B. (1974). *Societal structures of the mind.* Springfield IL: Thomas.

Freeman, L. (2011). Event planning tips: Ensuring attendees return next year. *Alaska Business Monthly, 27,* 28–31.

Frugal but classy event planning (2011). *Administrative Professional, 37,* 5.

Goldblatt, J. (2010). *Special Events: A new generation and the next frontier.* New York: Wiley.

Greenwell, T. C., Danzey-Bussell, L. A., & Shonk, D. (2013). *Managing sport events.* Champaign, IL: Human Kinetics, 2013.

Hanson, E. I. (1966). The budgetary control function. *The Accounting Review, 41,* 239–243.

Harvard Business Essentials (2002). *Finance for managers.* Boston, MA: Harvard Business School Publishing Corporation.

Herman, M. L., & Risser, J. (2009). *Managing special event risks: Ten steps to safety* (2nd ed.). Leesburg, VA: Nonprofit Risk Management Center.

Hildreth, W. B., & Miller, G. J. (1983). Risk management and pension systems. In J. Rabin, & T. D. Lynch, (Eds.). *Handbook on public budgeting and financial management.* (pp. 457–492) New York: Marcel Dekker, Inc.

Hofstede, G. H. (1967). *The game of budget control.* The Netherlands: Koninklijke Van Gorkum and Company.

Homans, G. C. (1958). Social behavior as exchange. *American Journal of Sociology, 63,* 597–606.

Huff, J. (2013, September). *Idaho Business Review's corporate guide to event planning: It's not too early to book your company's holiday event.* Retrieved from http://idahobusinessreview. com/2013/09/10/idaho-business-reviews-corporate-guide-to-event-planning-its-not-too -early-to-book-your-companys-holiday-event/

Huston, T. L., & Burgess, R. L. (1979). Social exchange in developing relationships: An overview. In T. L. Huston, & R. L. Burgess *Social exchange in developing relationships* (pp. 3–28). New York: Academic Press.

Idhammar, C. (2014). Visible and "hidden" costs. *PPI: Pulp & Paper International, 56,* 10.

Kenis, I. (1979). Effects of budgetary goal characteristics on managerial attitudes and performance. *The Accounting Review, 54,* 707–721.

Kilkenny, S. (2011). *The complete guide to successful event planning.* Ocala, FL: Atlantic.

Kimball, C. (2015). *Start your own event planning business,* (4th ed.). Berkeley, CA: Entrepreneur Press.

Kwiatoski, D. (2008). Planning a great event begins with having a clear "mission" …and having a good plan. *Hudson Valley Business Journal, 19,* 26.

Lambe, C. J., Wittmann, C. M., & Spekman, R. E. (2001). Social exchange theory and research on business-to-business relational exchange. *Journal of Business-To-Business Marketing, 8,* 1–37.

Lawson, H. (2009). A step-by-step program for planning special company events. *Vision Monday, 23,* 70.

Marquis, A. (2014). *Definition and example of step & fixed costs.* Retrieved from http://smallbusi-ness.chron.com/definition-example-step-fixed-costs-24318.html.

Masterman, G. (2014). *Strategic sports event management,* (3rd ed.). London: Routledge.

McCaffery, J. (2003). Confidence, competence, and clientele: Norm maintenance in budget prepa-ration. In A. Khan and W. Bartley Hildreth (Eds.). *Case studies in public budgeting and financial management.* (pp. 49–64). New York: Marcel Dekker.

Milani, K. (1975). The relationship of participation in budget-setting to industrial supervisor per-formance and attitudes: A field study. *The Accounting Review, 50,* 274–284.

Muller, M. (2015) The Mega-Event Syndrome: Why so much goes wrong in mega-event planning and what to do about it. *Journal of the American Planning Association 81* (1) , pp. 6–17.

Myers, S. A., Knox, R. L., Palowski, D. R., & Ropog, B. L. (1999). Perceived communication openness and functional communication skills among organizational peers. *Communication Reports, 12,* 71–83.

Polansky, S. (2018). What to do when you're expected to plan an event. *Wyoming Business Report. August 2018 Supplement Event Planning Guide, 8.*

Roloff, M. E. (1981). Five approaches: Social exchange theory. In F. G. Kline, & S. H. Evans (Eds.). *Interpersonal communications: The social exchange approach* (pp. 33–59). Beverly Hills, CA: Sage.

Simon, H. A., Guetzkow, H., Kometzky, G., & Tyndall, G. (1954). *Centralization vs. decentralization in organizing the controller's department.* Rochester, New York: Scholars Book Company.

Sprecher, S. (1998). Social exchange theories and sexuality. *Journal of Sex Research, 35,* 32–44.

Thibaut, J. W., & Kelley, H. H. (1959). *The social psychology of groups.* New York: Wiley.

Van der Wagen, L. & White, L. (2018). Event management: For tourism, cultural, business and sporting events. 5th ed. Melbourne, Victoria Australia: Cengage.

Walster, E., Berscheid, E., & Walster, G. W. (1973). New directions in equity research. *Journal of personality and social psychology, 66,* 1034–1048.

Waters, K. (2006). A practical step-by-step guide to organizing successful events. *Manager, 56,* 17–19.

Chapter 8

NEGOTIATION AND CONTRACTS: THE ETHICAL SIDE OF EVENT PLANNING

© Goran Bogicevic/Shutterstock.com

The business of event planning demands not just creativity and an understanding of fiscal matters, but also a knowledge of when and how to negotiate to achieve a need or a want as well an awareness of how contracts figure in event planning. Event planners must also have a sense of ethics that serves as their moral compass in negotiating agreements and writing contracts. These qualities are interdependent and rely on a thorough understanding of communication in addition to an approach to business crafted on honesty, consistency, and clarity. Successful event planners must also develop a writing skill set that equals their abilities in any other area, and they must be able to speak clearly in every human interaction they face, for each one is a form of negotiation. Whether it is a clear proposal, an unambiguous contract, or a negotiation with a significant commodity at stake, communication is an essential part of the event planner's job. Every one of these items requires exhaustive preparation and research in order to bring people together, connecting time zones and linking cultures (Canavor, 2011). The goals of the endeavor must be well-defined before negotiation or contract writing begins, since successful planning will influence the relationships that are to be built in the process (Fisher, Ury, & Patton, 2011). Above all, negotiating and contracting take time, effort, and optimism for success.

When you have finished reading this chapter, you will be able to

- describe a variety of methods that make negotiations successful;
- define the elements of a contract and indicate their importance;
- list the kinds of occurrences that can damage a contract;
- explain the ethical dilemmas that may occur in any negotiation.

Listening and Negotiating as Important Communication Tools in Event Planning

Lynn H. Turner, Ph.D., Professor, Communication Studies, Marquette University

In 2010, as the First Vice President of the National Communication Association (NCA), I planned the annual convention. It was held in San Francisco, and I began the process thinking about various ways that I could make the convention hospitable and welcoming. I was interested in offering experiences that would appeal to the diverse audience who attends NCA (from full professors interested in research, to undergraduate students just beginning to think about a career in communication, to communication practitioners). I was excited about the opportunities offered in San Francisco, and I was looking forward to providing our attendees with a positive experience.

However, my planning took a turn almost immediately when we discovered 10 months prior to the convention that our hotel site (along with most of the major hotels in San Francisco) was the subject of an ongoing labor dispute. The hotel workers there had been working without a contract for some time, and were organized by a group called UNITE-HERE. As of January 2010, UNITE-HERE had sponsored pickets at San Francisco hotels and was planning three-day rolling strikes. When I was at the hotel in late January for a planning meeting, I witnessed a sing-in in the hotel lobby ("Bad hotel" to the tune of Lady Gaga's song "Bad Romance," which was popular at the time). The dispute was not expected to be over by the time of our convention in November.

Almost immediately planning took on elements of negotiation—not with UNITE-HERE, but with NCA members and potential convention attendees who were in sympathy with the workers' plight and were concerned about attending a convention in a hotel that (a) was accused of exploiting its workers, and (b) could face disruptive activities and interrupted services during their visit. This situation was contextualized by the fact that two years earlier our convention in San Diego had been rife with dissention. Many members disapproved of the labor practices at our hotel site, and were also concerned that the owner of the hotel had provided monetary support for a ballot initiative that banned gay marriage in California. As a result, some people refused to attend that convention, and others met at alternative hotels in the area, refusing to enter the convention site. This convention was ultimately successful for most attendees, but left a reservoir of ill-will across the association that made me realize we had to be more proactive in dealing with the labor dispute in 2010.

We did the following things to navigate this planning challenge:

- Convened our site selection committee and increased its membership to include people holding a variety of positions on this topic and other topics about sites. We actively solicited their input and sought their support in speaking to those they represented.

- Communicated clearly with members through our association's online newsletter, as well as individually. I made a concerted effort, as did our Executive Director, Nancy Kidd, and our President, Dawn Braithwaite, to seek information, listen, be open to a diversity of opinions, and clearly explain our situation (See **Appendix B**). Some members wanted us to move the convention, and it was important to explain the financial implications of that choice.

- Communicated with other associations that are like NCA, and created a document for dealing with hotel labor issues that they have used as a model (See **Appendix C**).

- Provided alternate venues for those who wanted to attend the convention but not cross a picket line if there had been a strike called. We scheduled an Urban Communication Foundation Spotlight panel at the UNITE-HERE offices.

- Offered some programming about communication and labor disputes and about discourse that honors diversity and community.

- Published a tip sheet for members suggesting a variety of ways to support workers other than boycotting the hotel.

- Continuously published the following message:
  We understand that this is a difficult situation and the choices you are making are complicated. We want you to know that we are listening to your feedback and working hard to respond with what we believe are the most responsible and flexible options for the association and its members. We also understand that the workers and the hotel's management face difficult and complicated choices, and we are mindful that everyone's decisions reflect a delicate balancing act among competing concerns. Reprinted with permission from the National Communication Association. All rights reserved

Case study contributed by Lynn H. Turner. Copyright © Kendall Hunt Publishing Company.

When you have finished reading this chapter, revisit the case study and respond to the following question:

If you were planning this conference, how would you negotiate the situation with attendees' philosophical differences, the position of the workers union, and your own personal principles?

Negotiation

Negotiation: *Communication process in which people work to reach an agreement*

TIP

Utilize good negotiation strategies (such as advocated in *Getting to yes*), pause before speaking, keep the discussion on topic, and look at conflict with fresh eyes.

— Lynn Turner

Even though people negotiate every day, event planners in particular need to understand the art of **negotiation**, a communication process in which people work to reach an agreement. Event planners will be negotiating all aspects of the event, including items such as the venue, food, beverages, flowers, paper products, lighting, guest rooms, and much more. Negotiating a venue might be a logical first step, but it is important to realize that this is not always the case. Your client will determine what is most important and needed for the event. If the event requires a production team that needs specific lighting and sound, they might need to be available before a venue is chosen. Having a technology team available during the negotiation might actually be beneficial for all parties involved. Negotiations should not occur in a bubble, and having advice from experts in the specific fields can make an event successful (Goldberg, 2018). A common misconception about negotiation is that you are constantly trying to win a battle, yet the battle metaphor is not helpful because it views the negotiation as a win/lose situation. Putnam (2010) believes that negotiation offers an opportunity to generate creative options and discover new insights that you might not have found possible if you only view the process as a win/lose situation. Hopefully, you will do your best to negotiate an ideal price, but the art of negotiation is not about creating enemies. The process is about creating and maintaining clients who will work with you over your event planning career.

© Raywoo/Shutterstock.com

Fisher, Ury, and Patton's (2011) seminal work, *Getting to yes: Negotiating agreement without giving in*, offers three criteria to judge a negotiation fairly. Negotiations should (1) Produce a wise agreement if an agreement is possible. Both parties should be willing to do their research and decide what makes the best sense for everyone involved. If a client insists on a particular venue, for instance, your options for negotiating down the price might be limited. In some situations, such as if a venue is booked every Saturday in the summer for weddings, there will be no negotiation on price—it is what it is, without any adjustments. A well-researched event planner would know to suggest a date on a Friday or Sunday when the price might drop significantly due to the venue wanting to sell the space. (2) Be efficient. Figure out what is needed to create an event as opposed to what is wanted at the event. Knowing your client's needs and wants will help you create objectives that can guide you through the negotiation process. Receiving a discount at the hotel restaurant is a nice added bonus, but it should not make or break your contract with a hotel. (3) Improve on—or at least do not damage—the relationship with others. As an event planner, you never want to burn bridges with potential clients or vendors. Sales managers will remember how you treated them during the process and can damage your career if they are not willing to work with you in the future. These three principles are good guidelines to remember as you engage in various negotiations. Each negotiation will have its own unique characteristics, but the goal for each outcome is for all parties to feel satisfied at the end.

Negotiations should not be viewed as competitions where you always have to win, but rather as relationships in which both parties will sometimes need to give and take to move forward in the relationship (Cohen, 2002). Shapiro, Jankowski, and Dale (2001) state, "The best way to get what you want is to help the other side get what they want" (p. 3). During a negotiation, you do not have to be vicious to get results. Being mean only makes people hesitate to work with you in the future. A prime characteristic of an event planner is the desire to build relationships, not destroy them. Building rapport with others in the negotiation helps the process  move forward with success (Matusitz, 2013). Consider the event as a continual process of social interaction in which all parties constantly negotiate their own self-interest and the obligations of the moment (Ziakis, 2013). Imagine a scenario in which the event planner and the client would like the venue to be a little more accommodating in terms of space and price. Everyone involved has an interest in the outcome, and a balanced distribution of results would provide all parties with more than they had at the start. The venue does not want to lose the client; the event planner wants to demonstrate expertise and professionalism; and the client wants to preserve the budget as much as possible. Negotiating through this conversation demands research, patience, leadership, and careful listening on the part of all, particularly the event planner, who will usually lead the negotiation.

Tim Hindle (1998), founder of Working Words, a business communication consulting firm, states, "The art of negotiation is based on attempting to reconcile what constitutes a good result for you with what constitutes a good result for the other party" (p. 6). His book on negotiating skills, along with Benoiel and Hua (2009), both in the *DK Essential Managers* volume, are useful references for understanding the negotiation process. Hindle (1998) believes that negotiation is a skill anyone can learn. Additionally, he writes that the essential skills for a successful negotiation include five abilities:

1. the ability to define a range of objectives, yet be flexible about some of them;
2. the capacity to explore the possibilities of a wide range of options;
3. the power to prepare well;
4. the ability to engage in interactive competence, listen to and question other parties;
5. the capacity to prioritize clearly (p. 7).

These five characteristics will help you find common ground in the negotiation process, creating a successful outcome. In application to the role of the event planner, these abilities demand that event professionals prepare well before talking with vendors or sales managers and that they know the client's bottom line. Scripting a **negotiation storyboard** ahead of time will allow the event planner to foresee the kinds of challenges that may arise during any discussion. In many negotiation situations, rehearsal through storyboarding is commonplace and necessary (Cobb, Laws, & Sluzki, 2014).

Another key factor in negotiation is to be prepared, knowing what to expect during the negotiation. The more you know, the more power you will have to negotiate (Shapiro & Jordan, 2008). All event planners need to work on their research expertise to enhance their negotiation skills. In the early stages of your career, you will have to spend hours trying to ascertain the best price for the best product at a particular time of year, for instance. This is a tedious task, but it will provide invaluable advantages for all negotiations. For example, if you do not know the average cost of roses in the month of February, you will be missing the skills needed to discuss flower prices. How much can an expensive venue drop its price to host a small Friday wedding in January, but still make a profit from the event? What is the cost of ordering a larger number of monogrammed table napkins that your client could use for both appetizers and dessert? Answers to these questions are needed for your negotiation. The more you know, the better a negotiator you will become, and the more you negotiate, the more confident you will become at getting the best results for you and your client. Furthermore, event planners must thoroughly understand themselves so that they can pinpoint the qualities within that might be obstacles to successful negotiations (O'Brien, 2013). The desire to be the winner at any cost, an overabundance of pride, an inability to listen well, or susceptibility to flattery might all prevent the event planner from arriving at an amenable solution.

In the Business Insider of the *Houston Chronicle*, Feloni (2014) discusses the four most common negotiation mistakes. The first mistake is not listening. Those who do not listen cannot learn what the other side is asking. Great negotiators listen well in order to gain knowledge and then use this information for their benefit. The second mistake is going straight to the business aspect of the negotiations. Many negotiations are accentuated with various tensions, but engaging in non-business conversation or cordial chat at the outset can build trust and ease the tension in a negotiation. The third mistake is going into a negotiation without a clear sense of what is wanted in the outcome. Negotiators need to determine what the goals of the negotiation are—knowing exactly what they want will help them achieve their ideal results. The last common mistake comes from not having a best alternative prepared. Working from Fisher, Ury, and Patton's (2011) **BATNA** (Best Alternative to a Negotiated Agreement) strategy that articulates a fallback plan is indispensable in all negotiations. Event planners do not always get what they want, but having a backup plan allows them to walk away feeling satisfied.

As an event planner, your negotiation skills will constantly be put to the test, especially when you negotiate contracts. As you negotiate various elements of a contract, realize that you will usually be working with a sales team. Do not be intimidated by them. Yes, they are usually expert negotiators, but with practice, you will become good at preparing for and knowing how to navigate the negotiation. While others might have a dominant position in the negotiation, and the event planner might lack confidence at the start, researching sales techniques is one method that might strengthen the event planner's poise and self-assurance during the negotiation process. One tip is not to disclose your clients' budget up front. Consider a variety of fiscal scenarios and get multiple proposals so you can compare

© STILLFX/Shutterstock.com

prices (O'Brien, 2013). By doing this, you will be able to realize what is realistic for a budget. For instance, the cost of an early morning meeting featuring a smoothie bar including seasonal fruit may vary in price depending on the time of year your client hosts the meeting. The more proposals you get, the better prepared you will be in a negotiation. The company that charges the most to begin with might end up charging you the least if you can show them less expensive competitor rates. Use your research skills to find the best deals, and then be creative. For example, if a venue will not lower the cost of rooms, the sales team might be able to give you an overall discount if your final budget exceeds a certain dollar amount in catering, saving you more money in the long run. Think about your event as a large puzzle in which you have to negotiate each piece into the correct spot, creating the final product. Each puzzle piece or contract is important in producing the perfect event.

Contracts

Contracts are a very daunting process even to the seasoned professional (Stewart, 2007). Writing a successful proposal requires asking the right questions and actively listening to a client's answers before composition begins. Not only does this kind of writing demand a clear focus, but it also asks that the writer be attentive to details and forward-thinking in terms of services offered. Composing a legally binding contract requires a level of expertise, so it may be worthwhile to turn to an expert in the area (Brown, 2009). Interim emails, letters, and even short notes all need your close attention so that there are no points in time when communication breaks down. Whatever the document, though, you must read and reread it and craft it to address its purpose with clarity and transparency.

© de-focus/Shutterstock.com

Contract: *An agreement that stipulates what is expected of all parties and notes what will occur should a difficulty arise*

TIP

Establish multiple channels for those involved in the planning process to connect with one another. In addition to exchanging email information, share cell phone numbers so text messages can be sent in situations that require timely feedback.

—Candice
Thomas-Maddox

Clarity, applied to contracts, will produce good documents that ultimately protect all parties involved in an event. The **contract**, an agreement that stipulates what is expected of all parties and notes what will occur should a difficulty arise, is one of the first documents that initiates a relationship between client and event planner. The contract can help to address some challenging questions before problems can occur, and it serves to define the relationship from the beginning. Thus, it is imperative that the contract is fair to both parties and becomes a document of cooperation. One job of the event planner is to help the client understand any complicated clauses in a vendor's contract, for instance, clarifying each point and notation for transparency (Ernst & Young, Catherwood, & Van Kirk, 1992). In the ideal contract, of course, everything is clearly stated and each detail unambiguous. Certainly, it goes without saying that all parties involved must read and understand the entire document before signing (Kilkenny, 2011), paying special attention to the details. Be aware of any language that is at all equivocal. Are the names spelled correctly? Are the dates correct? Has the venue written down the same time that your contract states (Matthews, 2008)?

How easy it would be to begin working for a client without an actual signed contract. However, it is important that the event planner not perform any work until a signed contract is in hand. Good event planners spend time perusing a number of contract templates before settling on one that works in a variety of circumstances. They must restrain themselves from developing a working relationship with possible clients until that contract is satisfactorily submitted (See **Appendix D** for sample contract). Once a client has decided to work with you, you need to cement the relationship by sending a contract within a few days for signing (Ernst & Young, Catherwood, & Van Kirk, 1992). After the signed contract has been returned, the event planner can begin to develop strategies for the event.

Planners should realize that often there is not just one contract; there can be several, and sometimes these documents must be altered before the event is completed. At each change, whether proposed by the event planner or by the client, all parties must initial the document, and within a short period of time, the event planner should resubmit a newer version of the contract with the changes to the client for re-signing. At each juncture, including the first signing, you must include a date by which the client should sign and return two copies of the contract. Send copies of the contract through the mail for signatures, including a self-addressed stamped envelope for return. Sometimes event planners use email or programs that allow electronic signatures for contract return; if this is the case, a paper copy of each contract version must be kept on file for reference. Remember that all items on the contract are open to discussion until both you and your client have signed and agreed to the contract's terms and conditions. Every time a signature is affixed to a version of the contract, make sure there is a date accompanying the signature, and be certain that whoever has signed actually has the authority to do so. Generally, the person who signs checks to pay for your services should be the one to sign the contract. Finally, no parties should sign any contract if there is something in it with which they do not agree, in the hopes of negotiating that clause later (Matthews, 2008). Once the contract is signed, there is no guarantee that future changes can be made. After the contract is signed, the best event planners write down all of the applicable dates on a master calendar, usually color coding them according to the event planner's system (Kilkenny, 2011).

What are some other writing tips for a well-designed contract? The contract—whether it is your own or a vendor's—should include a clause in it stating that any fees not spelled out in the contract are not applicable. This will prevent a vendor, for instance, from assessing additional fees post-event. In the contract, be sure to clearly specify all dates and times (not 'three weeks before the event'). Once a contract is ready to be signed, make sure you review it with your sales staff as well as an attorney (Stewart, 2007). They are approaching the contractual relationship differently from you and may be able to see items that deserve more consideration. Because contractual laws vary from state to state, an attorney's opinion of the contract is helpful (Kimball & the Staff of Entrepreneur Media, 2015). If you are signing vendor contracts, remember that you can take a little time before you sign just to be certain that the agreement meets your needs and the needs of your client. In some cases, both you and your client may need to sign the contract (Kilkenny, 2011). If your producers or vendors have their own separate contract for you to sign, read it, compare it to your own version, and make certain there are no conflicting clauses. Furthermore, if there are differences from your preferences, be ready to negotiate the sections with which you do not agree. For example, hotels in New York City can end up charging over $7.70 for one cup of coffee after all of the fees are included (Stewart, 2007). A coffee break might not be cost-effective if it is not bundled with a food package, but it does not hurt to ask if morning coffee can be provided if the food and beverage budget exceeds a certain dollar figure. Often, before an event planner actually signs a contract with a vendor, such as a band or a photographer, the planner may require a presentation or portfolio. This portfolio will allow you to see the full spectrum of the vendor's work before signing on the dotted line (Ernst & Young, Catherwood, & Van Kirk, 1992).

Event planners often want to visit a site with their clients, but before that happens, contact the site manager and ask to see a copy of the standard contract ahead of time. That way, as you are visiting the site, you can be reviewing and amending the contract as needed. As you begin negotiations with the site or the venue, you must be certain that you are talking to a member of the staff who is authorized to make the decisions you need. Promises are easy to make when a large contract hangs in the balance, so do not be swayed by easy guarantees. Get them in writing on the actual contract.

© Imilian/Shutterstock.com

When building and keeping strong relationships with venue staffs, it is also acceptable to let them know that they are only one of several venues in the running with your client. A little competition is a good thing, though you do not want to manipulate or deceive competing site managers. Be direct and honest during your site search so that you can maintain positive relationships (Kilkenny, 2011).

What should a contract with a client include? There are several good templates available through the Internet, but in general, here are some minimal areas of consideration:

- the date of the contract;
- the date and time of the event;
- the name of the client or clients;
- signatures of all clients;
- contact information for clients: address, telephone numbers, email, signature authority;
- your fees, the first deposit, and a payment schedule;
- conditions and restrictions;
- detailed description of your services;
- contract terms, including liability and legal issues;
- your cancellation policy;
- 'Act of God' clause (Force Majeure/weather/etc.);
- termination conditions.

Rider: *A condition added to a contract that has already been signed*

In the best of all worlds, a solid contract enables events to run smoothly with no significant challenges. However, event planners must be prepared for any circumstances that compromise the contract. Once the contract has been written and signed by all parties, changes can also be made through the inclusion of a **rider**, a condition or clause added to a contract after it has been signed, and all signers must further agree to its stipulations (Silver, 2009). The contract between the event planner and the client is the beginning of the legal relationship between the two parties. Event planners need to be familiar with a variety of legal documents, including the following:

- Change orders
- Contracts
- Contract riders
- Confidentiality agreements
- Employer agreements
- Engagement agreements
- Invoices

- Leases
- Licensing agreements
- Proposals
- Purchase agreements
- Purchase orders
- Sponsorship agreements
- Work orders
  (Silvers, 2009, p. 60).

Additionally, an **indemnification** (or '**Hold Harmless**') **clause** in a contract protects one party from liability (Silvers, 2009). For example, if there is an event involving alcohol service, the event planner should include a Hold Harmless clause in the contract with the alcohol service vendor to ensure that the event planner cannot be held responsible for improper or illegal service. Contract plans must include contingencies for what to do if the client drops out or if an event is cancelled; other considerations include issues of security and protection, control of the venue, and breach of contract (Ernst & Young, Catherwood, & Van Kirk, 1992). **Breach of contract** occurs when one of the contract signers fails to uphold his or her part of the agreement (e.g., a check does not arrive on time, thus preventing the florist to be paid, who cancels the order); when one party does something against the intent of the contract (e.g., the florist substitutes yellow flowers when red flowers are not available); or when one of the parties refuses to perform what the contract stipulates (e.g., the band members decide they want a raised stage 12" high, and the stage at the venue is not high enough). What can be done about a breach—particularly when it is close to the event or even on the day of the event? Event planners can suffer extraordinary setbacks when breaches of contract occur and must rely on their communication skills to talk through uncomfortable situations in times of heightened anxiety and pressure. They must be direct and firm about the terms of the contract but stay cogent and forward-thinking until the event is over, looking quickly for alternatives or other solutions to the immediate problem. Some event planners feel comfortable enlisting the mediation of a neutral third party who might be able to discover a solution that is amenable to all parties. Staying in touch with all contract signees and making sure each contract is clear and comprehensible might help to prevent some breaches of contract, and of course, all planners need to learn from each episode and document concerns for the record. Hopefully, a clear contract spells out the conditions that are put into place should a breach occur (Matthews, 2008).

A **Force Majeure** or 'chance occurrence' clause can be written into a contract that substantially frees both parties from obligation when an extraordinary circumstance beyond their control, such as a war, strike, riot, crime, or an act of God (e.g., a hurricane, flood, or earthquake), prevents one or both parties from fulfilling their obligations under the contract. In a modern age of public challenges and threats, these kinds of clauses should be very clear in naming those who can actually define what constitutes the unanticipated and inescapable incidents that would cause cancellation of an event. The planner should be able to participate in the decision and the mediation regarding compensation (Kilkenny, 2011). Not all contractual signers will be agreeable to including a Force Majeure clause, so event planners who believe that this kind of clause is necessary will need to negotiate it into the contract through sound reasoning. Obviously, insurance for any catastrophe is necessary, yet may require negotiation skills for success. Investigating the wide range of insurance types is crucial for risk management.

Indemnification (Hold Harmless) clause. *A clause written into a contract that secures someone against any legal responsibility for his or her actions*

Breach of contract: *An occurrence in which one of the contract signers fails to uphold his or her part of the agreement*

TIP

Have a lawyer review your contracts before signing, if possible. The Force Majeure clause describes what happens when events occur beyond control. If a company is planning an event in Washington, D.C. at the same time that anthrax is found in a federal building, the Force Majeure clause might protect the company from forfeiting its deposit and fees already paid.

— Jeanne Persuit

© Kalinovskiy/Shutterstock.com

Force Majeure: *A chance occurrence beyond the control of the contractual parties that prevents one or both of them from fulfilling their obligations under the contract*

Ethics

Ethics applies to many areas of event planning including, but not limited to, contracts and negotiation, donated items with monetary value, beverage services, and collaborative programming (Burnham, 2012; McGarry, 2015). An ethical issue is described as something "one can raise a question about … [whether it] is right or wrong" (Neher & Sanden, 2007, p. 3). Moreover, **ethical issues** occur when behavior has a significant impact on others, and when these behaviors involve a conscious choice that can be judged by standards of right and wrong (Johannesen, Valde, & Whedbee, 2008). Jaksa and Pritchard (1988) believe that "ethics might be viewed as an umbrella term that refers to the study of a vast range of practical concerns that, although familiar to us, nevertheless are often not clearly understood and are often subjected to much controversy" (p. 4). The controversial component in ethics occurs when people do not understand why something is considered right or wrong. As an event planner, you will be constantly testing your ethics (Mancuso, 2008). Knowing where you stand on ethical issues will prepare you to engage in appropriate and well-considered responses to various ethical questions. For example, questions might arise about the appropriateness of accepting gifts. Do you accept a free weekend at a luxurious resort because you used the venue for one of your client's corporate retreats? Do you always refer your clients to a specific restaurant because you know you will receive complimentary dinners for all events you book? Other questions might focus on hiring vendors for specific client needs. Do you hire your friends at a professional photographer's rate when you know that they are not professionals? These are just a few of the endless possibilities of ethical questions that can occur on the job.

Ethical issues: *Problems that center on behaviors involving a conscious choice that can be judged by standards of right and wrong*

© Sarawut Aiemsinsuk/Shutterstock.com

No matter how one defines ethics, the key feature is that an understanding of ethics is needed in any profession, but especially in a career such as event planning where constant communication can create ethical issues. Questions of right or wrong, fair or unfair, caring or uncaring, good or bad, and responsible or irresponsible all stem from communication practices (Jaksa & Prichard, 1988). Communication is vital when thinking about ethics (Cooper, 2002). Martha Cooper (2002) argues that "communication is a means of ethical action, necessitated by the fact that power is embedded in all interactions" (p. 300). This approach recognizes that because power is inevitable in decision making, there must be an accompanying ethical impulse at the heart of making choices. Power implies responsibility (Arnett, 1987). As an event planner, you have the power and the responsibility to make choices that are beneficial to you and your clients without doing harm. People have not only a right to communicate, but an ethical responsibility in the process. The potential for ethical issues to arise is inherent in any instance of communication between people (Anderson, 2000; Johannesen, Valde, & Whedbee, 2008). Communication ethics focuses on how people communicate with others responsibly.

Communication ethics focuses on questions of practical concerns about how people should live their lives in relationship to others. **Communication ethics** is defined as "the philosophy of communication brought into engaged communicative application in the marketplace of ideas" (Arnett, Fritz, & Bell, 2009, p. 32). Communication ethics focuses on the "why" and the "how" of communicative interactions (Arnett, Fritz, & Bell McManus, 2018, p. 37). For Arnett, Fritz, and Bell McManus, communication ethics is a term that is applicable to everyday interactions with others. For example, understanding the 'why' behind an individual reason for planning an event will help you better figure out 'how' to plan the event. The National Communication Association (NCA), an organization that promotes the importance of communication in public and private life, prompts professional reflection on the importance of communication ethics. The NCA Credo for Ethical Communication states,

> *Questions of right and wrong arise whenever people communicate. Ethical communication is fundamental to responsible thinking, decision making, and the development of relationships and communities within and across contexts, cultures, channels, and media. Moreover, ethical communication enhances human worth and dignity by fostering truthfulness, fairness, responsibility, personal integrity, and respect for self and other. We believe that unethical communication threatens the quality of all communication and consequently the well-being of individuals and the society in which we live (para. 1)*

Reprinted with permission from the National Communication Association. All rights reserved.

Moreover, Kenneth Andersen (2005) stressed the importance of ethics in everyday professional and personal interactions when he delivered the NCA Carroll C. Arnold Distinguished Lecture, on *Recovering the civic culture: The imperative of ethical communication*. Event planners must understand that communication ethics will help guide the decision-making process. Additionally, creating some type of ethical guidelines or credo for your professional career will help steer your interactions as you encounter various ethical scenarios.

When examining your own ethical structure, it is also helpful to understand where your client stands on many different issues. Clients will have different goods that they protect and promote; as a result, understanding narratives (Arnett, Fritz, & Bell McManus, 2018) before you plan an event is imperative. Narrative structures guide decision-making processes and will help you determine what is needed to create the ideal event.

Communication ethics: *The philosophy of communication brought into engaged communicative application in the marketplace of ideas*

Narratives: *Socially agreed-upon ideas that are accepted as true or representative of the way the world and human life is constituted*

TIP

Be sure to understand the stories of your clients. When putting together an event, taking the time to process what clients want will help you create an event that responds to your clients' narratives.

— Stacey Haines

Narratives, working from MacIntrye (1984) and Fisher (1989), are socially agreed-upon ideas that are accepted as true or representative of the way the world is and human life is constituted. Narratives are based on tradition and history. MacIntyre (1984) emphasizes the importance of finding narratives in society with the assumption that individuals can find a common ground from which to work. MacIntyre advances the concept of narrative through philosophy. He believes that narrative structures give people an embedded response to the questions that reside within society. He states,

> *Man is in his actions and practices, as well as in his fictions, essentially a story-telling animal. He is not essentially, but becomes through his history, a teller of stories that aspire to truth. But the key question for men is not about their own authorship; I can only answer the question "What am I to do?" if I can answer the prior question "Of what story or stories do I find myself a part?" We enter human society, that is, with one or more imputed characters—roles into which we have been drafted—and we have to learn what they are in order to be able to understand how Others respond to us and how our responses to them are apt to be construed (p. 216).*

A person's identity is grounded in multiple narratives to make that person unique. Personal identity is developed in relationship to others; therefore, you can find answers in larger stories that situate people in roles within a larger framework of meaning. By understanding narrative as the background to ethics, you will be able to plan an event that incorporates the true nature of your client. Understanding the meaning behind traditions such as jumping the broom in an African American ceremony, a chuppah or the breaking of glass in a Jewish ceremony, or the sign of peace, communion, and genuflection in a Catholic ceremony, is important. When planning an event for an organization, you can find these ethical principles within a mission statement. Take, for example, the job of creating a fundraising event for the American Cancer Society. Understanding the organization's mission and identity will help your planning team create a healthy menu and entertaining activities that promote the vitality and well-being of individuals. Another national group called METAvivor, a non-profit organization that was established to help women with late-stage forms of cancer, produces an author's luncheon fundraiser each year to help benefit the cause. Stories about each featured woman who is battling cancer are told in real terms—so that those attending the function can understand the magnitude of cancer and empathize with survivors. The responsibility of the event planner is to understand the overall nature and tone of the event and plan accordingly, as some of the moments may be serious, touching, tender, and even

© Ekaterina Lin/Shutterstock.com

a bit melancholy. When planning events, pay particular attention to the narrative of your client or organization.

In today's society, where concern for multiple perspectives results in various choices, an impulse for ethical action is needed (Arnett, 1987; Arnett, Fritz, & Bell McManus, 2018). Clearly, there is much more to consider in the world of contracts, negotiation, and ethical behavior than simple words on a page or hasty conversations about choices. Good event planners take their time in helping the client make decisions, but also are painstaking in their own research, reading, and consideration. Well-laid plans produce successful events, but it takes thoughtful conversation, lots of study, and a great deal of self-knowledge. Preparing for a small, two-hour private event demands the same kind of commitment as a four-day music festival in terms of care and professional know-how. Event planners who do their homework will reap the benefits of this effort in an ever-expanding client base.

Key Terms

Negotiation

Negotiation storyboard

Best Alternative to Negotiated Agreement (BATNA)

Contract

Indemnification (Hold Harmless) clause

Breach of contract

Force Majeure

Ethical issues

Communication ethics

Narratives

Discussion Questions

1. How might you as an event planner explain the Force Majeure clause in a vendor contract to your clients? What examples could you give to illustrate what could possibly go wrong? Be realistic—an explosive volcano in New York City, for instance, is just not in the realm of possibility.

2. One of your vendors, who happens to be a friend, has offered to lower her rates if you use her multimedia services for your next three events. You have used her multimedia in the past but have not been entirely satisfied with the quality of her services. The discount is substantial. What is the ethical dilemma you face? What are the action choices that confront you? What are the possible outcomes of this scenario?

3. A vendor who had contracted to deliver the desserts to a reception you have been working on does not show up on the afternoon of the event. You have been consistently in touch with the vendor and paid a deposit for the desserts, so you are surprised to find out when you call that the phone has been disconnected. Discuss this scenario in terms of breach of contract. What are your choices—immediately and after the event? How would you handle this scenario? What do you need to know?

Activity

Find a template for a sample client contract. Compare the version you have found with those of others in the class and in **Appendix D**. Make lists of the similarities and differences. What conclusions can you form from this exercise?

References

Andersen, K. E. (2000). Development in communication ethics: The ethics commission, code of professional responsibilities, code for ethical communication. *Journal of the Association for Communication Administration, 29,* 131–144.

_____. (2005). *The Carroll C. Arnold Distinguished Lecture 2003: Recovering the civic culture: The imperative of ethical communication.* Boston: Pearson Education.

Arnett, R. C. (1987). The status of communication ethics scholarship in speech communication journals from 1915–1985. *Central States Speech Journal, 38,* 44–61.

Arnett, R. C., Fritz, J. M., & Bell McManus, L. M. (2018). *Communication ethics literacy: Dialogue and difference* (2nd ed.). Dubuque, IA: Kendall Hunt.

Benoliel, M., & Hua, W. (2009). *Negotiating.* New York: Penguin.

Brown, T. (2009). *Change by design.* New York: Harper Collins.

Burnham S. J. (2012). Training for tomorrow: Ethical issues in negotiating contracts. *Business Law Today,* 1. Retrieved from https://search.ebscohost.com/login.aspx?direct=true&db=edsjsr&AN=edsjsr.businesslawtoday.2012.12.06&site=eds-live&scope=site

Canavor, N. (2011). *Business writing in the digital age.* Thousand Oaks, CA: Sage.

Cobb, S., Laws, D., & Sluzki, C. (2014). Modeling negotiation using "Narrative Grammar": Exploring the evolution of meaning in a simulated negotiation. *Group Decision & Negotiation, 23*(5), 1047–1065. https://doi.org/10.1007/s10726-012-9334-2

Cohen, S. P. (2002). *Negotiation skills for managers.* New York: McGraw Hill.

Cooper, M. (2002) Decentering judgment: Toward a postmodern communication ethic. In R. L. Johannnesen, *Ethics in human communication* (5th ed.) (pp. 299–317). Prospect Heights, IL: Waveland Press.

Ernst & Young, Catherwood, D. W., & Van Kirk, R. L. (1992). *The complete guide to special event management: Business insights, financial advice, and successful strategies from Ernst & Young, advisors to the Olympics, the Emmy Awards and the PGA Tour.* New York: John Wiley & Sons.

Feloni, R. (2014, October). *The 4 most common negotiation mistakes—and how to avoid them.* Retrieve from https://www.businessinsider.com/most-common-negotiation-mistakes-2014-10

Fisher, R., Ury, W., & Patton, B. (2011). *Getting to yes: Negotiating agreement without giving in.* New York: Penguin Books. (original publication 1981)

Fisher, W. (1989). Narration as a human communication paradigm: The case of public moral argument. *Communication Monographs, 51,* 1–22.

Goldberg, L. M. (2018). Getting a seat at the table: The importance of involving the production team. *Sound & Video Contractor, 36*(6), 66. Retrieved from https://search.ebscohost.com/login. aspx?direct=true&db=a9h&AN=130115945&site=eds-live&scope=site

Hindle, T. (1998). *Essential managers; Negotiation skills.* New York: DK.

Jaksa, J. A., & Pritchard, M. S. (1988). *Communication ethics: Methods of analysis.* Belmont, CA: Wadsworth Publishing.

Johannesen, R. L., Valde, K. S., & Whedbee, K. E. (2008). *Ethics in human communication* (6th ed.). Prospect Heights, IL: Waveland Press.

Kilkenny, S. (2011). *The complete guide to successful event planning* (2nd ed.). Ocala, FL: Atlantic.

Kimball, C., & The Staff of Entrepreneur Media (2015). *Start your own event planning business: Your step-by-step guide to success.* Irvine, CA: Entrepreneur Press.

MacIntyre, A. (1984). *After virtue* (2nd ed.). South Bend: IN: University of Notre Dame Press.

Mancuso, J. (2008). *The everything guide to being an event planner: Insider advice on turning your creative energy into a rewarding career.* Avon, MA: Adams Media.

Matthews, D. (2008). *Special event production: The process.* New York: Routledge.

Matusitz, J. (2013). Interpersonal communication perspectives in hostage negotiation. *Journal of Applied Security Research, 8,* 24–37.

McGarry, B. (2015). Ethics and event planning: Some advice. *Campus Activities Programming, 48*(4), 12–13. Retrieved from https://search.ebscohost.com/login.aspx?direct=true&db=eue&AN =110434991&site=eds-live&scope=site

National Communication Association (1999). *Credo for ethical communication.* Retrieved from https://www.natcom.org/sites/default/files/Public_Statement_Credo_for_Ethical_Communication_2017.pdf

Neher, W.W., & Sandin, P.J. (2007). *Communicating ethically: Character, duties, consequences and relationships.* Boston: Allyn and Bacon.

O'Brien, J. (2013). *Negotiation for purchasing professionals.* London: Kogan Page Publishers.

Putnam, L. L. (2010). Communication as changing the negotiation game. *Journal of Applied Communication Research, 38,* 325–335.

Shapiro, R. M., Jankowski, M. A., & Dale, J. (2001). *The power of nice: How to negotiate so everyone wins-especially you.* Hoboken, NJ: Wiley and Sons.

Shapiro, R. M., & Jordan, G. (2008). *Dare to prepare: How to win before you begin.* New York: Random House.

Silvers, J. R. (2009). *Risk management for meetings and events*. New York: Routledge.

Stewart, K. (2007). Planning a conference? *Training, 44*(4), 31–35. Retrieved from https://search. ebscohost.com/login.aspx?direct=true&db=mth&AN=24996075&site=eds-live&scope=site

Ziakas, V. (2013). *Event portfolio planning and management: A holistic approach*. New York: Routledge.

Chapter 9

STAGING: SETTING THE SCENE FOR THE EVENT

Choosing the right space for an event and then making that space work to the client's advantage are skills that can be practiced and honed. Knowing how to incorporate and manipulate all the key components of staging will set you apart as an event planner. Clients will hear how well you presented an event, will see photographs of your events on social media, and will pass along word-of-mouth recommendations about your services and your ability to make a client's event unique. Getting there requires you to understand the dynamics of staging, and to begin, you have to work

© mambographer/Shutterstock.com

with a client to find the right place to hold that event. Selecting a venue and then all the supporting elements will help create an event that guests will not soon forget. The locale's accessibility, its facilities and services, its ambiance, and its cost (Shone & Parry, 2004) are just a few of the many considerations that the event planner will have to discuss with the client. To select a site from many that will be considered requires focus, thoughtful deliberation, and lots of experience.

When you have finished reading this chapter, you will be able to

- analyze the client's event needs for potential site selection;
- list ways to make guests comfortable in the space once a venue is selected;
- explain the relationship between good hospitality and a successful event.

CASE STUDY   Using Audiovisuals When Staging Your Event

Stacey Haines, President, Earl Beckwith & Associates

As the audiovisual management provider for a large pharmaceutical company's speaker training meeting series, our company was engaged to plan and produce a meeting with a unique staging and display screen scenario. Working closely with the company's event planning personnel, our first task was to make sure the appropriate space was assigned to accommodate the vision the company had for its general session. The general session is most often the focal point of the meeting, seating the full audience and providing the means for the presenters to deliver their message in the most effective and engaging way possible.

For this particular series of meetings, the concept was to build a stage with a catwalk extension so presenters could move into the audience. The display screens would be configured in a scoreboard-like fashion over the stage. The objective was to keep the audience fully engaged on the center of the room.

Understanding the client's vision was paramount to working with the meeting planner to contract for meeting room space to accommodate the audience of 300 people at round tables with extended staging and display screens to be hung from the ceiling over the stage. Working from the bottom up, a 2' stage, an 8' clearance from the stage to the bottom of the screen, and the 10' length of the display screen set the criteria for a room with a 20' ceiling. As this training meeting was part of a series, it was critical for each prospective venue to accommodate the ceiling height requirements.

Bringing in branding elements helps set the professional ambiance for corporate meetings. Incorporating color schemes depicting logos or corporate colors helps unify all the elements in the room. Projecting logos on the screens, dressing tables in linens reflective of the company's colors, wearing name tags that also showcase the company's identity, and offering attendees pens and pads that showcase the corporate logo all reflect thoughtful meeting branding.

Finally, when a meeting space is large, the overall audiovisual plays an important part in offering attendees an effective event. While the hotel's built-in audio can be used, clients often want to bring in external audiovisual teams so that the sound is crisp and appropriate. To add to the atmosphere of the room, music can be played before or after the meeting.

After reading this chapter, revisit the case study and respond to the following question:

How would audiovisual and staging elements change depending upon your audience for the event?

Staging the Event

Choosing the best venue for your event is one of the biggest decisions event planners will make. Assessing the needs of clients, the venue in which they want to hold the event, and the overall feel that the event should exude should be considered when selecting a host of items necessary to stage the event. Bowdin, Allen, O'Toole, Harris, and McDonnell (2011) state that the context in which the event takes place often can influence the overall success of the event simply because the environment should suit the organization and its attendees. Berridge (2012) writes that "modern event management is largely about delivery of experiences or experience opportunities" (p. 8). Moreover, Silvers (2004) believes event planners should address six aspects that will make an event memorable: "anticipation, arrival, atmosphere, appetite, activity, and amenity" (p. 6). Delivering an experience that attendees will remember requires selecting and staging a location that suits both the client and event planner: it should be a space that is comfortable, offers appropriate ambiance, and can hold the chosen number of guests.

© Eric Limon/Shutterstock.com

There are many questions you should ask before the actual planning begins. LoCicero (2008) and Wolf, Wolf, and Levine (2005) suggest using who, what, where, when, why, and how questions:

1. Who will be invited? If you know the number and **demographics** of your audience, then planning the tone, tempo, and design of your event will move smoothly. Considering the size of the space will determine the maximum number of people the room can hold, and in turn, you can get creative with the space itself to accommodate the guests.

2. What is the actual event? In today's world of event planning, you can create an experience for any occasion, so understanding the type of event will help you determine the ideal location and environment. Knowing what the client hopes to achieve will help you find a venue that correlates well with the client's desires.

3. Where will it be held? Location sets the atmosphere for how guests will perceive your event. Searching for venues that have the potential to meet the needs of the client is necessary, and you and your client must assess each venue until you find the best possible choice for the event.

4. When will it be held? Timing matters, and the season often dictates what you can and cannot do. Sometimes this question is answered merely by availability of the venue; at other times, the client will ask for a certain month, date, or year, and the event planner will have to work with the venue to pick a date that is suitable.

Demographics: *The composition of a certain group, often including statistical information*

5. Why is the event being held? The purpose of the event will help determine what is needed to make the event a success. Understanding the 'why' of the event will help you focus on what is important for the client or organization. Is the purpose to provide entertainment, offer instruction, encourage people to exchange information, or congratulate employees on a great year? Once the why is understood, you can put plans into place.

6. How will it be executed? Answering this question involves mapping out all of these integral components to set up the event in the right space that makes sense for all involved. How all of the staging elements (e.g., decorations, chairs, tables, music, and lighting) come together reflects thoughtful consideration of the event's vision.

7. How much is the budget? Money is the driver for how you design your event; once you figure out the maximum spending allowance, you can work within your means. A meager budget does not necessarily mean that the event will be less successful; it simply means that the event planner must be more creative in making choices that will impact the staging of the event.

Understanding the answers to these questions will make up the foundation of the event planning process.

Venue

Before event planners begin to investigate sites that may suit the client's vision, they should draw up a list of needs and wants for the space they will select. Choosing the venue is paramount in the beginning stages of planning an event (Shone & Perry, 2004). Once a thorough list is created, details such as how big or small the event will be, whether you will need

© 1000 Words/Shutterstock.com

seating for all guests, how you will want to serve food and beverages, and how to create the desired mood and configuration of the event space, you will then begin the hunt for the proper location. Some of these locations may be local; some may be in a different city, town, state, or even in another country.

Doing your homework prior to selecting the actual space is critical; you want to offer clients the best possible venues that will serve their needs. Taking time to walk through possible event locations will help you determine if the space is even workable. Finding a lovely location will not benefit you or the client if it cannot accommodate the right number of guests or if it is unavailable on the preferred date. Another consideration is parking: issues of parking costs and availability in urban centers, for instance, have caused both event planners and their clients to rethink venue choices (Dawes, 2018). Additionally, if you visit the venue during the summer, for instance, but the event will be held in early spring, you may want to ask to see photos of the venue taken during the season that matches the prospective event date (Lord, 2013). For example, if your clients want an intimate setting, a hotel ballroom will not offer them the proper venue. In the business setting, meetings will not run effectively or efficiently if the space does not flow well, offer good lighting, or is not safe for attendees. A venue that is unable to be decorated to reflect a theme because of regulations at the site may not make a bride and groom happy. Even major hotel venues are rethinking their space configurations to accommodate millennials and multigenerational visiting groups, as well as reorganizing hotel business spaces to reflect the changing needs of guests (Solomon, 2016). The event planner should know in advance how any particular venue might work for the client's needs in order to avoid disappointment and save time and energy.

The choice of venue helps set the tone of the event. A bride and groom may want to host their summer wedding in a renovated barn until they learn that it has no air conditioning; an east coast company may decide to have its conference on the west coast until it realizes that travel costs are prohibitive; and a fundraising group may want to hold its 5K race in the heart of the city until it realizes that there is no convenient place for participants and supporters to park. Moreover, the venue must suit the size of the event and the number of attendees. A venue that is too crowded or too empty will leave an impression. For example, crowds at a concert or a festival add to the energy of the event; however, a convention's breakout sessions that are sparsely attended may cast a negative light on the event planner. The event planner is responsible for creating a favorable impression for guests. Oriade, Robinson, and Gelder (2010) write, "No one wants to spend their day crammed into a small room becoming hot and uncomfortable" (p. 81). If there is a chance of discomfort, event planners will have to opt for other choices and readjust. An outdoor event may offer a charming setting, but event planners need to take into account the weather, including the possibility of sunburn, rain, mud, or other challenges. Be prepared to deal with last-minute weather patterns that pre-empt the best-laid plans (Hoyle, 2002). Considering all the possibilities ahead of time will help in anticipating guests' needs at the selected venue, including signage that sets the stage for a cheerful welcome and a clear pathway to the event site or to a registration space (Walker, 2017). Picking the space sometimes is not just about what is most pleasing visually because clients have a budget, and that can play an instrumental role in what they decide upon for their location. While many venues come with a high price tag, Diane Warner (2002) believes affordable options are available. There is a location that suits every event; often you just have to look a little harder for it. If a client has a vision for an event, your team can work to make it happen. Customizing a program to provide an event that matches a company's values and branding is essential if your event planning team wants to make an impact ("Putting the views in corporate event venues," 2017). Where can you turn to find the best venue for your client? Consider investigating spaces from the following list:

TABLE 1. *Event venues*		
Ballparks/stadiums	Country clubs	Open spaces/parks
Beaches	Exhibition/convention centers	Outdoor amphitheaters
Boats	Farms	Private homes
Chamber of Commerce sites	Historic properties	Resorts
Churches/synagogues/mosques	Hotels and inns	Restaurants
City/county properties	Local attractions	Theaters/cinemas
Colleges/universities	Museums	Theme parks
Conference facilities	Nightclubs	Vineyards/wineries/breweries

Determining the location of the event requires you to consider those who will be attending it. Flach (2017) writes, "The trend for unusual, multipurpose, aesthetically interesting locations has seen pop-ups, repurposed cathedrals and sustainable green spaces entering the market. And then there are the venues offering more than just a space for hire—breweries, cinemas and even a safari park are all investing in conference capabilities to lure in the corporate market" (p.47). First and foremost, event planners must ask themselves if the location suits the majority of the people—is it convenient? Is it easily accessible? Is it safe? Will it help facilitate the theme of the event? Once they have arrived at the event, can guests move about the space freely without constraint?

Convention and Visitors Bureau (CVB): *A not-for-profit organization that offers information and services to those from out of town*

If you are planning a large-scale meeting, conference or convention, a good tip is to work with the **Convention and Visitors Bureau (CVB)** in that location. Partnering with the CVB can assist event planners because it offers help through education and guidance, which can save both time and money as event planners have so many other tasks to juggle. Professionals who work in this field offer a spectrum of knowledge; they can help suggest a venue, book overflow hotels, and offer advice should there be a conflict or crisis. Those who work for the CVB work for the city or destination location and are not there to pressure event planners to use one particular venue, as they represent many possibilities in the destination location. For example, CVBs in Buffalo and Niagara, New York, were willing to provide the Eastern Communication Association with flights, travel accommodations, food samplings, and local entertainment in order to offer their destinations as possible locations for upcoming conventions. The job of the CVB is to provide a wide range of information about the locale. Moreover, CVBs have the credentials to assist in choosing venues that may be offsite, promoting attendance, serving as community and political liaisons, offering public relations services, and helping with onsite services (Convention and Visitors Bureau, 2013).

Travel

Just as it is important in real estate to consider 'location, location, location,' the same is true for hosting events. The location does matter. How easily guests can access it should be thoughtfully considered as they may travel from near and far to attend a conference, convention, or other event. Additionally, if guests are coming in from out of town, making things as convenient as possible will be more pleasing to them so they do not have to worry about transportation issues once they have arrived. When a convention takes place at a large hotel, for example, guests will typically stay in the hotel for convenience; being able to head downstairs from their rooms is an appealing draw for the convention. Whether it is a conference, a business meeting, or a wedding, reserving hotel rooms in advance will facilitate attendance and make travel coordination easier for guests. Event planners must know how to book a room block designated for the event, allowing for less expensive room rates and encouraging guests to stay in the same place. However, the event planner must make sure that the room block numbers can be met or the client will have to pay for a percentage of the unused rooms. Companies are also available to negotiate room block contracts for the event planner.

If a convention is very large, working with a travel agent might be helpful. Judy Allen (2009) suggests that event planners be aware of the length of time guests will be in transit. For instance, when relatives fly in for a wedding, it is always more desirable to consider holding the event in a convenient location; if at all possible, keep the ceremony site near the reception site. If a church, synagogue, or mosque is a distance from the reception site, for instance, it will require guests to travel between the two. A convention held in a city hotel as opposed to one on the outskirts of town will enable guests to dine in city restaurants and visit local attractions more easily. You and your client should determine travel needs before selecting a location.

Getting creative with transportation can make an event fun for guests. You may want to consider hiring limousines, minivans, trolleys, water taxis, or buses to ferry guests, which can extend the event experience. Be sure to look for reputable companies and book them early; during certain times of the year, transportation will be in high demand (Post, 2007). If some guests are using public transportation, make sure you have properly researched all public transit routes, and share those details with guests who may not be familiar with the site. Additionally, providing details about the price of transportation such as the cost from the airport to the hotel via taxi, ride sharing, or shuttle will help guests plan accordingly. Allen (2009) states, "If you're having an evening function, guests may be coming from work, or fighting rush-hour traffic …" (p. 150). Being able to help people in wheelchairs, in addition to those driving who may need handicapped parking,

will ease the minds of your guests by showing them you have considered their travel needs (Janner, 2003). Parking may be expensive for guests, especially if they have to pay fees for overnight or more than one day. Provide your guests parking information, such as maps or recommended parking garages in the area and their prices. All of these factors could influence what time you would like the event to begin. The job of the event planner is to examine all the transportation options in order to plan for stress-free travel.

Mapping the Space

Once event planners find what clients believe will be the best place to hold the event and have considered transportation necessities, it is a good idea to map out the space of the venue itself, keeping in mind that it should fit with the client's overall theme and vision. The physical factors of a setting often can trigger dissatisfaction among guests if the space is sub-par, but rarely does the setting contribute to an outstanding rating if it is adequate (Herzberg, 1966). In other words, these elements are taken for granted unless they stand out as objectionable. Figuring out the components of the event can help the client visualize how the space will be used. Making it easy for guests to move around is a necessary element of any event. By surveying the site and drawing a guide on paper, you will be able to place some of the components that are necessary to build upon the event's theme and help it coalesce (See **Appendix E** for a sample layout). In making your guide, take into consideration the size, weight, and volume of all aspects of your event (Goldblatt, 2014). For example, if you have a five-piece band, make sure you leave enough space so the dance floor is not on top of the band. Using a riser or a stage might be helpful if the room is able to support the size of the structure. Moreover, place decor on your design plan, because these elements can take up vital space. A balloon arch, for instance, would need to be strategically placed so that it welcomes guests but does not hinder guest movement.

Spatial context: *The space that is available at an event that influences guests' perception, cognition, and emotions*

Set the scene: *The act of making a space ready for an event*

People may not always be conscious of how the **spatial context** can influence perception, cognition, and emotions that they experience while attending and participating in an event (Bitner, 1992). Even an outdoor space may be called a room because, if planned correctly, it will feel as if it is a unified space. The saying '**set the scene**' refers to the idea of making something possible or getting it ready. Event planners must set the scene for each event they plan and give guests a unique experience that is pleasurable and entertaining. Allen (2009) states that by creating an event grid, you will have a "blueprint" (p. 80) that allows you to become acquainted with the space. Being able to see where everything is placed can ensure that the venue will have adequate space.

Cocktail hours and social parties require that you consider the number of people in the room in order to determine the placement of cocktail tables, the band or musicians, and any needed floor space for dancing or a silent auction table, for instance. Additionally, mapping out exactly where the bar should be will help with logistics. Keeping in mind that there will be suppliers who may come in and help set up the event (entertainment, caterers, florists, designers, servers, etc.), event planners will want to make sure there is enough room in the venue for them to move around to accomplish their work. Moreover, when evaluating the configuration of the room, keep in mind that it is people who warm up a place and make it feel more welcoming (Janner, 2003).

Hospitality and Seating

One of the greatest responsibilities of the hospitable host is to make guests feel welcome. Planning for this concern demands a knowledge of those who will be attending the event: how well do they know each other? How comfortable are they interacting with each other? Will there be a need to host some ice-breakers at the start of the event in order to encourage communication? Name tags are almost always indispensable, but beyond that, what level of interconnectedness will your client desire? The event planner will need to seek out this information during preparation for the event and then work with the client to determine how to make every guest feel welcome. Offering the best hospitality possible so that guests can enjoy and relax in the space provided is part of staging the event. Making guests feel comfortable at the event is another way planners can set the stage for the affair and position the event as a positive experience that attendees will remember fondly. The business of hospitality can be defined in terms of what you are providing guests and can include elements such as refreshments and meals, the look of the venue, and the way guests are treated (Brotherton, 1999; Brotherton & Wood, 2000; Kotler, Bowen, Makens, & Baloglu, 2017). Deciding how to configure and serve the food for the event is at the forefront of hospitality. Event planners will have to work within the confines of the space to figure out how to best serve food and provide drinks without the room or space feeling too crowded, chaotic, or confusing. Once your client has selected the room for the affair, the next step is to decide how the food should be served.

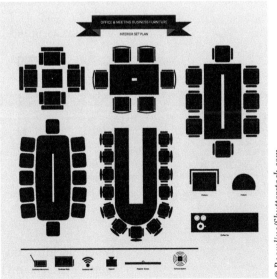

© Eric Limon/Shutterstock.com

Three primary ways to serve food include passed-tray service, buffet service, and a seated meal (Post, 2007).

Passed-tray service works beautifully for cocktail hours and private affairs. Servers, dressed in work attire, circulate around the room with a variety of items from which the guests can choose to eat. The trays may include fruit, cheeses, appetizers, shrimp, and other small bites. Guests typically stand while the food is being passed around the room, and you may want to consider having high-top tables where guests can place their drinks or normal-height tables where they can sit and converse while they eat. If you are serving the food buffet style, consider where to place the buffet station(s) to maximize the space. Placing buffet tables strategically around the room will force guests to get up for their meal. If, on the other hand, guests are being treated to a full-course, seated meal delivered by servers, they will be seated during dinner, and the servers will need room to move around easily. Being able to answer questions such as how much physical space is needed and how many tables and chairs are necessary can help event planners create a hospitable atmosphere and leave guests feeling comfortable at the event (LoCicero, 2008; Post, 2007).

Immediacy: *The perceptual availability of one person to another*

When deciding upon the type of seating your client prefers for the event, Mehrabian and Diamond (1971) describes **immediacy** as the perceptual availability of one person to another. They write that when people are in closer proximity to one another, conversation tends to build. Additionally, they note that people assume more immediate positions when they actually like one another. Therefore, thoughtful consideration of seating arrangements when planning an event can be another factor in how the guests perceive the event overall. Sometimes, guests will get to choose with whom they sit, such as during a reception or cocktail hour, and at other times they will not, such as at a large business function or a wedding. In that case, seating is assigned by the event planner and client working together, and

© elitravo/Shutterstock.com

as Judy Allen (2009) states, "When one of the objectives of the event is to bring key people together, guests are assigned strategically, not randomly" (p. 277). She also warns that people are apt to change locations by switching place cards to sit by people they know. Peggy Post (2007) offers some worthwhile suggestions event planners can use to help guide the seating arrangements. Consider who will be conversing in the setting; avoid placing one stranger at a table when the rest of the guests know each other; and seat guests who are disabled near the entrance or restroom for convenience.

When deciding on the layout of the room and the configuration of the tables, Mirisch and Harris (2013) suggest that you should consider whether 8 or 10 people will fit comfortably at a table. While it will affect the budget, fewer people at a table allows for a more comfortable setting; however, it could mean that you use up more floor space because there will be more tables. Tables are usually set to standard sizes, which means they are 72" to seat 10–12 people; 60" to seat 8–10 people; 54" to seat 6–8 people, and 48" to seat 4–6 people. In auditorium seating, it is proper to leave 18" between the back of the seat in one row and the front of the seat in the next row. Additionally, a good rule is to leave 36" between the edges of objects, such as between a buffet table and the closest seating; doing so will allow room on the floor for movement (Mirisch & Harris, 2013).

Event planners must take into consideration the age of guests when planning for seating. Offering guests a festive cocktail hour with delicious food and a full-service bar may be part of the plan, but if your guest population includes a number of elderly individuals, providing some seating may be necessary for their comfort. Asking senior citizens to stand for the majority of the event is not considerate, especially when the women and men may be in dress shoes. On the other hand, event planners must consider the placement of children at an event. For example, planning seating for children at a Mitzvah would require allowing enough room for the children to sit together at tables. Additionally, allowing the children extra room to move around among the guests or perhaps on a dance floor is something to consider.

TIP

Choose vendors who perform multiple duties. Venues with their own catering tend to be less expensive. Additionally, you know the food is being prepared fresh onsite.

— Matt Musgrove

© Milkos/Shutterstock.com

Decor and Theme

Part of staging the event requires you to make sure that "as guests arrive they know from the get-go they are entering a rarefied experience" (LoCicero, 2008, p. 222). Bowdin et al. (2011) state that creating an imaginary world gives guests something to participate in and remember. The approach to the event should contain some special elements of surprise, delight, and panache. Decorations and enhancements should add flair to the event. For example, if guests have to enter the event through a certain door, be sure to make the approach exciting for them; line a walkway with candles or lanterns for an evening cocktail reception on a golf course veranda; place a violinist on the lawn near the entrance for an outdoor wedding; or fashion a balloon tunnel through which employees enter for a corporate function. Of course, anything that will require a special set-up or creation on the site of the venue should be cleared with the site supervisor or coordinator, and it is a good idea to get this clearance in writing. Upon the guests' arrival, some events will require a check-in table, while others may have elegantly displayed place cards indicating table assignments. Knowing how to decorate the entrance and where to place all the key elements strategically should make a strong first impression on the guests.

© LiliGraphie/Shutterstock.com

Weaving the theme throughout the event can help guests appreciate it through their five senses (van der Meer, 2008). In addition, Edwards and Gustafsson (2008) state that "if the eating environment is to provide an 'appropriate atmosphere,' it is the aspects of the senses that must be manipulated" (p. 23). Consider having a signature cocktail and food (to taste), appropriate music (to hear), decorations (to see), lovely linens or favors (to touch), and flowers (to smell) at the venue.

Signature items specific to the event can be placed around the room. An ice sculpture depicting the corporate logo may be situated inside the ballroom; collectible items or books might be located near the entrance; large flower arrangements or event-specific centerpieces can liven up the room and be placed on tables; and banners and signs should be displayed strategically in the convention hall. To personalize their weddings, brides and grooms have displayed special guest books and tribute photo boards to thank their families and guests for coming. This gives guests something to look at while at the event and the opportunity to share stories while reminiscing. Paying careful attention to displays and artifacts that add personality to the event will remind your guests of the theme and hopefully have the power to create lasting memories (Mirisch & Harris, 2013; van der Meer, 2008).

Thinking through aspects of the guests' arrival times may require you to be cognizant of the physical aspects of the lobby, tent, room, ballroom, or meeting rooms. For example, a radio station that hosts corporate sponsors inside a large tent prior to a professional football game may place the alcohol table on one side of the tent and the food on the opposite side with table seating in the middle. This strategy encourages people to move around in the tent, which can help facilitate mingling among the guests. People who did not know each other prior to the event may strike up a quick friendship while standing in the beverage line and then meet up again at the carving station.

Ambiance: *All of the background features of an environment*

Ambiance

© Alex Andrei/Shutterstock.com

Event planners might consider devoting extra attention to those 'wow' factors such as ambiance, illusion, and enchantment if they want to make an especially compelling impression on guests. These intangible yet indispensable elements can easily move an event from good to great. If the goal is to produce enthusiastic responses to the event, paying careful attention to the details of the environment remains key.

There are many ways in which you can add ambiance to an event. Wall and Berry (2007) refer to **ambiance** as the cues in the service environment that contain non-human elements, whereas others refer to it as all of the background features of the environment (Johnson, Mayer, & Champaner, 2004; Lee, 2011; Simpeh & Simpeh, 2011). Ambiance sets the stage for your event and is exhibited in many different ways. As an event planner, your creative skills will take an event from ordinary to extraordinary. For example, fabric can be used to camouflage ugly walls, make a backdrop, create a special space, and even change the mood of a room. Additionally, linens come in all colors, fabrics, and styles, and you will be able to rent any type, either glamorous or simple, from a range of companies, or many venues will carry their own products. No matter where you get your linens, a steadfast rule is that all must go to the floor and cover the legs of the table (Wolf, Wolf, & Levine, 2005). Fabrics, however, are just one way to change the ambiance.

Lighting, as well, adds ambiance to an event and has the power to create a mood or change a mood as guests enjoy different aspects of the theme and the overall feeling you want to evoke. Using proper lighting techniques can be dramatic. There are different types of lighting, and many venues will help you decide what type works best at the location. **Backlighting** is used behind performers or speakers to make them visually stand out from the backdrop (Miziker, 2015). "**Atmosphere lighting**" is used to highlight things such as the food stations, sculptures, centerpieces, or other prominent features at the event. Atmosphere lighting can be used on fabrics to change the mood during the event. In addition to atmosphere lighting, "**intelligent**" **lights** automatically change positions, colors and patterns, and "**gobos**" are the plates used to customize names or patterns on a wall or floor (Wolf, Wolf, & Levine, 2005, p. 89). Moreover, a way to get the audience excited is to move a spotlight in a fast random fashion all around the room; this technique is referred to as a "**ballyhoo**" (Miziker, 2015, p. 20). For a high-energy event, consider special lighting effects that could be stimulating on the dance floor or during a live auction. For example, during an auction for a charitable organization, the celebrity hostess walked up and down the aisles encouraging attendees to bid on items to raise money; she was not daunted by this at all, and, in fact, had a spotlight on her at all times, so as not to put the focus on the people from whom she was trying to solicit money. The organizers knew spotlighting guests would be a little too intimidating and scare them away from bidding on items. For an evening event such as a reception, dinner or other special occasion, it is a good idea to dim the lights slightly. "Candles or lights controlled by dimmers is typically flattering, but do not have the light so low that people are in the dark," (LoCicero, 2008, p. 208), It is essential to provide enough light so that guests can read the program or menu. Today, battery-powered candles can take the place of lit candles should a venue not allow open flames.

Visiting the space and previewing how it will look during the hours of your event can give you ideas as to how to plan effectively for lighting, especially if your event begins in the daylight and moves into the evening. Mixing a combination of lighting is a good idea, as well; integrating incandescent and fluorescent light can strike the right balance, especially with events

Backlighting: *A type of lighting used behind performers or speakers to make them visually stand out from the backdrop*

Atmosphere lighting: *A kind of lighting used to highlight special features at an event*

Intelligent lights: *Lights at an event that can automatically change positions, colors and patterns*

Gobos: *Plates used to customize names or patterns through lighting on a wall or floor*

Ballyhoo: *A way to get an audience excited by moving a spotlight in a fast, random fashion all around the room*

such as conventions and meetings, where people sit for long hours, and eye strain is possible because they are looking at projection screens, writing, or working on computers (Worcester, 1999). Many people complain when there is not enough light by which they can read instructions or a bid sheet; therefore, striving to achieve a lighting balance that is beneficial but that also provides ambiance will benefit all involved. You can stage the lighting in small ways, but you will want to make sure the cost works within your budget. Getting bids from several vendors is important, since costs for the same job can vary greatly, as much as thousands of dollars. Since lighting packages can differ in size and complexity, be sure to compare all data you collect carefully before you make a selection (Matthews, 2007). If the technical choices you are presented with are beyond your scope, enlist the aid of a networking group or knowledgeable colleague to help in the decision making.

Music and Sound

TIP

Many built-in audio systems are old and not clear enough to meet a corporate client's expectation. Ask the venue if the audio system is new or old. We often get a surprisingly candid answer. Also remember that audio takes up a footprint on the floor space.

— Stacey Haines

Research on the effects of music on people is not surprising, and the results conclude that (1) music makes you feel emotional; you can experience joy, peacefulness, and even sadness and fear from it (Sloboda, O'Neill, & Ivaldi, 2001), and (2) physical and behavioral changes can occur, such as the urge to sing or dance, due to the effects of music (Bartlett, 1996; Scherer & Zentner, 2001). Music can be one of the most important aspects of staging the event, and if executed correctly, can make a lasting impression upon guests, maybe even give them chills at one point in the program. Staging the music is vital to the event's overall dynamics: a lovely cellist may play for guests and kick off the night at a cocktail hour; a DJ may help facilitate dancing at a wedding; and a band may begin a celebration at a large-scale function. When planning ahead for the musicians or DJ, consider whether the musicians need a riser on which to perform; placing the riser in a spot that best suits the guests can affect the sound in the room and the visibility of the band. By plotting out where the music or musicians will go, you will get a sense of the room dynamics. Ask the venue manager where other bands, DJs, or musicians have set up in the past. Also, if your client wants a dance floor, many people will estimate three square feet per person on the dance floor and an even larger space for the musicians so they can move around (Allen, 2009). Some venues will have a dance floor or supply one, so be sure to ask if you do not see one when you do your initial site check. If the venue does not have a dance floor, a party supplier can help provide one.

Additionally, when planning corporate or other business events, the particulars of the audio/visual set up for a business meeting or convention should be thoroughly considered, as the equipment can take up a good chunk of space. Check all sound systems and make sure they are functioning properly prior to the event; also, be sure the volume is loud enough for people to hear so they do not have to strain. Conversely, when considering a wedding atmosphere, for instance, watch the volume as well. Some people may not want to be in the room with loud, pounding dance music, so you may want to offer a place for them to get away from the noise, such as a lobby area, balcony, or adjacent room (Miziker, 2015). (For more information about audiovisuals, see Chapter 10).

The purpose of an event is for people to have a good time. Staging the event can help guests remember the event fondly when it is over. Sometimes it is the large, flamboyant touches you add to it, but often, it can be the small, personal touches, the thoughtfulness with which you planned it, and the hospitality that your client offered guests that make the event one that is remembered long after it is over. The strongest event planners know that success often comes in the most minor of details, and that happens when you are able to anticipate the needs of both clients and guests. Setting the stage with careful planning and forethought will help make each event memorable.

Key Terms

Demographics	Spatial context	Ambiance	Intelligence lights
Convention and Visitors Bureau (CVB)	Set the scene	Backlighting	Gobos
	Immediacy	Atmosphere lighting	Ballyhoo

Discussion Questions

1. Recall an event you attended in which the event's space, decor, and ambiance, seemed particularly well-coordinated. As you describe this event, think about what it took to make all of these elements come together so well.

2. Recall an event in which the mood did not match the setting. How did this affect the guest experience? What could have been done differently to make the staging more welcoming and appropriate?

3. We rely heavily on our senses when critiquing many events. Focus on all the senses to create an event that emphasizes these senses.

Activity

You have been selected as the coordinator of an event that is to be held to benefit blinded and injured veterans, 200 of whom will be the guests of honor at the event. Make a list of the primary concerns you must address when planning this event. How will staging this event make you think differently about the arrangements?

References

Allen, J. (2009). *Event planning: The ultimate guide to successful meetings, corporate events, fundraising galas, conferences and conventions, incentives and other special events.* Ontario, Canada: John Wiley & Sons Canada.

Bartlett, D. L. (1996). Physiological responses to music and sound stimuli. In *Handbook of music psychology* (2nd ed., pp. 343–385). San Antonio, TX: IMR Press.

Berridge, G. (2012). Event experience: A case study of differences between the way in which organizers plan an event experience and the way in which guests receive the experience. *Journal of Park & Recreation Administration, 30,* 7–23.

Bitner, M. J. (1992). Servicescapes: The impact of physical surroundings on customers and employees. *Journal of Marketing, 56,* 57–71.

Bowdin, G., Allen, J., O'Toole, W., Harris, R., & McDonnell, I. (2011). *Events management.* (3rd ed.). New York: Routledge.

Brotherton, B. (1999). Towards a definitive view of the nature of hospitality and hospitality management. *International Journal of Contemporary Hospitality Management, 11,* 165–173.

Brotherton, B., & Wood, R.C. (2000). Hospitality and hospitality management. In C. Lashley, & A. Morrison (Eds.). *Search of hospitality: Theoretical perspectives and debates.* (pp. 134–156). Oxford, United Kingdom: Butterworth-Heinemann.

Convention and Visitors Bureau (2013). Why meeting planners choose not to go it alone. *Successful Meetings, 62,* 1–18.

Edwards, J. A., & Gustafsson, I. (2008). The room and atmosphere as aspects of the meal: A review. *Journal of Foodservice, 19,* 22–34.

Dawes, J. "Event venues hear parking complaints." (2018). *Grand Rapids Business Journal, 36, 19,* 1–2.

Flach, C. (2017, November). The UK's top 10 corporate venues for your big HR event. *People Management,* 46–50.

Goldblatt, J. (2014). *Special events: Creating and sustaining a new world for celebration.* (7th ed.). Hoboken: New Jersey: John Wiley & Sons.

Herzberg, F. (1966). *Work and the nature of man.* New York: World Publishing.

Hoyle, L. H. (2002). *Event marketing: How to successfully promote events, festivals, conventions, and expositions.* Hoboken, NJ: John Wiley & Sons.

Janner, G. (2003). *Janner's complete speechmaker.* (7th ed.). London: Thorogood.

Johnson, L., Mayer, K. J., & Champaner, E. (2004). Casino atmospherics from a customer's perspective: A re-examination. *UNLV Gaming Research & Review Journal, 8,* 1–10.

Kotler, P., Bowen, J. T., Makens, J. C. and Blaoglu, S., eds. (2017). *Marketing for hospitality and tourism.* 7th ed. London: Pearson Education Ltd.

Lee, S. (2011). Evaluating serviceability of healthcare servicescapes: Service design perspective. *International Journal of Design, 5,* 61–71.

LoCicero, J. (2008). *Meeting and event planning.* Avon, MA: Adams Media.

Lord, M. (2013). *Things to consider before booking your wedding venue.* Retrieved from http://www.huffingtonpost.com/maggie-lord/things-to-consider-before_b_2951830.html

Matthews, D. (2007). *Special event production: The process.* New York: Routledge.

Mehrabian, A., & Diamond, S.G. (1971). Seating arrangement and conversation. *Sociometry, 34,* 281–289.

Mirisch, D., & Harris, G. (2013). *The charity event planning guide.* Los Angeles, CA: The Americas Group.

Miziker, R. (2015). *Miziker's complete event planner's handbook: Tips terminology, and techniques for success.* Albuquerque: University of New Mexico Press.

Oriade, A., Robinson, P., & Gelder, S. (2010). Delivering live events. In P. Robinson, S. Wale, & G. Dickson (Eds.) *Events management.* (pp. 72–112). United Kingdom: Cambridge University Press.

Post, P. (2007). *Emily Post's wedding planners for moms: How to help your daughter or son prepare for the big day.* New York: Harper Collins.

"Putting the views in corporate event venues," (2017). *Adweek, 58* (32), 8.

Scherer, K., & Zentner, M. (2001). Emotional effects of music: Production rules. In P. N. Juslin & J.A.Sloboda (Eds.). *Music and emotion: Theory and research.* Oxford University Press (pp. 631–392). Retrieved from http://psy2.ucsd.edu/~charris/SchererZentner.pdf

Silvers, J. (2004). *Professional event coordination.* Hoboken, NJ: John Wiley and Sons.

Shone, A., & Parry, B. (2004). *Successful event management: A practical handbook.* Boston: Cengage.

Simpeth, K. N., & Simpeh, M. (2011). Servicescape and customer patronage of three star hotels in Ghana's metropolitan city of Accra. *European Journal of Business and Management, 3,* 119–130.

Sloboda, J. A., O'Neill, S. A., & Ivaldi, A. (2001). Functions of music in everyday life: An exploratory study using the experience sampling method. *Musicae Scientiae,* 9–32.

Solomon, M. (2016). *The heart of hospitality.* New York: SelectBooks Inc.

van der Meer, A. (2008). *Modern bride survival guide.* Hoboken, N.J.: John Wiley & Sons, Inc.

Walker, J. R. (2017). *Introduction to hospitality.* 7th ed. Essex, England: Pearson Global.

Wall, E. A., & Berry, L. L. (2007). The combined effects of the physical environment and employee behavior on customer perception on restaurant service quality. *Cornell Hotel and Restaurant Administration Quarterly, 48,* 56–69.

Warner, D. (2002). *Great parties on small budgets.* Franklin Lakes, NJ: New Page Books.

Wolf, P., Wolf, J., & Levine, D. (2005). *Event planning made easy: 7 simple steps to making your business or private event a huge success.* New York: McGraw Hill.

Worcester, B. (1999). Casting light on meeting rooms. *Hotel & Motel Management, 214,* 50.

Chapter 10

THE EVENT: FROM SCRIPTING TO REFLECTING

The event date is set; plans are in motion; and now it is time to put it all together. Months of meetings and preparation are behind you, and the focus is on implementing all of your efforts to create a successful event. Moving forward requires schemata, the blueprints or plans of how event planners envision something, or, as Chesebro (2014) defines them, "mental filing cabinets" (p. 5). An **event schema** is the picture you register in your head of how different social settings play out (Schneider, 2014), and is essential for all pre-planning but also useful in particular for evaluating possibilities of what might happen during an event (Lawton & Weaver, 2015). For example, you might envision a sorority Halloween party a lot differently than a sorority end-of-the-year formal. The Halloween party might call for original costumes, music, and candy, but the end-of-the-year formal might include fancy dresses, a band, and a seated dinner. Developing a variety of schemata can help event planners anticipate the needs of the client and envision any complications during the process. In planning, you move from envisioning an actual event to the scripting process. Abelson (1976) defines a **script** as "a coherent sequence of events expected by the individual, involving him either as a participant or as an observer" (p. 33). Scripts answer the question, 'What comes next?' Think about attending a baseball game. The events throughout the game are scripted in a way that you know what comes next: the National Anthem will play; the visiting team will bat first; a song will play during the seventh-inning stretch; the home team will bat last if they find themselves behind in the ninth inning. Whether you are in Oriole Park at Camden Yards, PNC Park, or Fenway Park, the sequence of events generally remains the same. This chapter will cover many different parts of an event, from the beginning stages of scripting to reflection after the event concludes. All of these topics working together can create a memorable event for the client.

Event schema: *The picture that people register of how different social settings might play out*

Script: *A coherent sequence of events expected by individuals, involving them either as a participant or as an observer*

© Scott Lomenzo/Shutterstock.com

When you have finished reading this chapter, you will be able to

- develop a script for the variety of elements that bring the event together;
- list several ways in which information about the event is communicated to guests;
- explain what elements of invitation are essential for a successful event;
- create reflective opportunities for guests.

<table>
<tr><td>**CASE STUDY**</td><td>

Off the Script

</td></tr>
</table>

Elle Ellinghaus, Owner, Elle Ellinghaus Designs, LLC.

The wedding of Alexis and Bryce was going to be the most gorgeous wedding I had designed to date and by far one of the most relaxed and easiest weddings in terms of "day-of" work. I had my best production crew, favorite florist, fabulous caterer, and loads of my own assistants on this wedding with me, and this day could be nothing but stellar in theory. The bride and I had become very close, and she trusted my design and experience to create a jaw-dropping wedding for her and her handsome groom. To make it even better, it was a Sunday wedding, and there is something about being below the Mason-Dixon line on a Sunday that creates a peaceful state of mind.

The wedding was going to be held at a new venue that I had told the couple about, and I was sure to prepare them for a few things. One, that it was a new location, and as with all new venues, they most likely will have kinks to work out, so I could not "recommend" it, but it was a stunning site with a promising event staff. I also made sure we were not the first wedding of the season, so they could work out most of the problems on their first events. I reassured Alexis that I would be by her side every step of the way, but that the weather in October in North Carolina could be 80 degrees or 50 degrees. We needed to be sure to have funds set aside for bringing in heaters if needed. Lastly, I prepared her for an outside wedding and the uncertainties that come along with it. We spoke in detail about these things and decided to move forward with the venue.

The planning that goes into running an event starts on day one with your client. The bringing together of all the planning into one day begins in the third or fourth month. Two weeks before Alexis and Bryce's big day, the first major obstacle occurred. While we were doing a walk-through at the site, the staff told us we could no longer hang the stunning, custom-made, crystal chandelier I had designed for her wedding from the tent. However, we came up with something perfect, and made it not only work, but also look better than ever. We brought in a custom structure to hold the chandelier, and with the sheers we added to hide the hardware, it was going to look even more graceful as a focal point.

The days leading up to the event were calling for sunshine, slightly chilly, but lovely. The day before, we added the heaters we had prepared for in the beginning, and the next morning the wedding production began. I am always the first to arrive and last to leave at my events. Any of the assistants or planners at my company can tell you that an 18–24 hour day, two to three days in a row, is not out of the ordinary for us.

The day was going incredibly smoothly as my associate producers and I took a moment to go over logistics and look around at the flawless work that had been completed in record time. Then the band leader, who was a friend of the bride and groom, arrived, and the event quickly changed direction. Unfortunately, his lack of professionalism would be the cause of many difficulties throughout the event. He lashed out when he believed there would not be adequate power for his system. Had he discussed this with me first, he would have learned that we had already established sufficient power for his equipment.

The ceremony was perfect, the cocktail hour was flawless, and it came time to line up for introductions. I made my way over to the band leader to go over the timeline with him, but he had only notes scribbled down on a piece of paper. I had gone over the song choices, artists, and details with him months in advance, but he refused to listen to my expertise. Although I pleaded with him to stick to the bride's timeline, he simply laughed and ignored me. He preferred to "go with the flow" of the evening.

The wedding party was introduced and the first dance was to begin, a very specific version of a song for which the bride and groom had taken expensive dance lessons. The band leader, however, chose a different version of the song than what the happy couple expected, causing tears and disappointment. After that mistake, he agreed to review the rest of the event's timeline with me.

But I was mistaken if I thought he would actually cooperate. He took it upon himself to cue the best man to make the toast. This was another bad decision. First, the bride and groom were not seated, and second, the videographer and photographer were not even in the tent. Additionally, there was no champagne for the speaker nor was any lighting focused on the best man. I quickly had to rearrange the timeline, grab the videographer and photographer, and move the bride and groom back to the head table. Because of the band leader's arrogance, there were repercussions for his actions. The bride and groom have only a limited record of that priceless moment because the videographer and photographer captured only the last half of the speech. To make matters worse, the band leader had the audacity to sit at a table with the guests and enjoy the dinner, even though he was a hired vendor. When the bride came up to the band to request a song, and he was not there, she looked around and saw him eating at a table. The look on her face said it all.

At the end of the event, I was shocked to hear him ask me if we could work together again in the future. I told him we would keep him in mind for future events—although I probably never would enlist his help again—because you do not want to make enemies in the industry; you never know when your paths will cross again.

Contributed by Elle Ellinghaus. Copyright © Kendall Hunt Publishing Company.

After reading the chapter, revisit this case study and respond to the following question:

What are the clear benefits to scripting the event, and what problems can deviating from the script cause?

Scripting

Gantt chart: *An event management tool used to track the schedule of a project*

Event planners need to follow a script so that clients and event attendees know when specific parts of the event will occur. This does not mean that everything has to occur in the same order at every event, but there must be some sense of order to each event you plan. For example, most wedding guests expect cake to be served after dinner, not before, but the actual cutting of the cake could take place as soon as the couple walks in the door, after dinner, or in a private setting without the guests even viewing the process. As you plan events, you will need to think about balancing an anticipated routine against the client's desire for the uniqueness of the process. One way to help organize the development of the script is through a **Gantt chart**, an event management tool named after Henry Gantt, an American engineer who popularized the tool in the early 1900s. Most Gantt charts are used to track the schedule of a project, either in months or hours, and can be very detailed depending on the planner's needs. Some event planners continue to write Gantt charts by hand, but new software allows easy automation once the data is input. This kind of software encourages swift and timely revision as well. Gantt charts work primarily as bar graphs, and thus the visual picture is clear and simple (Milosevic, 2003; Shelly & Rosenblatt, 2009; Van Der Wagen & White, 2018).

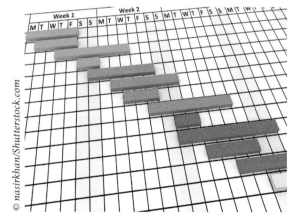

Activities occurring throughout the duration of the event (perhaps through weeks or months of a project, or merely through one entire day) are listed with an attached beginning and end time frame. The Gantt chart is typically customizable, and it demonstrates a logical sequence of events that helps event planners maintain the schedule they have mapped out with the client and gives a one-page overview of the entire event (See **Appendix F** for a sample Gantt chart). Because the Gantt chart is grounded in action, its main purpose is to show how projects actually get done. Thus, it is updated frequently as tasks are accomplished or changed. Day-of-event Gantt charts are highly structured and detail-driven (Timmreck, 2003; Van Der Wagen & White, 2018; Williams, 2017) and are used widely. Gantt charts can be helpful for scripting each aspect of the event, including food and beverage selection.

Food and Beverages

Making menu choices often comes months or years in advance of the event. In society, food expresses specific values and social significance, reflecting someone's opinion, the rules of the immediate society, and the client's expectations. Food, and thus a meal, is about more than just appeasing hunger; food makes a social statement in nearly every occasion. For any event, the client has to understand the guests' expectations about what will be served and respond to those social expectations. Because some societies are organized around anticipation of what occurs at mealtimes, negotiations about the menu begin with an ideal conception about attendees' expectations and then move on from there (Douglas, 2014). A meal format, or **menu**, is a way of "patterning dishes and items in time and space" (Douglas, 2014, p. 170), responding to the values, mores, and customs of the client's society. The event planner must understand that communication about food is actually more than just a conversation about a menu; issues of food are laden with expressions of ideals (Ali, Ferdinand, & Chidzey, 2017). Consider, for instance, the rapid development and wide acceptance of an enormous variety of ethnic cuisines that represent heritage, tradition, and values. Thus, choosing caterers, menus, and beverages can be far more complex than would first appear. A Greek festival, for instance, would bring the community together around a menu of gyros, spanakopita, moussaka, and baklava.

Planning a menu begins, as does most every component of an event, with a relationship: together with the client, the event planner must understand the needs of those who will be served and how those needs fit into the overall plan for the event (Booty, 2009). That means several components must come together in order to make **food decisions**: budget, catering, location, kitchen space, equipment, culture, presentation, and timing (Shiring, 2014). As the conversation about food begins, the event planner can help the client by preparing a list of typical questions and concerns. The questions fall into some general categories for consideration:

- Budget
- Size of locale/kind of service
- Pre-event food options
- Food choices/lifestyle
- Food allergies
- Dietary and religious restrictions
- Dessert options

Menu: *A meal format that patterns dishes and items in time and space*

Food decisions: *Choices that require event planners to examine the budget, catering, location, kitchen space, equipment, culture, presentation, and timing*

- Beverages
- Intermittent snack and/or coffee service
- Insurance/risk

Food should reflect the nature of the event (Ali, Ferdinand, & Chidzey, 2017; Devney, 2001, so food tastings are quite popular in helping to determine the catering choice. While a caterer may know a great deal about food, you are the one who understands the client's needs, so the conver-

sation among caterer, event planner, and client is as much about the budget and food tastes as it is about fulfilling the needs of the client in regard to trust, professionalism, clarity, and delivery. How well does the catering company listen to explicit and implicit wants of the client? Does the caterer understand the event demographics and offer possibilities in response to that knowledge (Booty, 2009)? Because these elements impact the budget, caterers should be respectful of all fiscal choices. Menu choices ultimately have one purpose: matching the client's desires with the caterer's abilities. Thus, the meal experience should be planned as a whole unit that includes service, food, beverages, comfort, atmosphere, and decor (Davis, Lockwood, Pantelidis, & Alcott, 2013). The best caterers understand this.

Besides setting up a tasting, check to see if the client is interested in viewing a caterer's portfolio or obtaining recommendations from previous clients. A caterer who has had experience in a wide variety of settings is ideal, but because the caterer's charges are usually three times the cost of the food itself, your client may have to choose between depth of experience and cost (Devney, 2001). Sometimes a caterer will create a bundled pack-

age that responds to the client's needs, but there may be room for only a little negotiation on the details in such a bundle (Shiring, 2014). These packages offer less expensive options than menus that are wholly personalized. But because the budget will always remain a priority, the event planner's job is to know what hidden charges and service fees will affect the bottom line. Additionally, there's no sense skimping on caterers who may not be properly credentialed or experienced even though their proposal may be enticing ("Sky Caterers: High-quality food at the right price," 2018).

The actual locale where the event is being held will influence the kind of food service offered. A good caterer will be familiar with the kitchen capabilities at the site (Shiring, 2014), the kind of service that can be offered there, and the number of staff that are needed. Do your research. Find out how well the caterer has worked with the venue or site and how well the company can solve problems of delivery (Mann, 2009). Since some sites have an 'approved' list of caterers, choices may be limited, but on the other hand, those vendors are knowledgeable about preparation and service at the site. The caterer should willingly participate in discussions about the set-up of the room, including details about the size of aisles between tables, a buffet as opposed to served or passed food, table linens, decorations, and food presentation (Ali, Ferdinand, & Chidzey, 2017; Devney, 2001).

Just as there are trends in fashion, food has its own trends, and good caterers know about new ways of serving, new foods, new designs, transformed eating patterns, and current food fashions (Davis, Lockwood, Pantelidis, & Alcott, 2013). Your client's guests may have special needs, such as gluten-free diets, religious restrictions, or vegan or vegetarian choices, and in some situations, the corporate culture itself actually dictates the kind of food chosen (Booty, 2009). For example, a heart-healthy foundation may be extremely conscientious about serving healthy choices at a black-tie gala. Because there is such a wide variety of possibilities in menu creation, the event planner must read every detail of the catering contract thoroughly and convey any hesitations to the client. The number of guests will also affect the kind of food chosen, since pricing will depend on those numbers, and an experienced caterer will also ask about the ages of the guests, since as people age, their appetites tend to decline, affecting the food production (Devney, 2001; Foskett, Paskins, Pennington, & Rippington, 2016). Depending on the number of children who may attend the event, a separate children's menu may be necessary and appreciated. These are details that event planners must have available at each catering consultation.

A beverage contract deserves in-depth consideration, and the event planner's job is to guide the client to choices that, again, address both the client's desires and the budget. Beverage choices are generally determined by the menu, so consultation is needed between those preparing and serving the food and those ordering and serving the beverages (Devney, 2001). Thus, it is important to trust that the beverage service vendor understands how wine, for instance, is paired with food, and how much to purchase for the event. Signature cocktails have become very popular in recent years and can reflect the theme of the event. For instance, a Pink Lady might be served at a breast cancer function to coordinate with the theme. In addition, another trend includes the pairing of local craft beers with the food on the menu. Usually there is a separate beverage contract if any form of alcohol is to be served, and caterers approach beverage service in many different ways. Is the company that will be providing beverage service equipped to handle the many tasks associated with serving? Responsible, professional bartending and pleasant service must be balanced against the client's budget, and this communication demands experience in personnel, standards, procedures,

and inventory (Shiring, 2014). Knowledge of the site is also vital for beverage service—not just for set up—but some sites do not allow alcohol to be served at all, so creative alternatives are necessary (Devney, 2001; Foskett, Paskins, Pennington, & Rippington, 2016). The company must consider providing equipment, as well as accounting for breakage, washing, serving, and more. All equipment rental charges should appear in the contract. There are also corkage charges associated with bringing in your own wine at some locales, and policies must be in place for enforcing drink limits, as well as handling intoxicated guests. Knowledge of state alcohol laws is important and should not be left up to the vendor. The event planner must be acquainted with the legal ramifications of alcohol service, as well as conditions for altering a beverage contract if service continues longer than planned (Davis, Lockwood, Pantelidis, & Alcott, 2013). Fees for beverage service vary widely, and often include one-time setting up and tearing down charges, as well as state, local, or city taxes, and gratuities, which are contracted per bartender (Shiring, 2014). Typically there is a 70% profit on alcohol, so if the budget needs tightening, there are choices among standard/house brands, call or name brands, or deluxe or premium brands (Davis, Lockwood, Pantelidis, & Alcott, 2013). Helping the client make informed beverage choices is a primary task of the event planner.

Finally, consider all the risks associated with food and beverage service. Ask to see the service vendor's insurance policies. This may mean consulting with an attorney if the limitations are too obscure, but coverage in the areas of food preparation and service and alcohol distribution is necessary (Devney, 2001). Is there a competent control system in place that addresses security, storage, theft, risk, and other unidentified possibilities (Davis, Lockwood, Pantelidis, & Alcott, 2013)? In addition, each state has developed laws for food safety, and thus safety procedures for serving food offsite should be part of the caterer's package. Some locales may also demand a written **Hazardous Analysis Critical Control Point (HACCP)** documentation, a food safety plan that addresses issues of contamination and risk (Booty, 2009; Surak & Wilson, 2014). Do not be afraid to ask questions about food or beverage service even after the contract is signed. Open and direct communication among all parties will help to ensure that the event is successful.

Hazardous Analysis Critical Control Point (HACCP): *A food safety plan that addresses issues of contamination and risk*

Invitations

Whether an event planner is coordinating a public event or a private affair, an **invitation** is necessary to set the tone for the theme and mood even before the event commences (Kadleck, 2006). Invitations can come in many forms, including traditionally printed invitations, postcards, evites, and flyers, among others. Whether you send a printed invitation or a digital one, you need to be able to guide the client in creating an invitation with an easy-to-read R.S.V.P. (Holtzman, 2014). **R.S.V.P.**, from the French Répondez s'il vous plaît (Respond if you please), allows the event planner to get an accurate representation of the number of event attendees. In addition, R.S.V.P. 'regrets only' is a popular trend that requires only those who are unable to attend to send a response back (Miziker, 2015). The invitations allow guests to get a sense of the event and decide whether they will attend.

In fact, in today's busy world, event planners are encouraging their clients to use save-the-date cards more and more as precursors to the actual invitation. These printed cards are distributed six months to a year in advance of an impending wedding, special function, or corporate convention, and are especially helpful when event planners must accommodate out-of-town guests (Ginsburg, 2014). The editor-in-chief of *Modern Bride* magazine offers suggestions for innovative save-the-date card such as magnets, puzzles, brochures, calendars, and bookmarks (van der Meer, 2008). Save-the-date cards are very popular and can help guests plan ahead for your client's event.

Invitations have the potential to evoke excitement about the event. For example, if a local Chamber of Commerce decides to host a high tea for businesswomen, in order to make the event warm and welcoming, the invitations might reflect that theme by incorporating an image of a teacup, a teapot, or flowers somewhere on the invitations with a matching elegant script font for the text. When the Leukemia and Lymphoma Society planned its annual fundraiser in Cleveland, it partnered with a graphic design firm and tackled the first impression the guests would receive: a sophisticated invitation on red cardstock with a red pocket and an elegant black tie completed the invitation to the Man, Woman and Business of the Year event (Kadleck, 2006). The results of the invitation design were noteworthy: attendance was 50% higher than in previous years (Kadleck, 2006). In addition to the look of the invitation, take care to word the invitation in a way that suits the client (Tobin, 2014). While the design is certainly important, guests will also read and interpret the language on the invitation, which can sometimes be personal, and at other times be formal or corporate in nature. The way invitations are worded, in conjunction with how they look, will help determine their personality (Friedland & Goodwin, 1998).

To get the best results, event planners should work with a vendor or printer to help design, create, and produce the invitation. Consider the client's preference for the look of the invitation, the weight and color of the paper, the type style, the ink color, and the way in which it will be printed. If

Invitations: *Printed or digital requests that set the tone of an event before it even begins, and ensure that guests are properly notified so they can build the event into their schedules in order to attend*

R.S.V.P.: *From the French,* Répondez s'il vous plaît *(Respond if you please), this request allows the event planner to get an accurate representation of attendees*

TIP

Work with your event planning team to have a backup plan in case far fewer or a great deal more guests than expected show up. View the unexpected as a message of opportunity, not of crisis, and respond accordingly.

— Janie Harden Fritz

an invitation requires innovative design elements, event planners may need to work with graphic artists to achieve the look the client desires (Ginsburg, 2014; Levy & Marion, 1997; Post, 2007). In much the same way you make a first impression on a job interview or at an initial client meeting, the invitation is the guest's first impression of your upcoming event. Of course, it is essential to double check the invitation's clarity and correctness before it is sent. Misspellings, dodgy production, and a lack of care when producing invitations will have a negative effect on guests when they open the invitation. Fashion designers, for example, spend countless hours creating innovative invitations to their theatrical fashion shows during Fashion Week in Paris, Milan, and New York, and each invitation represents a one-of-a-kind graphic keepsake that attendees cherish because it connects them to the event (Hawkins, 2017; Vienne, 2008).

Formal invitations for weddings, receptions, birthday parties, engagements, retirement parties, corporate holiday parties, or elegant corporate events may use engraving (deep-set) or embossing (raised or deep-set), print, or thermography, which is shinier and less expensive. The size and weight of the invitation may also incur additional postage (Post, 2007). Event planners must work closely with the client to establish the invitation budget in conjunction with the tone and theme of the event. Clients should establish a thorough invitation list and order more invitations than the number of potential guests. Clients can change their minds, invite people at the last minute, or make mistakes when addressing envelopes (Levy & Marion, 1997; Post, 2007). For the nominal fee that a few extra invitations incur, the cost is definitely worth it. Remember, you can hire a calligrapher to address the envelopes, which is more personal than a computer-generated label. To add an even more personal touch, have your client create customized postage stamps for the envelopes. When working with a printer, you can ask for a discounted rate if you order several of your printed pieces together, such as the save-the-date cards, the invitations, the R.S.V.P. cards, thank you notes, and ceremony programs, for instance. Additionally, for corporate events, printers may discount if you order large quantities, including, perhaps, printed favor bags, badges, and place cards. The cost of an invitation can vary depending upon the quantity you must order, but typically, the more you order, the lower the per-piece price (Kadleck, 2006). Invitations should include the specific locale's address, along with parking options and fees if appropriate. (Devney, 2001).

Suggest to your client the possibility of electronic invitations if they are appropriate. With the rise in social media, invitations sent to friends, acquaintances, or even strangers have become commonplace. Various software programs and websites make electronically inviting people to events easy (Holtzman, 2014). For some events, viral marketing could be an option, since electronic media can spread messages very quickly, and the practice is widespread (Woerndl, Papagiannidis, Bourlakis, & Li, 2008). Email invitations can be classified into two groups: (1) The long cycle, which requires sending multiple invitations over a two–six week period of time, and (2) The short cycle, which requires sending one or two invitations within a two–seven day period of time (Dupont, 2010). With either cycle, event planners will need to track the progress and effectiveness of the email invitations they send. Finally, when planning corporate invitations, consider using popular social media as well as business blogs and tagging (Rebelo & Alturas, 2011). Be sure to continuously build and maintain your database (Holtzman, 2014). One tremendous advantage to inviting guests to events electronically is the savings in cost. Guest management suites, operated through an app or a website, include a variety of elements, such as invitation lists, R.S.V.P.s, programs, and gift registries. These electronic databases are another way to help with invitation management.

Programs

Another piece that will take time to create and produce is the program. When guests arrive at the event, a schedule will help them feel more comfortable. Knowing exactly when the cocktail hour will begin, for example, or when the gun will sound for the race, is helpful when trying to organize even a few people or a larger crowd. The **program** is a printed guide that lists the order of the events, through which you can offer guests helpful information, as well as background notes about those involved with the event and the event's history (Miziker, 2015). For instance, a wedding program might include personal information from the bride and groom, including a welcome note, ceremony details, names of those involved in the ceremony, honored loved ones, and a meaningful story or quote (van der Meer, 2008). At a corporate event, such as a convention or a training seminar, a program will be vital to help move attendees from one place to another at specific times. Perhaps the ballroom at the hotel is being used for the luncheon, but several breakout rooms will hold working lunch training sessions. Attendees can refer to the printed program to see when and where they need to be. Event planners must pay careful attention to these details, as the success of the event will depend on what is communicated via the program.

Event programs come in a variety of dimensions, but keep in mind that the more intricate they are, the more they will cost. Elaborate programs can be quite pricey; a local printer may cost less, be more convenient, and have a faster turnaround time. Some clients may want to cut costs and produce programs inexpensively using their own computers, programs, and paper (Post, 2007). As the event planner, you will need to help guide your clients as to the type and style of program that might best suit them; you would

Program: *A printed guide that lists the order of the events, through which guests can receive helpful information, as well as background notes*

not want them to produce an amateurish program that does not match the quality of the invitations and decorations. Event planners should discuss with clients what they want to include in the event program. Organizations hosting local events may want to incorporate the schedule for the day, as well as a list of local donors and sponsors they wish to thank. Corporations could use the program as a public relations tool to promote the company's goodwill efforts, thereby educating attendees about the company (Carter, 2013). If people are paying money to attend the event, then understanding the foundation of the business is essential (Devney, 2001). The client may ask you to handle the project, which means you will have to collect information and then compose the appropriate program. Make sure the client reviews the draft for corrections or changes. Proofread the final copy carefully, scrutinizing it for any mistakes. A second or third pair of eyes is typically used, since it is easy for editors to overlook their own errors. Once the program is produced, it cannot be changed without costly reprinting, so be especially attentive to each line (Levy & Marion, 1997).

Programs offer guests and attendees a wonderful souvenir through which they can remember the details of the event (Post, 2007). The program at a graduation ceremony, for example, might include the keynote speaker's biography, along with the names of fellow classmates who are also graduating. Twenty years later, that college graduate may forget who his celebratory speaker was, but referring to the program kept in a special box or scrapbook will allow the graduate to reminisce.

Registration

Registration: *The first point of contact with your attendees and can serve as the command center for your event*

Registration is usually the first point of contact with your attendees and can serve as the command center for your event; as a result, the registration center needs to be situated in a prominent location. Most of your attendees will go to the registration table with all of their questions and concerns, so informed and friendly workers are needed at this station. The size of an event determines how many people should be working at the registration table. Usually a minimum of two people will be at the table at all times for a small- to medium-sized event (Miziker, 2015). In addition to people helping out with the registration process, a fully stocked registration table is another way to keep things organized (See Table 1).

TABLE 1. *Items at the registration table*	
Office Supplies	Pens, pencils, Sharpies, markers, staplers, staples, clear tape, duct tape, paper clips, extra name tags, calculator, envelopes, clipboards, scissors, rubber bands, Post-it notes, pad of paper, flashlight
Copy of contracts	Venue, catering, entertainment, vendors
Electronics	Tablets or iPads, computers, printers, ink cartridges, USB drives, power cords, extension cords, batteries of all types, camera
Personal items	Dental floss, mouthwash, headache medicine, allergy medicine, sewing kit, nail file, clear nail polish, makeup, brush and comb, hair supplies, feminine products, stain remover, first aid kit
Contacts	Contact names and phone numbers, venue liaison phone numbers, extra copy of the guest list, business cards
Financial/program	Cash box, starting cash (if guests are paying onsite), mobile payment reader, event programs, an extra copy of the program that does not leave the table

By keeping all of these items organized at the registration table, your attendees and workers will know precisely where to go when something specific is needed.

Registration can happen in many ways. At a small event, registration might consist of a check-off or sign-in sheet. If the event is large enough, however, attendees will need some way to identify themselves to others. Name tags or table cards can serve as both check-off sheets and identification markers. If name tags or table cards are used, print them out before the event and arrange them alphabetically by last name on the registration table to help the process flow smoothly. Avoiding a bottleneck at the registration table—the initial point of contact for the event—is essential for a good first impression (Devney, 2001; Miziker, 2015).

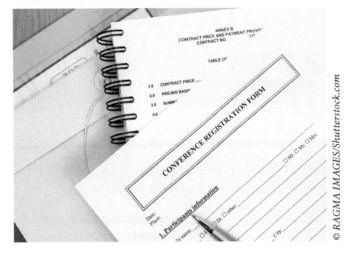

© RAGMA IMAGES/Shutterstock.com

You should also bring a computer and printer with all of the software ready to go for unexpected guests or misspelled names. Names should be printed in large, bold, block letters so they can be read from at least four feet away. This will remove the awkwardness that occurs if attendees forget names. If other information is needed, such as a person's affiliation, print it in small bold letters under the name. Plastic badge holders or branded lanyards are often used at large meetings or conventions. If you are considering using 'Hello, my name is …' adhesive tags, have lots of markers available at an adjacent table so that there is not a massive backup during registration (Wilcox, Cameron, & Reber, 2015). Another option is to purchase software that permits online registration. This type of software can allow instant confirmation of attendance, and since participants pay beforehand, the process is less labor-intensive and can expedite the registration process (Allen, 2002). There are many options for software, so conducting ample research on what will work best for you or your company is crucial.

Speakers, Guests, and Special Invitees

Another consideration event planners will have to manage is arranging for **special speakers, guests, or invitees,** individuals who attend functions as keynote speakers, dignitaries, community and government leaders, or honored members of families. The secret to making guests of any sort feel welcome and comfortable at an event is to place yourself in their shoes to discern what they would need. Offer the speaker your client has selected a few possible dates, explaining the purpose and theme of the event, describing the venue and the audience. Once the speaker has agreed to appear, planners should provide him or her with a list of important guests who also have been invited (Van Der Wagen, 2010). Event planners should not recommend or hire anyone they or their clients have not heard speak before or do not implicitly trust; some star speakers have notoriously outrageous demands, or they may be poor public speakers, and foreknowledge is essential in such cases (Smith, 2003).

© suradach/Shutterstock.com

Prior to the event, the event planner must be meticulous about coordinating details that will affect the speaker and the presentation. There are significant business protocols for international visitors that must be understood as well, including protocol for business cards, greetings, small talk, gift giving, religions, and cultures (Van Der Wagen, 2010). The role of the event planner is to pay attention to the logistics that might impact the comfort of the speaker or guest (Bowdin, Allen, Harris, McDonnell, & O'Toole, 2012). In preparation for the event, it is a good idea to ask speakers about their audiovisual needs, including, for instance, the kind of microphone preferred. Some different types of microphones include the shotgun, the handheld, the lapel or lavalier, the directional, and the wireless. Each serves a different purpose and will work better in a specific setting or space (Van Der Wagen, 2010). Knowing the area in which the microphone will be used is critical in choosing the exact kind of instrument. If there is an audiovisual presentation, have a wireless remote presenter available and make sure the speaker or an assistant knows how to use it. Help your client or designated presenter prepare a warm introduction, explaining why the speaker is present. If there is going to be a question-and-answer period, have some questions on hand in case the audience is reticent at first (Allen, 2009). Assessing attendance for the event ahead of time is important; if it appears that the event might be under- or over-attended, call to inform the speaker of the audience size. Staying in touch with the speaker in the time between the invitation and the event itself is necessary, and often occurs through the speaker's **gatekeeper,** someone who controls access to a particular person or locale. Send a parking permit or reserve a space ahead of time if the location demands it, and make sure the speaker has clear directions to the locale as well as your cell phone number. Arrange transportation if necessary, but keep the schedule flexible in case someone is

TIP

Lavaliere microphones look great but can be problematic with a house sound system because it takes a greater level of sound to make them work, and they tend to produce feedback. Handheld microphones or lectern microphones generally work better.

— Stacey Haines

running late, or be prepared to adjust it if needed. If the event is a major production, planners can arrange to have professional groomers available to do makeup and hair for the guest (Allen, 2009), and a check-in spot for the media should also be provided if they have been invited to the event (Gould, 2009). That means designating someone to greet and escort those media guests as well.

With practice, event planners will develop their own procedures for what occurs on the day of an event that features a special guest or speaker. The ultimate goal, once again, is to make the guest feel appreciated. As the speaker or guest arrives, make sure there is a greeter ready to welcome him or her, offering a beverage and pointing out the restroom facilities if necessary. If the speaker is giving a keynote address, and there is also a meal offered, make sure the meal is provided first (Allen, 2009). Your client should introduce the speaker or guest to other dignitaries present, and show the guest the place that has been reserved on the stage or near the podium. Try to make sure that all other honored guests are seated according to your client's wishes (Gould, 2009). With your client, take some time to review the event's agenda with the speaker, reminding him or her of the amount of time dedicated to the speech, including, perhaps, a question-and-answer session. Remember that you are in control of the event's pacing and will need to keep a watchful eye on the clock, since finishing on time is a goal. You will have worked out a signal with the speaker that indicates when the time is up. After the event is concluded, do not forget to thank the speaker or guest, perhaps with a gift or some other remuneration, and escort him or her back to where the event began. A personal thank-you note, sent the next day, is an excellent way to build a relationship.

Interactive Media

Scripting the event continues to evolve even after your client has selected guests and speakers. In the world of interactive media, a variety of digital media such as voice, text, images, audio, and video are combined into a multi-sensory and sometimes interactive presentation in order to communicate a specific message to those in attendance (Fearn, DeMuro, & Turner, 2019). The use of media has changed the manner in which events are presented as well as the methods people use to communicate. In some ways, the use of media has improved communication by making

© Matej Kastelic/Shutterstock.com

the message clearer and the delivery more engaging. Because most presentations that involve the use of media appeal to and stimulate many senses, information reaches the audience on several levels (Vaughan, 2014). Visual presentation technologies have grown enormously, and the event planner should have some knowledge of the differences, for instance, between front and rear presentation technologies, and how video-data projectors work (Fearn, DeMuro, & Turner, 2019).

The event planner must know and understand the many ways interactive platforms can work in different kinds of venues, or be in contact with a digital media company that is expert in the field. Controlling the content and course of information demands a very specific expertise, or a strong relationship with those who make a living in the industry. At the most basic, event planners must understand the terms and language used, the possibilities that exist for the wide variety of media use, and the integration of media into specific spaces. Of course, there are event production media service companies with whom a vendor relationship can be established for very specific needs, but they may exceed the budget of the client, so the event planner must at least have someone on site who can troubleshoot problems (Matthews, 2007). For example, consider a venue that is not prewired for an outdoor concert. Logistics such as where the video boards should be placed, where the speakers should be set up, and how the staging would allow for all audience members to view the musicians must all be in sync to offer the best show possible. Something as simple as knowing how to avoid microphone feedback can make a substantial difference to the success of an event.

Preparation and anticipation of complications is key when planning multimedia use. Projection and display equipment must be placed in such a way that all guests have a clear and unobstructed view of the media presentation. What resolution is optimum for the amount of light in the space? Who will control the pace of the presentation (Matthews, 2007)? These are all questions that the best event planners can answer. Checking sound quality and audio systems, amplification, screen size, lighting, and remote presentation devices ahead of time is critical (Agnew, Kellerman, & Meyer, 1996; Fearn, DeMuro, & Turner, 2019). For each phase of the presentation, trained technicians can perform a pre-event sound, presentation, and light check. Knowing the size of the room, the distance of the audience from the visual and sound elements, and the acoustics of the venue will aid in decision-making for your client (Matthews, 2007). If you are renting equipment from the site, make sure it is very clear in the contract what the costs are and who is responsible for repairing or replacing breakdowns. Event planners carry extra batteries, know the kind of lights used in display equipment, and are able to troubleshoot for issues of risk and safety (Matthews, 2007). While scripting for interactive presentations is imperative, gift-giving is another important aspect of the script.

Gifts

Issues of gift-giving in America have changed significantly in the last 130 years. Prior to that, the number of occasions on which gifts were actually exchanged was few, but as the economy of giving developed along with the rise of consumerism, the kinds of events for which gift-giving became the norm increased dramatically. Holiday gifts, wedding presents, birthday gifts—all of these offerings saw new popularity. Before that, money was the gift of choice (e.g., a dowry) until new gift-giving events evolved such as Mother's Day, Valentine's Day, graduations, christenings, and anniversaries. Household budgets after the turn of the previous century began to reserve a segment for gift-giving, and the tradition continues to affect business and personal lives (Rotman Zelizer, 1997). Most would agree that giving a gift is not just an economic exchange, but rather a gesture that has sentiment, and thoughtfulness, above all, continues to be relevant.

© elitravo/Shutterstock.com

Event planners must ask why the client is choosing to give a gift. What is the purpose of the gift and how does that purpose connect to the event itself? The number of reasons for **gift giving** in a business or personal setting is surprisingly high: for recognition, for gratitude, for community-building, for motivation, for increasing sales, for instance (Levy & Marion, 1997). The best event planners understand the gift-giving cultural expectations and assumptions of each group they are working with, and because event planners understand the key importance of being fluent in cultural and political manners, they avoid the chance of insulting guests or creating an awkward moment because of some unknown taboo in gifting. In most cultures, giving a gift is a sign of respect and appreciation, whether it is a business gift or a personal one. Choosing gifts demands time, effort, and consideration, as well as an understanding of the other's expectations. In business giving, if there is one gift, there must be something for everyone in the group, and in some cultures, the more senior the business rank, the more expensive the gift must be (Allen, 2010). Each business has a specific corporate image, and connecting gifts to the brand can help to extend that brand in a tasteful and memorable way. Know, however, that in some corporate cultures, there may be a prohibition on accepting gifts at all (Levy & Marion, 1997). For example, members of the media who attend an event are usually not permitted to accept gifts, as it is sometimes seen as a form of inducement. The best of intentions might backfire if the gift planning is not thorough, careful, and specific. Furthermore, there are gift codes attached to the geographic locale of many businesses, and that knowledge will be invaluable for successful event planners (Rotman Zelizer, 1997). For instance, will guests at a conference expect gifts to be delivered to their hotel room? Such gifts indeed offer a warm welcome, build community, and grow anticipation for conference events coming up, but event planners must include these items in the budget, remembering that there may be administrative charges and gratuities for the staff for delivery. Who will choose the gifts? Who will deliver them? Will all guests get the same product? These are questions to consider in the planning stage of the event. While some hotels may offer free welcome gifts, gift giving could be a costly investment if purchase is required (Allen, 2010).

Gift giving: *The action of giving a sentiment or token that allows for recognition, gratitude, community-building, motivation, and increasing sales in today's business and personal settings*

Similarly, on the personal or social event side, such as a wedding, guests have come to expect some sort of small gift or favor. While such gifts are certainly not required, because gifting in these situations is now such a common practice, it is difficult not to participate. One of the mistakes people make in this gift-giving area is waiting too long to make a decision or forgetting to include these costs in the budget. Help your client to make budgeting, choosing, ordering, and wrapping (if necessary) a priority. Favors or gifts that are personalized with a name and/or a corporate logo can demand more lead time than anticipated, so it is important that gifts appear as a line item in the budget from the start (Tutera, 2010). In any event, think about gifts in a way that they are not just required etiquette, but rather items that will evoke surprise, pleasure, and approval. Remember that all gifts need to be acknowledged in some way, since the giver has spent time and effort in selecting something appropriate.

Reflection

Reflection: *A process that allows people to turn their experiences into learning opportunities by thinking about what occurred*

The event is over, and a huge weight is lifted off your shoulders. Even though the guests have left and everything is cleaned up, there is still work to be done. Reflecting on your experiences will help you create stronger events in the future or perhaps even decide that the event was not worthwhile or beneficial in the future. **Reflection** is a process that allows you to turn your experiences into learning opportunities (Boud, Keogh, & Walker, 1985). Moreover, Gould and Baldwin (2004) believe that by participating in reflection, practitioners have the ability to recognize and avoid using ineffective methods the next time the same situation arises. The day after the event is the best time to start reviewing and typing your copious notes (Tull & Williams, 2017). This will allow you to develop an electronic debriefing file on each event that you plan. Make lists of what was effective and what could have been done better next time. For each ineffective scenario, create a 'next time' situation so that you do not make the same mistake twice. For example, you might realize that the coat rack was conveniently located by the registration table, but this caused a lot of congestion at the entrance of the event. Your 'next time' situation might remind you to give enough space between the registration table and the coat rack.

Another valuable way to reflect on your event is to get as much feedback as possible about various event details. For feedback to be useful, you need to know who to ask, when to ask, and how to ask. By answering these questions, you should be able to get a well-rounded response (Kirkland & Manoogian, 2004). If you are working with a group of people, ask them for feedback, and, if possible, include them in the reflection process. Other essential people to ask for feedback are the venue staff, vendors (e.g., florist, caterers), and your client. You can call them a few days after the event with a list of questions about their experiences, you could send them an electronic questionnaire, or occasionally you might choose to send a survey in the mail enclosing a self-addressed stamped envelope for convenience.

Each individual will notice different things that were effective and ineffective at the event, so the more feedback you have, the better your reflection process will be. Remember this is not a time to castigate yourself about all the things that went wrong; make sure you include positive scenarios so you can replicate your successes (Tull & Williams, 2017).

Even in this digital age, soon after your event is over, you should also start sending out personalized thank-you notes to your vendors, clients, and any special guests who attended the event. When writing these notes, try to be as specific as possible. If you can recall a certain moment of the event that was made extra special by someone, take the time to mention that moment in your appreciation. This will help ensure you are not creating generic thank-you notes that seem meaningless to the person receiving them. Thank-you notes are a way to show your appreciation and may lead to new or returning business. Going above and beyond what is expected of you after the event will help ensure a positive ending impression (Mancuso, 2008).

Italian fashion designer Giorgio Armani (2006), known for his painstaking quest for perfection in each creation, once said, "To create something exceptional, your mindset must be relentlessly focused on the smallest detail" (para. 13). His words should resound every day with the event planner who longs to create that near-perfect event in which all the details combine splendidly into one script that pleases the client, the guests, and the vendors. To do so is not impossible; such a script involves listening, planning, and reviewing each element that will affect the outcome of the event. Careful and conscientious attention to detail indeed demands a relentless focus but is well worth it in the end.

© Dusan Petkovic/Shutterstock.com

Key Terms

Event schema
Script
Gantt chart
Menu

Food decisions
Hazardous Analysis Critical
   Control Point (HACCP)
Invitations

R.S.V.P.
Program
Registration
Special speakers, guests,
   or invitees

Gatekeeper
Gift giving
Reflection

Discussion Questions

1. How can the details of food and beverage at a function make it memorable? Recall a time when you attended an event when the food and beverages made the event fun.

2. Think of a time you received an invitation in the mail for a family or corporate event, party, or wedding. How did that invitation set the tone for the event?

3. As an event planner, you will plan many functions of all varieties over the course of the year. What types of details and records would be beneficial for you to keep as you prepare for the future?

Activity

You are planning the end-of-year celebration banquet in Miami for your corporation's sales team. Over 350 salespeople received the trip as a reward and will be attending the celebration. Many of the salespeople will receive recognition and awards for reaching and exceeding their sales goals for that year. How would you script the event using the key outline provided below?

- Food and beverages
- Invitations
- Programs
- Registration
- Speakers, guests, and special invitees
- Interactive media
- Gifts
- Reflection

References

Agnew, P. W., Kellerman, A. S., & Meyer, J. (1996). *Multimedia in the classroom.* Boston: Allyn and Bacon.

Abelson, R. (1976). Scripting processing in attitude formation and decision-making. In J. S. Carrol, & J. N. Payne (Eds.), *Cognitive and Social Behavior* (pp. 33–46). Hillsdale, NJ: Lawrence Erlbaum.

Ali, N., Ferdinand, N., & Chidzey, M. (2017). Event Design. In N. Ferdinand & P. J. Kitchin (Eds.), *Events management: An international approach.* (2nd ed.) (pp. 67–93). Sage: London.

Allen, J. (2002). *The business of event planning: Behind-the-scenes secrets of successful special events.* Erobicoke, Ontario: Wiley.

_____. (2009). *The executive's guide to corporate events and business entertaining: How to choose and use corporate functions to increase brand awareness, develop new business, nurture customer loyalty and drive growth.* New York: John Wiley & Sons.

_____. (2010). *The business of event planning: Behind-the-scenes secrets of successful special events.* Hoboken, NJ: John Wiley.

Armani, G. (2006, October). *G & A: Giorgio Armani.* Retrieved from http://edition.cnn.com/2006/TRAVEL/06/01/milan.qa/

Booty, F. (2009). *Facilities management handbook.* Burlington, MA: Routledge.

Boud, D., Keogh, R., & Walker, D. (1985). *Reflection: Turning experience into learning.* New York: Routledge.

Bowdin, G., Allen, J., Harris, R. McDonnell, I., & O'Toole, W. (2012). *Events Management.* New York: Routledge.

Carter, L. (2007). *Event planning* (2nd ed.). Bloomington, IN: Author House.

Chesebro, J. L. (2014). *Professional communication at work: Interpersonal strategies for career success.* New York: Routledge.

Davis, B., Lockwood, A., Pantelidis, I., & Alcott, P. (2013). *Food and beverage management.* NY: Routledge.

Devney, D. C. (2001). *Organizing special events and conferences: A practical guide for busy volunteers and staff.* Sarasota, FL: Pineapple Press.

Douglas, M. (2014). *Food in the social order.* New York: Routledge.

Dupont, A. (2010). Get strategic with e-mail invitations. *Association Meetings, 22,* 26–27.

Fearn, N., DeMuro, J., Turner, B. (2019, March). Best presentation software of 2019. Retrieved from Techradar.Pro. https://www.techradar.com/news/best-presentation-software

Foskett, D., Paskins, P., Pennington, A., & Rippington, N. (2016). *The theory of hospitality & catering.* (13th ed.) London: Hodder Education Group.

Friedland, M., & Goodwin, B. (1998). *Invitations.* New York: Crown/Clarkson Potter.

Ginsburg, M. (2014). Smarter parties return. *Crain's Chicago Business,* 37, (5), 22.

Gould, M. (2009). *The library PR handbook.* Chicago: American Library Association.

Gould, N., & Baldwin, M. (2004). *Social work, critical reflection and the learning organization.* Burlington, VT: Ashgate.

Holtzman, B. (2014). Using event marketing to gain customers and buzz. *Inside Tucson Business, 24,* 2.

Kadleck, C. (2006). Chic invitations dressed to impress. *Crain's Cleveland Business, 27,* 15.

Kirkland, K., & Manoogian, S. (2004). *Ongoing feedback: How to get it, how to use it.* Greensboro, NC: Center for Creative Leadership.

Lawton, L. J. & Weaver, D. B. (2015, February). Using residents' perceptions research to inform planning and management for sustainable tourism: a study of the Gold Coast Schoolies Week, a contentious tourism event. *Journal of Sustainable Tourism*, 23 (5), 660–682 | Published online at https://www.coursehero.com/file/12589117/Using-residents-perceptions-research-to-inform-planning-and-management-for-sustainable-tourism/

Levy, B. R., & Marion, B. (1997). *Successful special events: Planning, hosting, and evaluating.* Burlington, MA: Jones and Bartlett.

Mancuso, J. (2008). *The everything guide to being an event planner: Insider advice on turning your creative energy into a rewarding career.* Avon, MA: Adams Media.

Mann, D. (2009). *Facility management: Human outsourcing solutions to clients.* New Delhi: Global India Productions.

Matthews, D. (2007). *Special event production: The resources.* NY: Routledge.

Milosevic, D. Z. (2003). *Project management toolbox: Tools and techniques for the practicing project manager.* New York: John Wiley & Sons.

Miziker, R. (2015). *Miziker's complete event planner's handbook: Tips, terminology, and techniques for success.* Albuquerque: University of New Mexico Press.

Post, P. (2007). *Emily Post's wedding planners for moms: How to help your daughter or son prepare for the big day.* New York: Harper Collins.

Rebelo, M., & Alturas, B. (2011, July). Social networking as a marketing tool: Study of participation in cultural events promoted by Facebook. *Academy of Marketing Annual Conference.* University of Liverpool Management School.

Rotman Zelizer, V. A. (1997). *The social meaning of money.* NJ: Princeton University Press.

Schneider, W. (2014). *Memory development from early childhood through emerging adulthood.* New York: Springer.

Shelly, G., & Rosenblatt, H. J. (2009). *Systems analysis and design.* Boston: Cengage.

Shiring, S. B. (2014). *Professional catering: The modern caterer's complete guide to success.* Clifton Park, NY: Delmar.

Sky Caterers: High-quality food at the right price (2018). *Caribbean Business*, 4 (42), 47.

Smith, P. J. (2003). *The dark side of the pyramid.* Arlington, VA: Xulon Press.

Surak, J. G., & Wilson, S. (2014). *The certified HACCP auditor handbook.* (3rd ed.) Milwaukee, Wisconsin: Quality Press.

Timmreck, T. C. (2003). *Planning, program development, and evaluation.* Burlington, MA: Jones & Bartlett Learning.

Tobin, L. (2014). *From yes to I do: The wedding guide for a modern bride.* Great Britain: Heron Books.

Tull, J. & Williams, N. (2017). Event Evaluation. In N. Ferdinand, & P. J. Kitchin. *Events management: An international approach.* (2nd ed.) (pp. 241–268). Sage. London.

Tutera, D. (2010). *The big white book of weddings: A how-to guide for the savvy, stylish bride.* New York: Macmillan.

van der Meer, A. (2008). *The modern bride survival guide.* New York: John Wiley & Sons.

Van Der Wagen, L. (2010). *Event management.* Ontario: Canada: Pearson Education.

Van Der Wagen, L., & White, L. (2018). *Event management: For tourism, cultural, business and sporting events.* South Melbourne, Victoria Australia: Cengage.

Vaughan, T. (2014). *Multimedia: Making it work.* (9th ed.) Berkeley, CA: Osborne/McGraw-Hill.

Vienne, V. (2008). R.S.V.P. (cover story). *Print, 62,* 66–73.

Woerndl, M., Papagiannidis, S., Bourlakis, M., & Li, F. (2008). Internet-induced marketing techniques: Critical factors in viral marketing campaigns. *International Journal of Business Science and Applied Management, 3,* 33–45.

Wilcox, D. L., Cameron, G. T., & Reber, B. H. (2015). *Public relations: Strategies and tactics.* (11th ed.) New York: Pearson.

Williams, N. L. (2017). Managing event projects. In N. Ferdinand, & P.J. Kitchin. *Events management: An international approach.* (2nd ed.) (pp. 94–119). Sage: London.

Chapter 11

EVENT TOURISM: CONNECTING EVENT PLANNERS TO THE TOURISM INDUSTRY

As you learned in Chapter 1, Bowdin, Allen, O'Toole, Harris, and McDonnell (2011) categorized events by size and impact. Event planners must be able to navigate their way through large-scale events as well as smaller-scale events they may be required to plan. Event planners may become involved in a hallmark event, festival, or concert that occurs annually or be invited to sit on an inclusive committee to bring a mega event to the city. Ritchie (1984) originally defined **hallmark events** as major one-time or recurring events developed to enhance a tourist destination, and whose uniqueness attracts attention. Event tourism has the potential to bring thousands of people to a city, boosting tourism and civic pride, and affecting the reputation of a city, town, county, region, or country. Therefore, planning the components necessary to create hallmark events that happen every year in the same city or location, as well as planning for mega events that yield a national or international audience, demands that professional event planners understand the purpose, function, and outcomes of these events.

Before event planners can leap into planning any destination events with many moving parts, they should understand the effects the event could have on tourism and on the locale.

When you have finished reading this chapter, you will be able to

- define event tourism and the role of the event planner;
- explain the importance of large-scale events within cities and communities;
- identify the elements necessary to generate sponsorships for event tourism.

Hallmark events: *major one-time or recurring events developed to enhance a tourist destination, and whose uniqueness attracts attention*

Planning Hallmark Sports Events

Morgan Cook, Senior Director of Women's Athletics, Corrigan Sports Enterprises

Corrigan Sports Enterprises (CSE) was established in 1991 with the goal of creating, managing, and implementing sports and event marketing opportunities for the corporate community. Based in Baltimore, MD, with another office in Oakland, CA, CSE develops and implements events throughout the entire country and maintains longstanding relationships with the corporate community in each market.

CSE's hallmark event, the Baltimore Running Festival, attracts 25,000 runners from all 50 states and more than 30 countries every year to the city in October. Other prominent properties include the Oakland (CA) Running Festival, the partnership with the Intercollegiate Women's Lacrosse Coaches Association (IWLCA), the Frederick Running Festival, and the Under Armour All-America Lacrosse Classic, to name a few.

The partnership with the IWLCA has landed CSE five of the largest girls' high school lacrosse recruiting tournaments in the nation. The IWLCA is a membership-led, nonprofit association representing the nation's intercollegiate women's lacrosse coaches within Divisions I, II, & III of the National Collegiate Athletic Association (NCAA) and the National Association of Intercollegiate Athletics (NAIA). The IWLCA is a 501c non-profit educational organization. The Capital Cup and Champions Cup each host 250+ teams from across the country, and the Presidents Cup attracts 350+ teams and boasts record numbers of college coaches each year. The newer events in the series include regional tournaments; the New England Cup and the Midwest Cup each attract 75–100 teams annually. All of these events fall within the domain of CSE.

© Morgan Cook

When developing the IWLCA Official Recruiting Tournament series, we had to consider many factors:

- The evaluation period of the NCAA recruiting calendar. Women's lacrosse recruiting is restricted to certain dates in the summer and fall. The dates for the tournaments had to fall within the open recruiting periods but also not conflict with other major tournaments.

- The choice of locations where the sport of lacrosse was established or rapidly growing.

- The choice of major tournament sites. Given the recruiting calendar, sites were selected based not only on the complex's availability to host a tournament on a preferred date, but also on the level of support the city was willing to provide to host our tournament.

- The logistics of the event. Factors considered when selecting sites included overall number of fields, including turf fields, lights, parking, number of hotel rooms in the surrounding area, and ease of travel/closest major airport.

The five official tournaments and their current host venues/cities are

- IWLCA New England Cup – University of Massachusetts, Amherst, MA
- IWLCA Junk Brands Champions Cup – River City SportsPlex and Clover Hill Athletic Complex, Midlothian, VA
- IWLCA Junk Brands Midwest Cup – Stuart Sports Park, Aurora, IL
- IWLCA Capital Cup – Calvert Regional Park, North East, MD
- IWLCA Brine Presidents Cup Presented by New Balance – International Polo Club Palm Beach, Wellington, FL (new venue starting with 2019 tournament)

Other complexes that have hosted the IWLCA tournaments include Disney's ESPN Wide World of Sports in Kissimmee, FL (Presidents Cup); Mercy Health SportsCore Two in Rockford, IL (Midwest Cup); and Voice of America Park in Hamilton, OH (Midwest Cup). These venues and cities were selected based on their ability and willingness to host thousands of athletes and their families in area hotels. In addition, we also considered available support from the local Convention and Visitors Bureau (CVB) and sports commission to help with hotel room rebates and subsidies and/or tourism grants to cover field rental fees or other operating expenses for the tournament. CSE is in constant communication with sports commissions across the country in search of new venues to host IWLCA events. Because of the highly competitive landscape of securing sports facilities and grants from sports commissions, CSE will negotiate contracts two to three years in advance of the tournament dates. Working through all of these moving parts allows event planners to navigate and execute these hallmark events successfully.

After reading this chapter, revisit the case study and respond to the following question:

How can event planners establish themselves routinely as the most successful choice for planning hallmark events?

Event Tourism

Today's large-scale events are created to attract visitors and yield attendance, whether those visitors are local or from afar. Events are often intermingled with the goals of cities and communities to bolster economies and create signature events that further promote the tourism industry. According to Getz (2008), "Events are an important motivator of tourism, and figure prominently in the development and marketing plans of most destinations" (p. 403). The role of event planners is to help create and manage events that figure prominently in communities and cities and have obvious strategic goals, such as bolstering a city or its image. Event planners should keep tourists in mind when planning large-scale events. Likewise, planners can use event tourism to their advantage to help garner interest and attract people to cities and communities (Getz, 2008).

When tourists visit a destination, they tend to spend time in that location, both before and after an event. If they are local, sometimes they spend the whole day; if they are from out of town, perhaps they spend several days in a destination. Therefore, Getz (2008) recognizes **event tourism** as an all-inclusive approach to creating, planning, marketing, and executing a special event. Event tourism also requires planners to recognize what Mill and Morrison (1985) termed '**drawing power**,' which refers to the distance people will travel to experience an event. Additionally, when considering event tourism, event planners should take into account the idea of promoting events for the outcome of creating a positive event image.

Tourism and events have been examined for centuries, but according to Oklobžija (2015), the study of event tourism is a relatively recent discipline, going back only a few decades. While events are often largely based on economics, there remains a certain amount of image branding that goes along with setting an event in a destination. Getz (2007) recognizes that the overall goals of event tourism can include the following:

1. events attract tourists (to specific places, and to overcome seasonality);
2. events contribute to place marketing (including image formation and destination branding);

TIP

Have fun with the experience! Stress and frustration can often get in the way of planning as we expect everything to be perfect. Remember that not everything will go according to plan, but enjoy that you have the ability to create fun, exciting events that leave an impact on others. Besides, that's what it's all about!

— Corrin Harris

Event tourism: *an all-inclusive approach to creating, planning, marketing and executing special events*

Drawing power: *the distance people will travel to experience an event*

3. events animate attractions and places, which essentially means that anyone with a park or facility is almost automatically in the events business; and

4. events can act as catalysts for other forms of development or improved capacity to attract tourists through infrastructure gains and more effective marketing (p. 19).

© dizain/Shutterstock.com

As events have the potential to be influential in a myriad of ways, event planners must also consider what motivates people to attend events. Destination events can bring joy to those who travel distances. Likewise, events set in particular locations have the power to draw attendees from afar and from the local, greater community. But why do people attend large-scale events? What is the psychology behind their attraction?

Event Tourism Attendance and Satisfaction

Bringing unique events to cities can help bolster a city's reputation and provide a memorable experience for attendees. Morgan (2006) found that attendees noted that the ability to discover something new was among one of the main reasons for attending a destination event. The ability to roam and find wonderful surprises was listed as a top reason for attending. Other reasons include to enjoy the escape and newness of an event; to overcome challenges; to spend time with family and friends; and to share cultural experiences and personal narratives (Morgan 2009). Moreover, people attend events that are new, staged in a different way, or offer a completely new concept. Take, for example, the Downton Abbey Exhibition that traveled from city to city, including New York, Washington, DC, and Boston, as well as a stop at the Biltmore in Asheville, N.C.. The exhibit promotes tourism and entices visitors to experience the actual set of the British series. Getz (2008) states, "Much of the appeal of events is that they are never the same, and you have to 'be there' to enjoy the unique experience fully; if you miss it, it's a lost opportunity" (p. 404). Therefore, attendees may have a certain perception of what a hallmark or large-scale event might be like, either from hearing from others, reading about it on the internet or in magazines and newspapers, or seeing promotional advertising. After attending the event, attendees may experience satisfaction or dissatisfaction because they have had their own expectations of an event, and in order for there to be satisfaction, those expectations must be met or exceeded. Gronroos (1990) suggests that perceptions gleaned from the event stem from technical or performance outcomes (such as how the staging and sound were), and functional, or process-related qualities of the event (such as the ease with which an attendee could move about and enjoy the event). However, Bowdin, Allen, O'Toole, Harris, and McDonnell (2011) suggest that there are so many other factors that can play a part in attendee satisfaction, such as the weather conditions and more personal issues that could be happening, such as whom an attendee is with and the nature of that relationship at the time. Internal motivations may also be a driving force in how an attendee experiences an event, including perception, learning and memory, motives, personality traits, and consumer attitudes. Neal, Quester, and Hawkins (2002) agree that consumer behavior is primarily driven by psychological motives. For example, you and your best friend travel a distance to attend a concert in a nearby city. The event is wonderful, but as the encore begins, your friend tells you she wants to get ahead of the traffic and leave before the final bow. You refuse, but now your perception of the event has completely changed, and you regret attending the concert with your friend, since her presence has altered your enjoyment of what was supposed to be a magical evening.

As event planners create and orchestrate large events, their goal is to impress visitors and to build an event that is memorable. With regard to positioning large-scale events as 'must attend' happenings, planners strive to create new and innovative opportunities that visitors may not have experienced elsewhere. Additionally, planners want to leave visitors with the ultimate pleasurable experience during their visit. O'Sullivan and Spangler (1998) identified several other factors of experience, including the stages of the event during which perceptions can change; the desire of the attendee to attend a particular event; and the ability to accommodate interpersonal relationships at the event. The notion of a fulfilling experience will drive the satisfaction, and that notion can mean different things to different people. When attendees enjoy something, they are more likely to return the next time the event is offered. For example, if attendees have a wonderful experience at the San Francisco Pride Festival one year, chances are they may already be making plans for the following year's event.

Strategic Planning and Event Tourism

Event tourism plays a role in tourism development, and event planners must understand that they should execute a strategic analysis before bringing events to destinations. Getz (2007) states that event tourism must be viewed from the demand and supply sides. The demand side requires planners to position the event with a positive destination image, and the supply side requires planners to develop, facilitate, and promote events to engage the potential audience. Hertanu and Boitor (2012) note that event tourism can have an effect on the economy either positively or negatively. On the positive side, revenue can be generated by boosting the economy through the event, and tourism can see a boon as well. On the negative side, the event expenses could be cumbersome. There is a great deal of planning and decision-making involved in building an event strategy for the masses.

TIP

Don't be afraid to challenge authority. If you see a potential problem, speak up!

— Nancy Willets

Before deciding to create any type of an event in a destination, event planners must conduct a SWOT analysis and a **feasibility study**. The SWOT analysis is a good starting point in strategic development for event tourism because it allows planners to decide if the event's strengths, weaknesses, opportunities, and threats permit the event to go forward (Bowdin, Allen, O'Toole, Harris, & McDonnell, 2011). Additionally, a feasibility study, sometimes referred to as a pre-event evaluation, is vital to the decision-making process as to whether or not to hold an event in a specific location. Getz and Page (2016) suggest that a feasibility study should be executed prior to an event and then be considered in conjunction with the project planning of an event. Moreover, it is important not to commit to any event until all facets of the study have been examined and the event is deemed acceptable in terms of cost, benefit, sound reasoning, marketability, and management. Take, for example, the Grand Prix car race held in Baltimore for the first time in September, 2011. After the failure of the event, an economic study found that the promoters' projections fell short of the anticipated revenue (Brumfield, 2011), and the city severed its contract with the promoters. Baltimore city and other vendors never received payment as debts rose to over $3 million (Jackson, 2011). This type of catastrophic failure traces its origins to a lack of a thorough feasibility study and SWOT analysis.

© duckeesue/Shutterstock.com

Feasibility study: *a research project that examines new or untested ideas through best practices in research, design, budget planning, coordination, and evaluation*

When considering the integration of a hallmark or large-scale event into an existing place, event planners will have to take into account many factors that could affect the outcome of the event. Creating a deliberate checklist in which planners can address specific parameters necessary to guide the event will help determine whether or not it is feasible. Considerations might include some of the following:

INITIAL CHECKLIST

- ☐ Place of event
- ☐ Venue (indoors or outdoors)
- ☐ Budget considerations
- ☐ Current infrastructure
- ☐ Projected attendance
- ☐ Time of year of event
- ☐ Sponsorship
- ☐ Volunteers
- ☐ City/Town/County support
- ☐ Managerial needs
- ☐ Saftey needs
- ☐ Travel
- ☐ Transportation

Event planners rely on lists like this one to guide their pre-planning visions and decisions.

When events move into the global arena, they are sometimes referred to as mega events, which take on a much larger scope. Getz's (2007) definition of **mega events** is as follows: "Mega events, by way of their size or significance, are those that yield extraordinarily high levels of tourism, media coverage, prestige, or economic impact for the host community, venue, or organization" (p. 25). These large-scale events often affect whole economies and are the result of competitive bidding. They are also deemed 'mega' events according to their "size, significance, levels of tourism, media coverage and prestige" (Getz, 2005, p. 18). The Olympics, World Cup, and World's Fairs are examples of these types of mega events.

Mega events: *Events that yield extraordinarily high levels of tourism, media coverage, prestige, or economic impact*

© lazyllama/Shutterstock.com

TIP

Listen to all constituents and establish your primary and secondary goals for the event to make sure you meet all expectations.

— Julie Wagner

Müller (2015) states that there can be symptoms and consequences to bringing mega events to cities, and that it is important to understand the benefits of hosting these mega events before deciding to become a host city. Some challenges to producing a mega event could include overpromising the benefits of hosting the event, underestimating costs of the event, hosting an event that is too large for the size of the city, and creating an event that does not benefit the public. Additionally, Müller cites consequences of planning mega events that could damage the actual reputation of the event in any given city, thus the need for proper analysis and consideration prior to selection and confirmation. Consequences for choosing a city that does not suit the mega event can include a loss of trust with citizens, budget shortfalls and profiteering, displacement, and either oversized or unfinished infrastructures. For example, the 2016 Summer Olympics in Rio de Janeiro were fraught with troubles including uninhabitable housing, infrastructure delays, and environmental issues including air and water pollution, and public safety and disease (Ward-Henninger, 2016).

However, for the most part, mega events are thought to be more positive than negative for a city. For that reason, Chen, Qu, and Spaans (2013) suggest that an analysis of the host city for a possible mega event should include a holistic examination of the site and not be concerned with only economic and political aspects. A combination of elements including, but not limited to, economic, social, environmental, and others should be considered in the decision making. Mega events should be designed not just with short-term goals in mind, but also by looking at long-term, lasting, and positive outcomes for the host city.

Getz (2008) distinguishes between mega and hallmark events by noting the global orientation of the former. Holding a mega event often requires a bid for the location (such as the Super Bowl or Olympic Games) as opposed to a hallmark event that exists in conjunction with the place, and is, in fact, tied directly to it. Hallmark events become synonymous with a place because of their unique quality, the spirit that the event embodies, their reoccurrence, and the recognition they bring, either long or short term (Ritchie, 1984). Rizzi and Dioli (2010) suggest these events can be defined as "events that are meant to be temporary, highly visible and often expensive projects aimed at attracting a large number of extremely focused visitors in a relatively short time span, but able to change people's ideas about a city" (p. 302). Examples of hallmark events include the Wimbledon tennis championships, Mardi Gras in New Orleans, Oktoberfest in Munich, and the Boston Marathon. Other hallmark event examples include the Miami Book Fair, founded in 1984 by Miami Dade College and community partners, and recognized as the nation's top literary festival (About us, 2016), as well as the Nantucket Food and Wine Festival, which has been in existence for over 20 years, and which opens the summer season on the island.

© Trong Nguyen/Shutterstock.com

Quite often, hallmark events are created and driven by economic factors and social benefits and then become a staple event in a city. People are enticed to come from the local region or from all over the world, and the decision to attend is often based solely on intuition and interest (Roslow, Nicholls & Laskey, 1992). For example, Carnivale in Venice is a perfect example of the spirit an event can bring to a city. Venetian masks are part of the culture in Venice, passed down for generations (Adams, 2014). While most people dress in Venetian masks and elaborate costumes, any costume is appropriate when attending this large masquerade ball that takes over the city

© Lois GoBe/Shutterstock.com

for several days. American travel writer Sheila Buckmaster (2012) writes glowingly about her eighth annual visit to Carnivale dressed as Charlie Chaplin, recounting all the reasons she cannot miss this hallmark event that yields three million visitors annually (Adams, 2014), gives the city an economic boost in tourism, and provides visitors with lasting memories year after year of both the place and event.

Event Sponsorship

Large-scale events often require funding from sponsors in order to be successful. Sylvia Allen (2016) defines **event sponsorship** as "an investment, in cash or in kind, in return for access to exploitable business potential associated with an event or highly publicized entity" (p. 44). In order for events to have monetary support, sponsorship is needed and often available at different levels. Event planners should look for ways to subsidize costs of the event. Securing sponsorship is a way to help events flourish and provide the

Event sponsorship: *an investment, in cash or in kind, in return for access to exploitable business potential associated with an event or highly publicized entity*

necessary monetary factions to create a worthwhile and meaningful event. Allen's (2016) approach to sponsorship success includes a 12-step process that can help event planners think about potential sponsors and how to ascertain partners for events. The following steps can help ensure sponsorships that add meaning:

1. *Take inventory*—Figure out what would be a value to a sponsor, and what will add value to sponsors, whether it is on the marketing side or hospitality side.

2. *Develop your media partners*—Media partners are an important aspect and should be treated the same way as sponsors. Work to make sure your event offers the chance for media partners to increase their non-traditional revenue.

3. *Develop your sponsorship offerings*—Organize sponsorship opportunities into categories that work, such as title sponsor, presenting sponsor, or partner. These opportunities will have value associated with each and offer a great deal of exposure.

4. *Research your sponsors*—Do your research about possible sponsors. Make sure that the event's vision and the sponsor's vision are in alignment.

5. *Make initial sponsor contact*—Reach out to sponsors, most importantly decision makers at the company to see if the event is a good match. Talk directly to the person in charge. Explain the event and how it will benefit the business.

6. *Go for the appointment*—After a brief discussion about the event and how the business may fit into the plan for sponsorship, send along a formal package that explains in detail the sponsorship opportunity.

7. *Be creative*—Think of how the business can benefit from being associated with your event and all the opportunities that may be possible. Be in the 'yes' business to see how you can make a sponsorship happen.

8. *Make the sale*—Ask directly if the potential sponsor is ready to strike a deal. Figure out a way to close the sale that will make the sponsor happy to be a part of the event.

9. *Keep the sponsor in the loop*—Work with the sponsor's public relations team to develop collateral material that helps spotlight their involvement. From flyers to posters to press releases and invitations, event planners should work directly with the sponsors.

10. *Involve the sponsor in the event*—Invite the sponsors to be on site, to attend exhibits or background events associated with the larger event, to have a booth on site, or whatever else may suit their needs.

11. *Provide sponsors with a post-event report*—After the event, give sponsors an overview of the event, including attendance, press coverage, feedback, and general analysis compiled into a formal report.

12. *Renew for next year*—Provided everything went rather well, event planners should see if sponsors are willing to jump on board for the next event (p. 44-47).

While garnering sponsorships is not always easy and takes a great deal of time, research, and patience to find the right fit, it is an important aspect to producing large events. Sponsors who would like to be involved in events enjoy the exposure they gain. Furthermore, in order for sponsors to benefit from the partnership, it is important for sponsors to be active participants in the event and communicate with their target audience (Sözer & Vardar, 2009). In some cases, sponsorship will be a harder sell than in others; sometimes potential sponsors will not understand the reach and prestige or positive association they may receive from being connected to a large-scale event, and event planners will be required to help them understand the benefits of such an association.

Exposure through events can help companies link to well-known entities and other brands whose vision and mission are much like their own. Sponsorships can elevate brands, and events rely on sponsorships for success. **Sponsor sincerity** suggests that consumers link the level of authenticity to how much the event or sponsorship benefits and supports the community or cause (Rifon, Choi, Trimble, & Li, 2004). While some sponsors may be better suited than others for specific events, it is in the event planner's best interest to attract and secure sponsors that have the potential to be connected for years to come. For example, Southern Bancorp in Arkadelphia, Arkansas, partnered with Downtown Arkadelphia to improve the look of downtown, believing that when hotels, restaurants, and attractions are full, the entire community benefits from the partnership (Lahouze, 2018). Promoting the town and its events required sponsorship from Southern Bancorp, in addition to the joint event planning of several groups. The collaboration orchestrated promotions, including a craft beer festival and catfish cook-off that have boosted the attendance by about 7,000, which includes mostly out-of-town visitors (Lahouze, 2018).

Event planners must make sure that sponsors are treated to extra-special care and given the VIP treatment. "Corporate sponsors often want specific hospitality services for themselves and their guests, even to the point of having private and exclusive areas and mini-events" (Getz & Page, 2016, p. 249). Arranging for these types of perks is important to sustaining sponsorship and to securing new ones. As sponsorship is vital to the overall budget and execution of the event, sponsors expect a certain level of pampering and care. Planners must work with each sponsor to facilitate a healthy relationship and ensure it is a win-win for both the event and its generous sponsors.

Marketing the Event Location

Convention and Visitors Bureaus (CVBs) and **Destination Marketing Organizations (DMOs)** are two cost-free groups event planners should consider using when bringing larger groups of people to a city. Event planners must understand these terms, which are often used interchangeably. Convention and Visitors Bureaus (CVBs), hotels, and other large venues

---

Sponsor sincerity: The belief that consumers link the level of authenticity to how much the event or sponsorship benefits and supports the community

---

Convention and Visitors Bureaus (CVBs) A not-for-profit organization that offers information and services to those from out of town

Destination Marketing Organizations (DMOs): A bureau or group whose job is to promote a specific locale as an interesting and viable place to visit

have the capacity to attract organizations and entice them to hold their meetings and conventions in their destination. Moreover, there are 256 convention centers in the United States, and over 60 million people attend conventions and conferences, while 30 million people attend U.S. trade shows annually (Kotler, Bowen, Makens, & Baloglu, 2017). Destination Marketing Organizations (DMOs) can offer event planners a variety of solutions and opportunities that can be incredibly helpful when tasked with planning at large venues with many moving parts (Palmer, 2017).

© CrackerClips Stock Media/Shutterstock.com

Palmer (2017) strongly suggests that planners who work with CVBs know what types of questions to ask when deciding upon a location for their meeting, conference, or convention. Asking the right questions can make a big difference. Questions to consider might include the types of possible savings a CVB can provide an organization; innovative suggestions creating a brand for the conference or convention; types of partnerships available for the organization; ways to take the event to new heights; and assistance in selling the destination to decision makers. For example, Visit Detroit, the city's CVB, worked diligently with conference planners to educate and expose them to the city's vast resources, local business, and tourism (Palmer, 2019). CVBs are a wealth of information for event planners and can offer attendees unique, exciting, and authentic experiences that help sell the event (Crocker, 2017).

Convention: *a large, purposeful gathering of people with common interests or goals*

Today, cities such as Louisville, Baltimore, Minneapolis, and Salt Lake City are expanding their convention spaces and increasing the number of hotels to attract new organizations and groups (Fredericks, 2019). A **convention** can be defined as a large, purposeful gathering of people with common interests or goals. While the big cities such as New York and San Francisco draw conventions based on their notoriety and allure, other cities are emerging as places to go for conventions and meetings. With culinary experiences, cool neighborhoods, and vibrant art scenes, some of the smaller cities are connecting with planners and showcasing their personalities. For example, representatives of the Eastern Communication Association flew to Buffalo, New York, to evaluate the location as a possible site for a future convention. While some may have had a negative perception of the city as being a small town lacking vibrancy, the CVB worked hard to dispel any preconceived notions. From its Frank Lloyd Wright structures to its world-renowned art collections, to its extensive culinary offerings, "Unexpected Buffalo," the city's theme, wowed the selection committee, and the city was selected without hesitation (Visit Buffalo Niagara, para. 1, 2019).

CVBs often help organizations help book convention centers. Brymer, Brymer, and Cain (2017) note that conventions, tradeshows, and large-scale meetings have the capacity to help the global economy by bringing people to cities for either work or pleasure. In North America, there are over 13,000 conventions held annually; additionally, on a global scale, there are approximately 25,000 to 30,000 conventions that take place each year (Brymer, Brymer, & Cain, 2017). As a testament to the popularity of traveling to a city to attend a convention, there is a rise in new convention and meeting properties being christened, and in 2015 alone, there were more than 18 new properties established all over the world (Woolard, 2015). Convention-goers may have many different motives for attending events. According to Bagdan (2013), some of these motives may involve a sense of completion at having attended, a sense of identity, a chance to escape from the daily grind, an opportunity to learn more about a culture, or the chance to be able to say they attended the convention or trade show.

Popular destinations for conventions and trade shows include Orlando, Las Vegas, Chicago, New York, San Diego, Atlanta, Dallas, and Nashville (CVENT.com, 2019). **Trade shows** are typically industry-driven opportunities to showcase products or to promote awareness of a business or organization. When event planners have to make decisions about where to hold an event, they must remember that the venue makes money by renting its space, including exhibit halls, meeting rooms, and ballrooms, and most venues have over 150,000 square feet available for these types of grand-scale gatherings (Brymer, Brymer, & Cain, 2016). Event planners must work with event managers at hotels or convention centers to help coordinate and decide what would be best for their organization's convention. Event tourism grows by bringing people into a city, facilitating the need for hotels, registration for the convention, transportation such as the bus, subway or ride share fares to get around, and restaurants. Convention and trade show attendees may also visit other popular sites in town, increasing tourism. Conventions typically bring in large numbers of people, and cities are finding ways to entice event and convention planners and thus increase revenue in their cities.

Trade shows: industry-driven opportunities to showcase products or to promote awareness of a business or organization

Volunteers

One of the most difficult challenges event planners face is soliciting and securing volunteers to help with large-scale events. Volunteers are key to the operation and execution of events to help the event run smoothly. In fact, volunteers may be the first connection an attendee makes at an event (Kilkenny, 2011). Understanding volunteer motivation is part of an event planner's role. Motivating volunteers who would not otherwise be paid, but give up their time freely to help the event be a success, is a challenge event planners face.

Johnson's (2015) research with managers in non-profit organizations found that managing volunteers is not without difficulty, including the following: (1) getting volunteers to take responsibility and act; (2) fostering effort and interest; and (3) ensuring a commitment from responsible volunteers

© Danny E Hooks/Shutterstock.com

with efficient follow-up skills. Soliciting volunteers can be a challenge, and often the same people volunteer to help over and over again. Proper solicitation and training of volunteers must happen prior to the actual execution of the event, and planners are tasked with securing as many volunteers as possible to ensure a seamless experience.

Connecting with employees, corporate partners, and members of the city or town is a good place to start when seeking volunteers. Ralston, Lumsdon, and Downward (2005) studied event volunteers and concluded that people volunteer for events for the following reasons: to share in the excitement of the event, to be a part of a unique experience, to get a chance to meet interesting people, and to take advantage of the opportunity to connect with others and be part of a team. Additionally, event planners should select a person or team of people who will conduct the training of volunteers (Kilkenny, 2011).

Moreover, Gardó, Granizo, Moreno, and Imizcoz (2013) found that unpaid workers are vital to the smooth execution of events, yet volunteers must feel some level of satisfaction that meets both their functional and emotional needs when signing on to volunteer. They also found that if volunteer needs are met, there can be a certain amount of loyalty that results in an attachment to that event, and volunteers will be eager to be involved year after year. As an example, many who volunteer to work the Masters in Augusta, Georgia, one of the four major tournaments in men's professional golf, have been doing so for years. To be associated with such a prestigious golf tournament and to be able to be on site where the best golfers from around the world compete in an annual tournament to win the coveted 'green jacket' is a thrill for many volunteers. Because of that particular association and esteem, they continue to volunteer year after year. In his seminal study, Chelladurai (2006) noted that economically, volunteers in sport were valued at over $50 billion, and that 20% of volunteers in America were connected to events in both sport and recreation. Overall, American volunteers comprise about 8 billion hours' worth of work, with a value estimated at $203.4 billion (Cardinali and Paquin, 2019). Therefore, it is vital that event planners not only learn what helps motivate volunteers, but also implement recruitment and training that adds value to their time and commitment.

TIP

Over-communicate. No matter how much you think you are communicating with people during the event planning process, it probably is not enough. It is essential to be proactive and keep the event planning team, vendors, partners, etc. informed throughout the process to avoid mishaps.

— Chris Daley

Accessibility, Safety, and Security at Events

Bowdin, Allen, O'Toole, Harris, and McDonnell (2011) state that events are highly susceptible to risks and hazards. Therefore, while event tourism is exciting, and it is thrilling to see large-scale events populated by people from all over the world, it is important to consider putting safety and security measures into place. Organizing large-scale events requires event planners to investigate permits, purchase insurance, and formulate emergency plans that must be put into effect. Preparedness is an event planner's greatest ally in pulling off an event intended for hundreds or thousands of people.

O'Roarke and Murphy (1995) suggest that accessibility is one of the first concerns an event planner should address. Access roads in and out of the area or city must be considered. People who reside in the area should not be displaced or inconvenienced because of an event that will take place in their city or town. Contingency plans and a clear path for emergency and delivery vehicles should be part of the planning. For mega events, having the space to land a medevac helicopter for dire emergencies is a necessity. O'Roarke and Murphy (1995) also found that planning for Woodstock '94 required the planners to evaluate fire safety for the music festival, as the event was taking place in the pastures of Ulster County, New York. Additionally, the planners constructed safety plans including maintaining a fluid water supply, making hazmat preparations, providing medical care on site throughout the festival, securing effective apparatus and equipment that might be needed, providing pads for medevac helicopters to land, and hiring people to monitor campfires during the event. Those who would be on site providing medical care should be licensed medical providers. Planners also established an on site command center that was in operation 24 hours a day during the three-day festival. Professionals from state and local police, state health agencies, EMS, and the U.S. Coast Guard were brought in to serve at the command center.

© mark reinstein/Shutterstock.com

Event planners should conduct a site visit to preplan for events. Krebs (2001) recommends sketching a site map, which should include the venue, outdoor locations, and emergency exit locations for attendees. Meeting with involved city and local agencies is imperative, and making a quick note of where the closest hospital is located is always a good idea. For hallmark events such as marathons, races, rallies, and other outdoor events, weather could become an issue. Do you have contingency plans for inclement weather? On hot days, do you plan for water stations? In cold weather, are there places for people to warm up? Is there an ample number of bathrooms for attendees to access? These are just some of the questions event planners should consider when designing safety precautions.

There are two key ways to begin planning for large-scale events (Krebs, 2001). First, assemble an event team to help you with the safety planning. Designate who will be in charge of the different aspects of the event, and stay in close contact with them. Meet frequently to stay up to date on the precautions for the event. Make sure proper accommodations, safety, and security measures are put into place. Use a checklist such as the one in this chapter to tick off items that could be important in providing a safe, pleasant, and meaningful experience for event attendees.

BASIC PRE-CHECKLIST FOR PLANNING LARGE-SCALE EVENTS

- ☐ Review overall plan
- ☐ Work with city/municipal leaders
- ☐ Establish venue/event plan
- ☐ Determine ticketing vs. free event
- ☐ Obtain and complete permits/applications needed
- ☐ Assess venue for people with special needs
- ☐ Conduct facilities review including all safety aspects
- ☐ Assess transportation in and out of site
- ☐ Plan for crowd management & work with law enforcement
- ☐ Create vehicles for communication regarding event information and welfare
- ☐ Secure medical team and first-aid
- ☐ Solicit and approve all vendors
- ☐ Manage restrictions for music and entertainment
- ☐ Approve amusements, attractions, displays, and special staging
- ☐ Provide ample sanitary facilities & waste management
- ☐ Hire volunteers and train them accordingly
- ☐ Work with local media for promotion

Finally, security at events should be at the forefront of every event planner's mind with regard to large-scale events. In Katie Gibson's interview (2016) with Juliette Kayyem, the Belfer Lecturer in International Security at Harvard Kennedy School, and a former official in the federal Department of Homeland Security, Kayyem states that we are a totally different nation after the horrific events of 9-11, and that security has become a part of our everyday lives—whether it is regarding traveling, getting on trains, or attending large-scale events. Event planners should work closely with security teams, including local and state law enforcement; federal law enforcement, such as the Department of Homeland Security; and other government bodies to help manage events that attract tourists from all over the world. Connors (2007) created a report for the U.S. Department of Justice's Office of Community Oriented Policing Services that still today offers approaches for best practices regarding national and regional events that can be tailored to various sizes of planned events. This report, available online, can help event planners become acquainted with a variety of scenarios that can heighten their awareness of the possible threats that could potentially unfold at an event. Being fully aware of threat possibilities can help event planners manage risk. While this chapter mentions risk management only briefly, it is vital that event planners working with large-scale events be well-educated regarding the safety of event attendees.

Jobs for Event Planners in the Event Tourism Industry

Event tourism gained ground in the 1980s (Getz, 2008), and today, the most recent statistics validate the importance of event tourism. In 2018, travelers spent $1.1 trillion, which generated $2.5 trillion in economic output and 15.7 million American jobs (U.S. Travel Association, 2018, para.1). Four out of five domestic trips were taken for leisure purposes. Business travel supported 2.6 million jobs, while meetings, events, and incentive travel supported 1.1 million jobs (U.S. Travel Association, 2018, para.1). With California as the number one travel destination in the United States with nearly 1 million tourism jobs out of 14 million in the country, it is not difficult to understand how event tourism is a vast and growing industry (Easter, 2017). Therefore, event planners have many options within the event tourism industry. So where do event planners find jobs? Walker (2016) suggests that many jobs in the industry can be found in hotels and resorts, corporations, associations, the government, and nonprofit organizations. Finally, as event planners rank #21 as Best Business Jobs in U.S. News & World Report (2019), and as event tourism continues to grow, those who are interested in pursuing this avenue of work are in a good position to join the ranks of other contented career professionals who enjoy working in this field.

People have attended events for centuries, from the Olympic Games to festivals that have been established in cities all over the world, to conventions, conferences, and sporting events, just to name a few. As Queen Victoria stated in her letters published by His Royal Majesty the King, "Great events make me quiet and calm, and little trifles fidget me and irritate my nerves," (Benson & Esher, 1907, p. 197). Although Queen Victoria ruled over a hundred years ago, she understood what made an event worthwhile for people, as well as what might keep them coming back and visiting again. Take for example, the Great Exhibition of 1851, her husband Prince Albert's grand event, during which over six million people visited the newly erected, but temporary, Crystal Palace to see great culture and industry. That singular event set in motion the World's Fairs and catapulted it to be regarded as one of the most successful events ever staged; in fact, it was heralded as a defining moment for England during the Industrial Revolution (Johnson, n.d.). This legendary example showcases the power of a unique event that draws crowds from distances and leaves them in awe. As Queen Victoria lamented, no one wants to attend an unpleasant event or one that has not been thoughtfully planned and executed. Forethought, skill, and planning, along with an understanding of what drives event tourism, are required to ensure a seamless large-scale event that brings people to town, leaves them satisfied by having attended, and makes them want to come back and visit again soon.

Key Terms

Event tourism

Drawing power

Mega events

Hallmark events

Feasibility study

Event sponsorship

Sponsor sincerity

Convention and Visitors
  Bureau (CVB)

Destination Marketing
  Organization (DMO)

Convention

Trade shows

Discussion Questions

1. What made you want to attend a particular large-scale event initially? What are some of your impressions of that event?

2. Think about a convention that comes to a nearby city. What makes people want to attend that convention? Research to see how long the convention has been in existence. Why do you think it continues to thrive in that location?

3. What type of event planning job interests you within the travel tourism industry (e.g., planning soccer tournaments or travel abroad trips with groups of student athletes)? Why?

Activity

Create a hallmark event for a nearby town or city in your area that would bring tourists from across the region. Craft a feasibility study that includes the following:

- What is the overall strategy and outcome desired for the event?
- Who is the target audience?
- Is the event paid or free?
- For how many days will the event take place?
- Who might be appropriate sponsors for the event? Why?
- What types of security and municipal planning might be necessary?
- Will hotels, restaurants, and shops be impacted by this event? If so, how?

References

About us (2016). Retrieved from https://www.miamibookfair.com/about/

Adams, W.L. (2014). What's with those mysterious masks? The dark drama of Venice Carnival. CNN. Retrieved from http://edition.cnn.com/travel/article/whats-with-those-mysterious-masks-the-dark-drama-of-venice-carnival/index.html.

Allen, Sylvia (2016). 12 steps to sponsorship success, *Parks & Recreation*, p. 44–47.

Bagdan, P. (2013). *Guest service in the hospitality industry.* Hoboken, NJ: John Wiley & Sons, Inc.

Benson, A.R., & Esher, V. (1907). *The letters of Queen Victoria: A selection from her majesty's correspondence between the years 1837 and 1861.* New York: Longmans, Green, and Co.

Bowdin, G., Allen, J., O'Toole, W., Harris, R., McDonnell, I. (2011). *Events management.* London/New York: Routledge.

Brymer, R.A., Brymer, R.A., Cain, L. (2016) *Hospitality: An introduction.* Dubuque, IA: Kendall Hunt.

Brumfield, S. (2011, November). AP Exclusive: Grand Prix Short of Projections. *Bloomberg Business Week.* Retrieved from https://web.archive.org/web/20131214035805/http://www.business-week.com/ap/financialnews/D9QPVRTG0.htm

Buckmaster, S. (2012). Charlie Chaplin's Venice. *National Geographic Traveler.* Retrieved from https://www.nationalgeographic.com/travel/city-guides/venice-traveler/

Business Dictionary. *Feasibility study.* (n.d.), Retrieved from http://www.businessdictionary.com/definition/feasibility-study.htm

Cardinali, D., & Paquin, N, (2019, April). Value of volunteer time rose 3 percent in 2018. Retrieved from https://philanthropynewsdigest.org/news/value-of-volunteer-time-rose-3-percent-in-2018

Chelladurai, P. (2006). *Human resource management in sport and recreation.* Champaign, IL: Human Kinetics.

Chen, Y., Qu, L., & Spaans, M. (2013). Framing the long-term impact of mega-event strategies on the development of Olympic host cities. *Planning Practice & Research*, 28, 340–359.

Connors, E. (2007). Planning and managing security for major special events: Guidelines for law enforcement. *Office of Community Oriented Policing Services, U.S. Department of Justice.* Retrieved from https://www.hsdl.org/?view&did=482649

Crocker, M. (2017). 10 ways CVBs help meeting planners create stellar programs. *Successful Meetings*, 66, 16.

CVENT.com. (2019). CVENT's top 50 meeting destinations in the United States. Retrieved from https://www.cvent.com/en/marketing/top-50/2017-top-destinations-us.php.

Easter, M. (2017, May). California tourism industry grows for the 7th straight year, report says. Los Angeles Times. Retrieved from https://www.latimes.com/business/la-fi-ca-economic-impact-20170504-story.html.

Fredericks, K. (2019). Up-and-coming meeting destinations in 2019. *Successful Meetings*. Retrieved from http://www.successfulmeetings.com/Strategy/Meeting-Strategies/Emerging-Popular-Event-Destinations-aurora-Kissimmee-baltimore/

Gardó, T.F., Granizo, M.G., Moreno, F. A., & Imizcoz, E. F. (2014). Measuring socio-demographic differences in volunteers with a value-based index: Illustration in a mega event. *Voluntas: International Journal of Voluntary and Nonprofit Organizations, 25*, 1345–1367.

Getz, D. (2005). Event management and event tourism (2nd ed.). New York: Cognizant.

Getz, D. (2007). Event studies: Theory, research and policy for planned events. Oxford: Elsevier.

Getz, D. (2008). Event tourism: Definition, evolution, and research. *Tourism Management, 29*: 403–428.

Getz, D. & Page, S. (2016). *Event Studies: Theory, research and policy for planned events*. London/New York: Routledge.

Gibson, K. (2016). 15 years after 9/11, how has national security changed? Retrieved from https://www.hks.harvard.edu/research-insights/policy-topics/international-relations-security/15-years-after-911-how-has

Gronroos, C. (1990). *Services management and marketing: Managing the moments of truth in service competition*. Lexington, MA: Lexington Books.

Herțanu, A., & Boitor, A.-B. (2012). S.T.E.P. analysis on event tourism. *Bulletin of the Transilvania University of Brasov. Series V: Economic Sciences*, 25.

Jackson, A. (2011, November). Baltimore Grand Prix organizers hit with $600,000 tax lien. *Baltimore Business Journal*. Retrieved from https://www.bizjournals.com/baltimore/news/2011/11/21/baltimore-grand-prix-organizers-hit.html

Johnson, B. (n.d.) The great exhibition 1851. *Historic U.K.: The History and Heritage Accommodation Guide*. Retrieved from https://www.historic-uk.com/HistoryUK/HistoryofEngland/Great-Exhibition-of-1851/

Johnson, T. (2015). Converting volunteers from joiners to stayers. Retrieved from https://www.wildapricot.com/academy/expert-webinar-series/converting-volunteers-from-joiners-to-stayers/

Kotler, P., Bowen, J., Makens, J., Baloglu, S. (2017). *Marketing for hospitality and tourism*. Harlow, Essex, England: Pearson Education Limited.

Krebs, D. R. (2001). Ems preplanning for large public events. *Fire Engineering, 154*, 16.

Kilkenny, S. (2011). *The Complete Guide to Successful Event Planning*. Ocala, Fl: Atlantic Publishing Group, Inc.

Lahouze, A. (2018). Carrie Price: Small town, big events. *Independent Banker, 68*, 102.

Mill, R. & Morrison, A. (1985). *The Tourism System*. Englewood Cliffs, NJ: Kendall Hunt.

Morgan, M. (2006). Making space for experiences. *Journal of Retail & Leisure Property, 5*, 305–313.

Morgan, M. (2009). What makes a good festival? Understanding the event experience. *Event Management, 12,* 81–93.

Müller, M. (2015). The mega-event syndrome: Why so much goes wrong in mega-event planning and what to do about it. *Journal of the American Planning Association, 81,* 6–17.

Neal, C., Quester, P., and Hawkins, H. (2002) *Consumer Behaviour.* 3rd edition. Sydney, McGraw-Hill.

Oklobdzija, S. (2015). The role of events in tourism development. *BizInfo Journal, 6,* 83–97.

O'Rourke, J. J., & Murphy Jr., J. J. (1995). Woodstock '94: Fire planning for large public events. *Fire Engineering, 148,* 74.

O'Sullivan, E. and Spangler, K. (1998) *Experience marketing: Strategies for the new millennium.* State College, PA: Venture.

Palmer, A. (2019). How meeting planners can get more from CVBs and DMOs. Successful Meetings.

Palmer, A. (2017). The key to better meetings. *Successful Meetings, 66,* 12–16. retrieved from http://www.successfulmeetings.com/Strategy/Meeting-Strategies/convention-visitor-bureaus-meetings-sustainability-destination-marketing/

Ralston, R., Lumsdon, L. and Downward, P. (2005) The third force in events tourism: Volunteers at the XVII Commonwealth Games. *Journal of Sustainable Tourism, 13,* 504–519.

Rifon, N.J., Choi, S.M., Trimble, C.S., and Li, H. (2004). Congruence in sponsorship: The mediating role of sponsor credibility and consumer attributions of sponsor motive." *Journal of Advertising, 33,* 30–42.

Ritchie, J.R. (1984). Assessing the impact of hallmark events: Conceptual and research issues. *Journal of Travel Research, 23,* 2–11.

Rizzi, P. & Dioli, I. (2010). Strategic planning, place marketing and city branding: The Italian case. *Journal of Town & City Management, 1,* 300–317.

Roslow, S., Nicholls, J. A. F., & Laskey, H. A. (1992). Hallmark events and measures of reach and audience characteristics. *Journal of Advertising Research, 32,* 53–59.

Sözer, E. G., & Vardar, N. (2009). How does event sponsorship help in leveraging brand equity? *Journal of Sponsorship, 3,* 35–42.

U.S. News & World Report. (2019). Best business jobs. Retrieved from https://money.usnews.com/careers/best-jobs/rankings/best-business-jobs

U.S. Travel Association. (2018). U.S. travel answer sheet. Retrieved from https://www.ustravel.org/system/files/media_root/document/Research_Fact-Sheet_US-Travel-Answer-Sheet.pdf

Visit Buffalo Niagara. (2019). Home page. Retrieved from www.visitbuffaloniagara.com

Walker, J. (2016). *Exploring the hospitality industry.* Upper Saddle River: N.J.: Pearson.

Ward-Henninger, C. (2016, July). Here's a list of all the issues surrounding the 2016 Rio Olympics: From Zika to robberies to polluted water, there are plenty of issues in Rio. Retrieved from https://www.cbssports.com/olympics/news/heres-a-list-of-all-the-issues-surrounding-the-2016-rio-olympics/

Woolard, H. (2015). 18 new meeting properties christened in 2015. Retrieved from https://www.smartmeetings.com/news/82521/18-new-meeting-properties-christened-2015.

Chapter 12

CONFLICT AND CRISIS: DEALING WITH UNEXPECTED ISSUES

Conflict and crisis communication skills are essential in any field, and those able to handle difficult situations are sought-after employees in almost any industry (Ulmer, Sellnow, & Seeger, 2017). Some of the best event planners are able to handle conflict and crisis situations while staying calm under pressure. Conflict situations in event planning usually deal with people and can include anything from unhappy guests or irresponsible vendors to careless staff members. The difference between a conflict and an argument is that an **argument** relies on a logical order that is grounded in reason, research, and evidence (Putnam & Fairhurst, 2001), whereas **conflict** is situated in perceptions, goals, and values (Putnam & Poole, 1987), and involves heightened senses and emotions (Arnett, Bell McManus, & McKendree, 2018). Arguments are usually easier to deal with and most of the time can be resolved through some type of rational analysis. There is a greater sense of personal involvement in a conflict, and many times conflicts can lead to hurt feelings (Guerrero & La Valley, 2006). A **crisis**, on the other hand, can be the most difficult situation to address because it includes unexpected, unique moments that can cause high levels of uncertainty and chaos (Ulmer, Sellnow, & Seeger, 2017). This chapter will discuss conflict and crisis, and it will give you options to work through both conflict and crisis situations.

Argument: *A rhetorical approach that relies on a logical order that is grounded in reason, research and evidence*

Conflict: *A sizeable disagreement situated in perceptions, goals, and values and involves heightened senses and emotions*

Crisis: *A challenging event that includes unexpected, unique moments that can cause high levels of uncertainty and chaos*

When you have finished reading this chapter, you will be able to

- explain the components of various definitions of conflict;
- list styles for conflict management;
- summarize the best practices and human qualities in crisis management.

© bikeriderlondon/Shutterstock.com

CASE STUDY — Conflict, Crisis, Confusion, and Commitment

Jeanne M. Persuit, Ph.D., Associate Professor, Department of Communication Studies
University of North Carolina, Wilmington

I was a marketing communication manager at Cutler-Hammer, a division of Eaton Corporation, responsible for the Integrated Marketing Communication (IMC) of all of the electrical distribution and control products we manufactured for commercial purposes. For example, a building on a college campus would need panelboards, switchboards, safety switches, and circuit breakers, and we wanted the electrical contractors who installed these systems in the building to buy Cutler-Hammer products to install. One of the big events we attended yearly was the National Electrical Contractors' Association (NECA) trade show. We spent a significant amount on our presence at this trade show since it allowed us to meet and entertain our biggest customers. In addition to the 40' × 40' booth at the trade show, we had a golf outing, small client dinners on Friday night, and a big client dinner on Saturday night—the last event of the trade show. Planning for the event began 10 months in advance. Our presence at NECA was intended to show our customers the strength, collaboration, and reliability of Cutler-Hammer's products and people. With site visits completed and a planning team of six, I was ready for anything.

Or so I thought.

NECA is held in October every year, and in 2001 NECA celebrated its 100th anniversary in Washington, D.C. I had been planning for about nine months and was finalizing details when the attacks of September 11, 2001, happened. I remember I was having an NECA update meeting with my boss when his secretary interrupted the meeting to let us know the World Trade Center buildings had collapsed.

The thing I remember most about that time, besides the sadness and fear, was the confusion everyone felt. Everyone was fragile, tentative, and unsettled. Despite this, we heard from NECA that they had confirmed with Washington, D.C. authorities that they could still hold the trade show. Plans were on, and we were committed.

The United States invaded Afghanistan in late September, 2001. We waited again to hear if NECA would move forward, which it did. I confirmed the International Trade Center—Ronald Reagan Building—as the site of our closing banquet and booked the Georgetown University Pep Band to play after dinner. The golf outing at the Tournament Players Club (TPC) in Potomac, Maryland, at Avenel Farm was set for Friday morning, and the booth space was coming together with everything ready to ship. Surely, I thought, this would be the end of any concerns we would have about the event being canceled.

Again, so I thought.

On October 15, 2001, Senator Tom Daschle's aide opened a letter that contained anthrax. This would be one of several letters sent that contained anthrax spores, and the letter addressed to Daschle infected two postal workers who handled it, killing both. Federal office buildings were shut down to be swept for anthrax spores. Some of my co-workers who were attending NECA expressed concerns about being in the city at this time. My contact at the International Trade Center called me to make sure I knew that, as a federal building, the Center could be closed at any time if the FBI suspected anthrax; this could mean no closing banquet and no refund on our deposit.

We were a week away from the conference on October 22. My leadership team met to review the latest information and made the call to go forward with the events. If NECA was not canceling, neither would we.

What I remember most about that weekend was that while the event had some minor problems (as all events do—no event will be perfect), it met our objectives to connect with our clients in a meaningful way. The Georgetown University Pep Band began their after-dinner music with John Philip Sousa's "Stars and Stripes Forever," which brought the house down. Our attendees were honored to participate in this event, and my planning team was proud of our efforts.

Contributed by Jeanne M. Persuit. Copyright © Kendall Hunt Publishing Company.

After reading this chapter, revisit the case study and respond to the following question:

What indicators are present when an event turns from conflict mode to crisis mode, and how do you determine the appropriate response?

Conflict

Conflicts are messy, and many scholars have articulated different definitions of what exactly a conflict consists of (Arnett, Bell McManus, & McKendree, 2018; Cahn & Abigail, 2014; Hocker & Wilmot 1978/2013; Mortensen, 1974; Pearce & Littlejohn, 1997). After examining various definitions, Linda Putnam (2006) states that "conflict centers on incompatibilities, an expressed struggle, and interdependence among two or more parties" (p. 5). Through her research, she found that there are usually five components that unite the definitions of conflict:

1. Scope—incompatible interests, goals, needs, desires, values, and beliefs;
2. Nature of action—expressed struggles, dissonance, tension, and frustration;
3. Relationship—the connections between persons and their interdependence;

4. Communication—the distribution of symbols, acts, and exchanges of messages;

5. Context—elements that give rise to conflict, such as limited or scarce resources, which are regulated by one's culture (Putnam, 2006, p. 7).

These five components can be seen throughout the event planning process. For example, a client might want to schedule a baby shower at an historical landmark that is also a restaurant. She believes this venue is the perfect place, whereas the individuals who are actually paying for the shower believe that the restaurant is overpriced and serves bad food. Both parties have different goals for the shower. Tension starts to build as you try to please the people who are paying for the event as opposed to the guest of honor. There is an expressed struggle between the mother-to-be and those giving the shower. As you communicate with both parties, you might feel as if you are at a standstill. The continued exchange of messages among all parties might become difficult to manage if everyone wants something different. The expectant mother might believe the baby shower should meet her needs, but the friends believe they should be accommodated if they are paying the bill. As the event planner, your job is to stop the conflict before it spirals out of control. There are many ways to approach this situation, but the best option would be to make everyone walk away believing they are getting what they want, even if it is not exactly what was stated at the beginning of the conversation. One of many options might be to choose the same setting, but negotiate a less expensive caterer for a brunch when the restaurant is usually closed.

Many times emotions play a large role in conflict situations. Emotions such as anger, jealousy, hurt, and guilt have the potential to fuel conflict situations (Guerrero & La Valley, 2006). However, in an organizational setting, one needs to keep emotions in check. Event planning is a career that deals with heightened emotions in organizational settings (Allen, 2009). Kramer and Hess (2002) believe that in such a context there are six emotional rules that those involved need to follow. Individuals should (1) express emotions in a professional manner, maintaining control over feelings; (2) express emotions to improve circumstances, seeking to prevent or correct problems; (3) express emotions to the appropriate person at the proper time and in a fitting manner; (4) express emotions to assist and support others; (5) express emotions that are appropriate to their organizational role; and (6) curtail the impulse to express emotions for personal benefit, but which are detrimental to others. As an event planner, it is important to keep your emotions under control during the planning process. The stress associated with an event will heighten emotions from all parties involved; as a result, you need to know in advance how you will handle a situation before you react to a conflict.

TIP

Expect the unexpected and remember, your priorities are not someone else's priorities. This will help you manage the stress associated with change, conflict, and chaos that often goes along with event planning.

— Angela Corbo

Thomas and Kilmann's (1974) seminal research on conflict has identified five different styles for handling a conflict:

1. **Avoiding** takes place when individuals intentionally remove themselves from the situation. The person will do anything to avoid the situation and might cause further damage for all parties involved.

2. **Accommodating** occurs when one is always willing to give in to the other person at any cost. This person is seen as a pushover and can be persuaded to do just about anything.

3. **Competing** focuses on a constant struggle of who is going to win the conflict. A competitive person will always want the last word.

4. **Compromising** requires both parties to make sacrifices to accommodate the other. Both people will feel as if they are winning something and losing something else.

5. **Collaborating** demands creating positive alternatives for everyone involved and is the optimal method. Collaboration is a constructive response to conflict (Rusbult, Johnson, & Morrow, 1986); however, this style is the most difficult to implement (Canary & Cupach, 1988).

As an event planner, you may deal with many people who have varying styles of handling a conflict, but your job is to create a space that allows for some type of collaboration. Suppose, for example, you are working with a bride whose entire family wants to be involved in the planning process. This situation is fraught with various types of conflict. The bride might be *avoiding* her father because she does not want to talk to him about increasing the budget. She is also *accommodating* her mother because she does not like her grandmother's lace veil but will wear it for family tradition. The bride is *competing* with her sister whose luxurious wedding the previous year set an extravagant precedent, and she refuses to settle for anything less. She might be *compromising* with her fiancé on a final guest list. As the event planner, it is your job to make this situation work not only for the bride, but also for the entire family. Using your creative skills to solve conflict through some type of *collaboration* will produce a win/win situation for all those involved. You might not always make everyone happy, but your job is to make as many people as possible happy so that everyone is excited to participate in and attend the wedding.

Conflict Management Methods

LoCicero (2008) believes that in the event planning industry, common mistakes such as missing materials, problems with food or drink, untrained staff, lack of leadership, attendance issues, equipment malfunctions, and unclear goals can be avoided to prevent a conflict situation. Conflict occurs for many reasons, but when it takes place during the event planning process, some type of resolution or management needs to occur as soon as possible. There are many ways to handle a conflict situation. **Conflict resolution** focuses on examining the facts of the situation to solve the issue, whereas

Avoiding: *In conflict situations, a behavior that occurs when individuals intentionally remove themselves from the situation*

Accommodating: *In conflict situations, a type of behavior that occurs when one is always willing to give in to the other person at any cost*

Competing: *In conflict situations, the act of striving to gain something, focusing on the struggle of who is going to win a conflict*

Compromising: *In conflict situations, behavior that requires both parties to make sacrifices to accommodate the other*

Collaborating: *In conflict situations, the optimal method of creating positive alternatives for everyone involved; a constructive response to conflict*

> **TIP**
>
> For every Plan A, you must have a Plan B. But your Plan B must have a Plan C, D, E…
>
> — Kristen Schultz

Conflict resolution: *A strategy that focuses on examining the facts of the situation to solve the issue*

conflict management works from a dialogic approach that looks at the conflict from all sides, uncovering various assumptions of what is fair in a particular situation (Yungbluth & Johnson, 2010). Both methods of dealing with conflict are needed and can be used in a variety of situations. This section will examine several approaches used in working through conflict.

In *Managing conflict through communication*, Cahn and Abigail (2014) suggest an **S-TLC** acronym of "Stop, Think, Listen, and Communicate" (p. 79) to deal with various conflicts. During a conflict situation, it is helpful to stop what you are doing and "take a time out" to evaluate the situation (p. 79). The stopping step allows for a de-escalation of the situation. Thinking makes you process what has transpired. Thinking through the process will keep you from making any irrational decisions. Listening forces you to see the other side of the situation. As discussed in Chapter 2, listening will help you use the other person's comments as a way to make informed, rational decisions. The last step, communicating, gives you the opportunity to voice your thoughts about what matters to you in a particular situation. Many people will communicate first, but in this model, communication is deliberately placed last so that you do not say something inappropriate. Remember, once something is communicated, it cannot be taken back; no matter how many times you say, 'I am sorry; I did not mean to say that,' your words have been said and cannot be erased, so choose them carefully.

Arnett, Bell McManus, and McKendree (2018) in *Conflict between persons: The origins of leadership* suggest making a conflict map. The **conflict map** is based on the assumption that you need to understand what matters in a particular conflict situation. Not all conflicts are logical; as a result, looking at the big picture will help you focus on what is important in the situation. The conflict map offers a visual representation that consists of four elements:

1. the persons who are included in the conflict;
2. the context of the conflict;
3. an understanding of the larger background of the conflict;
4. the ethical significance/importance attached to the content of the conflict (p. 146).

These coordinates offer a constructive way to view the conflict and provide a coherent structure in which one can process the entire situation. By creating an interpretive map, all parties will be able to visualize an outcome for the situation.

In *Bullies, tyrants & impossible people: How to beat them without joining them*, Shapiro, Jankowski, and Dale (2005) use a **NICE** acronym: "Neutralize" emotions, "Identify" the type, "Control" the encounter, and "Explore" options when dealing with people who enjoy creating conflict situations (pp. 9–11). Neutralize emotions in order to maintain control over the situation. Sometimes your emotions get the best of you, and you end up doing things that you regret when emotions control the situation. Identify three types of difficult people: (1) Situationally difficult, those who make the circumstance controversial; (2) Strategically difficult, those who believe being unreasonable will make them effective; and (3) Simply difficult, those whose personalities exude conflict. By recognizing the type, you will have a greater understanding of how to handle each conflict situation. Control the encounter in order to be smart about the situation. When you are in control, you can think clearly and use

© romakoma/Shutterstock.com

techniques that will help improve rather than escalate the conflict. Lastly, explore options in order to make a win/win collaborative decision for all parties involved. The more options you have, the greater chance you will be able to move forward and resolve the conflict situation. For example, you arrive at a local golf course at 5 a.m. for a charity fundraiser, only to find that someone forgot to charge the golf carts your guests will use. As you start to panic, consider using the NICE acronym. First, *neutralize* your emotions by taking a deep breath and trying to think clearly. This is a small hurdle that you will have to overcome, and you will discover that there is a solution to the problem. Next, *identify* the type of people you are working with as being situationally difficult. Someone did not follow through with the task that was assigned, and now this mistake has become your problem. As you *control* the encounter, you need to figure out a way to get the carts charged before players begin to arrive in two hours. You make your way into the clubhouse and speak to the course manager and the golf pro who both suggest there is time to charge the carts enough to get the outing started. Meanwhile, you *explore options* with the pro shop personnel to figure out a plan. Once the retail stores open, a designated employee will purchase additional batteries and switch them out when the existing batteries in the carts die. This might not be an ideal situation, but it is a way to handle and find a solution to the conflict.

Pachter and Magee (2000) in *The power of positive confrontation: The skills you need to know to handle conflicts at work, at home, and in life* use a **WAC'em** acronym: *What* is really bothering you? *Ask* other people to do something or change something. *Check in* with others to see what they think about the changes (p. 66). This WAC'em model examines conflict through perspectives of both the self and others. There are many times people will take conflict out on the wrong person. For example, you might yell at the staff at an event when you are having a conflict with the client, causing more issues instead of getting at the heart of the problem. By confronting others, you are giving yourself the opportunity to explain your thoughts about the situation and allowing them to explain theirs. By using the work of Cahn and Abigail (2014), Arnett, Bell McManus, and

WAC'em: *An acronym for What is really bothering you? Ask the other person to do something or change something. Check in with the other person to see what he or she thinks about the changes*

McKendree (2018), Shapiro, Jankowski, and Dale (2005), and Pachter and Magee (2000), you now can choose from multiple styles of handling various conflict situations. The next section will discuss the move from a conflict to a crisis situation.

Crisis

With a rise in national and international crisis situations, the field of communication plays a fundamental role in helping find clarity in the midst of catastrophe (Bell, 2010; Ulmer, Sellnow, & Seeger, 2017). Crisis situations can occur at any time and at any event you host. According to Hermann (1963), there are three defining characteristics of a crisis situation. The first is surprise. During a crisis situation, there is no foreshadowing; the incident is unexpected and takes everyone by surprise. The second characteristic is a threatening circumstance that goes above and beyond the traditional problems an organization faces on a daily basis. This threatening circumstance can cause harm to the organization and potentially the community. The third characteristic of a crisis is the short response time. In a crisis situation, there is no time for a thorough discussion of what to do next. Decisions are made quickly, and action needs to occur sooner rather than later.

Matthew Seeger, Timothy L. Sellnow, and Robert R. Ulmer (1998), whose work in crisis communication has been extensive (Seeger, 2006; Seeger, Sellnow, & Ulmer, 2003; Sellnow & Seeger, 2013; Sellnow & Ulmer, 1994; Sellnow, Ulmer, & Snider, 1998; Ulmer, 1999; Ulmer, Seeger, & Sellnow, 2007; Ulmer, Sellnow, & Seeger, 2017), offer insight into the importance of communication in a crisis situation. They offer a working definition of an **organizational crisis** as "a specific, *unexpected*, and *nonroutine* event or series of events that create high levels of *uncertainty* and *threaten* or are perceived to threaten an organization's *high-priority goals*" (Ulmer, Seeger, & Sellnow, 2007; p. 7). This definition resonates with event planners because during an event, a crisis situation can threaten the occasion's overall goals. For example, an event can be ruined because of the weather. What happens if you have planned a fundraiser and there is a hurricane, blizzard, or tornado? Or what happens if a fire breaks out in the kitchen, and your venue for the wedding needs to be evacuated? Crisis situations occur, and it is important you offer a response to the situation that does not create more chaos for your clients. Moreover, Ulmer, Sellnow and Seeger (2017) articulate the importance of turning a crisis situation into a learning opportunity that will create a better business.

Organizational crisis: *A specific, unexpected, and non-routine event or series of events that create high levels of uncertainty and threaten or are perceived to threaten an organization's high-priority goals*

Crisis Response

A crisis takes people by surprise; however, event planners should create various responses to potential crisis situations because the threatening nature of crisis must be addressed as quickly as possible, and brainstorming possible solutions in the middle of a crisis situation is usually not feasible (Ulmer, Sellnow, & Seeger, 2017). Even though you will be creating backup plans for all of your events, the reality is that you cannot control everything. However, this does not mean there should not be backup plans. Yes, there should be a Plan B for various situations, such as what you will do if lightning occurs during your pool party, but if all your backup plans have been exhausted, you need to switch to crisis response. The crisis response has three objectives: (1) to shape attributions of the crisis; (2) to change perceptions of the organization in crisis; and (3) to reduce the negative effect generated by the crisis (Coombs, 2007). The more information you have about the situation, the better your perspective will be on how to move forward. In any crisis, there is a need to blame someone for the situation. As the event planner, your goal is to make sure you are not perceived as part of the problem but rather as part of the solution. The negativity generated by the crisis will be profound; however, staying positive throughout the situation and offering a response will put people at ease. Consider the effects of a guest drinking too much at an event, whether it is a corporate event, wedding, or private party. When alcohol is being served at an event, an event planner must consider all tactics to manage people who may have had too much to drink. If the event were held at a local winery—perhaps it is a celebration of a successful quarter for a department in a corporation—event planners must plan for transportation to and from the event. Someone who has consumed too much wine still has to get home. In this scenario, proper bus or limousine transportation might be a good idea, in addition to having designated drivers or taxis on hand when guests have returned from the winery. A crisis can occur if someone has too much to drink, becomes unruly or unmanageable, or absolutely refuses to get on the bus and tries to drive home. Event planners do not want to be responsible for a guest's drunk driving citation, or even more catastrophic, responsible for the guest recklessly killing someone. While people cannot always be controlled, having the best plans—and contingency plans—in place will help avoid a potential crisis situation. In addition, having effective communication skills during a crisis situation can help save lives (Van Der Wagen & White, 2014).

© Kinga/Shutterstock.com

Working with the Centers for Disease Control, research developed by the National Center for Food Protection and Defense, research from various scholars, and work affiliated with the North Dakota State University Risk and Crisis Communication Project, Seeger (2006) developed 10 best practices for crisis communication. The research was based on observations, experience in crisis response, case study analysis, and empirical investigations. A panel of experts from the National Center for Food Safety and Defense created and reviewed these best practices, and after making refinements, they released the final combinations of 10 best practices.

1. Process approaches and policy development—communication is an integral part of crisis communication and should be incorporated into all parts of the process. As you plan events, communication about crisis situations needs to be an ongoing and integrated part of the planning process.

2. Pre-event planning—having a plan in place is crucial. A plan serves as a reminder of potential problems and can act as a guideline for employees to follow in preventing or dealing with a crisis. As you plan your events, keep in mind what you would do in case of an emergency.

3. Partnerships with the public—the public is a legitimate and equal partner that should be informed and educated throughout the event. The public may also serve as a resource rather than a burden. If you are planning an event that has any ties to the community (e.g., fundraiser or outreach program), keeping your audience informed about the situation is beneficial. The attack on the Boston Marathon and its aftermath is a good example of how the public helped respond to a crisis.

4. Listen to the public's concern and understand the audience—an organization must listen to the concerns of the public and take these fears into account. In any crisis situation, people will have different views about what is important or what needs to be communicated. During a crisis situation in event planning, listening to your audience as well as to your colleagues and clients will help you make informed decisions about how to proceed.

5. Honesty, candor, and openness—these ideas can be seen as a whole. Honesty should be used in all cases, for lying will not help the situation; candor deals with the issue of communicating the truth even when the truth may reflect negatively on the organization; and openness is defined by accessibility and immediacy that goes beyond a mere response. The continuum of honesty, candor, and openness should be at the forefront of your communication while planning an event.

6. Collaborate and coordinate with credible sources—planners and other communicators should continually seek validation that allows their sources to communicate and collaborate effectively with all stakeholders. Coordination is critical and should not break down during a crisis event. Just as you use collaboration and coordination to make an event a success, you will also use these ideas to move beyond the crisis.

7. Meet the needs of the media, and remain accessible—effective use of the media is necessary to reach the general public and will help assure that no one is misinformed about the event. The more you can communicate at regular intervals with the media, the more apt

they will be to help you as needed. Developing sincere and honest relationships with members of the media benefits everyone.

8. Communicate with compassion, concern, and empathy—true compassion, concern, and empathy will enhance credibility of the message and the perceived legitimacy of the messenger before and after the event. For example, Tony Hayward, former CEO of British Petroleum (BP), lacked true compassion, concern, and empathy in his public communication following a devastating oil spill, resulting in formidable and long-lasting backlash from the public. On the other hand, Gerry Cahill, CEO of Carnival Cruise lines, made an emotional and obviously sincere apology after an unexpected week-long disaster aboard the Carnival Triumph. Cahill remained in command, accepting full responsibility, praising his crew, owning the failure, and never once minimizing what had occurred. Compared to Hayward, Cahill's public acknowledgement that the passengers were, in fact, the greatest sufferers (rather than the company) demonstrated his leadership, compassion, and empathy in ways far different from anything that occurred with BP.

9. Accept uncertainty and ambiguity—there will always be some level of uncertainty. Dealing with uncertainty in event planning, a field in which everything is planned, is difficult, but there is no need to add stress over what you cannot control. Take a positive approach and focus on what you can do; return to the uncertain areas later.

10. Messages of self-efficacy—tell people what they can do to reduce harm. These messages will decrease some of the uncertainty in a crisis. As the event planner, you are the leader of the event, and enlisting others to assist in the crisis will help organize the circumstance. Do not be afraid to issue orders to others in a polite yet firm way.

These 10 best practices act as general guidelines offering an effective crisis communication plan and response to a crisis situation. By keeping these 10 steps in mind, you will be more prepared and hopefully remain calm if a crisis should ever occur at one of your events.

In times of conflict or crisis, perceptions about the relative seriousness of the situation can vary widely. The labels of conflict or crisis are socially constructed, meaning that definitions of each depend upon those caught up in the immediate circumstances. At the start of an escalating situation, the event planner should ask who actually defined the occurrence as a conflict or crisis (Hilhorst, 2013). Those involved in an event may have a different perspective about the relative importance of what is happening, and their perceptions are not always logical or consistent. Since moments of conflict or crisis can heighten feelings of mistrust, which in turn influences and escalates other emotions, the difference between a relatively minor conflict and something else of considerable importance is easily confused.

© xtock/Shutterstock.com

Event planners cannot always expect rational responses when dealing with clients in conflict or crisis, since most people read a situation through a lens distorted by their own desires (Eadie & Nelson, 2001). The event planner's job is to maintain a clear and balanced perspective of the situation's relative importance and priority. For instance, during a two-day corporate business retreat, the event planner finds out that the keynote speaker is stranded in another city when storms ground all flights. Arranging for the speaker to arrive in time for the next morning's agenda would be impossible, and the corporate organizers are distraught over this turn of events. The event planner's job is to de-escalate the situation by offering a variety of alternative possibilities to the organizers, including, perhaps, rescheduling the keynote speaker to a later date, consulting the local chamber of commerce for a last-minute replacement, or substituting a different session in place of the keynote. Although some retreat-goers may be disappointed, it will be the event planner's job to diffuse negative thinking and keep the retreat a positive and enjoyable experience. After an unforeseen event occurs, it is important to document as much information as possible. Van Der Wagen and White (2014) state, "Assembling stories and evaluating data on events provides a useful legacy for future event planning and implementation" (p. 251). Documenting all of the details after any crisis or conflict situation is necessary to plan for future emergencies.

Calm Under Pressure

In either a conflict or crisis situation, all event planners need to know how to remain calm under pressure. Event planners typically can face the unknown at every turn during an event. Remaining calm when the unexpected occurs is critical for success in this field. This characteristic develops through adulthood and can be cultivated if event planners find that they are uncomfortable during pressure-filled situations. While some people thrive in moments of stress, most need training to become adept in times of conflict or crisis. Because stress occurs when the demands exceed a person's capacity to react (Cohen, Kessler, & Gordon, 1997), psychological and biological changes occur within (Menkes, 2013). In moments of stress, the sympathetic nervous system is activated, sending a cloud of hormones through the brain, ultimately working to destroy your ability to maintain clarity of thought (Menkes, 2013). Thus, a good first response might be to step outside when the trouble situation occurs, breathe some fresh air, splash some cold water on your face, and try to relax through some deep breathing (Amen, 1999). These physical steps might help control an unwanted emotional response.

© VGstockstudio/Shutterstock.com

Another way to begin dealing with stress is by identifying clearly and succinctly the cause of the pressure. Ask yourself questions; ask questions of those in the situation with you, so that you are fully armed with as much information as possible (Amen, 1999). Since pressure often comes from uncertainty, seek information before choosing a course of action (Menkes, 2013). Ask for clarification when possible to determine exactly how much control you have in the moment. If you feel uncertain about what choices to make, try creating some quick 'what if?' scenarios in your head that offer distinct possibilities for action (Amen, 1999). But in any event, do not wait for conditions to change; maybe the decision you make in the moment of pressure will not necessarily be the best one every time, but it will still offer a course of action that allows you to move forward (Melnick, 2013). In moments of extra pressure, making a decision that significantly affects outcomes is difficult at best. When you might not be able to make a decision, one possibility is to analyze the costs and benefits of any choice (Amen, 1999). For example, your clients are worried that if they invite the former beloved CEO to their end-of-the-year celebration, the new CEO might feel uncomfortable; however, if they do not invite the former CEO, it might cause a great deal of uncertainty among attendees. In this scenario, you will need to help your clients analyze the costs and benefits of each choice, offering suggestions including an assurance that you will work hard to accommodate both parties. Though there is no guarantee of the outcome of the situation, it is important to create options for the clients.

The issue of control during a conflict or crisis means walking a delicate balance between understanding what is happening and wanting to change the outcome. Event planners should know that there are some elements that can be controlled, and those are the details that deserve your attention. Melnick (2013) writes that there is always something you can do to make a situation more workable, and that it is possible to turn obstacles into opportunities once you have enough information. Focusing only on the stimuli that are relevant and in your own controllable domain will give you a greater shot at reducing stress.

If the stress is coming from another person and a response is demanded, listen carefully to what the person is saying, paying special attention to the nonverbals before responding. What you say in a moment of conflict or crisis can define the path that will resolve the stress, so make a plan before you speak, and stick to just one main point as you respond, offering adequate support for your decision without any extra embellishment (Amen, 1999). As you explain your solution or course of action, speak strongly and directly, clarifying what is going to happen. Avoid repeating yourself; conclude when you have made your summary statement. These practices will not only address the immediate situation, but will also build your own confidence in your ability to function when pressured. Event planners who function well under pressure ultimately become stronger leaders, and their clarity of thought will continue to develop despite adversity (Menkes, 2013). Other suggestions? Get mentors whom you admire for their ability to be strong under pressure, but also trust yourself in less important,

stressful situations to practice making the kind of decisions that will empower you in the future and prepare you for when the tough times come along. Finally, make it a point to remember each time when your ability to function under pressure was successful. These images of success will serve as guideposts for the future (Menkes, 2013). Event planners need to remember the occasions during which they felt successful, such as when the CEO congratulated them for a well-planned corporate function.

All event planners need to know exactly what their own personal style is in conflict and crisis situations. A conscious inventory of past reactions to stress will help you to understand what works and what does not. There are, in fact, choices you can make in handling stress. In some cases, people work in conditions in which their physical or emotional health is constantly under fire because of the stress; such work situations are not unlike that of the event planner. But with deliberate and conscious thought, you do not have to let pressure affect your health or decision-making powers (Newman, 1999). Making decisions under pressure, staying calm when no one else is—these characteristics will become part of your brand when you develop them fully.

Learning to listen and come to terms with the voice that rules your inner core, the "calm, confident and connected inner self" (Payne, 2012, p. 4), will enable you to balance job performance with self-satisfaction and ethical decision-making. Odd hours and unpredictable working times, common in the lives of event planners, are among the most stressful modern work variables in this century (Henley & Lambert, 2014). Good event planners are attuned to internal and external signals that may indicate incoming stress, and have developed methods to handle a response. What agitates you? What are your weak spots that trigger even greater tension? Perhaps it may not be the external environment that is providing the stressor; in fact, that stress may be coming from you, from your typical responses to events around you. For example, it is common for every client and every event planner to want a 'perfect' event, but as any seasoned event planner knows, imperfections are a common part of the process. Making 'perfect imperfections' is a stressful part of the solution, but it is a regular part of the job. For instance, a stark white wall at the event venue might not match the off-white decor. As your client makes the outrageous demand to have the wall painted before the event, your stress level rises. Instead of handing your client a can of paint, you realize the wall can be covered with beautiful drapery that makes the event even more glamorous. As you look back on the event, it is easy to realize that the number of sleepless nights and stressful meetings about the wall color were unnecessary. Learn from the conflict; file away your reaction so that you can grow as a result.

As the world population continues to grow, and new technologies continue to advance, conflict and crisis situations become inevitable (Perrow, 1999). Understanding how to manage chaotic situations is a must in the event planning industry where conflict and crisis situations are going to happen. Maintaining a calm presence is contagious. A calm demeanor offers others in the situation a lifeline by which they can tailor their responses to yours. A calm presence also gives you time to plan through the immediate situation and work with those around you to formulate responses that might be effective (DuBrin, 2013). Though it may not be your first response in a conflict or crisis, the ability to remain composed can be learned and developed with practice (Barbato, 2010). Unanticipated events in this field will be a regular occurrence, and having a strategy in place for the unexpected will provide you with a sense of calm if you have done your preparation. While effective event planners appreciate the importance of preparation, they also must understand that no amount of preparation can cover every contingency, and that their own personality must be able to develop alternatives with only a second's notice (Shapiro & Jordan, 2008). Moreover, personality types might be an indicator of the ability to adapt in a moment filled with turmoil. Strong problem-solving and decision-making abilities are helpful in maintaining a calm presence, and personality tests including the Myers-Briggs Type Indicator (MBTI®) could prove useful in determining a specific personality type that is more adaptive to quick change (Briggs Myers, 1998; Briggs Myers, McCaulley, Most, 1985). Conflict and crisis are inevitable parts of event planning; by using the tactics covered in this chapter, you will find greater success in times of uncertainty.

Key Terms

Argument	Accommodating	Conflict resolution	NICE
Conflict	Competing	Conflict management	WAC'em
Crisis	Compromising	S-TLC	Organizational crisis
Avoiding	Collaborating	Conflict map	

Discussion Questions

1. You are planning an outdoor event in your town center, and your contact at the CVB has a reputation for being a very difficult person with whom to work. This person is hypercritical, close-minded and a control freak. How would you manage working with this person in order to have a good experience and be successful in your planning?

2. Describe the last conflict situation you were in. How did you handle it? Describe the last crisis situation you were in. How did you handle it?

3. Create a backup plan for an outdoor festival if the weather reports are calling for a tornado.

Activity

By using the conflict management methods of Cahn and Abigail (2014), Arnett, Bell McManus, and McKendree (2018), Shapiro, Jankowski, and Dale (2005), and Pachter and Magee (2000), examine a conflict that is happening on campus, in your organization, or in the news. Use their research to help reach a resolution to the problem.

References

Allen, J. (2009). *Event planning: The ultimate guide to successful meetings, corporate events, fundraising galas, conferences and conventions, incentives and other special events.* Hoboken, NJ: John Wiley and Sons.

Amen, D. G. (1999). *Change your brain, change your life.* New York: Crown Publishing Group.

Arnett, R. C., Bell McManus, L. M., & McKendree, A. G. (2018). *Conflicts between persons: The origins of leadership* (2nd ed.). Dubuque, IA: Kendall Hunt.

Barbato, P. (2010). *Inspire your career: Strategies for success in your first years at work.* London: Insomniac Press.

Bell, L. M. (2010). Crisis communication: The praxis of response. *Review of Communication, 10,* 142–155.

Briggs Myers, I. (1998). *Introduction to Type®: A guide to understanding your results the MBPT instrument.* Washington, DC: Consulting Psychologists Press.

Briggs Myers, I., McCaulley, M., & Most, R. (1985). *Manual: A guide to the development and use of the Myers-Briggs Type Indicator.* Washington, DC: Consulting Psychologists Press.

Cahn, D. D., & Abigail, R. A., (2014). *Managing conflict through communication* (5th ed.). New York: Pearson.

Canary, D. J., & Cupach, W. R. (1988). Relational and episodic characteristics associated with conflict tactics. *Journal of Social Science and Personal Relationships, 5,* 305–322.

Cohen, S., Kessler, R. C., & Gordon, L. U. (1997). Strategies for measuring stress in studies of psychiatric and physical disorders. In S. Cohen, R. C. Kessler, & L. U. Gordon. *Measuring stress: A guide for health and social scientists* (pp. 3–28). New York: Oxford University Press.

Coombs, W. T. (2007). Protecting organization reputations during a crisis: The development and application of situational crisis communication theory. *Corporate Reputation Review, 10,* 163–177.

DuBrin, A. J. (2013). *Handbook of research on crisis leadership in organizations.* Northampton, MA: Edward Elgar Publishing.

Eadie, W. F., & Nelson, P. E. (2001). *The language of conflict and resolution.* Newbury Park, CA: Sage.

Guerrero, L. K., & La Valley, A. G. (2006). Conflict, emotion, and communication. In J. G. Oetzel, & S. Ting-Toomey (Eds.), *The Sage handbook of conflict communication* (pp. 69–96). Thousand Oaks, CA: Sage.

Henley, J. R., & Lambert, S. J., (2014). Unpredictable work timing in retail jobs: Implications for employee work-life. *Industrial & Labor Relations Review, 67,* 986–1016.

Hermann, C. F. (1963). Some consequences of crisis which limit the viability of organizations. *Administrative Science Quarterly, 8,* 61–82.

Hilhorst, D. (2013). Disaster, conflict and society: Everyday politics of crisis response. In D. Hilhorst (Ed.). *Disaster, conflict and society in crisis: Everyday politics of crisis response* (pp. 1–15). New York: Routledge.

Hocker, J. L., & Wilmot, W. W. (2013). *Interpersonal conflict* (2nd ed.). Dubuque, IA: W. C. Brown. (Original work published 1978).

Kramer, M. W., & Hess, J. A. (2002). Communication rules for the display of emotions in organizational settings. *Management Communication Quarterly, 16,* 66–80.

LoCirero, J. (2008). *Meeting and event planning: From trade shows and conventions to fundraisers and galas—everything you need for a successful business event.* Avon, MA: F & W Publications.

Melnick, S. (2013). *Success under stress: Powerful tools for staying calm, confident, and productive when the pressure's on.* New York: AMACOM.

Menkes, J. (2013). *Better under pressure: How great leaders bring out the best in themselves and others.* Boston, MA: Harvard Business Press.

Mortensen, C. D. (1974). A transactional paradigm of social conflict. In G. R. Miller, & H. W. Simons (Eds.), *Perspectives on communication in social conflict* (pp. 90–194). Englewood Cliffs, NJ: Prentice Hall.

Newman, J. E. (1999). *How to stay cool, calm and collected when the pressure's on: A stress control plan for business people.* New York: AMACOM.

Pachter, B., & Magee, S. (2000). *The power of positive confrontation: The skills you need to know to handle conflicts at work, at home, and in life.* New York: MFJ books.

Payne, S. G. (2012). *The joy of work: How to stay calm, confident & connected in a chaotic world.* Bloomington, IN: Balboa Press.

Pearce, W. B., & Littlejohn, S. W. (1997). *Moral conflict: When social worlds collide.* Thousand Oaks, CA: Sage.

Perrow, C. (1999). *Normal accidents: Living with high-risk technologies.* Princeton, NJ: Princeton University Press.

Putnam, L. L. (2006). Definitions and approaches to conflict and communication. In J. G. Oetzel & S. Ting-Toomey (Eds.), *Sage handbook of conflict communication* (pp. 1–32). Thousand Oaks, CA: Sage.

Putnam, L. L., & Fairhurst, G. T. (2001). Discourse analysis in organizations: Issues and concerns. In F. M. Jablin & L. L. Putnam (Eds.), *The new handbook of organizational communication: Advances in theory* (pp. 78–136). Thousand Oaks, CA: Sage.

Putnam, L. L., & Poole, M. S. (1987). Conflict and negotiation. In F. M. Jablin, L. L. Putnam, K. H. Roberts, & L. W. Porter (Eds.), *Handbook of organizational communication: An interdisciplinary perspective* (pp. 549–599). Newbury Park, CA: Sage.

Rusbult, C. E., Johnson, D. J., & Morrow, G. D. (1986). Impact of couple patterns of problem solving on distress and nondistress in dating relationships. *Journal of Personality and Social Psychology, 50,* 744–753.

Seeger, M. W. (2006). Best practices in crisis communication: An expert panel process. *Journal of Applied Communication Research, 34,* 232–244.

Seeger, M. W., Sellnow, T. L., & Ulmer, R. R. (1998). Communication, organization, and crisis. *Communication Yearbook, 2,* 231–275.

————. (2003). *Communication and organizational crisis.* Westport, CT: Quorum Press.

Sellnow, T. L., & Seeger, M. W. (2013) *Theorizing crisis communication.* West Sussex, UK: John Wiley & Sons.

Sellnow, T. L., & Ulmer, R. R. (1994). Ambiguous argument as advocacy in organizational crisis communication. *Argumentation & Advocacy, 31,* 138–150.

Sellnow, T. L., Ulmer, R. R., & Snider, M. (1998). The compatibility of corrective action in organizational crisis communication. *Communication Quarterly, 46,* 60–74.

Shapiro, R. M., Jankowski, M. A., & Dale, J. (2005). *Bullies, tyrants & impossible people: How to beat them without joining them.* New York: Crown Business.

Shapiro, R. M., & Jordan, G. (2008). *Dare to prepare: How to win before you begin.* New York: Random House.

Thomas, K. W., & Kilmann, R. H. (1974). *Thomas-Kilmann conflict mode instrument.* Tuxedo, NY: Xicom, Inc.

Ulmer, R. R. (1999). Responsible speech in crisis communication: The case of General Motors vs. Dateline NBC. *Free Speech Yearbook, 37,* 155–168.

Ulmer, R. R., Seeger, M. W., & Sellnow, T. L. (2007). Post-Crisis communication and renewal: Expanding the parameters of post-crisis discourse. *Public Relations Review, 33,* 130–134.

Ulmer, R. R., Sellnow, T. L., & Seeger, M. W. (2007). *Effective crisis communication: Moving from crisis to opportunity.* Thousand Oaks, CA: Sage.

Ulmer, R. R., Sellnow, T. L., & Seeger, M. W. (2017). *Effective crisis communication: Moving from crisis to opportunity* (4th ed.) Thousand Oaks, CA: Sage

Van Der Wagen, L. & White, L. (2014). *Human resources management for the event industry* (2nd ed.) Abingdon, United Kingdom: Routledge.

Yungbluth S. C., & Johnson, S. E. (2010). With respect to emotion in the dominion of rationality: Managing conflict through respectful dialogue. *Atlantic Journal of Communication, 18,* 211–226.

Chapter 13

INTEGRATED MARKETING COMMUNICATION: PROMOTING THE EVENT

In an era where collaboration among those in the world of business can pose some definite challenges to those knowledgeable about communication, it is even more important for professionals in the field of event planning to be able to integrate their knowledge of organization, marketing, scheduling, public relations (PR), promotions, advertising, and communication smoothly and seamlessly into one total and cohesive package that offers clients a framework for engagement and success. Event planners must know and apply principles of integrated marketing communication (IMC) in every event they plan for clients; in the competitive world of today's events, it is not enough to understand marketing theories. Professionals must practice every principle on a regular basis, and all practitioners should approach the application of IMC principles from a generalist perspective, rather than a territorial one (Schultz, Patti, & Kitchen, 2013). Engaging clients, guests, consumers, and other shareholders requires a determination to integrate the many aspects of communication into a well-thought-out plan. This chapter seeks to construct such a plan.

© Jacob Lund/Shutterstock.com

When you have finished reading this chapter, you will be able to

- define IMC and its components;
- develop an integrated marketing plan for an event;
- select the proper channels for reaching an event audience.

Strut Your Mutt

Angie Corbo, Ph.D., Chair & Associate Professor, Widener University

Our pets are part of family life, and they certainly add adorable content on Instagram and Snapchat. Dogs on a college campus seem to bring happiness for those who just can't help themselves from interacting with a furry friend.

Students enrolled in COMS 375: *Event Planning & Campaigns* launched Strut Your Mutt—a dog Halloween Parade complete with prizes, to fulfill a course requirement. The students' goal was to encourage the university president to enter her dogs into the contest. The event was open to all canine-loving faculty, staff, and students. To our delight, the president was enthusiastic about the idea, and her dogs attended the event in costumes.

As with all events, the event planners conducted a SWOT analysis as a first step. They found the following:

- *Strength:* A dog Halloween Costume Parade offers a light-hearted social event and provides a perfect visual to add to the university website during the fall term. This shared interest creates a sense of community and a fondness for the university brand.
- *Weakness:* As a new event, a strong IMC promotion is needed to encourage participation. Another (unexpected) weakness was feline fans complained that we did not offer a costume party for cats.
- *Opportunity:* This is a perfect event to allow the university president to interact with students, faculty, and staff in a relaxed atmosphere on a Friday afternoon.
- *Threat:* Risk management needed to approve the event and help draft a participant agreement form. The success of this outdoor event was contingent upon nice weather!

The student organizers created, implemented, promoted, and evaluated the success of their 'original campus event.' Once students gained approval to proceed with the event, they referred to the RACE model as a planning guide.

- *Research:* Halloween traditions often include costume parties for people of all ages. In recent years, pet costumes are widely available in retail stores and online. The event planning students believed this event would be well-received on our dog-friendly campus. They informally surveyed students and faculty and believed they would have a minimum of 20 participants for this inaugural event.
- *Action:* The planning phase of this event introduced several challenges. Students resolved the risk management with the following language: "The participating member of the campus community must accompany their pet(s) during the event. Participants must agree that the dog will remain on-leash throughout the event and

that any disagreeable dog will be asked to leave." This outdoor event required sound and special arrangements with the Office of Multi-Media Support. The event planners secured a rain date location and included this information on all promotional materials. Students also managed additional layers of the organizational infrastructure including registration, judging, and prizes. They designed the entry application, collected the registration fee (with cash, check, and Venmo options), recruited judges, created a judging rubric, and sought donations for pet-friendly prizes. The registration fee covered any minor expenses for the event, and the remaining balance was donated to a local animal shelter.

- *Communication:* Strut Your Mutt promotional material was highly creative, through visual material transmitted via traditional and social media. Students launched an IMC campaign through university and personal social media accounts; a media advisory to local media; promotional flyers; and consumer-generated media. Student planners partnered with University Relations, campus organizations, Greek life, and other campus online influencers to promote the event. Consumer-generated media increased closer to the event as participants waged friendly competitive banter with each other. Local media covered the event.

- *Evaluation:* The event was a success by most standards! Participants (human and canine) enjoyed themselves. The university president requested this to be an annual event. The original group of students recommended several changes for future years. They encouraged prizes for small, medium, and large dogs. They also recommended that dogs be judged on their costume and 'performance' in modeling the costume. The outdoor venue works well but the sound system connection was poor in the original space.

Strut Your Mutt was a success as it mirrored the campus culture and had support from key stakeholders on campus, including a new sponsor, the Public Relations Student Society of America (PRSSA). The event planners' creativity, thorough planning, and professionalism resulted in a new tradition on campus.

Contributed by Angie Corbo. Copyright © Kendall Hunt Publishing Company.

After reading the chapter, revisit this case study and respond to the following question:

What other integrated marketing communication possibilities are available for incorporating a feline-friendly campaign?

Integrated Marketing Communication

Integrated Marketing Communication (IMC) emerged in 1980 as a natural evolution in the fields of business and communication. During a time of changing and increasing demands in the marketplace, there was a need to move towards a more strategic and integrated form of communication (Du Plessis, van Heerden, & Gordon, 2010). Grounded in communication theory (Fitzpatrick, 2005; Kliatchko, 2005), IMC connects public relations, marketing, and advertising. In 1960, Berlo examined the importance of communication as a process. IMC, which many understand as a process, works to reclaim the importance of communicative content—in other words, the message is important. Moreover, one consistent strategic communicative message that reaches a target audience is the essential characteristic of IMC (Pelsmacker, Geuens, & Bergh, 2001). A study by Kitchen, Kim, and Schultz (2008) looked at IMC in the United Kingdom, the United States, and South

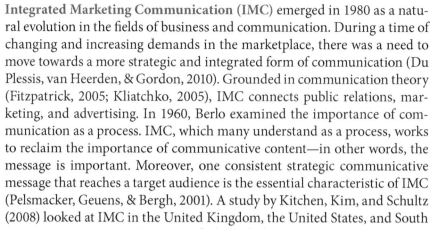

Korea, and showed that IMC is not just another management fad, but that the concepts behind the field of IMC are being consistently implemented by advertising and PR agencies. Another study by Batra and Keller (2016) offers a comprehensive look at how traditional and new media affect consumer decision-making, offering specific criteria through which a marketing plan can be assessed. In addition, Kliatchko and Schultz (2014) have found that in today's society of constant communication, IMC is the major theme behind many client-based organizations, even though practitioners might not always call what they do IMC.

IMC has many different names in the marketplace, including "integrated thinking, integrated planning, integrated marketing, full service, 360, or simply integration" (Kliatchko & Schultz, 2014, p. 380). Additionally, IMC has many different definitions. One definition of IMC that works for the field of event planning is as follows:

> *IMC is really all about planning in order to deliver a consistent message. Effective IMC should certainly encourage strong customer relationships, but it does that through effective planning in order to develop an integrated communication program that will optimize specific communication objectives that lead to a desired behavior on the part of a target audience (Percy, 2008, p. 8).*

In the planning of events, all communicative interactions can lead to a greater understanding of what the client needs and wants. Talking to people and understanding what they desire and require is necessary in any field that deals with human interaction, but especially in event planning, where you are constantly communicating with others to create a successful event. The goal of IMC is to build long-term relationships through effective two-way interactive communication (Blakeman, 2009). For example, when communicating with an organization that is planning a business retreat, you need to learn more about the company than just what they want at their event. Through various discussions, you might learn about the important connections the organization has with the community, for instance. Thus, a nice touch might be to incorporate a community service project in the middle of the day during the retreat. After a few hours, the mind and body get tired of being in the same location. By taking a break from the traditional business-style meeting and helping to serve lunch at a local soup kitchen, employees might be invigorated for the evening sessions. Understanding the identity of an organization allows you to offer unique touches that incorporate some of the organization's mission, vision, and values, and will create lasting memories for your client. Appreciating the importance of an integrated marketing approach to communication will allow you to comprehend more than just what is needed at an event. To build a brand, to increase customer loyalty, to draw attention to changes within a client's company, event planners and their colleagues in marketing fields must understand the ways in which new methods of marketing communication can be implemented (Keller, 2016).

Don Schultz and his colleagues (1993) believe IMC is a way to view the process as a whole instead of as multiple parts, making all forms of communication relevant and connected. IMC is constructed in a manner similar to the well-known phrase, "The whole is more than the sum of its parts" (Aristotle, Trans. 1984; Mill, 1843/1875; Wertheimer, 1912/1961). IMC is the whole, and communication is the glue that holds all the parts together. Before one thoroughly understands the whole, however, it is important to understand all of the parts.

Public Relations

The multifaceted field of public relations is a growing commodity for any organization (Daugherty, 2003). The Public Relations Society of America (PRSA) (2012) defines **public relations** as "a strategic communication process that builds mutually beneficial relationships between organizations and their publics" (The Public Relations Society of America, "What is public relations?" para. 3). Public relations is about making a lasting, positive connection with the community, but what does an actual public relations professional do? According to the Occupational Outlook Handbook of 2018, various duties are performed by public relations specialists, such as writing news releases for the media, determining ways to reach an audience, helping clients communicate, developing and maintaining identity/brand, writing speeches, evaluating/creating advertising and other promotional material, and fundraising. Event planners will learn to use all of these skills to their advantage over the course of their career. The public relations media and methods employed by the event planner must align with the experience that is being created. Branding for a casual event

Public Relations (PR): *A strategic communication process that builds mutually beneficial relationships between organizations and their publics* demands a different kind of PR than what is demanded for a formal gala, for instance (Barrow, 2017).

Before you begin promoting an event, it is necessary to understand the process of public relations. Marston (2012) describes the process through the RACE acronym:

R—**research** the situation; the more information you know, the more possibilities for successful execution will occur;

A—**action** or planning what is going to be done; allows you to map out your approach;

C—**communication** with the public allows you to inform, persuade, and motivate others;

E—**evaluation** of the project offers a systematic assessment of your task and provides accountability for your actions and opportunities for improvement the next time you engage in the process.

RACE: *A technique involving research, action, communication, and evaluation used to understand the process of public relations*

Press kit: *Items produced and used for a variety of public relations purposes, including items such as a press release, backgrounder, and brochure*

These steps are vital for understanding the processes of public relations. Another component of the public relations composite is the **press kit**, items that are "produced and used for a variety of public relations purposes" (Bivins, 2008, p. 76). The press kit may include a press release or media advisory announcing your event; a backgrounder, which is a one- or two-page treatment on the history of the company and/or event; brochures and/or pamphlets that inform the public about the event; a fact sheet; and any promotional photos that the media is permitted to use. While public relations tools can help promote an event, marketing allows you to focus on the consumer.

Marketing

Marketing: *The science of combining the understanding of human psychology with deliberate and scientific analysis to promote or sell products or services*

Almost every event that is designed to promote a brand or a special occasion must begin with a marketing plan. Corporations in the United States have invested more than $300 billion a year in every kind of event, touching on the realms of education, promotion and production, hospitality, and many more (Saget, 2006). Thus, event marketing continues to grow substantially every year, with spending in the United States reaching $37 billion in 2012 (Miller & Washington, 2012) and $565 billion worldwide in the same year (Cespedes & Prasad, 2015). With decades of research (Alderson, 1957; Bartels, 1970; 1988; Keller, 2016; Kotler, 1997; Nicosia, 1966; Pickton & Broderick, 2005; Vargo & Lusch, 2004), **marketing** has now become a science, combining understanding of human psychology with deliberate and scientific analysis; the result is that marketing must seek to develop a plan that does not just identify and reach the target audiences, but satisfy them as well (Hoyle, 2002; Keller, 2016). A marketing plan must be thoughtful, holistic, and detailed, relying on imagination and innovation as well as true market research. "Knowing the story behind your business, and knowing how to make that story include your customer is vital to your overall marketing message" (Cockrum, 2011, p. 231). Building a marketing plan can be a formal process or one more informal, but the plan needs time to take shape and demands the input of everyone involved in the event (Masterman & Wood, 2006). McCarthy's (1960) four p's of marketing (product, price, place, and promotion) and variations on the p's of marketing (profit, positioning, people, and process) make up a strategy for achieving a desired outcome (Oguejiofor, 2014). The p's of marketing help the event planner understand this process as a multifaceted endeavor that takes time, effort, and energy. A successful marketing plan depends on the ability to build and sustain relationships with all the shareholders in the event in order to gain their trust and contribution (Saget, 2006). Thus, if the marketing plan is going to succeed, it needs to communicate a strategy to everyone in the organization as well as to those customers the client hopes to reach (Batra & Keller, 2016; Masterman & Wood, 2006). "One essential difference between a business that fails or is perpetually anemic and one that survives and prospers, is how successful they are with their marketing …" (Corbett, 1996, p. 1). The most effective event marketers have a large toolbox of creative and emotional marketing skills that can reach the consumer on many levels (Gupta, 2003; Kotler & Zaltman, 1971).

Hoyle (2002) mentions several aspects of preparation to consider as the marketing plan begins. First, the marketing team must understand the client thoroughly. Performing a **SWOT analysis** (strengths, weaknesses, opportunities, and threats) with the client can be a starting point for the development of a marketing plan. This kind of research, often called discovery, demands that event planners learn all they can about the company for whom they are marketing an event. This knowledge can dramatically affect the marketing plan (Saget, 2006) as well as the relationship with the client. In her study of event marketing, Allison Saget (2006) interviewed Brian VandenBroucke, CEO and senior creative director of Articulate Creative Communications, Inc., who notes:

SWOT analysis: *A process that includes analyzing the (S) strengths, (W) weaknesses, (O) opportunities, and (T) threats with the client as a starting point for the development of a marketing plan*

> *Real discovery is the art form of asking questions with intense purpose, curiosity, and enthusiasm. Real questions provide real answers to guide your program as a whole—ultimately ensuring its success. Real discovery provides a program which aligns both your strategic and creative plans (Saget, 2006, p. 19).*

Discovery demands open and honest communication with not just one person on the client side, but with a range of voices that can offer insight and clarification. Once the communication occurs, the event planner can begin to build objectives based upon the information obtained from the client, sharing those objectives at each point along the event journey. Understanding the client's personality is key to designing the kind of event that is appropriate, brand-consistent, and impressive.

Armed with this client knowledge and understanding, the event planner can then turn attention to discerning who the client's competition is in hopes of finding a way to make any particular event different from what the competition is doing (Hoyle, 2002; Oana, 2018). For instance, your client wants you to plan an event, perhaps a gala, to raise money for the company's underserved partners in the community. Formal galas have become commonplace in the last decade, so you will need to look at how other major fundraisers have used such an event to raise money and awareness for particular causes, and then brainstorm for ideas that distinguish your upcoming event from similar ones. Will there actually be a gala at all? You may find that some people or markets must actually be persuaded that there is value in attending an event in terms of their time and money (Hoyle, 2002). Perhaps contributors, many of whom might have frantic lives, would be willing to buy a ticket to an event for which they could just stay at home and relax instead of facing the stress of finding babysitters, dressing up, and heading out to a venue that may not be terribly convenient. Instead of planning a sumptuous dinner for them at a pricey hotel, you might consider sending pizza and a movie to their home on the night of the non-event. Knowing your target audience and thinking outside the box could provide you with a wealth of unique ideas for event planning. The event planner's job is to design a strategy that will ultimately meet the agreed-upon marketing objectives (Masterman & Wood, 2006). An ever-expanding competitive marketplace offers a greater number of creative challenges to the event planner, so that more effective marketing strategies are needed to distinguish one event from another (Koo, Byon, & Baker, 2014). Market research about the target audience will reveal a great deal of information about the customer, and your job is to discern how to reach that customer most directly (Hoyle, 2002; Keller, 2016), finding a fit between the marketing plan, the brand of the client, and the kind of event you want to produce (Zarantonello & Schmitt, 2013).

© dotshock/Shutterstock.com

The next step in the plan would be to carefully estimate how much money is available for the event itself. The budget almost always dictates the kind of event that can take place, so knowledge of the finances is crucial before proceeding further. When the budget is limited, event planners may have to find new marketing strategies that capitalize on the use of resources (Koo, Byon, & Baker, 2014). In this instance, creativity and thoughtfulness are tremendously important; the success of a marketing plan may depend upon effectively reaching the customers' emotions (Masterman & Wood, 2006), which can occur even when the budget is constrained. An event such as a simple bake sale might produce large profits if the marketing is effective. People may be willing to pay $5 for a large homemade cookie or $30 for a pie if they know that all the proceeds are benefitting a child with cancer. Following your detailed business plan, and not allowing anything to derail it along the way, will demand focus, communication with the client, and steadfast 'eyes on the prize.'

Once the objectives, market research, and finances are in place, how will the event planner ultimately reach the audience? Depending upon the budget, there is an enormous variety of methods. Social media, target marketing, digital media, and e-commerce are some of the most effective modern methods of gathering customers. Today, consumers seem to be less influenced by traditional marketing methods like advertising (Martensen, Grønholdt, Bendtsen, & Jensen, 2007), and are turning to other outlets (Batra & Keller, 2016). Attracting sponsors to an event demonstrates the importance of media buys and hospitality to draw in possible consumers (Hoyle, 2002). For example, a company looking for a **return on investment (ROI)** might choose to sponsor a luncheon that offers high visibility. Creating and maintaining a positive event image will help the success of the event and strengthen the popularity of the client's brand, so if the event planner is trying to build brand equity through the event, every opportunity to promote the brand must be sought (Zarantonello & Schmitt, 2013). Think about creating an event on campus. How can you get other college students excited to attend your event? One way might be to consider offering complimentary branded giveaways, since people love free promotional items such as t-shirts, water bottles, sunglasses, and hats. How do you get the word out so people actually attend the event? Perhaps instead of hanging posters in classrooms around campus, you create special invitations for professors to hand out in their classes. Reach out using social media—tweet about the event, create a promotional Facebook page, design a Snapchat filter or open an Instagram account for the event, and send text messages encouraging attendance. Think of other ways to enhance participation. Invite the marching band to play the school fight song to kick off the promotion, or perhaps the dance team can get people moving. Incorporating some of these possibilities will help market and advertise the event.

Advertising

Event planners must understand the nature of advertising and how to use it to their advantage. Often, word of mouth and public relations are not enough to publicize your event, so you and your client may decide that purchasing time or space in a medium is a good option. Whether you are placing an advertisement in a print publication, scheduling a promotion to run on local or satellite radio, television or streaming services, or using digital media, you are buying advertising. In today's ever-changing world, definitions of advertising come in various forms and styles, and as social media continue to expand and flourish, these definitions continue to evolve.

TIP

Event planners must find creative ways to make the client's logo the most prominent feature of the promotion. Don't be afraid be inventive and keep an open mind when brainstorming and planning.

— Charles Steinberg

Return on Investment (ROI): *The benefit an investor derives that is the result of an investment of a resource*

However, one definition that accurately represents the nature of advertising comes from Thomas Bivins (2008): "**Advertising** is the controlled use of media ensuring that your message reaches your audience in exactly the form you intend and at the time you want. Advertising can be print, broadcast, or Web-based" (p. 5). The operative word in this definition is that it is "controlled" (p. 5). If you direct a press release to local media about your upcoming event, you are not guaranteed that the media will cover it, nor are you guaranteed that the media will put the correct spin on it. However, when you purchase advertising, you have more control; you can purchase a specific time and space and direct a message to an intended audience. Therefore, advertising has an enormous potential to help inform an audience or customers of the details of your upcoming event.

Keeping the client's advertising in line with the event, and sending a message that is tailored to an audience, can help position your client's event effectively. Al Ries and Jack Trout (2001) define positioning in the following way: "**Positioning** is not what you do to a product. Positioning is what you do to the mind of the prospect. That is, you position the product in the mind of the prospect" (p. 3). David Ogilvy (1985), who was hailed as one of the most creative and successful advertising men, describes positioning in his own words: "Positioning is 'what the product does, and who it is for'" (p. 12). For example, positioning involves the way you advertise your event to consumers and helps define what they should think of your event. If you are planning a 5K fundraising run for a hospital, you will want to position that event as entertaining, worthwhile, and healthy, and also as a way for people to give back to the community. If you are planning a black-tie gala months later for that same hospital, you might want to position that event to consumers as another way to connect to a good cause by attending an elegant night out that includes dinner, drinks, music, and a live band. In both of these examples, the hospital itself is considered a **brand**, the "image" or personality of your product, service, or event (Ogilvy, 1985, p. 14). The hospital's brand might be one of continued community commitment along with superior health care. If the aforementioned statement is accurate, then supporting the local hospital would be something many consumers would want to do by attending its advertised events. In that case, they are attaching themselves to the brand. "The ultimate act of branding is to take something—a product or service—and make everyone aware of it, and its purpose or intent" (Arnell, 2010, p. 32). Connecting the event to the brand in a way that makes sense is an important advertising strategy.

Positioning: *Not what you do to a product, but what you do to the mind of the prospect; that is, you position the product in the mind of the prospect*

Brand: *The "image" or personality of a product, service, or event*

Advertising is a means by which the client's message will reach consumers. Figuring out which method of advertising would be most beneficial is a

strategic decision you will want to make with your clients. Whether event planners are designing ads themselves, utilizing a freelance graphic artist, or working directly with an advertising agency, the client should have a desired outcome from the placement of advertising. Before the advertising placement begins, however, the advertisement itself must be created. But just how creative must advertising be? How can you capture the attention of consumers for your client's event? Ogilvy (1985) writes, "I do not regard advertising as entertainment. When I write an advertisement, I don't

© littleny/Shutterstock.com

want you to tell me you find it 'creative.' I want you to find it so interesting you buy the product" (p. 7). In the case of the event planner, Ogilvy would create an advertisement so strong that consumers sign up to attend the event right away. If that were the outcome, he would consider that successful advertising.

Like Ogilvy (1985), Marsh, Guth, and Short (2009) suggest that effective advertising requires event planners to write persuasive messages, and that these messages should get consumers to act. In today's over-communicated society, advertisements must be positioned correctly so they penetrate the clutter and noise that bombard the consumer every day (Keller, 2016; Ries & Trout, 2001). People today are constantly being invited to attended charitable events, join groups on social media, participate in community service activities, and chair social committees in the community. While it is noble to want to craft an innovative, 'look at me' ad, what is more important is to "develop one clear message for your ad" (Marsh, Guth, & Short, 2009, p. 116). However, in order to create such a piece, you must spend some time researching to draft a strategic message. See how other types of events like yours have been promoted through advertising. How were these ads constructed? How were they built? What color schemes were used? Did they reflect the overall theme of the event? Likewise, if the client is new to you but has been orchestrating the same event consistently for several years, you will want to see what advertisements have been put together in the past so you can effectively analyze their value and not repeat something that has already been done. Doing your homework is imperative when creating advertising. You will not produce successful advertising if you do not properly do your research (Ogilvy, 1985). By understanding your client and conducting research, you will begin to generate ideas for an advertising campaign that meets the needs of the client and effectively promotes the event.

TIP

Keep your stakeholders in mind when planning your strategic messages. Do your research. Know who they are, what they like, and how to incorporate them into the event.

— Julie Wagner

Remember, one of the keys to advertising an event is that you cannot discount consumers who already believe in the event or have attended it in the past. "Your existing customers are your best prospects for re-selling, cross-selling or up-selling" (Corbett, 1996, p. 25). If event attendees have a great time at your function, their positive comments may help garner new attendees the next time you plan an event. "To gain the loyalty and trust of consumers, your message—conveyed through advertising or marketing—has to be authentic. It has to be simple and boiled down in essence" (Arnell, 2010, p. 32). Keeping your message strong when creating and placing advertising can further help solidify clients while, at the same time, make and keep them happy and effectively brand each event you produce. Effective advertising with strong messaging will successfully promote events.

Promotions

As with any public relations, marketing, or advertising activity, promoting the event in a thorough and consistent manner is vital. Your client's company name, logo, or brand is an important part of the promotions plan, and whether obvious or subliminal, brand awareness must be part of that plan. Consider the message that the brand conveys and how that message can be best communicated. What are the goals of this communication (Hoyle, 2002)? As you begin to conduct research on what promotional materials are needed, you should list the advantages and disadvantages of various methods of engagement. For example, will you be sending formal invitations, e-vites, emails, social media blasts, or will you be hanging posters in selected locales or advertising in papers (Public Relations Student Society of America, 2014)? There are many ways to publicize an event; in fact, the choices may become overwhelming, so sticking to a plan will keep you on track. The Public Relations Student Society of America (2013) offers a few suggestions for promoting events on a college campus, including creating videos, speaking to professionals, working with the media, and relying on personal relationships for word-of-mouth promotion. Considering a variety of promotional strategies will help event planners reach their niche market.

Good promotions as part of the marketing plan depend on sensory stimulation, for research has shown that experiential contact means the most to consumers. Giving them a hands-on experience makes a lasting emotional impression (Zarantonello & Schmitt, 2013). You can work to reach the target audience through giveaways, and there are a myriad of vendors who will work with you creating promotional items. You can use creative materials to their best advantage by making use of every available space and every surface to stimulate the consumers' connection between the company's image and the event. This amount of work means that you might want to consider building a relationship with print and production vendors on whom you rely consistently for products, and with time, the relationship might even positively impact prices you are given. Ask other planners, vendors, and production houses for advice about design, artwork, copy writing, photography, production, printing, and distribution. Full-service creative agencies also specialize in promotional materials, and though they

TIP

Ask vendors for several references and look at reviews online. Anyone can say they are great, but their clients know them best.

— Matt Musgrove

can expand the budget more than might be advisable, you can portion out some of the deliverables to an agency very reasonably. Alcohol companies, in particular, may provide excellent examples of strategic placement, so take a lesson from them and think outside the box for new promotional ideas. You must work consistently to reinforce the client's message through all your promotional pieces, and the customer will ultimately sense this consistency (Saget, 2006).

In addition to promoting the event itself, there are also many times that events themselves are promotional. Promotional events are used to boost visibility, expose products, raise funds, and increase awareness about a cause, a product, a brand, or an occasion. One of the major skills needed for developing promotional events is the ability to do something unique. Grand openings and ribbon cuttings can be very ordinary if there is not some type of excitement that brings people to the event. When the International Spy Museum in Washington, D.C., first opened its doors, there was not just an ordinary ribbon cutting; instead, acrobats dressed in black climbed down the outside of the building for all to see. A sense of mystery and excitement made guests feel as if they were part of a spy movie during the opening. This dramatic opening was nominated for a variety of awards for its creativity and style (International Spy Museum L'Enfant Plaza, 2019).

© Tinseltown/Shutterstock.com

Other options for promotions include using celebrities, respected politicians, and community leaders to attract attention; however, these choices can be very expensive (Mirisch & Harris, 2013; Wilcox, Cameron, & Reber, 2015). Mirisch and Harris (2013) state, "Celebrities add 'glitz and glam' to an event, generating excitement and attracting media" (pp. 12–13). Celebrities will certainly bring awareness to an event, but it is important to match each celebrity personality to a cause. For example, Julia Louis-Dreyfus, actress and humanitarian who has become a spokeswoman for breast cancer awareness through Key to the Cure (Nagelberg, 2017), might be invited to open a new breast cancer wing in a prestigious hospital. Her association with the cause creates a sympathetic connection for consumer giving. However, the event planner must be aware that celebrity guests can also easily distract attention from the real reason the event is being held; instead of focusing on the event, guests instead are enthralled by the celebrity and miss the point completely. Additionally, balancing the finances of securing a prominent, high-profile figure against the outcome of such choices requires experience, careful examination, and well-considered decisions.

Social Media

Event planners can effectively utilize social media networks to promote events in many different ways. In today's tech-savvy world, anything that is promoted digitally is called social media. Kane, Alavi, Labianca, and Borgatti (2014) define **social media** as "information technologies which support interpersonal communication and collaboration using Internet-based platforms" (p. 275). While many people may use social media passively,

Social media: *Information technologies which support interpersonal communication and collaboration using Internet-based platforms*

others believe that it can be a compelling tool that allows users to engage in expanding online content (Sweetser & Lariscy, 2008) (p. 178). Social media helps keep the conversation going and is a way to extend discussion even after the physical event has taken place (Fletcher, 2011). An added benefit of social media is that it is a relatively low-cost endeavor and allows you to connect to existing traffic and sites that consumers are already using (Friedman, 2012). Furthermore, over half of events use social media strategies to help strengthen attendance at meetings. Planners have been pleased with the use of social media to promote events, and in 2017, the results were impressive: 47% of planners said social media helped bolster their events at meetings; 87% said Facebook was the most useful platform to promote events at meetings; and 84% said some or all of their events use social media at the actual event for meetings (Alonzo, 2017).

Social media allows businesses to bolster their company's personality through a light, self-aware tone where innovation matters (Gilette, 2010). Statistics regarding social media usage suggest that social media interactions have the power to inform large numbers of people. Smith (2019) found that of the 7.7 billion worldwide population, there are 3.5 billion active social media users. In fact, social media users grew by 202 million between April 2018 and April 2019. Since social media platforms operate on a global scale, they are changing consumer behavior (Dutta, 2010). As a result of this trend, businesses are creating multi-platform strategies in order to reach their overall marketing goals. **Consumer-generated media**, another term for social media, are quickly growing into a most significant factor in influencing consumer behavior "including awareness, information acquisition, opinions, attitudes, purchase behavior, and post-purchase communication and evaluation" (Mangold & Faulds, 2009, p. 358). Social media have a profound influence on promotion, visibility, and branding, and yet there are still some in managerial or decision-making positions who remain ambivalent about the usefulness of a social media profile. In fact, only 48% of planners use 'some' social media to promote events, and 42% say they have no formal strategy (Alonzo, 2017). "To guide managerial decision making and academic research for IMC, an updated, comprehensive, dynamic frame-work is needed that captures the full range of outcomes of interest as well as the various temporal sequences involved" (Batra & Kelly, 2016, p. 129) in developing a media campaign. Selecting the best platforms for promotion is key to gaining visibility and event recognition. Overall, event planners should consider selecting both traditional and social media avenues that work to strategize their event promotion.

Some of the most popular choices for event planners to publicize events include Facebook, Twitter, Instagram, Pinterest, LinkedIn, YouTube, Snapchat, blogs, and others. Through these platforms, planners can promote upcoming events and make connections with other social media users. The benefit of promoting your client's events through social media is that you have the power to expand your potential reach. "Your viewer could be the person next door or the person in Algeria" (Marsh, Guth, & Short, 2009, p. 98). Businesses must be mindful to vet their social media content with

Consumer-generated media: Another name for social media

the same vigor that they would scrutinize any other message that would go public (Kelly, 2010), and event planners should create informative and intriguing messages to share with followers. Event planners should structure social media content to be adaptable and adjusted based on how users interact and share feedback and ideas in an open manner (Klepek & Starzyczna, 2018). Today, social media users are connected not just to those in their personal networks, but also to unknown sources who share opinions, recommendations, and experiences regarding goods and services (Ratchford, Talukdar, & Lee, 2001). With opportunities to reach clients not readily available through traditional media, the possibilities are endless and continue to evolve and change every day.

© Quka/Shutterstock.com

In order to connect people to your events through social media, be sure to use language and incentives that help followers understand the meaning and nuances of the events you are promoting. Kotler and Keller (2012) examine the importance of the information that is shared among users—as well as between users and brands—that include both rational and emotional reasons as to why a user might engage with a brand or event. For example, a city neighborhood hosts outdoor Friday night movies during the summertime. An incentive for the event might include a coupon for a free ice cream cone on the event's Facebook page, while the language used in the messaging of the post might include an explanation of the event and its importance within the community. Schiffman and Kanuk (2004) believe that communication through social media has the power to blur interpersonal communication and impersonal communication. Therefore, users often feel a sense of belonging and connection through social media interaction. Creating clever and clear messages that invite interaction requires event planners to understand their role in promoting their client's event on social media. Writing engaging headlines, using photos to capture attention, providing hyperlinks, and making every word in the text count are some of the ways you can bolster your audience and get them interested in events you are promoting. Additionally, creating **hashtags**—the pound sign followed by a word or phrase—on social media can help your client and guests associate with your event by connecting keywords and conversation topics; using these hashtags is a way for users to find, identify, follow, and become connected to your company or organization (Drell, 2014). Event planners should use hashtags strategically to help users find and connect with the business' brand. For example, over the last several years, the Eastern Communication Association (ECA) has used the hashtag #ECA, followed by the year (for instance, #ECA19), for its annual convention. The hashtag is updated annually, and convention attendees use that hashtag throughout the five-day conference to tweet about sessions, panels, and colleagues along with hot topics in communication. Understanding these different promotional tools will enable you to market or grow your brand recognition in ways that you may never have thought possible.

Hashtag: *The pound sign followed by a word or phrase, used on social media to identify messages on a specific topic*

While setting up and managing social media is time-consuming and requires a constant effort, the event planner's goal of promotion on social media is to foster engagement and create curiosity. Therefore, it will be beneficial to develop several platforms and tie them all together. Rosenholm (2019) suggests creating a content team to coordinate all social media efforts whereby diversified messages could be constructed in advance. She also recommends recruiting local influencers to help reach new audiences, as well as utilizing the many additional functions such as 'stories' and ITV to showcase complementary content. For instance, one of the first things an event planner should do is set up a website (Friedman, 2012), and through that website, cross-promotion can occur. From their website, planners can link to their Facebook, Instagram, YouTube, Pinterest, and Snapchat accounts, for example. When planning events for clients, it would be beneficial if both the event planner and the client promote the event. **Cross-promotion**, a method of marketing that targets buyers of a product with an offer to purchase a related product, can be instrumental in getting the word out about a client's event. For example, your client, who is organizing a 5K run to raise awareness for a charity, might consider offering the first 100 people to register a race towel, hat, and shirt with branded logos of the charity and the sponsors. An article in Marketing Week documents ways in which brand partnerships that can cross-promote are often a highly effective way of marketing on a tight budget (Bacon, 2016). The cross-promotion benefits all involved through social media and website links.

Social media is integral to your success and the success of your clients, and connectivity on many levels matters. Consider writers who want to attend a writing conference. They may use social media for the following reasons: (1) To learn about the event through the convention website; (2) To register for the event online via the website; (3) To follow the convention and the activities leading up to the event on Facebook, Twitter, LinkedIn, or the convention site and blog; (4) To make connections at the conference and add them to their LinkedIn accounts; (5) To post updates on their own Facebook, Twitter, and LinkedIn pages; (6) To use an app on their smartphones that offers the schedule of the conference; (7) To upload interesting speaker videos to YouTube; and (8) To write about the convention experience on their blogs. All of these platforms help connect people to the event. Similarly, you as the event planner should be coordinating the same type of social media strategies as you plan, organize, and then execute events. Connecting people through social media and understanding why these connections should be made must be at the forefront of an event planner's thinking. For example, "if vendors or exhibitors are part of the convention, social media can help increase the benefits of their participation" (Friedman, 2012, p. 15). A prominent publisher, Kendall Hunt, is traditionally one of the exhibitors at a National Communication Association (NCA) convention. NCA's social media intern for the convention, who works directly for the convention's event planner, should post photos and text to the NCA blog, tweet messages, upload photos to Instagram, and create videos for YouTube that help promote Kendall Hunt's presence, among many other publishers in attendance. The intern's job is to make all the

Cross-promotion: A method of marketing that targets buyers of a product with an offer to purchase a related product

TIP

Just as an event planner pulls all ideas together, IMC brings together many components of promotion. In the communication discipline, it is imperative to understand the parts that make up the whole, and the whole is greater than the sum of the parts.

— Jeanne Persuit

publishers feel appreciated for their sponsorship. Event planners must realize the connections they are making though social media—both large and small scale—have the potential to generate more awareness for all types of events.

While social media is an essential tool for event promotion, it can also glorify an event in an untruthful way. For example, Billy McFarland and Ja Rule, the organizers of the Fyre festival, used social media to create an event that was impossible to produce with the resources they had available. Billy McFarland and Ja Rule paid social media influencers Kendall Jenner, Bella Hadid, Hailey Baldwin, and Emily Ratajkowski to promote an extravagant concert experience by using a simple orange block, which flooded Instagram, creating a buzz about the Fyre festival. Jenner was reportedly paid $250,000 to announce the festival lineup and offer a promotional discount code (Gonzales, 2019). The Fyre festival was branded as the next Coachella, offering big-name musicians, luxury villas, and fine dining. Guests paid up to $250,000 for an all-inclusive VIP experience but were soon disappointed when they arrived at an island that did not have the supplies necessary to host all of the guests. The event used disaster tents as guest rooms, served cheese sandwiches as the gourmet meal, and produced no musical appearances (Ohlheiser, 2017). Hulu and Netflix both created documentaries describing how social media influencers artificially inflated the Fyre festival to an epic event that never happened (Kleinman, 2019). The Fyre festival is a good social media case study in over-promoting and over-promising luxuries for an event, and a good lesson for event planners to heed.

The keys, then, to planning a successful event are based on elements of integrated marketing communication, including clear communication with the client in order to understand the objectives and target audience, development of a creative marketing plan that addresses these objectives, and attention to the budgetary constrictions. This can be a hefty task for the event planner, but with good communication, strong organization, a little experience, and more than a dash of creativity, communicating to a variety of public consumers about an event can be one of the most thrilling experiences in the business. Bell McManus and Rouse (2016) state, "As the event planning industry continues to grow, the need for understanding IMC becomes imperative" (p. 49). To find new and interesting ways to engage consumers on behalf of your clients, to entice them to an event for which you have collaborated with a diverse group of interested parties, to meet the challenge of innovation in a world not easily impressed—these are the tasks of the modern event planner who understands the importance of integrated marketing communication in event planning.

Key Terms

Integrated Marketing
  Communication (IMC)
Public Relations (PR)
RACE

Press kit
Marketing
SWOT analysis
Return on Investment (ROI)

Advertising
Positioning
Brand
Social media

Consumer-generated media
Hashtag
Cross-promotion

Discussion Questions

1. Think of a recent event you have either attended or wanted to attend. Identify and examine its integrated marketing communication components (public relations, marketing, advertising, promotions, and social media). How did the use of these components work together to enhance the event?

2. You are promoting a celebration weekend for children at your local zoo with events scheduled for both Saturday and Sunday, and entrance tickets are half-price for children and parents. Keeping in mind integrated marketing communication strategies, create a plan that promotes awareness in the weeks leading up to the event and generates attendance for the event.

3. You have been hired as the event planning company for the grand opening of a new Town Center (outdoor shopping complex) in your town, replete with eateries, retail stores, and a new multiplex movie theater. There has never been anything like this in your rural town before, and excitement is building. What types of integrated marketing communication strategies might benefit the community in order to best educate them on the new Town Center?

Activity

Your event planning company has been hired to orchestrate the city's 5K "Run Across the River." The route will take runners across a well-known and iconic bridge and into the historic district for a scenic tour. Streets will be closed for several hours on Saturday from 7 a.m. until noon.

Since this is the first time you have worked with the city as a client, perform a **SWOT analysis** (strengths, weaknesses, opportunities, and threats) as a starting point for the development of a marketing plan for this event. Consider aspects of IMC as you develop the plan.

Strengths:

Weaknesses:

Opportunities:

Threats:

References

Alderson, W. (1957). *Marketing behavior and executive action*. Homewood, IL: Richard D. Irwin.

Alonzo, V. (2017, September). Social media trends at meetings for 2017. Successful Meetings. Retrieved from http://www.successfulmeetings.com/Infographic/Social-Media-Trends-at-Meetings-for-2017/

Aristotle. (Trans. 1984). *Metaphysics*. In Jonathan Barnes (Ed.), *The complete works of Aristotle: The revised Oxford translation* (Vol. 2, pp. 1552–1728). Princeton, NJ: Princeton University Press.

Arnell, P. (2010). *Shift: How to reinvent your business, your career, and your personal brand*. New York: Crown Publishing Group.

Bacon, J. (2016). Getting the most out of cross-promotion. *Marketing Week (August 11)*. Retrieved from https://www.marketingweek.com/2016/08/11/how-to-get-the-most-from-cross-promotion-opportunities/.

Barrow, D. (2017). Are you hosting an event or creating an experience? *Campus Activities Programming*, *49*(6), 12–13.

Bartels, R. (1970). *Marketing theory and metatheory*. Bel Air, CA: Richard Irwin Press.

_____. (1988). *The history of marketing thought* (3rd ed.). Columbus: Publishing Horizons.

Batra, R, & Keller, K.L. (2016). Integrating marketing communications: New findings, new lessons, and new ideas. *Journal of Marketing*, *80*, 122–145.

Bell McManus, L. M., & Rouse, C. (2016). An integrated marketing communication approach to event planning. In J. M. Persuit & C. L McDowell Marincheck (Eds.). Integrated marketing communication: Creating spaces for engagement. (pp. 37–51). Lanham, MD: Lexington Books.

Berlo, D. K. (1960). *The process of communication*. San Francisco: Rinehart.

Bivins, T. (2008). *Public relations writing: The essentials of style and format*. New York: McGraw-Hill.

Blakeman, R. (2009). *The barebones introduction to integrated marketing communication*. Lanham, MD: Rowman & Littlefield.

Cespedes, F.V. & Prasad, P. (2015, March). Get more from your event spending. Harvard Business Review. Retrieved from https://hbr.org/2015/03/get-more-from-your-event-spending.

Cockrum, J. (2011). *Marketing: 101 low and no-cost ways to grow your business online and off*. Hoboken, NJ: John Wiley & Sons, Inc.

Corbett, M. (1996). *The 33 ruthless rules of local advertising*. Houston, TX: Breakthru Publishing Inc.

Daugherty, E. (2003). Strategic planning in public relations: A matrix that ensures tactical soundness. *Public Relations Quarterly*, *48*, 21–26.

Drell, L. (2014). Hashtags and infographics and videos! Oh my! *Marketing Insights, 26*, 40–47.

Du Plessis, F., van Heerden, N, & Gordon, C. (2010). *Integrated marketing communication* (3rd ed.). Pretoria: Van Schaik Publishers.

Dutta, S. (2010). What's your personal social media strategy? *Harvard Business Review, 88*, 127–130.

Fitzpatrick, K. R. (2005). The legal challenge of integrated marketing communication (IMC): Integrating commercial and political speech. *Journal of Advertising, 34*, 93–112.

Fletcher, M. (2011, January). How to…use social media and keep the event alive. *Conference & Incentive Travel*, 12.

Friedman, S. (2012). Using social media and other technologies to promote and enhance your franchise convention. *Franchising World, 44*, 15–16.

Gilette, F. (2010, June). Twitter, Twitter, little stars. *Bloomberg Businessweek*, 64–67.

Gonzales, E. (2019, April). Kendall Jenner responds to her Fyre Festival involvement for the first time. Retrieved from https://www.harpersbazaar.com/celebrity/latest/a27028770/kendall-jenner-fyre-festival-responds/

Gupta, S. (2003). Event marketing: Issues and challenges. *UMB Management Review, 15*, 87–96.

Hoyle, L. H. (2002). *Event marketing: How to successfully promote events, festivals, conventions, and expositions.* New York: John Wiley & Sons.

International Spy Museum L'Enfant Plaza. (2019). Awards page. Retrieved from https://www.spymuseum.org/press/awards/

Kane, G. C., Alavi, M., Labianca, G., Borgatti, S. P. (2014). What's different about social media networks? A framework and research agenda. *MIS Quarterly.* 38, 275–304.

Keller, K. L. (2016). Unlocking the power of integrated marketing communications: How integrated is your IMC program? *Journal of Advertising, 45*(3), 286–301.

Kleinman, Z. (2019, January). Has Fyre festival burned influencers? Retrieved from https://www.bbc.com/news/46945662

Kotler, P., & Keller, K. L. (2012). *A framework for marketing management* (5th ed.). Harlow: Pearson

Kelly, S. (2010, April). Herding social media. *Treasury & Risk*, 30–32.

Kitchen, P. J., Kim, I., & Schultz, D. E. (2008). Integrated marketing communications: practice leads theory. *Journal of Advertising Research, 48*, 53–546.

Klepek, M., Starzyczna, H. (2018), Marketing communication model for social networks. *Journal of Business Economics & Management.* 48, 500–520.

Kliatchko, J. (2005). Towards a new definition of Integrated Marketing Communications (IMC). *International Journal of Advertising, 24*, 7–34.

Kliatchko, J. G., & Schultz, D. E. (2014). Twenty years of IMC. *International Journal of Advertising, 33*, 373–390.

Koo, S. K., Byon, K. K., & Baker III, T. A. (2014). Integrating event image, satisfaction, and behavioral intention: Small-scale marathon event. *Sport Marketing Quarterly, 23*, 127–137.

Kotler, P. (1997). *Marketing management: Analysis, planning, implementation and control.* NJ: Prentice Hall.

Kotler, P., & Zaltman, G. (1971). Social marketing: An approach to planned social change. *Journal of Marketing, 35*, 3–12.

Mangold, W. G., & Faulds, D. J. (2009). Social media: The new hybrid element of the promotion mix. *Business Horizons, 52*, 357–365

Marsh, C., Guth, D., & Short, B. (2009). *Strategic writing: Multimedia writing for public relations, advertising, and more.* Boston, MA: Pearson.

Marston, J. (2012). *The nature of public relations.* Whitefish, MT: Literary Licensing.

Martensen, A., Grønholdt, L., Bendtsen, L., & Jensen, M. (2007). Application of a model for the effectiveness of event marketing. *Journal of Advertising Research, 47*, 283–301.

Masterman, G., & Wood, E. (2006). *Innovative marketing communications.* Oxford: Elsevier.

McCarthy, E. J. (1960). *Basic marketing: A managerial approach.* Homewood, IL: Irwin.

Mill, J. S. (1875). *A system of logic, ratiocinative and inductive: Being a connected view of the principles of evidence and the methods of scientific investigation.* London: Longmans, Green, Reader, and Dyer. (Original work published 1843.)

Miller, R. K., & Washington, K. (2012). Event and experiential marketing, In R. K. Miller, & K. Washington (Eds.). *Consumer Behavior* (pp. 427–429). Atlanta, GA: Richard K. Miller & Associates.

Mirisch, D., & Harris, G. (2013). *The charity event planning guide.* Los Angeles, CA: The Americas Group.

Nagelberg, R. (2017). 15 celebrities with breast cancer. Retrieved from https://www.healthline.com/health/celebrities-with-breast-cancer#5

Nicosia, F. M. (1966). *Consumer decision processes: Marketing and advertising implications.* New Jersey: Prentice-Hall.

Oana, D. (2018). Integrated marketing communication and its impact on consumer behavior. *Studies in Business and Economics, 13* (2), 92–102.

Occupational Outlook Handbook (2018). *What public relation specialists do.* Retrieved from http://www.bls.gov/ooh/media-and-communication/public-relations-specialists.htm#tab-2

Ogilvy, D. (1985). *Ogilvy on advertising*. New York: Random House.

Oguejiofor, K. E. (2014). *Explaining effective marketing in contemporary globalism: An exponential tutorial*. Bloomington, IN: Trafford.

Ohlheiser, A. (2017, April). The complete disaster of Fyre Festival played out on social media for all to see; NOT MY FAULT says organizer Ja Rule. Retrieved from https://www.washingtonpost.com/news/the-intersect/wp/2017/04/28/the-complete-and-utter-disaster-that-was-fyre-festival-played-out-on-social-media-for-all-to-see/?utm_term=.447b2817318e

Pelsmacker, P., Geuens, M., & Bergh, J. (2001). *Marketing communication*. London: Prentice Hall.

Percy, L. (2008). *Strategic integrated marketing communication: Theory and practice*. Oxford: Buttworth-Heinemann.

Pickton, D., & Broderick, A. (2005). *Integrated marketing communications* (2nd ed.). Harlow, England: Financial Times/Prentice Hall.

Public Relations Society of America. (2012). *What is public relations?* Retrieved from http://prdefinition.prsa.org

Public Relations Student Society of America. (Dec. 2014). *Let's party! Five steps to planning a successful holiday event*. Retrieved from http://progressions.prssa.org/index.php/2014/12/15/planningaholidayevent/

_____. (Aug. 2013). *A blueprint to planning the perfect event*. Retrieved from http://progressions.prssa.org/index.php/2013/08/13/a-blueprint-to-planning-the-perfect-event

Ratchford, B.T., Talukdar, D., & Lee, M.S. (2001). A model of consumer choice of the internet as an information source. *International Journal of Electronic Commerce, 5*, 7–21.

Ries, A., & Trout, J. (2001). *Positioning: The battle for your mind*. New York: McGraw-Hill.

Rosenholm, K. (2019). 9 social media tips for event marketing. *Business NH Magazine, 36*, 30.

Saget, A. (2006). *The event marketing handbook: Beyond logistics and planning*. Chicago: Kaplan Publishing.

Schultz, D., Patti, C. H., & Kitchen, P. J. (2013). *The evolution of integrated marketing communications: The customer-driven marketplace*. New York: Routledge.

Schiffman, L. G., & Kanuk, L. L. (2004). Consumer behavior (8th ed.). Prentice Hall.

Smith, K. (2019, June). 126 amazing social media statistics and facts. *Brandwatch*. Retrieved from https://www.brandwatch.com/blog/amazing-social-media-statistics-and-facts/#section-2

Sweetser, K., & Lariscy, R.W. (2008). Candidates make good friends: An analysis of candidates' uses of Facebook. *International Journal of Strategic Communication, 2*, 175–198.

Vargo, S. L., & Lusch, R. F. (2004). Evolving to a new dominant logic for marketing. *Journal of Marketing, 68*, 1–17.

Wertheimer, M. (1961). Experimental studies on the seeing of motion. In T. Shipley (Ed. & Trans.), *Classics in psychology* (pp. 1032–1089). New York: Philosophical Library. (Original work published 1912).

Wilcox, D. L., Cameron, G. T., & Reber, B. H. (2015). *Public relations: Strategies and tactics.* (11th ed.). New York: Pearson.

Zarantonello, L., & Schmitt, B. H. (2013). The impact of event marketing on brand equity. *International Journal of Advertising, 32,* 255–280.

Chapter 14

LEADERSHIP: EMPOWERING OTHERS IN EVENT PLANNING

Most people who are successful in their careers exhibit a degree of leadership at some point, but this particular characteristic is essential in every event planner. Leadership requires not just vision and energy, but a willingness to take on responsibility, exercise patience, and motivate others to fulfill their potential. Moreover, Jeff Weiner, the CEO of LinkedIn, describes three qualities that make great leaders: (1) they are clear about the vision, (2) they are brave, and (3) they are effective communicators (Feloni, 2015, para. 7–11). All of these characteristics are needed for leaders to be successful at their job. Through the planning process, you will have to adjust your leadership style to accommodate the needs of your client and the demands of the event (van der Wagen, 2006), as well as the skills of your employees. In the midst of the energy and chaos of an event, it is the planner who must maintain control, order, and forward progress. As Rudolph Giuliani (2002), the former mayor of New York who served as an exemplary leader throughout the September 11 crisis, stated, "Leadership does not simply happen. It can be taught, learned, developed" (p. xii). Research on leadership indicates that through education, training, and effort, you can become an effective leader (Daloz Parks, 2005; Doh, 2003; van der Wagen, 2006). A study at the University of Birmingham in the United Kingdom, for instance, found that medical students who believed themselves to be significantly lacking in medical leadership skills learned the necessary leadership abilities through a combination of discussion about case studies and extra support from mentors and colleagues (Matthews, Morley, Crossley, & Bhanderi, 2018). Focusing on developing leadership skills is imperative if the event planner is to flourish in the field. Event planners will develop their leadership skills over time, having to be decision makers, constantly evolving as they work at their craft. All who are involved in an event will look to the event planner for guidance, answers, and leadership.

When you have finished reading this chapter, you will be able to

- explain the importance of leadership in the field of event planning;
- describe how leadership and motivation can impact the client's vision of the event;
- analyze the connection between leadership and emotional intelligence.

CASE STUDY Leading the Way to the Baltimore Book Festival

Rosalind Healy, Chief of Staff, Baltimore Office of Promotion & the Arts

The Baltimore Office of Promotion & The Arts (BOPA) is a 501(c)3 non-profit organization that produces events and arts programs and serves as the Baltimore City Arts Council. In the past, BOPA has orchestrated or assisted with large-scale city events. The activities include the Ravens Rally Super Bowl Send-Off and the Ravens Super Bowl Victory Parade in 2001 and 2013; Miss USA Pageant in Baltimore; Baltimore's Celebration of the Army-Navy Game & Festivities; the Star Spangled Salute to Michael Phelps in 2008; the Star-Spangled Sailabration in 2012; the NFL Kick-Off in 2013; and the Star-Spangled Spectacular in 2014, which included the city's largest fireworks display.

Our former executive director, Bill Gilmore, visited Edinburgh, Scotland in 1994 and came across that city's Book Festival. He was so inspired by what he experienced that he wanted to create a book festival in Baltimore. At that time, we were looking for a new event idea to bring to the Mount Vernon area. Baltimore Mayor Kurt Schmoke's slogan for Baltimore was "The City that Reads," so a book festival would be the perfect new event for the city. As the city's event arm, BOPA took the leadership role in getting the event up and running and on its way to be a signature city event. The Baltimore Book Festival was launched the following year in 1995.

To launch this new special event, we needed to consider many things:

- Choosing a date that did not conflict with another major event in Baltimore City;
- Choosing a location that would be unique but accessible for people to attend;
- Gathering a committee of people who could help move the project forward and give it some status in the literary world;
- Gaining support for city services for a signature event;
- Reaching out to exhibitors and vendors who sell books, publish books, or have a book hook;
- Engaging the community, neighbors, and surrounding institutions;
- Creating programs and elements that would attract sponsors and/or funders;
- Making it free and fun for families, book lovers, festival lovers... everyone!

We chose the end of September because it is a time when the weather is still nice, and the major event and festival season is over. Fall is also the time of year authors are on tour promoting their new books. With many publishers and authors in New York City, Baltimore is a quick day trip on the train. Over the years, our proximity to New York has resulted in many great authors participating in the festival.

BOPA selected the Mount Vernon neighborhood in midtown Baltimore as the unique venue. The festival footprint included the four beautiful parks that border the iconic Washington Monument—the nation's first Washington Monument. The location was easily accessible by car, public transportation, and foot. Fortunately, the Mount Vernon area was rich with institutions including the Walters Art Museum, the Peabody Conservatory, Agora Publishing Company, Center Stage Theatre, *The Baltimore Sun* newspaper, the Maryland Historical Society, and the Enoch Pratt Free Library. All of these institutions have become valuable partners over the years and integral to the festival.

We reached out to partners, including Citylit, Johns Hopkins Press, and Baltimore Reads to help shape the programming of the event. It was important to have these partners help with the programming since they were the subject matter experts. To give the event literary clout, we also reached out to Baltimore-based authors Anne Tyler, author of *The Accidental Tourist*, and Taylor Branch, author of *The King Years: Historic Moments in the Civil Rights Movement*, to be honorary chairs of the event in the early years.

The first year we actually went door to door looking for bookstores, publishers, and authors to join us for the weekend. As a startup event with no track record, many of our exhibitors and vendors participated for free. The neighbors were accustomed to small, one-day events such as the Flower Mart and even filming of commercials and movies that would displace their parking and impact them for a short amount of time. However, the Book Festival was the first three-day event for the Mount Vernon neighborhood that would impact them for a week with set up and break down. It was important to meet with the community groups and get them excited about the event while listening to their concerns. The possibility of losing their free residential parking was an obstacle we had to work through. Luckily, we were able to secure parking for participants in a nearby lot for the festival weekend, and the neighbors were pleased to hear they would not be displaced for the event.

By the 19th year of the festival, the event attracted many well-known authors and large crowds. The festival was outgrowing the venue. That same year, the Washington Monument required major renovation work, and much of the monument circle area was not available for the festival's anchor programming tents. After much debate, we realized we needed to find a new festival location for the year or take a year break. The festival was moved to Baltimore's Inner Harbor—not the same quaint venue as Mount Vernon, but certainly a picturesque backdrop of the city, with four times the square footage for exhibitors and vendors. The festival's 20th anniversary was in

2015, and we returned to the Inner Harbor, where the event exhibitors, authors, businesses, locals, and tourists had been pleased. BOPA's leadership created this historic event for the city, and it was their leadership that grew the event in 20 years to become a major festival for the book arts.

At the end of 2018, we discussed moving the Baltimore Book Festival to later in the fall to accommodate changes in the publishing industry with books being published closer to the end of the year. We also took into consideration moving the Light City Festival to later in the year when it gets darker earlier. These discussions led to the creative concept of illuminating our city with literature and ideas during the day and with spectacular works of light art at night. Besides creating an even greater event experience for the public, uniting the two festivals is more cost efficient for BOPA and our many city partners. The Light City/Baltimore Book Festival will now take place in November.

Contributed by Rosalind Healy, 2019. Copyright © Kendall Hunt Publishing Company.

After reading this chapter, revisit the case study and respond to the following question:

Using the Light City/Baltimore Book Festival as an example, how could you take the lead in creating a neighborhood event that promotes collaboration between your institution and the surrounding neighborhoods?

Leadership

The debate continues to rage over whether event planners—or anyone, for that matter—can learn leadership skills or if leaders are born. In the end, most of the research points out that leaders are self-made, through hard work and attention to their own development (Arvey, Zhang, Avolio, & Krueger, 2007; Greenwell, Danzey-Bussell, & Shonk, 2014; Tracy & Chee, 2013). In fact, one study indicated that leadership skills are only about 30% genetic (Arvey, Zhang, Avolio, & Krueger, 2007). There are many different definitions of leadership, and various schools across the country teach leadership skills. Theorists including Barnard, Deming, Fayol, Maslow, Weber, and Smith have shaped definitions of leadership. Blanchard (2009) defines **leadership** as "the capacity to influence others by unleashing their power and potential to impact the greater good" (p. xvi). Bennis (2009), who underscores the basics of leadership, states that leadership requires a guiding vision, passion, integrity, and maturity, with additional qualities of trust, curiosity, and daring. Notable researchers James Collins and Jerry Porras (1994) offer a definition of leadership that is both inclusive and detailed:

> Leadership was defined as top executives who displayed high levels of persistence, overcame significant obstacles, attracted

Leadership: *The capacity to influence others by unleashing their power and potential to impact the greater good.*

dedicated people, influenced groups of people toward the achievement of goals, and played key roles in guiding their companies through crucial episodes in their history (p. 262).

While the definitions of leadership may vary, a strong leader must provide guidance and direction.

In addition to definitions of leadership, there are also many styles of leadership including **autocratic**, which focuses on one person holding all the power to make decisions; **bureaucratic**, in which the procedures and rules guide one's action; **charismatic**, which focuses on infusing energy and eagerness into team efforts; **democratic**, in which there is a participatory factor in the decision-making process; and **laissez-faire**, in which there is a hands-off approach to guiding people. All of these styles of leadership can ebb and flow with different events (Adeniyi, 2007). Event planners must be present, be able to see how an event could be created, and ask questions about how it could unfold—including the positives and the negatives. They must motivate, work well with others, and be trustworthy enough to see the event through to completion. To do so effectively, event planners must function as leaders, no matter what type of style they utilize.

Those who wish to be leaders in the field of event planning and management must pay attention to two important variables: coordinating the event with precision and making sure that all who are involved in planning and executing the event are motivated and satisfied. In support of this division, studies conducted at the Ohio State University (Ohio State Leadership Studies, 1962) and at the University of Michigan (Katz, Maccoby, & Morse, 1950) reduced all the qualities of a leader into these same two dichotomies: leaders complete tasks effectively, and they exhibit concern for the satisfaction of those with whom they work. With attention and care, the event planner can find success in these two areas through persistence, charisma, motivation, and goal-orientation (Antonakis & Day, 2018; Bryman, 1992; Muller & Turner, 2010). Leadership can help an event planner produce a successful event and enable the planner to motivate staff and even clients to be efficacious workers (Greenwell, Danzey-Bussell, & Shonk, 2014). Leaders are those who sustain the vision and at the same time manage the elements of the event while keeping staff and clients satisfied. Event planners must guide with vision and passion and be willing to delegate tasks to others.

Delegation of Responsibility

While leaders must learn that running a successful event demands the delegation of responsibilities, in order to inspire collegial trust, planners should nevertheless be willing to complete any task they would assign to someone else (White, 2006). Assigning the most menial tasks at an event to one of the staff working the occasion would be easy, but leaders should resist the urge to keep themselves apart from the grind and pitch in right alongside everyone else working the event. Setting tables with placecards,

Autocratic leadership: *A type of leadership style that focuses on one person holding all the power to make decisions*

Bureaucratic leadership: *A type of leadership style in which the procedures and rules guide one's action*

Charismatic leadership: *A type of leadership style that focuses on infusing energy and eagerness into a team's efforts*

Democratic leadership: *A type of leadership style in which there is a participatory factor in decision-making process*

Laissez-faire leadership: *A type of leadership style in which there is a hands-off approach to guiding people*

TIP

Grow leadership skills. Sometimes while planning an event you may need to take on a project outside of your expertise or make a critical decision. Use these opportunities to elevate yourself as a professional and learn new skills. If you remain confident in yourself as you face these situations, they will help you grow into a leader.

— Chris Daley

© *Peshkova/Shutterstock.com*

hanging bunting, trimming flowers, and putting together a coat rack—if all of these tasks are important, and if event planners want to inspire trust in those with whom they work—they must become a part of the event's interaction. Balance is key: micromanaging every task is counter-productive, but detachment and aloofness accomplish the opposite effect of what the event planner hopes. Becoming a part of the staging, for instance, means collaborating with everyone involved in the process. Good leaders are willing to hand over some power to their staff but also step up to take responsibility for whatever happens as a result of management decisions (Getz, 2012). However, leaders know that the amount of control they offer to others depends upon an assessment of the skills of those with whom they are working. At times, this relationship is collaborative; at other points, event planners must delegate and oversee tasks (Greenwell, Danzey-Bussell, & Shonk, 2014). Assessing for the right touch at every instance requires some experience, but also a sense of knowing what your colleagues can and will do.

In an interview conducted by Greenwell, Danzey-Bussell, and Shonk (2014), Talty O'Connor, the founder and president of Covey Communications Corporation, spoke about the power of **delegation**, noting that the more responsibility and authority people are given, the more they will give in return. Delegating responsibilities gets staff members eager to participate in the event. Leaders, however, must teach others how to pay attention to the details; it is not fair to assume that any employee can see what needs to be accomplished in every situation. Hire good people who, when trained, do not need micromanaging (Greenwell, Danzey-Bussell, & Shonk, 2014). But delegation means far more than merely assigning tasks to others. Leadership demands that successful event planners know the limits of each employee's abilities and work within those boundaries. For instance, some staffers may not have well-developed interpersonal skills but are outstanding in the area of logistics; it would thus make sense not to put these employees at a 'Meet and Greet' registration table, and instead place them in a position supervising deliveries and attending to room details. However, unless you know the people with whom you are working, a mistake like this could be a costly one. Identifying those colleagues who can handle additional duties and then giving them the chance to prove themselves is a win/win situation for all. Leaders thus must be attentive to developing the next generation of leadership through their assessment of their employees and colleagues (Caramela, 2017). In addition, delegation includes making sure that all who are working the event share in the vision and the event outcome, for "vision comes alive only when it is shared" (Westley & Mintzberg, 1989, p. 22). Leadership and vision are inextricably linked in the creation of successful events.

Delegation: *The act of giving over work responsibilities in varying degrees to co-workers or helpers*

TIP

Have more people assisting than you think you need. Write an excruciatingly specific task list with assignments. Then add one or two additional pairs of hands to help with the unexpected. I promise, you will be happy to have the extra bodies.

— Sandy Hillman

Vision

Leaders are initially responsible for providing a **vision** of how to achieve a specific set of event outcomes. They must determine how to make decisions and know who has the final authority (Blanchard, 2009). Having a

vision is an essential component of leaders, alongside communication skills, character, and boldness (Antonakis & Day, 2018; Williams, 2013). Because event planners must communicate with a variety of constituents, they must be capable of influencing people in each of these areas, understanding all the stakeholders and their needs. Strong leaders can connect all these diverse goals and focus on the event's vision. Their task starts with creating a vision that is communicated clearly and imaginatively, using a variety of media and reacting to the responses of the stakeholders. For instance, your client, a new specialty and theatre costume design conglomerate, is planning to host a week-long

Haunted House around Halloween week. This event will showcase a wide range of the costumes, props, and special effects the company has available for rental, and while the idea is an interesting one, you are worried that the company has not completely developed its vision for the event. What is the role of the event planner in such a circumstance? First, a careful conversation with the company's team might unveil some unspoken goals, and as you probe for more details, you are able to compile a much more comprehensive picture of what they hope to accomplish. You will need to walk the team through a visualization of each part of the plan, including how such an event might unfold, as well as all the possible challenges it might present. Your list to the company's team might include the difficulty of finding actors who are consistently available, the challenge of finding a suitable space for such a project, and the necessity of a marketing plan that can make such an event successful. Brainstorming with the team will enable them to see beyond their initial idea, measuring the advantages and disadvantages of moving the vision to the next stage.

Leaders must be dynamic and collaborative since they should be able to appeal to the specific needs of everyone involved. They understand and can articulate clearly what their clients want and translate those ideas into a comprehensible vision. These leaders, considered strategic visionaries, take old practices and make them new through their understanding of the issues and their innovative methods. Leaders energize their clients and staff and are themselves energized by those with whom they are working, so their imagination is crucial, strengthened by the ideas of others. Thus, leaders must be good listeners, attuned to the input of their staff and clients and ready to adapt the vision when necessary. A vision may take a while to develop or it may occur extemporaneously, so leaders must be patient,

TIP

Be the diplomat to merge competing visions while staying true to the primary constituent's goals and vision (e.g. CEO, sales, bride)

— Julie Wagner

© 360b/Shutterstock.com

relying on their self-confidence and imagination to persevere (Westley & Mintzberg, 1989). Yet if the event is to be successful, the best event planners know they will need to adjust their vision and style based upon the way the event planning is going (Antonakis & Day, 2018; van der Wagen, 2006).

The vision itself must be content-heavy, not just filled with ideas of what might happen. An event planner could develop a client's vision for an opening of a new museum with a small collection of Impressionist paintings, for instance, an event complete with sketches of Paris and the Seine, a multimedia presentation that focuses on Impressionist history, and space decorated as the Rue Bonaparte. Leaders focus on the delivery of concrete products or services through the vision, and while they are brilliant and artistic storytellers, planners must also balance the artistic vision with solid management skills (Westley & Mintzberg, 1989). Leaders know that event planning is all about balance: developing the art without forgetting the finances. Artistic creativity cannot be stifled in order to accommodate the budget, but neither can the finances be compromised in favor of creativity. At times, one or the other of these factors may take precedence, and event planners know that their leadership vision during the event can depend upon many variables, including the numbers and personalities of the staff with whom they are working, the budget itself, the client's wishes, and other factors beyond the control of the event planner (Getz, 2012). All of these variables will affect the vision of the event and how it unfolds, yet few leaders can achieve their goals without perseverance and self-confidence.

Perseverance and Self-Confidence

Perseverance: *Persistence or determination to accomplish a task*

Perseverance is another element of leadership that is essential to the event planner. According to Maxwell (2011), perseverance is comprised of seven characteristics. These include the following:

1. Perseverance means succeeding because you are determined to, not destined to.
2. Perseverance recognizes life is not a long race, but many short ones in succession.
3. Perseverance is needed to release most of life's rewards.
4. Perseverance draws sweetness out of adversity.
5. Perseverance has a compounding effect on life.

6. Perseverance means stopping not because you're tired but because the task is done.

7. Perseverance doesn't demand more than we gave but all that we have (pp. 128–134).

Leaders persevere toward excellence in every deliverable, whether it is in the communication of the vision, in the routing of day-of-event tasks, or in the debriefing surveys that follow an event. The choice to be the best at what you do is the first step to becoming a top-notch leader, but it requires commitment and consistency (Tracy & Chee, 2013). Leadership also necessitates conscious choices, for there are many moments when it would be easy to agree to something that is good enough. Reputations, however, are made through a choice to be the best in every situation.

Bolstered by passion, purpose, and focus, you can sustain the decision to be excellent throughout your event planning career if you are committed to bringing the best possible product to your clients. You can maintain this kind of commitment despite obstacles and setbacks because you have made a choice to keep the vision alive and in focus (Orlick, 2008). "The vision is the destination, and your leadership is the driver on the road towards that objective" (Ferreira, 2018). For example, a last-minute change in the number of available breakout rooms for a conference you are planning throws a wrench into the afternoon plans. Complying with the conference hotel liaison and asking for a partial refund, while enlarging the group size in each breakout room to accommodate the smaller number of available spaces, would be simple enough. But your commitment to providing the best possible experience for the conference-goers means that your dedication to excellence drives you to persevere in finding alternative rooms per the contract that had been signed. This perseverance to excel at every job will help establish your reputation as the best. Achieving excellence in every area of event planning may not be possible right away, so perhaps the best path in the beginning is to focus on one or two areas in which excellence is achievable, such as service or creativity. The rest will follow once the path toward distinction has begun. Look at the example of young Walt Disney, hoping to begin his career when he was told by a news editor that his ideas were neither creative nor original; or consider that Michael Jordan, one of the top professional basketball players of all times, never made the cut for his high school basketball team (Neck, Manz, & Houghton, 2019). Those who can persevere when confronted with obstacles can still go on to become leaders in their field.

© MateusandOlivia/Shutterstock.com

Self-confidence: *The ability to believe that you can accomplish a specific series of tasks successfully*

Self-efficacy: *The idea that people believe in their own ability to accomplish something*

In leadership, **self-confidence**, or the ability to believe that you can accomplish a specific series of tasks successfully, demands a strong sense of self-knowledge that often hinges on experience and a sense of **self-efficacy**

TIP

When making a decision, sometimes you lead with your head (what is the smart or safe answer?); other times lead with your heart (based on emotion), but if they are not decisive, go with your gut!

— Kristen Schultz

(Greenacre, Tung, & Chapman, 2014). As Chapter 4 stated, self-efficacy is the idea that people have a belief about their own abilities to accomplish something. The concept relies heavily on ideas about what people believe they are capable or not capable of doing. Event planners must develop confidence in order to be successful with both clients and staff. Leaders who want to become more confident in what they can accomplish pay attention to the feedback they get after every decision they make and internalize that knowledge for the next set of challenges they face. Leaders rarely start out as confident, secure people; "choosing to learn from the experience requires exploring the leader you've become and clarifying the leader you want to be. It also involves suffering through temporary embarrassment and insecurity" (Treasurer, 2017, p. 1). As self-confidence increases, leaders tend to repeat the behaviors that made them feel more confident, and this is how self-confidence continues to grow (Bandura, 1990). Event planners might gain confidence by measuring themselves against the competition to see how they themselves might fare in the same situation. For instance, confident event planners often take advantage of open invitations to events planned and executed by other event planning firms to compare their own vision, design, implementation, and crowd satisfaction (Buckingham & Coffman, 1999). This kind of feedback and evaluation can help event planners gain confidence as well as new ideas. Successful leaders will work to instill confidence in their employees in order to build the business and share authority (Krames, 2002). Furthermore, having a sense of emotional intelligence allows event planners to utilize the characteristics necessary for effective leadership.

Emotional Intelligence

In a digital world where some people communicate exclusively through online text, understanding the art of emotional intelligence is particularly essential for leadership (Bariso, 2018). **Emotional intelligence (EQ)** demands being judicious about emotions, having the ability to rely on one's own emotional resources during periods of stress, change, conflict, and even chaos. Those who are emotionally intelligent are able to create a climate that enables them to encourage innovation, create vision, develop sustainable relationships and increase performance (Goleman, Boyatzis, & McKee, 2013), all characteristic of leaders. Practically speaking, event planning leaders who are emotionally intelligent can easily read signals that come from a client or co-worker and are also aware of what their own cues are indicating (Schutte, Malouff, & Thorsteinsson, 2013).

Leadership demands a level of emotional intelligence if competent communication is to proceed. Gail T. Fairhurst and Robert Sarr (1996) believe "leadership is a language game, one that many do not know they are playing … even though most leaders spend nearly 70 percent of their time communicating …" (p. xi). Leaders know that many factors can disrupt clear communication. The client's emotional location, your own perceptions, as well as external factors in the environment, can all put up barricades to successful conversation. You can overcome some of these obstacles easily enough, but others require more attention and thought. Emotionally intelligent leaders are not only able to balance both emotion and reason (Mayer & Salovey, 1997), but they are also able to frame messages that are effective for the situation at hand (Fairhurst, 2011). Fairhurst and Sarr (1996) describe **framing a message** as the way in which you manage meaning by actively choosing a set of words for a particular context. Framing consists of "language," "thought,"

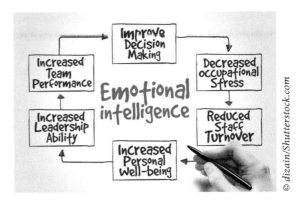

and "forethought" (p. 7). Leaders must manage all three of these components before messages are articulated. **Language** helps categorize and classify thoughts; through language, you are able to communicate with others. **Thought** is a reflection process that allows people to strategically create an insightful message. **Forethought** is a means of anticipation for spontaneity. Great leaders will have to communicate at any time and almost anywhere; as a result, they must have the skills necessary to offer insightful communication for the particular context. Moreover, Fairhurst (2011) believes that emotionally intelligent leaders will

1. Recognize a framing opportunity when emotions run strong;
2. Prioritize listening amid the framing, especially when dialogue is key;
3. Treat toxic emotions as an exercise in framing and an opportunity to manage them productively;
4. Reflect and treat their own emotions as data, joining reason and emotion to facilitate the right kind of decision making and framing for the benefit of those involved (pp. 119–120).

Strong leaders will develop the communicative skills necessary to proceed with emotional intelligence. For instance, a novice event planner, hired just out of college, is tasked with planning a day-long festival celebrating a small town's birthday, complete with food trucks, games, and music. However, the event planner neglected to consider the audience's demographics, and chose music only familiar to her own generation. When the festival-goers began to leave the event early, the event planner did not pick up on the cues that the music drove them out. Her level of emotional intelligence, and her ability to be judicious about others' experiences, caused the event to suffer.

Utilizing the skills of emotional intelligence through any interpersonal interaction will help develop a stronger leadership style, and, like leadership skills, emotional intelligence can be learned (Cherniss & Goleman, 2001; Northouse, 2018). Emotional intelligence, or the knack for "meeting the world with honest, creative engagement" (Arnett, Bell McManus, & McKendree, 2018, p.129), demands skills beyond average. Those who consistently demonstrate emotional intelligence are more "adaptable" (Akerjordet & Severinsson, 2007, p. 1410) and "high-performing" (Burgess, 2005, p. 97). The ability to collaborate well with others and build relationships

Framing [a message]: *The way in which meaning is managed by actively choosing a set of words for a particular context; consists of language, thought, and forethought*

Language: *In connection with Emotional Intelligence, the set of skills that help people categorize and classify thoughts*

Thought: *In connection with Emotional Intelligence, a reflection process that allows people to strategically create an insightful message*

Forethought: *In connection with Emotional Intelligence, a means of anticipation for spontaneity*

often depends on the degree of emotional intelligence the listener has developed (Arnett, Bell McManus, & McKendree, 2018). More specifically, certain qualities contribute to a heightened degree of emotional intelligence. Mayer and Salovey (1997) note four specific assets of emotional intelligence: "perceiving," "assessing," "understanding," and "regulating" emotions (pp. 10–14). (1) **Perceiving** demands that you are able to recognize and label the emotions that you or someone else is experiencing; (2) **Assessing** requires that you are able to produce emotions that help you make a decision; (3) **Understanding** means that you will be able to appreciate how your emotions cause you to act in a certain way; and (4) **Regulating** your emotions requires that you offer others evaluation and accept critique in a suitable way (Mayer & Salovey, 1997). These assets are essential for the event planner. For example, as an event planner you will be working with clients whose emotions may negatively influence their behavior in ways that you must understand. Despite the heightened emotional drama, event planners must maintain equilibrium to make sound decisions. Imagine, for instance, that you are responsible for situating trade show participants in a given space, but when you arrive for set up, the space for one particular vendor is not large enough to accommodate the exhibit. As emotions become heightened, you must remain level-headed, think it through, and present a solution to the problem. By offering responses based upon your experiences with trade shows, you can ease the tension that may exist and come to some mutually acceptable solution. Leaders have the ability to turn problems into opportunities. The research of Sheep, Fairhurst, and Khazanchi (2016) discusses how leaders can use the tensions in an organizational setting to produce innovative solutions; in addition, Putnam, Fairhurst, and Banghart (2016) explain the importance of leaders seeing the difference that occurs in all aspects of an organization and producing creative insights from that. The tensions that occur in the event planning industry should give rise to unique and creative solutions.

Goleman, Boyatzis, and McKee (2013) worked extensively in the corporate world, examining the domains of emotional intelligence and their associated competencies and found clusters of qualities, as the Competency Framework indicates. The researchers make a point that these competencies are not innate talents; rather, the leaders they studied demonstrated that the qualities are learned and derived. Their research also indicated that even the best, most emotionally intelligent leaders do not demonstrate the entire range of characteristics; instead, they tended to show leadership styles based on a handful of these qualities clustered together (Goleman, Boyatzis, & McKee, 2013, p. 39).

Perceiving: *In the context of Emotional Intelligence, the ability to be able to recognize and label the emotions that you or someone else is experiencing*

Assessing: *In the context of Emotional Intelligence, the ability to be able to produce emotions that help you make a decision*

Understanding: *In the context of Emotional Intelligence, the ability to appreciate how emotions cause you to act in a certain way*

Regulating: *In the context of Emotional Intelligence, the ability to offer others evaluation and accept critique in a suitable way*

Competency Framework

	Awareness	**Management**
Self	**Awareness** Emotional self-awareness Accurate self-assessment Self-confidence	**Self-Management** Emotional self-control Transparency Adaptability Achievement Initiative Optimism
Social	**Social Awareness** Empathy Organizational awareness Service	**Relationship Management** Inspirational leadership Influence Developing others Change catalyst Conflict management Building bonds Teamwork and collaboration

Diagram 05.
Competency Framework

Leaders should not confuse Emotional Intelligence (EQ) with a person's **Intelligence Quotient (IQ)**, a value that measures someone's ability to perceive and process information meaningfully. While both measure some aspect of a person's self, one (EQ) measures the ability to understand emotion, and the other (IQ) measures the ability to understand information. Successful leaders need to rely on both measures in the appropriate situation. To be able to make sense out of a sometimes frenzied state of affairs means understanding the emotions of the moment and finding the appropriate response that satisfies everyone involved (Goleman, Boyatzis, & McKee, 2013).

> Intelligence Quotient (IQ): *A value that measures someone's ability to perceive and process information meaningfully*

Some may fear that the qualities of emotional intelligence are set in place before adulthood; however, with time and practice, those who work at it can, in fact, continue to develop emotional intelligence throughout their lives (Goleman, Boyatzis, & McKee, 2013). This means unlearning old habits, and the motivation to be cued in to others' emotions must be strong and sustained if change is to occur (Schutte, Malouff, & Thorsteinsson, 2013). Learning emotional intelligence coincides with most of the research that indicates leaders themselves can be created and developed (Daloz Parks, 2005; Doh, 2003; van der Wagen, 2006). While many people have a clear set of values, for instance, and understand how others

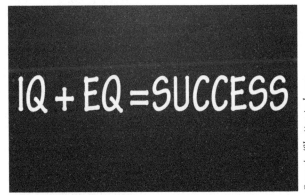

© woaiss/Shutterstock.com

form their own standards, the emotionally intelligent leader knows that self-reflection and self-awareness help to maintain these standards in the workplace.

Paying attention to the client's emotional state, language, and nonverbals will enable the event planner to understand what the client wants and needs, and thus take the lead in building the relationship. A person's communication, negotiation, and leadership skills all need to be grounded in understanding the human component of intelligence (Jenson, 2014). A definite connection exists between career adaptability and success and the degree of emotional intelligence (Coetzee & Harry, 2014). Fall, Kelly, MacDonald, Primm, and Holmes (2013) also found that business students getting ready for careers needed a heightened degree of emotional intelligence in order to succeed inter-culturally and to reduce their communication apprehension. James C. McCroskey (1970) coined the term **communication apprehension**, which refers to an anxiety syndrome that occurs when people anticipate or participate in communication. This anxiety is not limited to the classroom or to public speaking situations; in fact, Cristobal and Lasaten (2018) found that communication apprehension influences nearly every other aspect of learning and life. Event planners must be sensitive to any apprehension a client or an employee is experiencing, and understanding how to regulate one's emotions so that they are appropriate for any situation is essential. This skill demands an insight into emotional intelligence and the ability to use that knowledge in career leadership.

Event planners with an elevated degree of emotional intelligence can rely on their own emotional resources during periods of strain and anxiety. Thus, leaders who exhibit these assets are skilled at perceiving, assessing, understanding, and regulating emotions, and these four areas of control offer the event planner strengths in adaptability, listening, and self-awareness (Mayer & Salovey, 1997). The assets of emotional intelligence are set in place early, but leaders can learn them with time and determination (Goleman, Boyatzis, & McKee, 2013). Developing these qualities of leadership in the professional workplace can give the event planner a much-needed edge over the competition.

Motivation

Besides considering the connection between leadership and successful execution of events, good leaders also understand how to motivate and engage staff and colleagues. In the 1960s, McGregor investigated different sources of **motivation** and hypothesized about Theory X and Theory Y as explanations for motivational sources. **Theory X** looks at coercion, intimidation, and regulation as factors that motivate workers, and the theory also includes management styles that allow permissiveness and seek only harmony among the work force. However, **Theory Y** posits that if people find their work important, they will be self-motivated and creative. The job of the manager is to create a space in which people want to work

Communication apprehension: *Fear associated with communicating with another person*

TIP

Subscribe to industry publications (online or hard copy) for current trends, people in the news, and economic status of the industry

— Linda Paris

Motivation: *The reason a person acts or behaves in a particular way*

Theory X: *A theory of management that examines coercion, intimidation and regulation as factors that motivate workers*

Theory Y: *A theory of management that examines spaces in which people want to be creative, find new and different solutions to problems, and use their imagination to help the organization*

hard, be creative, find new and different solutions to problems, and use their imagination to help the organization. McGregor established that this capacity to excel creatively is found in every population group more widely than was ever perceived. Finding ways to help employees share a commitment to excellence and rewarding them for achievement are the most effective motivators leaders can use, much more than pressure and control (McGregor, 1960). How does this process of operational motivation begin?

Good supervisors learn to inspire by positive reinforcement in order to develop motivation within the employees themselves. This demands that employers get to know their employees well, finding out what makes them excited about their job. For instance, one staffer might truly find inspiration in clear organization, effortless lists of event attendees, and database management. These efforts might often go overlooked in the planning and management of an event; they are not high profile and sometimes are even invisible. However, supervisors must be attentive to every job performed excellently and acknowledge each part of the event plan that was successful. No event occurs successfully without a strong organizational undergirding, but if that work is low-visibility, then it could be easily overlooked. Giving the organizational job to the worker who feels the most satisfaction performing it will trigger that person's internal motivation, and thus matching talents, skills, and desires to each staff member's task list will more easily tap into employee self-motivation. This matching includes certain special projects that may arise from time to time, and event planners can assign the tasks to employees who would benefit from the extra assignment because they might see it as a chance to demonstrate their ability and skills (Collins & Porras, 1994). Leaders who can inspire and demonstrate that they value creativity and risk-taking among their employees will find that their employees live up to the challenge of experimentation and forward thinking (Bennis, 2009).

Leaders also must find ways to build community among their staff in an effort to encourage shared motivation and empowerment. For instance, Proctor & Gamble encourages its employees from their early grooming days to purchase shares of stock in the employee program, thus getting them literally to 'buy in' to the company and demonstrate their psychological commitment to and belief in the culture and values of the organization (Collins & Porras, 1994). Such stock options are, of course, a form of reward, but they also encourage employees to define themselves as integral parts of the organization because they own part of it. Leaders who can find ways to help their staff members to define themselves as more than just employees but rather forge an identity integral to their self-efficacy will reap the benefits of a highly motivated workforce. In an event planning company, this would mean working collaboratively with employees defining and refining the brand, requesting their input and opinions about even minor collaterals like company letterhead, web presence, advertising, and community service. Leaders know that employees who believe in and are vested in the success of the organization will be more apt to act with motivation and excitement (Maxwell, 1993). Empowering employees closest to

TIP

Have specific goals in mind. Make sure your event addresses them. Think and act strategically.

— Sandy Hillman

the work by offering them more authority, collaborative opportunities, and chances to feel they are important will encourage confidence and motivation (Krames, 2002). Nowhere is there room for condescension and leader arrogance, which can turn colleagues away from the project or event at hand and dissuade them from choosing leadership roles for themselves. Keeping the ego in check while motivating others is the mark of a great leader (Treasurer, 2017).

Leaders also know that motivation often hinges on being identified publicly as one who can handle additional responsibilities. Finding opportunities for staff members to demonstrate competence will whet their appetite for even greater charges (Maxwell, 1993). Leaders must regularly and publicly acknowledge accomplishments of their employees, and this depends on knowing who does what well, going beyond typical performance management (Buckingham & Coffman, 1999). For instance, when planning for an upcoming event, one of the staff members suggests a shift in the registration process that not only saves money, but also saves time and energy and can be repeated in the future for other events. Make sure when the event is over and the debriefing is underway, you give that employee's idea full spotlight. Perhaps initiating an annual awards ceremony is one way to acknowledge valuable contributions that deserve recognition. Giving positive feedback is certainly known as a pillar of performance management, but doing so in front of all the staff is essential. Additionally, if an opportunity arises in front of the client to acknowledge the work of your staff, that is equally motivating. However, if you need to offer negative feedback, and that does necessarily occur as events are planned and executed (Northouse, 2018), it should generally be given in private if motivation is to remain intact. Finally, if it works in your environment, consider giving staff members who want the challenge leadership roles for each event, and creating a title for this role may give validity to their new assignment (Bennis, 2009). Would one of your employees appreciate being named the pre-function chair for an upcoming event? Leaders might recognize such a title as an opportunity to further motivate a co-worker. In addition, it is important to let all your co-workers know exactly what the big picture is. Leaders who keep the vision to themselves without sharing with the team how all of the details fit together prevent others from seeing how their work benefits the vision (Ferreira, 2018).

Setting realistic but ever-changing expectations is one of the most basic motivators of leaders with vision and goals (Northouse, 2018). Of course, this demands knowing what your staff members are capable of doing, but it also means steadily increasing those expectations with help and encouragement. Send employees who seem interested to professional seminars as a reward for exceeding expectations. A variety of professional development seminars and webinars are available in the event

planning field, including classes and workshops offered by the Event Planners Association, a national organization located in Lake Forest, California, with chapters in New York City and Chicago (Event Planners Association, 2019). Locally, event planners can consult a variety of professional organizations that have chapters in nearly every major city and that sponsor a number of professional development opportunities, which can be accessed through the Event Planners Lounge—www.plannerslounge.com—a clearinghouse for a wide assortment of event planning opportunities. Moreover, trade shows sponsored by MPI, Meeting Professionals International (Meeting Professionals International, 2019), include the World Education Congress and the Professional Education Conference-North America. These opportunities present a myriad of meetings, shows, and workshops that can help motivate and encourage your staff members. Another possibility comes from the International Special Events Society (ISES) Eventworld® which offers an Institute for Professional Development each summer. ISES is possibly the leading event planning continuing education event in the nation. Or perhaps you might consider sending valued and motivated employees to Event Solutions Idea Factory, a four-day trade show for event planners that is both educational and social. Networking opportunities and leadership training sessions abound during the event, and staffers who have a particular interest in one aspect of planning, such as decor, can find what they need at this extravaganza. One-on-one coaching chances are available at most of these national events as well. Consider also the National Association of Catering Executives organization, which organizes an annual conference, the Catering Executives Conference, for caterers, event planners, and industry vendors and suppliers. During this conference, event planners can not only learn about industry trends and can gain insights into food and beverage services, but they can also share leadership stories and network in a professional setting. Finally, consider attending conferences where communication is the main focus, such as the annual National Communication Association (NCA) convention, as well as any of the regional or state communication association conferences.

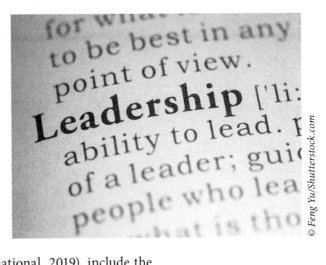

© Feng Yu/Shutterstock.com

Leadership is much more than simply the ability to be a director or an administrator. Event planners must develop the aptitude for leadership because they are constantly working within the decision-making process with clients, who will rely on them for guidance, experience, professionalism, and tenacity. Consider leadership to be a muscle that you can train, develop, flex, and put to use over and over again. Good leaders are delegators and visionaries; they have perseverance, self-confidence, a high degree of emotional intelligence, and can motivate employees. They lead by example but never hesitate to take advantage of opportunities to learn new tactics, skills, technologies, and collaborative techniques. Ultimately, success in event planning will come much more easily as leadership proficiencies are developed.

TIP

Plan an event that is within your budget. Many times on large-scale, free events, we think big and have various stages, attractions, and decor. If a sponsor or funding source does not get secured, we are forced to review what was planned and decide where we can cut the budget. In the leadership role, you sometimes need to make tough decisions on content, scale, and/or decor. It needs to be done without any negative effect on the event. Don't spend money that you don't have.

— Rosalind Healy

Key Terms

Leadership

Autocratic

Bureaucratic

Charismatic

Democratic

Laissez-faire

Delegation

Vision

Perseverance

Self-confidence

Self-efficacy

Emotional Intelligence (EQ)

Framing

Language

Thought

Forethought

Perceiving

Accessing

Understanding

Regulating

Social competence domain

Intelligence Quotient (IQ)

Communication apprehension

Motivation

Theory X

Theory Y

Discussion Questions

1. Imagine you have a client who is unable to make decisions easily—or sometimes unable to make a decision at all. As an event planner, you know your client's indecision will eventually pose serious setbacks to getting the event running. What can you do to change this scenario? How can your leadership skills help your client get past the hesitation that is slowing down the planning progress?

2. Your client, the new CEO of a mid-level technology firm, will be the keynote speaker at the company's annual retreat, which you are planning. He suffers from a severe case of communication apprehension and would like to get someone else to stand in for him at the event. You know such a substitution would communicate the wrong message to the company, which is relying on him for new leadership and vision. How will you address this problem? What kinds of leadership skills will you rely on to make this event a success?

3. Develop a plan for helping your client's employees become more skilled at carrying out smaller in-house events—not the large-scale events you help plan annually, but events like company birthdays, employee anniversaries, and special holidays. As an event planner, you should have several strategies for this kind of employee development. As a leader, what is your vision for growing these special events?

Activity

You are working with two clients—one, the president of a local historical preservation society, and the other, the director of special events for the county that will be celebrating the 100th anniversary of an historic Civil War-era mansion and parkland. The two personalities are at odds at almost every turn in the planning and execution of the celebrations that will center on the mansion's historic anniversary. At issue? Finances, authenticity, kinds of events, invitees, preservation of the mansion—everything you can think of has become an issue between these two. As an event planning leader, you must find a way to encourage these sides to work together for a successful event. What is your strategy?

References

Adeniyi, M. A. (2007). *Effective leadership management: An integration of styles, skills, & character to today's CEO.* Bloomington, IN: Author House.

Akerjordet, K., & Severinsson, E. (2007). Emotional intelligence: A review of the literature with specific focus on empirical and epistemological perspectives. *Journal of Clinical Nursing, 16,* 1405–1416.

Antonakis, J., & Day, D.V. (2018). *The nature of leadership.* 3rd ed. Thousand Oaks, CA: Sage.

Arnett, R., Bell McManus, L., & McKendree, A. (2018). *Conflict between persons: The origins of leadership.* (2nd ed.). Dubuque, IA: Kendall Hunt.

Arvey, R. D., Zhang, Z., Avolio, B. J., & Krueger, R. F. (2007). Developmental and genetic determinants of leadership role occupancy among women. *Journal of Applied Psychology, 92*(3), 693–706.

Bandura, A. (1990). Perceived self-efficacy in the exercise of personal agency. *Journal of Applied Sport Psychology, 2,* 128–163.

Bariso, J. (2018). *EQ, applied: The real-world guide to emotional intelligence.* New York: Borough Hall

Bennis, W. (2009). *On becoming a leader.* (4th ed.). Cambridge, MA: Perseus.

Blanchard, K. (2009). *Leading at a higher level, revised, and expanded edition: Blanchard on leadership and creating high performing organizations.* Upper Saddle River, NJ: Prentice Hall.

Bryman, A. (1992). *Charisma and leadership in organizations.* Thousand Oaks, CA: Sage.

Buckingham, M., & Coffman, C. (1999). *First, break all the rules.* New York: Simon and Schuster.

Burgess, R. C. (2005). A model for enhancing individual and organizational learning of "emotional intelligence:" The drama and winner's triangles. *Social Work Education: The International Journal, 24,* 97–112.

Caramela, S. (2017, September). 4 ways to define leadership. *Business News Daily.* Retrieved from https://www.businessnewsdaily.com/3647-leadership-definition.html.

Cherniss, C., & Goleman, D. (2001). *The emotionally intelligent workplace: How to select for, measure, and improve emotional intelligence in individuals, groups and organizations.* San Francisco: Jossey-Bass.

Collins, J. C., & Porras, J. I. (1994). *Built to last: Successful habits of visionary companies.* New York: HarperCollins.

Coetzee, M., & Harry, N. (2014). Emotional intelligence as a predictor of employees' career adaptability. *Journal of Vocational Behavior, 84,* 90–97.

Cristobal, J. & Lasaten, R. (2018). Oral communication apprehensions and academic performance of grade 7 students. Asia Pacific Journal of Multidisciplinary Research, 6, (3), 5–16.

Daloz Parks, S. (2005). *Leadership can be taught: A bold approach for a complex world.* Boston, MA: Harvard Business School Publishing.

Doh, J. P. (2003). Can leadership be taught? Perspectives from management educators. *Academy of Management Learning & Education, 2*, 54–67.

Event Planners Association. (2019). *Providing a foundation for success.* Retrieved from eventplannersassociation.com.

Fairhurst, G. T. (2011). *The power of framing: Creating the language of leadership.* San Francisco, CA: John Wiley & Sons.

Fairhurst, G. T., & Sarr, R. A. (1996). *The art of framing: Managing the language of leadership.* San Francisco, CA: Jossey-Bass.

Fall, L. T., Kelly, S., MacDonald, P., Primm, W., & Holmes, C. (2013). Intercultural communication apprehension and emotional intelligence in higher education: Preparing business students for career success. *Business and Professional Communication Quarterly, 77*, 412–426.

Feloni, R. (2015, July). LinkedIn CEO Jeff Weiner describes 3 qualities that make a great leader. Retrieved http://www.businessinsider.com/linkedin-ceo-jeff-weiner-on-being-a-great-leader-2015-7.

Ferreira, S. (2018, February). 4 ways to share your vision and lead a successful team. *Inc. Com.* Retrieved from https://www.inc.com/stacey-ferreira/4-ways-to-share-your-vision-lead-a-successful-team.html.

Getz, D. (2012). *Event studies: Theory, research and policy for planned events.* London: Routledge.

Goleman, D., Boyatzis, R., & McKee, A. (2013). *Primal leadership: Unleashing the power of emotional intelligence.* Cambridge, MA: Harvard Business Press.

Greenacre, L., Tung, N. M., & Chapman, T. (2014). Self-confidence, and the ability to influence. *Academy of Marketing Studies Journal, 18*, 169–180.

Greenwell, T. C., Danzey-Bussell, L. A., & Shonk, D. (2014). *Managing sport events.* Champaign, IL: Human Kinetics.

Giuliani, R. (2002). *Leadership.* New York: Hyperion Books.

Jenson, K. (2014). Intelligence is overrated: What you really need to succeed. Retrieved from http://www.forbes.com/sites/keldjensen/2015/02/10/intelligence-is-overrated-what-you-really-need-to-succeed-continued/

Katz, D., Maccoby, N., & Morse, N. (1950). *Productivity, supervision, and morale in an office situation.* Ann Arbor, MI: Institute for Social Research.

Krames, J. A. (2002). *The Jack Welch lexicon of leadership.* New York: McGraw Hill.

Matthews, J.H.; Morley, G.L.; Crossley, E.; & Bhanderi, S. (2018). Teaching leadership: the medical student society model. *The Clinical Teacher* 15 (2), pp. 145–150.

Maxwell, J. C. (1993). *Developing the leader within you.* Nashville, TN: Thomas Nelson Publishers.

_____. (2011). *Beyond talent: Become someone who gets extraordinary results.* Nashville, TN: Thomas Nelson Publishers.

Mayer, J. D., & Salovey, P. (1997). What is emotional intelligence? In P. Salovey and D. Sluyter (Eds.), *Emotional development and emotional intelligence: Implications for educators.* (pp. 3–31). New York: Basic Books.

McCroskey, J. C. (1970). Measures of communication bond anxiety. *Speech Monographs, 37,* 269–277.

McGregor, D. (1960). *The human side of enterprise.* New York: McGraw Hill.

Meeting Professionals International (2019). *When we meet, we change the world.* Retrieved from www.mpiweb.org.

Muller, R., & Turner, J. R. (2010). *Project-oriented leadership.* Surrey, England: Gower.

Neck, C.P., Manz, C.C., & Houghton, J.D. (2019). Self-leadership: The definitive guide to personal excellence. Thousand Oaks, CA: Sage.

Northouse, P. (2018). Introduction to leadership: Concepts and practice. 4th ed. Thousand Oaks, CA: Sage.

Ohio State Leadership Studies (1962). *The leader behavior description questionnaire.* Columbus, OH: Personnel Research Board, The Ohio State University. (Original publication 1957)

Orlick, T. (2008). *In pursuit of excellence* (4th ed.). Champaign, IL: Human Kinetics.

Putnam, L. L., Fairhurst, G. T., & Banghart, S. (2016). Contradiction, dialectics, and paradoxes in organizations: A constitutive approach. *The Academy of Management Annals, 10,* 65–171.

Schutte, N. S., Malouff, J. M., & Thorsteinsson, E. B. (2013). Increasing emotional intelligence through training: Current status and future directions. *The International Journal of Emotional Education, 5,* 55–72.

Sheep, M. L., Fairhurst, G. T., & Khazanchi, S. (2016). Knots in the discourse of innovation: Investigating multiple tensions in a reacquired spin-off. *Organizational Studies, 38,* 463–488.

Tracy, B., & Chee, P. (2013). *12 disciplines of leadership excellence: How leaders achieve sustainable high performance.* New York: McGraw Hill.

Treasurer, B. (2017). A leadership kick in the ass: how to learn from rough landings, blunders, and missteps. Oakland, CA: Berrett-Koehler Publishers.

Van der Wagen, L. (2006). *Human resource management for events: Managing the event workforce.* Oxford: Elsevier.

Westley, F., & Mintzberg, H. (1989). Visionary leadership and strategic management. *Strategic Management Journal, 10,* 17–32.

White, J. (2006). *Excellence in leadership.* Downers Grove, IL: InterVarsity Press.

Williams, P. (2013). *Leadership excellence: The seven sides of leadership for the 21st century.* Uhrichsville, OH: Barbour Publishing.

Chapter 15

ENTREPRENEURSHIP: STARTING YOUR OWN EVENT PLANNING BUSINESS

In an ever-competitive world where business owners face the challenge of setting themselves apart from others, deciding to be an entrepreneur takes a lot of gumption and drive. **Entrepreneurship** requires vision and innovation, and it surely takes a certain amount of creativity to invent your own brand and deliver to the client what you have promised. Nussbaum (2013) points to Apple as being the most highly regarded company in terms of its creativity because of its originality and its ability to satisfy aspirations and empower customers with its innovation. Decision making with regard to entrepreneurship is vital, and management consultant and

Entrepreneurship: *The act of starting and managing one's own business*

author Peter Drucker (1985) writes, "… everyone who can face up to decision making can learn to be an entrepreneur and to behave entrepreneurially. Entrepreneurship, then, is behavior rather than personality trait. And its foundation lies in concept and theory rather than intuition" (p. 26). Being able to make that first decision to start your own company is the beginning of entrepreneurship.

© KeyStock/Shutterstock.com

When you have finished reading this chapter, you will be able to

- explain the advantages and disadvantages of becoming an entrepreneur;
- list the steps in developing a solid business plan;
- establish a strategy for marketing and branding your business.

Launching a Communications Agency Involved with Events

Chris Daley, Principal and Founder, Whirlaway

After working for over a decade at a successful entrepreneurial public relations agency, becoming my own boss was the logical next step as I launched Whirlaway, LLC, a communications agency specializing in public relations and marketing. During my 15-year public relations career, my role has often been to serve as an event planner, or part of the support team implementing media relations and social media strategies for events. Whirlaway works with clients across various industries, and typical events my company plans are press conferences, influencer gatherings, product launches, grand openings and professional workshops. Whirlaway provides marketing or public relations support for fundraisers, sporting events and networking functions.

At any point during the year, my company is involved with either planning and/or promoting different sized events. In most cases, client events are connected with the organization's public relations and marketing strategies. Events can serve as a tactic to build brand awareness, connect with a target audience or serve as a revenue source. By offering event support services, I knew there would be a lot of opportunities to grow Whirlaway. The event industry continues to boom, and there is a large demand from organizations or individuals seeking professional assistance to make their event successful. Having the professional experience, I know there are a lot of opportunities to generate new business for Whirlaway by offering event support services.

Prior to launching the company, my entrepreneurship process began by conceptualizing the brand. I did not want to name the company after myself, so I thought through creating a brand name that exuded confidence while resonating with the communications industry. I wanted the brand name to tell a story and distinguish itself from other agencies. I settled on the name Whirlaway because it was inspired by horse racing's 1941 Triple Crown champion, and the definition of "Whirl" relates to the current state of the public relations industry.

After the branding process was complete, I created a business plan for Whirlaway. This is a vital step that all entrepreneurs should begin with even if the plan primarily serves as a personal document. Creating a business plan gives your new company direction and brand guidelines. Through the process, you will identify new business opportunities and places to focus your energy so that you can create a path to short-term and long-term success.

Specific components of Whirlaway's business plan were the mission and vision statements, analysis of the market landscape, identification of competition, financial goals, brand style guide, marketing plan and action items to complete during year one of operation. Because Whirlaway does not have any employees except for me, the business plan serves as an internal guide. Every few months I review it and make adjustments as the company evolves.

When you have established a vision for your company, it is important to create and implement a business development plan. Whirlaway's business development plan started with a description of ideal clients in line with the agency's services and capabilities. The ideal client descriptions I created were centered around industries, services needed and budget size. Once an initial list of potential clients to approach was established, I began cold outreach and tapped into my professional network to look for introductions and referrals.

To support business development, I created a marketing plan for Whirlaway to generate brand awareness for the new company as well as the services I provide. I built a website and launched social media platforms including Twitter, Instagram, and LinkedIn. The platforms showcase my expertise, offer samples of work and serve as branding tools. Additionally, I was able to secure media coverage about the launch of Whirlaway after distributing a press release that garnered attention and reached new client prospects.

Whirlaway is off to a successful start, already working with ideal clients seeking event planning help in addition to public relations services, including managing promotions and providing other support services. A great entrepreneur learns how to adapt to different situations and people. During the event planning process, you will experience all types of hurdles, including people who work differently than you, and management of your time and tasks. An entrepreneur also knows how to adapt to challenging environments and can figure out the best way to communicate with all types of people.

After reading the chapter, revisit this case study and respond to the following question:

If you were to start your own event planning business, what would some of the benefits and hurdles include?

Entrepreneurship

There are many successful entrepreneurs in the event planning industry, from those who run large firms to those who run their own small businesses. The term entrepreneur is a widely used French word dating back to the 1700s, originally referring to someone who was commissioned to complete a particular project by an individual who had money to invest (Raj, Walters, & Rashid, 2011). Since its inception, the term **entrepreneur** has evolved into the simpler idea of someone who starts a new business. Entrepreneurs are able to identify an opportunity and develop it into a new

Entrepreneur: *A person who starts a new business*

© bleakstar/Shutterstock.com

Exploratory phase: *A time of brainstorming and researching to ascertain if starting a business is the right career path*

venture or project (Burke, 2006). Entrepreneurs must exercise "vision and alertness" for ongoing business opportunities if they are to succeed (Kirzner, 2015, p.57). They are able to build and create an ideal from within and are considered one of the driving forces behind changes in society and industry. Entrepreneurs need to understand the evolving economy and the changing industry in which they work. Usually before individuals decide to create their own business, they will go through some type of **exploratory phase** where they are brainstorming and researching to ascertain if starting a business is the right career path. Both knowledge and motivation are usually the driving factors in opening one's own business (McMullen & Shepherd, 2006). Entrepreneurs have many responsibilities because they participate in various tasks, including starting the new venture, managing production, marketing the company, directing the business process, organizing finances and supervising people (Douglas, 2009). Being able to manage all of these tasks requires entrepreneurs to embody various qualities.

Qualities of an Entrepreneur

One way to gain an understanding of entrepreneurship is to examine some of the inherent qualities of the entrepreneur. People who want to create and manage their own businesses are typically sociable leaders who are interested in others. They are goal-oriented and usually motivated enough to accomplish any tasks necessary to reach that goal. Their communication skills are strong and natural, and friends and colleagues often turn to them for advice and opinions. Entrepreneurs are driven from within to succeed, and are both flexible and innovative. Business owners in the field of event planning have a strong vision of what an event should look like, and their motivation carries them to the finish. Their ability to innovate pushes them to develop new ideas and re-evaluate older ways of accomplishing tasks. Constantly searching for improvements, entrepreneurs are not satisfied with the status quo because they can see possibilities where others cannot (Bowser, 2010). Burns (2016) notes six characteristics of many entrepreneurs: "a high need for autonomy; a high need for achievement; an internal locus of control; drive and determination; creativity and innovation; and a willingness to take measured risks" (p. 82). The entrepreneurial job demands determination, dedication, and superior decision-making skills (It's all none of your business, 2000). Thus, "the entrepreneur is the aggressive catalyst for change in the business world" (Frederick, O'Connor, & Kuratko, 2019, p. 9). Additionally, successful entrepreneurs are likely to go the extra mile, both for their business and for their clients. Connors and Smith (2014) believe that when you go the extra mile and give extra effort to your business, wonderful opportunities can happen, thereby setting you apart from the crowd.

Many entrepreneurs are risk-takers who are not afraid of failure, or at least they can confront their fears and still push forward. Brené Brown (2018) states, "Not enough people are taking smart risks or creating and sharing bold ideas to meet changing demands and the insatiable need for innovation" (p. 8). Yet they are not reckless in their decision-making; in fact, one of their strengths is calculating the risk in any decision, and they are able to make a sound choice when appropriate. Once a decision is made, many business owners can see the path ahead of them clearly and feel no regrets about where they are heading (Burns, 2016; Cooper & Vlaskovits, 2013). A competitive desire to be the best drives them to take risks where a less adventurous soul might falter (Frederick, O'Connor, & Kuratko, 2019; Pfister & Tierney, 2009). Event planning entrepreneurs have a desire to grow their business in relation to the market share, yet while profits are tangible incentives, many entrepreneurs are motivated instead by the desire to excel among their peers (Bowser, 2010). Successful business owners are guided by a code of ethics that will become a part of their brand and provide a sense of integrity to their clients, their team, and their colleagues. This kind of integrity demands a heightened sense of self-honesty and personal reflection on a regular basis. Entrepreneurs can make mistakes, but they do not let their mistakes offer roadblocks to forward movement; self-actualized event planners who work independently cannot afford to dwell in regrets and remorse (Raffiee & Feng, 2014).

© Victor Soares/Shutterstock.com

These characteristics are not necessarily indicators of an entrepreneurial spirit, but are generally shared qualities of those who do own their own businesses. Entrepreneurs are passionate about their plans, their clients, and their vision for what lies ahead (Cooper & Vlaskovits, 2013). Both realists and visionaries, they are unwilling to concede that any job is beyond their scope with the proper planning and help. However, there is no room in the entrepreneurial spirit for egotism or pigheadedness, since ultimately they themselves must answer to each outcome. Optimistic by nature and creative by design, entrepreneurs in the field of event planning channel their energy and inspiration into each project for success (Bowser, 2010).

Finally, entrepreneurs are aware of the full scope of the arena in which they work and are vigilant in learning what they can do to broaden their knowledge of the occupation, keeping in mind that they are small players on a very large playing field (Bowser, 2010). Realizing the need for constant growth, they are good at meeting others, understanding the necessity of operating among colleagues and peers in order to grow the business and address current trends (Frederick, O'Connor, & Kuratko, 2019). Entrepreneurs believe in

© docstockmedia/Shutterstock.com

relying on their contacts, professional organizations, and other associates to keep them connected and effective. They are good networkers and understand the importance of professional liaisons. Furthermore, they are not just detail-oriented perfectionists; they are big-picture thinkers as well who constantly self-assess their learning curve (Gladstone, 2007) and seek to grow professionally. This entrepreneurial mindset consistently infuses an individual's approach to innovation and growth (Frederick, O'Connor, & Kuratko, 2019). These characteristics are certainly indicative of the spirit of the entrepreneur, and those who demonstrate these qualities might easily be enticed into starting their own business, but it is important to determine the advantages and disadvantages of starting one's own business before beginning the move.

Advantages of an Entrepreneurial Life

© mangostock/Shutterstock.com

Owning your own business might sound like it offers innumerable advantages, and for the right person, that is true. Such a pathway allows event planners to be their own supervisor, using their skills and understanding in ways that they determine necessary. This kind of creative freedom is tempting in a world where much is regimented and controlled by others (It's all none of your business, 2000). Entrepreneurship offers the opportunity to develop great insight into one's own identity through hard work and self-examination (Roman, 2007), and to be in control of one's own work life is certainly alluring. Being able to challenge yourself and determine your own success is a terrific incentive for many who have a unique vision for their careers. Creating a work/life balance is possible when you control your own professional path and destiny in order to make a vision come true (Abreu, Oner, Brouwer, & van Leeuwen, 2019; Pfister & Tierney, 2009). In fact, being the person who sets the rules can be seen as very freeing for those who might chafe under others' structures. However, it should be noted that a wide range of variables may affect the entrepreneur's satisfaction, well-being, and success, including personality characteristics, geographic location, class status, and health (Abreu, Oner, Brouwer, & van Leeuwen, 2019).

Other advantages are perhaps less obvious but equally important. The pride in creating and managing your own brand is reinforced daily in conversations with clients and colleagues. Each day is a new one, filled with novelty of your own selection and creation. For instance, an event planner might be meeting a client in the morning, and in the afternoon creating centerpieces for an upcoming event. At 5 p.m., the event planner might head to a networking mixer at the local Chamber of Commerce, and then finish out the evening by stuffing gift bags for a weekend function. Building

TIP

Resourcefulness is essential. Ingenuity will help you figure out how to do that which you don't know how to do, and that which others say can't be done—but can be.

— Charles Steinberg

a company that will be a testament to your posterity can be a factor in the entrepreneurial choice, and working in an environment over which you have control is also mentioned as highly important by entrepreneurs (Mitchellette, 2007). In fact, many of the advantages of entrepreneurship are clearly linked to autonomy and motivation (Abreu, Oner, Brouwer, & van Leeuwen, 2019; Kuratko, 2017) To be directly connected to clients in a personal and deliberate way may also induce some to this life, for the corporate world often tends to draw creative spirits away from the heart of the action. Working where you choose and taking on the clients who appeal to you in some way also might be reasons to start your own firm. Finally, those who can survive the daunting initial years may find great job security and financial independence within their reach (Ernst & Young, Nissenbaum, Raasch, & Ratner, 2004).

Disadvantages of an Entrepreneurial Life

Starting your own business is no easy task and certainly not for the faint of heart. This kind of effort requires enormous stamina and hard work, often without an immediate vision of success. Those who want to become entrepreneurs must certainly have the drive to be their own boss and the patience to make that happen, but more than patience, they need to understand that owning and running their own business demands a seven-day-a-week commitment if the business is to flourish (Roman, 2007). They must develop a "tolerance for failure" (Kuratko, 2017, p. 34), learning from each experience and resetting expectations as they learn. Starting your own business comes with a high degree of risk, for according to the U.S. Department of Labor, six out of 10 new firms survive at least two years, slightly more than half at least five years, and a quarter stay in business 10 or 15 years or more (U.S. Department of Labor, 2019). Risk taking and the capacity to remain calm through the storm of a new business venture are two intertwined qualities that entrepreneurs generally demonstrate (Gladstone, 2007; Roman, 2007). Without these, the danger is that growth will be stymied because owners are too anxious to make any changes that might impact the business, even when change is demanded. "Your own fears will be your biggest limitation" (Roman, 2007, p. 41), and so unless you are willing to face uncertainty boldly, choose another career path. Be aware that entry mistakes are common among those who desire to begin a new venture, and examining the predictors of success carefully with some detachment will be vital (Burns, 2016; Santarelli & Vivarelli, 2007).

Those who want to start their own business because they see big profits may need to rethink their goals. There is enormous liability for financial risk in a start-up company; often owners must pledge on their personal net worth in order to secure financing. Viability can be delayed well beyond the formative years of the company, and incomes vary widely among entrepreneurs. Profit-making takes patience and stamina for the long haul, so entrepreneurs must be able to look ahead beyond the initial slow growth and maintain a steady hand (Ernst & Young, Nissenbaum, Raasch, & Ratner, 2004). In addition, uncertainty also stems from the fact that there is no true template upon which you can build a successful business; while there are, of course, many tips of the trade that may help you, including the development of a solid and sustainable business plan (Frederick, O'Connor, & Kuratko, 2019), there is still a great deal of pressure in every decision that comes from an absence of rules for absolute success (Pfister & Tierney, 2009). This lack of an established system for financial attainment can contribute to the sense of social isolation that the entrepreneur might face. Often, new businesses begin with only one or two principal owners, which can leave entrepreneurs feeling lonely and far too independent. With a jam-packed work schedule that may leave little time in the early years for breathing—much less a vacation—owners might begin to feel overwhelmed, another one of the reasons that many entrepreneurs do not make it past year five (Mitchellette, 2007). When time is limited, often the family or personal life suffers the most (It's all none of your business, 2000).

Finally, consider the fact that in the event planning business, at least at first, you will be responsible for every one of the tasks that needs to be done. Not only must you be able to converse interpersonally with clients, but you will create their design elements, organize and administer their social media, arrange transportation, conduct public relations, book venues, manage your own billing and finances, set up and tear down actual events—just to name a few of the tasks that will fall to you (Pfister & Tierney, 2009). All of the work comes back on your shoulders, and this includes even the unpleasant jobs you may have been able to avoid in the past. The entrepreneurial spirit may be sorely tried at 2:15 in the morning as you are emptying trash cans and cleaning up debris. Thus, consider carefully the complete range of advantages and disadvantages before you make the jump into entrepreneurism.

The Hybrid Approach

If the disadvantages outweigh the positive features, there are other options to becoming an entrepreneur. One alternative choice is to remain in a salaried job in an existing organization while beginning a new venture part-time. This hybrid model of entrepreneurship seems ideal for someone who may want to start more slowly without a large capital investment. By reducing what is put at risk—the full-time salary—some entrepreneurs have found that this model is more forgiving. Research has found that employing this **hybrid entry model** for at least a year prior to full-time entrepreneurial self-employment can increase the success rate of the business (Folta, Delmar, & Wennberg, 2010; Furr, 2016). Because costs are limited, risk is limited, and this model may offer a sound alternative to those who hesitate to take that first, hugely committal step. This conclusion applies generally to those who are beginning an entrepreneurial career in a field different from their previous job, in which there is no competition for clients. However, entrepreneurs who are developing ventures in the same

Hybrid entry model: *A career plan in which one remains in a salaried job in an existing organization while beginning a new venture part-time*

field as their full-time employment may face legal action, including signing a **non-compete clause**—a legal term in which an employee agrees not to start a similar profession in competition with a current employer—that serves to protect the original company's property, in this case, the client list. The best advice? Hire an attorney to sort out the advantages and disadvantages of such a restrictive clause before signing (Baron & Shane, 2007).

To add an additional part-time job as event planner to a full-time career path takes some ingenuity as well as some good choices. Teaming up with other successful planners as an adjunct on their staff is certainly an option, or putting together your own cohort of those connected to the profession is another choice (Moran, 2010) as you begin to think about full-time or part-time work as an event planner. For example, you may have a particular caterer, videographer, or printer with whom you might be able to forge a good working partnership as you become more independent. Your training and experience may be lacking in one or two areas, but putting a team together might help solve the problem. The growth potential, even for part-time event planners, continues to show steady increases (Palmer, 2014), depending on the niche market, the kind of services provided, and the commitment level of the event planner. Moran (2010) suggests asking questions before making a decision. These could include questions that focus on your own strengths and abilities, your financial situation, the time commitment you can make and your ability to network. Perhaps the honest answers to these questions can help you decide if the hybrid model approach or a full-time leap is the best choice.

TIP

Passion is not a learned skill, but an innate one. But you can learn skills to sustain your passion in the demanding profession of event planning.

— Kristen Schultz

The Business Plan

If you decide that being an entrepreneur is for you, your first step is to begin thinking in terms of the business. Initially, entrepreneurs must concentrate on developing a sound **business plan** that embraces the vision for the company or enterprise. This plan must examine the value that will be offered to clients and how that value will translate into a clearly thought-out brand identity (Joseph, 2004). Hindle and Mainprize (2006) write, "With a good plan in hand, an entrepreneur should not let a lack of resources inhibit his or her pursuit of opportunity," (p. 7). As entrepreneurs develop a business plan, the brand must not only become a part of the fabric of the business, but also a part of the entrepreneurs themselves. Because of their desire, creativity, and hunger for the new undertaking, many entrepreneurs may want to proceed full steam ahead into the venture without laying the strong foundation that is the business plan. Put the business plan in writing so that it becomes a cornerstone document to use when temptation to veer from the plan strikes (What to do when starting a new business, 1995).

Business plan: *A written framework that embraces the vision for the company or enterprise, including its goals for its niche market and market analysis*

© *Marlon Lopez MMG1 Design/ Shutterstock.com*

Think about the niche you are attempting to fill and how the values you want to convey address that particular niche. But remember that as time passes, your vision might evolve into something other than what it was at the start. Be open to that. Performing a market analysis will enable you to prioritize your goals in light of what you find is missing from the niche you want to carve out for your business (Burns, 2016; Frederick, O'Connor, & Kuratko, 2019; Gladstone, 2007). A solid five-year plan is an absolute necessity before even thinking about logos, storefront rentals, and client services. While a business plan may not furnish all the answers, it will help you to steer the course and stay on track to develop the vision that will guide your business (Burns, 2016; Collins & Porras, 2002). The business plan will help you create the first impression you want to convey, because you will have spent time mapping a strategy for the business and the brand.

Vesper and Vesper (1993) suggest that writing a business plan requires imagination, information, and analysis. Entrepreneurs who want to start their own company must take into consideration possible risks and contingency plans so that all aspects of planning are covered. O'Brien (2010) further elaborates by offering 10 tips to creating a successful business plan:

1. Purpose—decide on the intention of the business and the role you want to play in it;
2. Market analysis—research and write an evaluation of the market trends; map out your strategy for getting ahead;
3. Competitive landscape—study the other organizations that make up your competition and examine the environment at the moment;
4. Financial and business objectives—determine your financial commitments and construct a financial projection as you begin your business;
5. Marketing strategy—once you have determined your financial responsibilities, create a sound marketing plan for generating business;
6. Operations—use your office space to your advantage and invest in what you will need to make your business a success;
7. Systems and processes—create good habits that will lead to success, such as setting your work hours, reading about your business and the industry, and managing your time;
8. Action steps—in order to reach your business objectives, create lists and check them off as you go; these activities will turn into palpable business results;
9. Timeline—set up a schedule that will help guide you to reach your overall business objectives;
10. Analysis of performance—stay true to your business plan for positive results, but be honest about where you can improve next time (p. 12).

Entrepreneurs must be willing to engage all of the previous tips in detail to maximize the scope of the business they wish to launch. Remember that there is a plethora of research for those who want to start their own business (Joseph, 2004; Kuratko, 2017; Mitchellette, 2007; Raffiee & Feng, 2014), so the more research you conduct, the better informed you will become.

Branding Your Business

Once the business plan is under construction, event planners must brand themselves in order to market their services. Influencing others' perception of your brand is challenging at best, but with a carefully thought-out business plan, you will be able to communicate your message clearly (Joseph, 2004). Morgan (2011) suggests personal **branding** whereby you "quietly and steadily distinguish yourself through quality delivery that adds incremental value to the client. Anticipate, innovate, and excel at execution" (p. 61). Furthermore, it is imperative that entrepreneurs are able to verbalize why your company is one to consider securing to help plan events. Simon Sinek (2009), states, "People don't buy what you do, they buy why you do it" (p. 58). This statement, Sinek says, is the main reason businesses fail—simply because they are unable to communicate the 'why' part of the equation. People choose to work with successful companies or buy their products because they understand what the business believes simply because consumers understand why they do what they do. Sinek uses the examples of Apple, Southwest Airlines, and Harley Davidson as companies that supremely understand 'why they do what they do.' They do not just focus on the 'what' and 'how' of the company's strategy. Therefore, event planners who start their own businesses must be able to offer clients something they need and to communicate the unique 'why' component of their business to clients. Judy Allen (2002) recognizes that branding has become a vital marketing tool, and that clients want to know the character, integrity, and quality of the event planning company with which they will do business. Event planners can think of their brand as the image or personality they wish to create by answering questions such as the following:

Branding: *The process of distinguishing a product, service or person through quality delivery that adds incremental value to the client by anticipating, innovating, and excelling at execution*

- What services and innovation can you offer that other companies may not?
- How can you distinguish yourself from other event planners?
- Why is your event planning company unique?

These are all good questions to ask and can help you find your business niche. Furthermore, branding takes time because building relationships takes time. Cockrum (2011) states that "the best ideas for spreading your brand and increasing your customer base are more about relationships and trust than they are about spending money on the correct advertising or marketing. The best ideas are free ideas" (p. 289). Creating a plan to brand your business simply takes forethought and creativity. There are numerous ways to promote your business; you just have to know which ones might be best for your particular event planning business. Burns (2016) suggests that the brand should be unique and memorable, and promoting it is the entrepreneur's main task. Encouraging clients to associate the brand with the business is the first step on the road to success. Consider, for instance, ESPN's annual award ceremony, the ESPYs, that recognizes yearly achievement by sports teams and athletes. Because ESPN was already strongly established as a brand, the ESPY awards, which began 14 years after the launch of ESPN, could rely on an established audience that lifted the event to success.

Being able to frame your company in the right context will help your brand as well. Erving Goffman (1986), who put forth the theory of **framing**, explains that people have their own sets of beliefs about the world around them that make up their framework. "These 'frames' are there, whether we are aware of them or not, and people with Creative Intelligence have a knack for turning frames a bit to the side, spinning them around, or maybe even tossing them all together, changing the way we view the world and our place in it" (Nussbaum, 2013, p. 88). Framing, an essential communicative tool, focuses on how to communicate a message strategically (Fairhurst, 2011; Fairhurst & Sarr, 1996). Tom Kelley (2001) believes that in today's business environment, senior executives are more likely to frame their companies' needs in the context of innovation, with innovation taking the starring role of many corporate decisions and initiatives. Similarly, entrepreneurs should learn how to frame the benefits provided by the products or services provided, relying on some kind of qualitative or quantitative measurement system to assess their efficacy (Charette, Hooker, & Stanton, 2015). Being able to frame your company in the right manner will help people see its value and personality.

In a comparable way, Arnell (2010) believes that when you brand your business, you are primarily concerned with creating emotions. He suggests targeting positive emotions to "unlock a sense of wonder, to package an uplifting sense of fun" (p. 60). Event planners should consider having a strong **vision statement**—a picture of what an organization wants to achieve over time—or **mission statement**—a formal summary of the goals and values of a company (Corbett, 1996). Allowing your clients to know exactly how you see your company on a daily basis, and what its goals are for the future as you grow and develop, will better acquaint them with your unique understanding of the event planning industry. Once you have created your vision or mission statement, you should begin to develop all the promotional materials necessary to market their business. Consider what benefits your company offers a client that other companies may not. "Benefits can build brands" (Marsh, Guth, & Short, 2008, p. 116), and event planners should incorporate those messages into the pieces they create. Developing a **logo** offers event planners the opportunity to brand their companies with a recognizable symbol. Antonelli (2014) suggests that the logo represents the solid foundation of the brand and "conveys expertise, establishes brand promise, and creates an expectation for quality" (p. 6). Therefore, the logo should easily identify the company's brand as well as meet the needs of all those who are involved (Van der Wagen & White, 2018). Additionally, event planners should consider how the logo will look in different sizes, on different paper, and on all online platforms. Consider thoroughly the logo color, shape, and size before making a final decision. If you do not have the skills to create a logo yourself, you may want to hire a freelance graphic artist to create one for you. Once you choose a logo, you will have to plan the different types of public relations and marketing collaterals you want to produce. Consider several pieces in order to formalize your business, including business cards, stationery, and a brochure marketing your services. Additionally, companies such as Staples now help small businesses build their

© Rawpixel/Shutterstock.com

brands through design services, by which businesses can create all of their marketing materials through one company (Staples Inc., 2015).

Business cards should look professional and consistently reflect your company's brand identity (Van der Wagen & White, 2018). Put your company's name, logo, and title on your business card, and include all contact information necessary, including your business address, office telephone number, mobile telephone number, email address, website address, and social media accounts. Online companies can inexpensively print standard-size business cards and will ship directly to you. Consider using two colors on your cards to help them stand out. Popyk (2015) states that business cards are a way to make connections with others and leave them with a way to reach you. He writes, "Leave them everywhere. Hand them out to everyone" (p. 56). Handing out cards confirms your connection, and business cards offer potential clients the chance to remember your name and your brand.

Moreover, a printed brochure may be a helpful promotional piece that you can leave behind with potential clients. Bivins (2008) suggests planning your brochure by considering your intended audience and what they should learn from it. Will it be informative or persuasive? Brochures can be created in different sizes and shapes, so do not feel limited to using the standard 8½" by 11" tri-fold format; allow yourself the creativity to develop the brochure so that it suits the written content and the ways in which it will be used by the client. Brochures should contain relevant information written in clear, concise language, and include testimonials from clients and photographs depicting past events your company has produced. Include your company's contact information, website, and social media accounts on the brochure so that it can drive clients to your business.

Branding Your Business through Social Media

Using social media to connect with potential clients to generate business is vital in today's business world. Brand building through social media is an important aspect of positioning your event planning business. The goal is to have potential clients and customers engage with you and feel something for your business. Thus, you might consider building your brand using the 'daring' acronym:

- Dependable: your clients know that you will get the job done correctly and on time
- Attentive: you understand that attention to details can make or break an event
- Resourceful: your portfolio reflects a wide and diverse client base because you can communicate well
- Identifiable: your corporate identity is easily recognizable
- Nimble: your company is flexible and adaptable
- Groundbreaking: you create innovative and unique events as an entrepreneur.

As an event planning entrepreneur, using the 'daring' acronym can help you build a brand that makes your business extraordinary. Knowing how to connect the organizational vision through social media requires a careful fashioning of a concise, direct and engaging message, and that takes knowledge, time, and creativity. But the rewards continue to remind you that engagement with the public is essential in a time when consumer mentalities desire an immediate response. Not only can customers connect with your company through social media, but they can also communicate with each other, multiplying your company's visibility and strengthening the profile (Mangold & Faulds, 2009). Event planners need to have a clear understanding of every type of social media and how each can work in your favor for developing a prominence in the virtual world.

Successfully built and administered websites and social media platforms are incredibly valuable and the best way for consumers to garner information about your product or services. Bailyn (2012) states that the digital world has now become central, and he writes the following:

> The currency of the Internet is changing from one based on links—the symbol of trust in the eyes of search engines—to a currency of likes, comments, pins, retweets, shares and video responses. Simply put, virality is the new decider of business (pp. 3–4).

Bailyn's hypothesis is true; it is vitally important that event planners create the means to do business via the Internet, including through their website, blogs, and social media outlets. Creating a website can be simple or more complex, and depending on your resources, you will have to determine which avenue suits your company best. Services are available to build websites, but you must pay for their time and creativity, and then afterwards, for training so that your company can manage the website itself. However, there are other platforms, such as blogging platforms, that allow you to have an online presence using their software, including WordPress, Blogger, Wix, and Tumblr, for instance. While these applications have been established as blogging web sites, many businesses use their templates and alter the configuration to make them work as a website. Costs can vary; some of these templates are free, while others cost a minimal amount of money. Select a domain name that is the company's name or something related to it; you will want it to work to your company's advantage.

Promoting your company properly on the website will mean creating categories of information about your business. Turn consumers into fans by having them connect to your brand (Arnell, 2010). So how does one go about building relationships and fans? Start by building your online presence. On your website, include an 'About the Company' tab, and post your vision and mission statements prominently. Let people know who you are, what type of event planning business you run, where you are located, when you started your business, and how potential clients can get in

touch with you. Keep your text succinct and precise, as successful web-based sites are often low on text and high on images. Strong websites feature your online portfolio, including information about your clients and samples of your work, along with current client testimonials (Bly, 2009). Showcase your work with photographs and videos of past events you have created, but be sure to check with your client for permission to share their professional work on your website. The Forbes Communications Council (2017) suggests that you showcase your work with videos of events you have planned, even a live stream of an event, as well as working towards a cohesive presentation of every collateral related to your brand. Anything you can do to build up your brand will help your identity. Display the logo on the website's front page, and it is imperative to include phone numbers and email addresses so clients can get in touch with you. Including a blog area is not a bad idea; this will allow you to connect with people by telling stories about your events, and narratives allow your brand's personality to shine. However, be sure to keep the blog current, and schedule your posts to run on specific days.

Creating a business Facebook page and an Instagram account where you can post pictures of your events, showcase your clients, and talk about your brand is the perfect way to promote your work. Set up your own Twitter account to connect with local businesses and customers, and tweet photos, news, and tips about event planning. YouTube is another popular social media site; post videos of your best events and link them to your website, Facebook, Instagram, and Twitter accounts. Creating a LinkedIn account for you as the business owner of your event planning company will help you connect with potential clients.

In addition, it may be worth investigating some reliance on **influencers**, those individuals who have power over potential customers through postings on Instagram and YouTube, for instance. Marketing activities can be built around the social media presence of these individuals who can affect purchase decisions by virtue of their relationship with their audience. This means that event planners and their team must know their audience, monitoring social media accounts of the competition and sharing your own event content in ways that set you apart from others. Enlisting social media influencers can help spread the word about your company with low cost and achievable success (Krost, 2017).

One of the best attributes of using social media is that there is typically zero to minimal cost involved in marketing your event planning company. While it does take time and strategy, targeting potential clients through social media can lead to increased business and customers who feel connected to your brand. Spreading the word through social media as to what you can provide your clients can help them feel better about any one of those categories and will enable them to connect to your brand. Finally, be sure to investigate how to optimize your placement in various search engines. When potential clients are searching for an event planner via the Internet, you will want your business to show up early in their search.

Networking

Another free way to spread the word about your business is through networking. **Networking** is the process of developing and nurturing relationships with professional organizations, local chambers of commerce, educational institutions and service organizations, and practicing professionals. Networking will be an important tool as you begin to foster relationships for business development, for new vendors, and for all sorts of professional resources. Never overlook an opportunity to work with others in the profession in order to form these alliances and relationships; join committees, volunteer at conferences, take advantage of speaking engagements so that you can demonstrate your competence (Maslowski, 2005). Event planning is about developing relationships: with professional organizations, with local chambers of commerce, with educational institutions and service organizations, and with practicing professionals in your own field. For instance, there may be times when your event planning skills will be needed to help local city and community organizations plan large-scale events. These types of working relationships will enable event planners to gain exposure and credibility. Attending professional conventions in the field of event planning will help you assess your own skills on a regular basis to ascertain that you are indeed keeping up with the latest trends and accreditations. "Networking begins with taking the time to begin a conversation" (Chichester, 2014, p. 163),

and it can take place over dinner, with drinks, before a conference breakout session, or during an event. For some younger entrepreneurs, networking can be intimidating and challenging, but it is still a necessary component of business growth. Perhaps, as a new college graduate, you have been invited to attend a business workshop, and though it would be easier and more comfortable to sit next to the few people you know, forcing yourself to sit at a table with people you do not know might offer the potential for unexpected opportunities. Most importantly, when networking, be yourself, and do not try too hard to impress others. Just tell people what you do and a little bit about your business as you mingle and converse; that usually works best (Dickison, 2011).

Rittscher (2012) offers six ways to make professional connections that are vital for business growth. Her suggestions include the following:

1. Start with a plan—Figure out who your business will need to connect with and how others can help you.
2. Be selective with your efforts—Be mindful of your time (an important commodity) and know where you spend it in order to best target your efforts.
3. Use the "hostess principle"—Do not be afraid to walk up to someone, stick your hand out, form a connection, and make everyone around you comfortable.
4. Make a real connection—When making connections, make sure they are authentic and sustainable and will last for a long time.
5. Build and keep your network current—Today's contact lists are the connections you will make through social media.
6. Pay it forward by helping others to achieve success—A hallmark of good leaders is their ability to be honest, trustworthy, and caring about the well-being of others (paras. 2–7).

Being able to network appropriately and with good intention will help set you apart and position your business in the best way possible. Proper networking helps you open doors and then keep them open.

Finally, becoming an involved participant or holding an officer position in an event planning professional association or organization is also a great way to network with those in your field. Professional associations and organizations serve the needs of new professionals and those already in the industry and provide continuing education to further develop their careers (Kaweckyj, 2009). Volunteering within those organizations allows you to make connections that will serve you immediately and in the future. Following is a list of some associations that may provide good networking opportunities:

American Marketing Association (ama.org)	International Association of Venue Managers (iavm.org)
American Society of Association Executives (asaecenter.org)	International Branding Association (internationalbranding.org)
Association for Talent Development (td.org)	International Festivals & Events Association (ifea.com)
Association of Travel Marketing Executives (atme.org)	International Special Events Society (ises.com)
Association of Fundraising Professionals (afpnet.org)	Marketing Research Association (marketingresearch.org)
Destination Marketing Association International (destinationmarketing.org)	Meeting Professionals International (mpiweb.org)
Event Planners Association (eventplannersassociation.com)	National Association for Catering and Events (nace.org)
Event Service Professionals Association (espaonline.org)	Professional Convention Management Association (pcma.org)
Exhibit and Event Marketers Association (tsea.org)	Sales and Marketing Executives International (smei.org)
Hospitality Sales and Marketing Association International (hsmai.org)	Society of Government Meeting Professionals (sgmp.org)
The International Association of Conference Centers (iacconline.org)	Trade Show News Network (tsnn.com)

These associations provide learning opportunities and may connect you with a mentor.

Mentorship

Mentoring: *Process through which a senior and more experienced person offers advice and consultation to someone newer in the field*

Mentoring matters because it can impact your business in many ways (Patel, 2014). **Mentoring** is a process-driven phenomenon where there is a senior, wise, and more experienced person offering advice and consultation to someone (Nandram & Samsom, 2008). This process is a way to support new entrepreneurs in overcoming many of the obstacles that exist in creating a business (Sullivan, 2000). "Mentoring is the process by which one person (the mentor) encourages another individual (the mentee) to manage his or her own learning so that the mentee becomes self-reliant in the acquisition of new knowledge, skills and abilities, and develops a continuous motivation to do so" (Klasen & Clutterbuck, 2002, p. 16). Choose **mentors** who have expertise in the skills you lack (Ebrahimi, 2013), and slowly build relationships with those whom you trust: bankers, graphic designers, attorneys, industry specialists—these people can offer practical advice and guidance as your business evolves (What to do when starting a new business, 1995). Klasen and Clutterbuck (2002) suggest that mentors can provide support and help guide mentees using various methods, including setting goals, offering advice, encouraging initiative, fostering decision making, and helping to solve challenges. Because mentors have often lived through many of the same entrepreneurial experiences, they are able to offer their time and expertise as mentees grow and develop.

Mentor: *An experienced or trusted advisor*

Do not be afraid to ask others for help, advice, insights, and opinions, since you cannot expect to be proficient in every area of the business, even after you have gained some experience. Many people do not reach out to mentors because "(1) they do not know where to start; (2) they are too proud; and (3) they believe it is a waste of time" (Patel, 2014, para. 6). For example, you may reach out to someone with whom you have worked in the past, such as a professor, a supervisor, or an established self-starter, for advice. This person could serve as an inspiration to you, and when asked, is typically willing and honored to help others launch a career. With the assistance of mentors whom you have carefully selected, you will be able to make wise decisions that are based partly on your creative instincts as well as on the advice of people you trust (Roman, 2007). Regular and honest self-evaluation through this growth process is another important task: look at the wish list you created at the beginning of the journey and assess where you are at various milestones along the way. Flexibility, honesty, and goal-orientation will propel you forward (Gladstone, 2007).

Whether or not you choose to become an entrepreneur depends upon your ability to accept risk, maintain a patient and constant work ethic, access your creativity and networking skills, and develop your vision far into the future. Research may indicate that the uncertainty and fear of failure connected to a start-up company may not just keep creative people from beginning their own company, but it may also contribute to the high rates of new business failure (Raffiee & Feng, 2014). The data on new business failure rates is well-known in the business world (Mitchellette, 2007; U.S. Department of Labor, 2019). However, the rewards of an entrepreneurial life are clear and motivating. Entrepreneurs are innovative and offer new business ideas and concepts; they invest money into their businesses that can potentially reap large returns (De Nardi, Doctor, & Krane, 2007). Look at the passion and independence that drive you, but also make sure you enter into a new venture with eyes wide open. With a strong business plan and a clearly defined set of goals, you are more likely to succeed in your entrepreneurial undertaking. Bearing the responsibility of a start-up is definitely daunting, but if the freedom of the venture draws you like a magnet, then you may be one of those fortunate entrepreneurs who makes a go of it and enjoys the experience.

Key Terms

Entrepreneur	Business plan	Mission statement	Mentor
Exploratory phase	Branding	Logo	Mentoring
Hybrid entry model	Framing	Influencer	
Non-compete clause	Vision statement	Networking	

Discussion Questions

1. What qualities do you have that you share with entrepreneurs? Does being an entrepreneur appeal to you? Why or why not?

2. Why is networking important to the growth and sustenance of an entrepreneurial event planning company? Discuss ways in which you could establish and sustain connections through networking.

3. If you were to create your own event planning company, how would you differentiate yourself from other companies who do similar work? Why would branding be vital to your company's success?

Activity

After many years of working as an event planner, you have decided to become an entrepreneur and open your own event planning company. Using the steps below as a guide, begin to build and brand your company.

1. Give your company a name, a logo, and create its vision and mission statements.

2. List the things you would do before you officially launch your company by creating a bullet-point business plan.

3. Come up with at least 10 organizations, businesses, or community groups you would want to network with over the next year.

4. Draft an outline of what you would want to include on the new website for your company.

References

Abreu, M., Oner, O., Brouwer, A., & Leeuweng, E. (2019, July). Well-being effects of self-employment: A spatial inquiry. *Journal of Business Venturing* 34 (4), 589–607.

Allen, J. (2002). *The business of event planning*. Ontario, CAN: John Wiley & Sons.

Antonelli, D. (2014, May). Logo literacy: How a great logo informs branding and drives business. *Hudson Valley Business Journal* 6–8.

Arnell, P. (2010). *Shift: How to reinvent your business, your career, and your personal brand.* New York: Random House.

Bailyn, E. (2012). *Outsmarting social media: Profiting in the age of friendship marketing.* Fort Wayne, IN: Que Publishing.

Baron, R. & Shane, S. (2007). *Entrepreneurship: A process perspective.* Boston: Cengage.

Bivins, T. (2008). *Public relations writing: The essentials of style and format.* NY: McGraw Hill.

Bly, R. W. (2009). Set up a Web site to sell your services: Here's a rundown of what key elements to include and how to drum up business. *Writer, 122,* 41–42.

Bowser, J. (2010). *Eight traits of successful entrepreneurs.* Retrieved from http://www.mbda.gov/ blogger/starting-business/8-traits-successful-entrepreneurs do you have what-it-takes

Brown, B. (2018). *Dare to lead: Brave work, tough conversations, whole hearts.* NY: Random House.

Burke, R. (2006). *Project management: Planning and control techniques.* China: Everbest.

Burns, P. (2016). *Entrepreneurship and small business: Start-up, growth and maturity.* London: Palgrave/Macmillan.

Charette, P., Hooker, N.H., & Stanton, J. L. (2015). Framing and naming: A process to define a novel food category. *Food Quality and Preference, 40, Part A,* 147–151.

Chichester, M. (2014). Making connections to develop a professional network. *Nursing for Women's Health, 18,* 163–167.

Cockrum, J. (2011). *Free marketing: 101 low and no-cost ways to grow your business online & off.* Hoboken, NJ: John Wiley & Sons.

Collins, J., & Porras, J. (2002). *Built to last: Successful habits of visionary companies.* New York: HarperCollins.

Cooper, B., & Vlaskovits, P. (2013). *The lean entrepreneur: How visionaries create products, innovate with new ventures, and disrupt markets.* Hoboken, NJ: John Wiley & Sons.

Connors, R., & Smith, T. (2014). *The wisdom of Oz.* New York: Penguin Group.

Corbett, M. (1996). *The 33 ruthless rules of local advertising.* Houston, TX: Breakthru.

De Nardi, M., Doctor, P., & Krane, S. D. (2007). Evidence on entrepreneurs in the United States: Data from the 1989–2004 survey of consumer finances. *Economic Perspectives, 31,* 18–36.

Dickison, S. (2011). Networking: A how-to guide for both introverts and extroverts. *Writer, 124,* 10–12.

Douglas, E. (2009). Perceptions-looking at the world through entrepreneurial lenses. In A. L. Carsrud, & M. Irännback (Eds). *Understanding the entrepreneurial mind: Opening the black box* (pp. 3–22). New York: Springer.

Drucker, P. (1985). *Innovation and entrepreneurship.* New York: Harper & Row Publishers.

Ebrahimi, R. (2013, November). *Why entrepreneurs need good mentors.* Retrieved from http://www.forbes.com/sites/rodebrahimi/2013/11/14/why-entrepreneurs-need-good-mentors/

Ernst & Young, Nissenbaum, M.; Raasch, B. J., & Ratner, C. L. (2004). *Ernst & Young's personal financial planning guide.* Hoboken, NJ: John Wiley & Sons.

Fairhurst, G. T., (2011). *The power of framing: Creating the language of leadership.* San Francisco, CA: John Wiley & Sons.

Fairhurst, G. T., & Sarr, R. A. (1996). *The art of framing: Managing the language of leadership.* San Francisco, CA: Jossey-Bass.

Folta, T. B., Delmar, F., & Wennberg, K. (2010). Hybrid entrepreneurship. *Management Science, 56*, 253–269.

Forbes Communications Council (2017, August). 12 ways to communicate your brand to customers for increased recognition. Retrieved from https://www.forbes.com/sites/forbescommunic ationscouncil/2017/08/30/12-ways-to-communicate-your-brand-to-customers-for-increased-recognition/#fc293a41b5f6

Frederick, H., O'Connor, A., & Kuratko, D. F. (2019). *Entrepreneurship: Theory/Process/Practice.* (5th ed.). South Melbourne, Victoria, Australia: Cengage.

Furr, N. (2016, March). Hybrid business models look ugly, but they work. Retrieved from https://hbr.org/2016/03/hybrid-business-models-look-ugly-but-they-work.

Gladstone, J. (2007, April). Laying the foundation for your own PR firm. *Public Relations Tactics,* 17.

Goffman, E. (1986). *Frame analysis: An essay on the organization of experience.* Boston, MA: Northeastern University Press.

Hindle, K., & Mainprize, B. (2006). A systematic approach to writing and rating entrepreneurial business plans. *Journal of Private Equity, 9*, 7–22.

It's all none of your business. (2000). *American Music Teacher, 49*, 77–80.

Joseph, J.M. (2004). Making the leap: Starting your own firm. *Journal of Financial Planning, 17*, 44–50.

Kaweckyj, N. (2009). Networking within your professional association. *Dental Assistant, 78*, 12.

Kelley, T. (2001). *The art of innovation: Lessons in creativity from IDEO, America's leading design firm.* New York: Random House.

Kirzner, I. M. (2015). *Competition & Entrepreneurship.* Chicago and London: University of Chicago Press.

Klasen, D., & Clutterbuck, D. (2002). *Implementing mentoring schemes, a practical guide to successful programs.* Burlington, MA: Butterworth-Heinemann Lincere House.

Krost, C. (2017, Sept.). Want to use influencer marketing for your next event? Here's how. https://www.forbes.com/sites/forbescoachescouncil/2017/09/14/want-to-use-influencer-marketing-for-your-next-event-heres-how/#445b94246e80. Accessed Feb. 12, 2019.

Kuratko, D.F. (2017). *Entrepreneurship: Theory, process and practice.* (10th ed.). Boston: Cengage.

Mangold, W. G., & Faulds, D. J. (2009). Social media: The new hybrid element of the promotion mix. *Business Horizons, 52*, 357–365

Marsh, C., Guth, D., & Short, B. P. (2008). *Strategic writing: Multimedia writing for public relations, advertising and more.* Boston: Pearson/Allyn and Bacon.

Marshall, D. R., Davis, W. D., & Dibrell, C. (2016). Work to work enrichment: Employee innovation through hybrid entrepreneurship. *Academy of Management Proceedings 2016,* https://journals.aom.org/doi/abs/10.5465/ambpp.2016.11318abstract

Maslowski, I. (2005). The power of one: The challenges—and solutions—to growing your own business. *Public Relations Tactics, 12,* 12

McMullen, J., & Shepherd, D. A. (2006). Entrepreneurial action and the role of uncertainty in the theory of the entrepreneur. *Academy of Management Review, 31,* 1332–152.

Mitchellette, R. J. (2007). *Entrepreneurial decision making: A must-read for every aspiring entrepreneur.* Bloomington, IN: Xlibris Corporation.

Moran, J. S. (2010). *How to start a home-based event planning business.* Lanham, MD: Rowman & Littlefield.

Morgan, M. (2011). Reaching your career goals. *Strategic Finance, 93,* 16–61.

Nandram, S. S., & Samsom, K. J. (2008). *The spirit of entrepreneurship: Exploring the essence of entrepreneurship.* Berlin, Germany: Springer.

Nussbaum, B. (2013). *Creative intelligence: harnessing the power to create, connect, and inspire.* New York, NY: HarperCollins.

O'Brien, T. (2010). Time for an upgrade: Creating a 10-part business plan for career success. *Public Relations Tactics, 17,* 12.

Palmer, K. (2014). *The economy of you: Discover your inner entrepreneur and recession-proof your life.* New York: AMACOM.

Patel, S. (2014, November). *Why every entrepreneur needs a mentor.* Retrieved from http://www.forbes.com/sites/sujanpatel/2014/11/12/why-every-entrepreneur-needs-a-mentor/2/

Pfister, R. E., & Tierney, P. T. (2009). *Recreation, event, and tourism businesses: start-up and sustainable operations.* Champaign, IL: Human Kinetics.

Popyk, B. (2015). Non-traditional advertising ideas that work. *Music Trades, 162,* 56.

Raffiee, J., & Feng, J. (2014). Should I quit my day job?: A hybrid path to entrepreneurship. *Academy of Management Journal, 57,* 936–963.

Roman, L. M. (2007). There's no business like your own business. *RN, 70,* 38–43.

Raj, R., Walters, P., & Rashid, T. (2011). *Events management: Principles and practices.* Thousand Oaks, CA: Sage.

Rittscher, S. (2012). *Six keys to successful networking for entrepreneurs.* Retrieved from http://www.forbes.com/sites/susanrittscher/2012/05/31/six-keys-to-successful-networking-for-entrepreneurs/

Santarelli, E., & Vivarelli, M. (2007). Entrepreneurship and the process of firms' entry, survival and growth. *Industrial and Corporate Change, 16,* 455–488.

Schulz, M., Urbig, D., & Procher, V. (2016). Hybrid entrepreneurship and public policy: the case of firm entry deregulation. *Journal of Business Venturing, 31,* 272–286.

Sinek, S. (2009). *Start with why.* NY: Penguin.

Staples, Inc. (2015, February). *Staples brings brands to life with professional logo design Services.* Retrieved from http://www.businesswire.com/news/home/20150212005707/en/Staples-Brings-Brands-Life-Professional-Logo-Design#.VXOnHUajIgQ

Sullivan, R. (2000). Entrepreneurial learning and mentoring. *International Journal of Entrepreneurial Behavior & Research, 6,* 160–175.

U.S. Dept. of Labor, Bureau of Labor Statistics. (2019). *Survival rate of new firms.* Retrieved from http://www.bls.gov/bdm/us_age_naics_00_table1.txt

Van der Wagen, L., & White, L. (2018). *Event management: For tourism, cultural, business and sporting events.* South Melbourne, Victoria, Australia: Cengage.

Vesper, J.F., & Vesper, K.H. (1993). Writing a business plan: The total term assignment. *Bulletin of the Association for Business Communication, 56,* 29–32.

What to do when starting a new business: Checklist (1995). *Journal of Accountancy, 179,* 34.

APPENDICES

APPENDIX A

Event Budget—Expenses

Totals	
Total Income	$
Total Expenses	$
Total Profit/Loss	$

Site Rental:		
	Projected	Actual
Rental Fees		
Insurance		
Staff		
Equipment		
Total	$	$

Advertising:		
	Projected	Actual
Print		
T.V./Radio		
Total	$	$

Programming:

	Projected	Actual
Fees		
Hotels		
Travel		
Total	$	$

Decorations:

	Projected	Actual
Lighting		
Total	$	$

Total Expenses

	Proposed	Actual
Total	$	$

Event Budget—Income

Tickets:

	Projected	Actual
Adults		
Children		
Other		
Total	$	$

Advertisements:

	Projected	Actual
Total	$	$

Sales:

	Projected	Actual
Merchandise		
Food		
Total	$	$

Total Income

	Proposed	Actual
Total	$	$

APPENDIX B

National Communication Association

National Office
1765 N Street, NW
Washington, DC 20036

202-464-4622
fax 202-464-4600
http://www.natcom.org

October 14, 2010

Dear Colleagues,

We write once again to keep you apprised of recent developments regarding the labor situation at the Hilton San Francisco Union Square, NCA's headquarter convention hotel for 2010. As you likely recall, the collective bargaining agreement between United Here! Local 2, which represents approximately 800 workers at our convention hotels, expired in August, 2009. Since that time, both of our convention hotels and their workers have continued to operate under the terms of the expired agreement while working toward ratification of a new contract. For additional background information about this situation, please refer to our earlier correspondence.

Yesterday, the union called a limited strike to last for 6 days at the Hilton San Francisco Union Square. This strike is scheduled to end at 4:00 a.m. on Tuesday, October 19, at which time workers will resume their regular duties at the hotel. We have no reason to believe that another strike is imminent at the Hilton. The hotel is currently functioning normally with sufficient staff and continues to offer its usual services and maintain its operating standards.

The union has called a few short-term strikes at various hotels in San Francisco during the last fourteen months. It has not been the union's practice to have more than one strike at a single hotel within a short time period, but rather to move among different hotel locations in the city. The one previous three-day strike at the Hilton took place in April, 2010.

Our strong hope is that negotiations can be completed to both the workers' and management's satisfaction by the time we meet next month. However, given that the situation is currently in flux, we want to remind you that NCA has developed a number of options for different scenarios. One option is alternate meeting space at the San Francisco State University Downtown Campus, and there is still space available at this location. For more information about SFSU as well as details on relevant programming, electronic options, and amended registration policy and services, please visit the Convention Session Alternatives webpage.

The number of attendees registered to join us in San Francisco continues to be comparable with recent years. Our room block at the Hilton is almost full, and rooms are still available at the Parc 55 hotel. Parc 55 is not under boycott or threat of strike by the union at this time, and we do not expect it to be when our convention is held.

We understand that this is a difficult situation, and the choices we all are making are complicated. We want you to know that we are listening to your feedback and working hard to respond with what we believe are the most responsible and flexible options for the association and its members.

We continue to monitor the situation on a regular basis, and we will keep you informed on a regular basis. You might know that we created a dedicated webpage last spring that includes the most up to date information available to us as well as links to the union, hotel, and city to help keep you abreast of developments. We hope you will visit it, and of course you should always feel free to contact us directly with your questions and concerns.

We look forward to an excellent convention that responds to our attendees' intellectual and professional needs.

Best,
Dawn O. Braithwaite, NCA President
Lynn H. Turner, NCA First Vice President and Primary Convention Planner
Nancy Kidd, Executive Director

APPENDIX C

NCA 2010 Convention in San Francisco
Onsite Considerations in the Event of a Labor Action

The collective bargaining agreement between United Here! Local 2, which represents approximately 800 workers at our convention hotels, expired in August, 2009. Since that time, both of our convention hotels and their workers have continued to operate under the terms of the expired agreement. There have been two strikes of short duration at the Hilton San Francisco in recent months and a few small demonstrations. We have no reason to believe there will be any actions while we are meeting in San Francisco, but we are providing you with the following information in the event of a labor action.

Communications

We are committed to keeping attendees up-to-date on any actions that may occur while we are onsite. We will be enacting an email and text message alert system to notify attendees if any action does occur during the convention. If you would like to sign up for either or both services, please visit the Cyber Café and access the San Francisco Update Web page at www.natcom.org/SFUpdates. You will find an opt-in form for email alerts as well as information on how to add your mobile phone to the text message alert list.

Personal Security

Both the Hilton San Francisco security staff and the San Francisco Police Department are responsible for the safety of guests. The main entrance to the Hilton San Francisco (O'Farrell Street) is the area where an action would most likely occur. A section of this entrance will be kept clear for guests entering and exiting the hotel under any circumstances. There are also additional entrances to the Hilton San Francisco on Taylor Street and Ellis Street (via the Hilton parking entrance) available for guest use. An attendee may request a Hilton San Francisco hotel security staff escort to exit/enter the building at any time. Please notify the Hilton San Francisco security staff (dial 415-771-1400 ext. 6200 from any outside line or dial extension 6200 from any Hilton house phone) if you would like an escort. If you have any other security concerns, please contact a member of the NCA national office staff.

Hotel Operations

The Hilton San Francisco has a comprehensive plan for covering areas of hotel operation that may be affected by an employee walkout or slow down. During a three-day employee walkout in April and a more recent six-day walkout in October, the hotel experienced minimal operational disruption.

APPENDIX D

Sample Event Planner Contract

Host: _____

Title: _____

Company: _____

Phone: _____

Email: _____

Fax: _____

Address: _____

Planner: _____

Event: _____

Company: _____

Phone: _____

Email: _____

Fax: _____

Address: _____

This document serves as a binding contract between **{Host's Name}**, hereafter known as "Host," and **{Planner's Name}**, hereafter known as "Planner," signed **{date}**. The Host desires to engage the services of the Planner for the **{Name}** event on **{date(s)}** at **{location(s)}**. Both parties agree to abide by the following conditions:

1. The Event will be as follows: **{Description of event.}**
2. The Planner will be in charge of the following aspects of the event: **{Attach addendum detailing every aspect for which the Planner will be responsible.}**
3. The Host will pay the Planner $**{amount}** for all services rendered or **{number}** hours of work, with the option to negotiate further payment for more hours worked. The Planner will be given an initial amount of $**{amount}** for **{fees, deposits, and down payments, etc.}** The Planner will receive the additional **{amount}**% at the completion of the event.
4. In addition to event design, Planner's duties will include but not be limited to **{drawing up contracts for venue/vendor, and putting down deposits, etc.}**
5. Necessary lodging/travel costs incurred by the Planner **{will/will not}** be covered by the Host.
6. The Planner agrees to use Host's company logo and no other where desired.
7. The Host agrees to acknowledge the Planner's services in **{place, aspect}**, including the Planner's logo.
8. The Host will not enter into any contracts on behalf of the Planner or without the Planner's knowledge and consent.

9. If the Host cancels within {**days**} of the event they will be refunded {**amount**}% of the original fee. If the Host cancels within {**days**} of the event they will receive {**amount**}%, and after {**days**} no refund will be given.

10. If the Planner cancels, {**he/she**} will either provide a substitute planner or refund the full fee, minus the cost of nonrefundable deposits.

_____   _____

(Host's Signature)   (Planner's Signature)

_____   _____

(Date)   (Date)

APPENDIX E

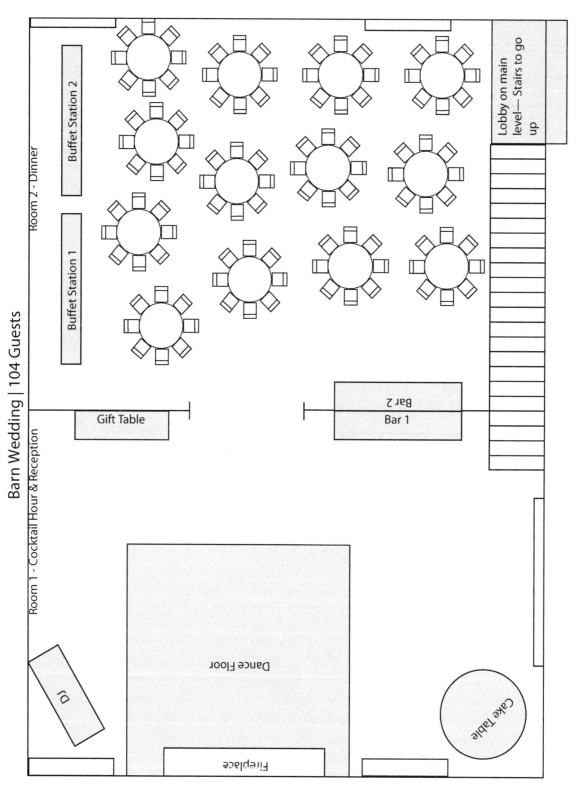

Corporate Meeting & Post-Meeting Reception | Hotel

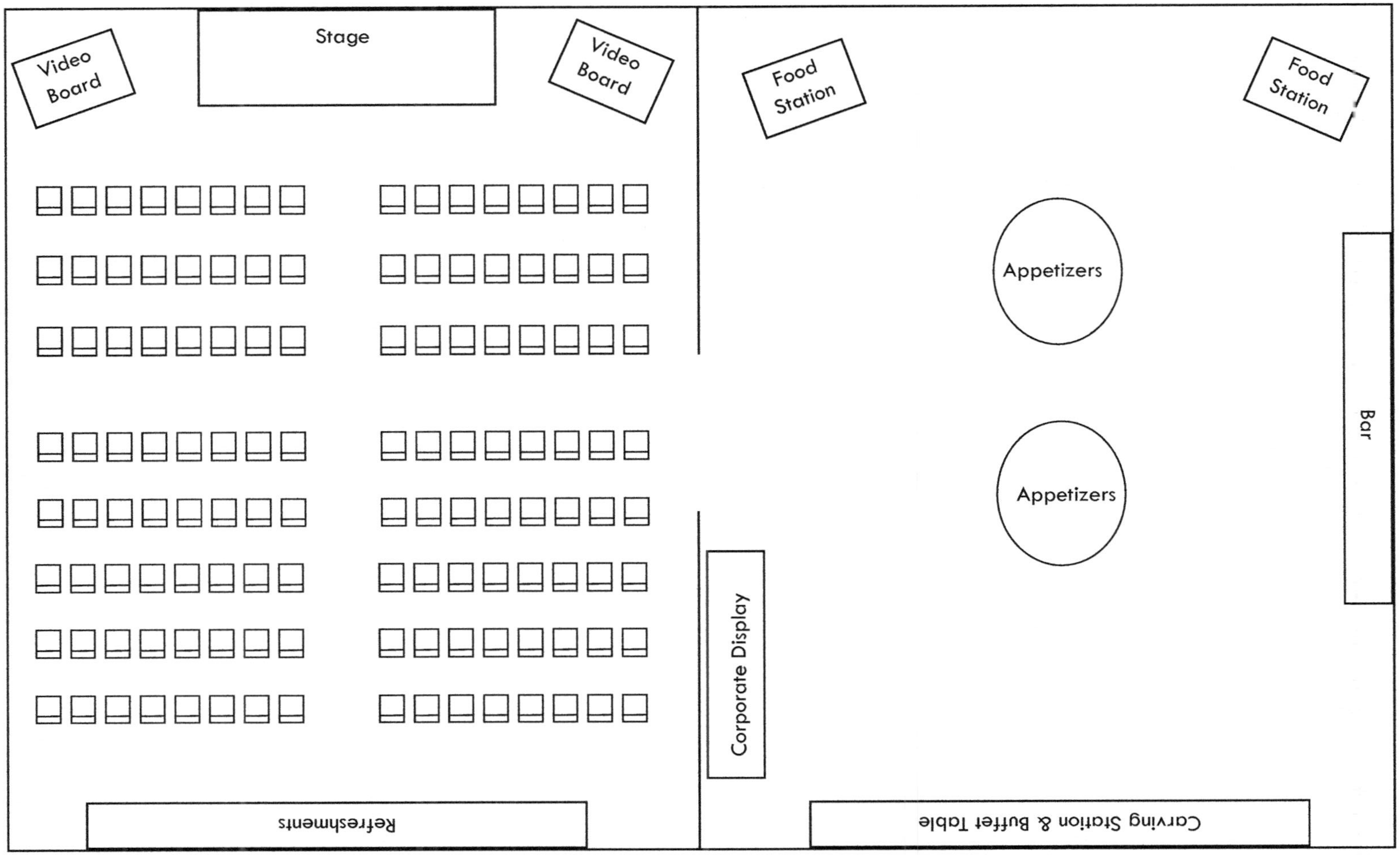

Bar

Food Station

Food Station

Appetizers

Appetizers

Carving Station & Buffet Table

Corporate Display

Video Board

Stage

Video Board

Refreshments

APPENDIX F

Smith/Jones wedding	7	8	9	10	11	12	1	2	2:30	3	3:15	3:30
										CEREMONY		
Staff set up at site	■	■	■	■	■	■	■	■				
Table decorations					■	■	■	■				
Florist set up				■	■	■	■	■				
Band set up at site					■	■	■	■				
Lighting set up					■	■	■	■				
Cake & treat set up					■	■	■	■				
Caterer set up						■	■	■	■	■		
Photobooth set up							■	■	■	■		
Bartender set up							■	■	■	■		
Photographer/video	■	■	■	■	■	■	■	■	■	■	■	■
Bride/Groom prepare										■		
Ministers arrive/in place								■	■	■	■	
Photos of wedding party								■	■	■		
Ceremony /staff ready										■		
Guests to reception												
Bar opens for guests												
Photobooth opens												
Wedding party entrance												
Bride/Groom first dance												
Toasts wedding party												
Dinner served in buffet												
Bride/Groom cut cake												
Other dances in party												
Dancing open for all												
Bride/groom off												
Guests depart												
Staff clean up/depart												

3:45	4	4:15	4:30	4:45	5	5:30	6	7	8	9	10	Smith/Jones wedding
	COCKTAIL HOUR/RECEPTION	▓	▓	▓	▓	▓	▓	▓	▓			
												Staff set up at site
												Table decorations
												Florist set up
												Band set up at site
												Lighting set up
												Cake & treat set up
												Caterer set up
												Photobooth set up
												Bartender set up
▓	▓	▓	▓	▓	▓	▓	▓	▓	▓	▓		Photographer/video
												Bride/Groom prepare
▓												Ministers arrive/in place
	▓	▓										Photos of wedding party
	▓											Ceremony /staff ready
	▓	▓	▓	▓								Guests to reception
	▓	▓	▓	▓		▓	▓					Bar opens for guests
	▓	▓	▓	▓	▓							Photobooth opens
												Wedding party entrance
												Bride/Groom first dance
					▓							Toasts wedding party
					▓	▓						Dinner served in buffet
							▓					Bride/Groom cut cake
												Other dances in party
							▓	▓				Dancing open for all
									▓			Bride/groom off
												Guests depart
												Staff clean up/depart

APPENDIX G

Additional Case Studies

Listening as the Key to Understanding Your Stakeholders

Julie Wagner, Vice President, Community Affairs,
CareFirst BlueCross BlueShield (former Community Relations Director, Baltimore Orioles)

The event can be great, the weather could be terrific, the attendance could be outstanding, the food might be delicious, and the event could be flawless, but if you have not listened to your clients and achieved their goals and their vision, then you have not succeeded at presenting an effective event.

What makes an event a success is knowing what your clients want to achieve; you have listened to their desires and goals in terms of executing a successful event. For example, the All-Star Celebration in 1993 was the first time Major League Baseball extended the All-Star experience beyond the three-day break to include community partners and citizens beyond the ballpark. For this week-long celebration, the Baltimore Orioles had several clients, the primary one being Major League Baseball and others including members of civic, local, and state groups. Several entities had to come together and listen to a variety of ideas being presented in Baltimore for the week-long festivities by the All-Star Week Committee. When people assemble for this type of brainstorming committee, they must listen to all ideas in order to come away with the best ones. Listening to ideas and suggestions takes time. The event planner's job is to listen carefully and identify whom the primary and secondary stakeholders are and determine how to meet their objectives.

In the All-Star Week example, the primary stakeholders were Major League Baseball, who had awarded Baltimore the All-Star Game and celebrations, and the ownership of the Baltimore Orioles (because it was their reputation at risk). In order to satisfy Major League Baseball, the committee clearly identified goals and met many times to set objectives, including the following: providing housing for more than 1,000 people; planning a gala; facilitating the All-Star FanFest experience; hosting the All-Star workout day and Home Run Derby; and producing the actual All-Star Game. A million details went into the planning and coordinating of baseball's mid-season showcase. The overall goal was to welcome guests to all events, transport them with ease, and provide a great takeaway experience. To achieve these goals, we listened to the stakeholders and instituted training for 1,000 volunteers and hotel staff, engaged cab drivers by providing hats with All-Star logos for them to wear, created All-Star Week schedules with all the events listed, collaborated with the state to assist with ease of transportation at the airport, and worked closely with the city to spotlight Baltimore's image.

Our secondary stakeholders included state and local officials, members of the tourism industry, minority community leaders, and various prominent Baltimore figures important to the Orioles. By listening to input from the Baltimore community, the committee focused on offering an experience that extended beyond the ballpark. Making the All-Star celebration accessible and inclusive for those who did not have a ticket to the game was the number one priority. In this way, the Orioles and the secondary stakeholders achieved that goal. The Orioles and their event planners brought people to Baltimore City; fans visited museums, bars, and restaurants; a free outdoor concert engaged the public; and the Orioles honored Baltimore's rich Negro League history with a celebration both on the field and at All-Star FanFest, which tens of thousands of people attended.

Contributed by Julie Wagner. Copyright © Kendall Hunt Publishing Company.

Managing Teams through Collaborative Interpersona Communication

CASE STUDY

Sandy Hillman, President, Sandy Hillman Communications

Several years ago, one of our major clients bought an even larger company. Integrating cultures is always a difficult thing to do, but this particular acquisition was fraught with potential problems, particularly with employees at all levels. Our solution was to create a series of employee events that would introduce them to and define their new ownership. Strong interpersonal relationships and communication skills were key to getting the C-suite (a term that refers to corporate officers and directors) to agree to this strategy and ultimately executing dozens of events across the country. First, upper management was concerned about becoming the central focus of the merger and exposing themselves to 100,000 employees over the course of the first 10 days they owned the business. Based on our long-term relationship and their faith in our decision-making, they agreed to move forward with our idea.

From beginning to end, the success of this effort was all about communication: initially, to get CEO buy in and to get all of upper management at the newly acquired entities to embrace the notion of their new boss coming into "their" territory and galvanizing "their" troops. In order to develop a supportive environment, we met with management in every single property and upper management from the to-be-acquired company. We gained their trust and collaboration through transparent, continuous in-person and written communication. They were privy to everything we were doing from speeches to internal web strategy to employee gifts. They were advised about every aspect of the complex all-employee events, including audio-visual, lunches, dinners, decor, and transportation. There were no surprises. They felt included rather than excluded. In the end, they became internal boosters because we were diligent and dedicated to fostering trust and support through collaborative interpersonal communication.

The internal team was only one part of the event management equation. External resources were extensive. We hired and managed no less than 10 consultant teams each with major responsibilities, all of whom had to be seamlessly integrated into the production process, which was ultimately nineteen events over 10 days in different locations around the country. A number of the consultants had similar skills so each thought their expertise and ideas should prevail. Our interpersonal communication skills were put to the test with these associates as we worked to make these bicoastal teams collaborative. All parties had to stay in their own lanes and deliver exactly what we were expecting. No deviation. That took disciplined communication. We had to be both forceful and sensitive, keeping everyone motivated, excited, and invested in the effort. In the end, the result was triumphal, and each team—whether internal or external—would tell you that it was their work that was responsible for the extraordinary results.

CASE STUDY

Under Armour's Fall Family Fun Day at Padonia Park Club

Matt Musgrove, CEO and President, Padonia Park Club

Whether we are planning an event or are in the business of hosting and catering events, we wish we had endless budgets, but this is usually not the case. Many factors come into play when it comes to budgeting for a large or small event. Often the host planning the event has to start pricing out different costs before a budget can even be established. Rarely, if ever, is the budget unlimited, even when the host's pockets are deep.

The average cost of a wedding in the United States, for instance, is over $25,000. Typically the first question that a bride and groom ask when they call a venue is, "What are your prices?" Weddings are often the first event they are planning together, and they are not sure where to start. When calling venues and vendors, clients should let them know what their budget is up front, for any kind of event. Many people are concerned that by doing this, they are going to be taken advantage of, but being honest allows both parties to decide if collaboration will work.

An event budget is broken down into categories of standard costs for each part of the event. Many times the client will choose the venue first, as a date must be set for the event, and vendors can be selected based on their availability on that date. Key budgeting categories for the client include the following:

- Venue
- Catering—food and beverage
- Decorations
- Entertainment—photographer, DJs, florist, performers, etc.
- Insurance and Taxes
- Printing
- Labor
- Other—Something always comes up and adds to the budget, no matter how much planning occurs.

© Matt Musgrove

Budgets demand a great deal of creativity in applying the numbers. In 2013, Under Armour, a Baltimore-based sports and apparel company, was looking to host an appreciation event for its employees. The company wanted a themed event on a Saturday in October. What better theme for an October event than Halloween? The company wanted to invite 3,000 of its Baltimore-based employees to the event, so finding a large venue was the first task. Under Armour called Padonia Park Club.

Padonia Park Club is a 30-acre country club that hosts hundreds of social and corporate events annually. The venue is located about 25 minutes north of the employees' work location in Baltimore. In addition to costs, clients should consider travel time, transportation, and parking. With thousands of guests attending, plenty of parking was required, which the venue could accommodate. Many guests also use public transportation, so a shuttle bus was arranged to run between the venue and the nearby bus and train stations. Transportation problems at the beginning of an event can ruin the entire day for guests.

In choosing Padonia Park Club, the host was able to include venue and catering costs within one company, a move that will usually save the host money. The club itself performed all of the catering under the leadership of their executive chef, whose simple yet custom-designed menu made the event welcoming and cost-effective. Additionally, Padonia Park Club has amusement amenities including sports fields, paddle boating on a lake, a baseball diamond, and room for other activities. These amenities also save the host from bringing in additional amusements via an outside vendor. If you are able to find venues and vendors that perform multiple duties, it allows for substantial savings.

Padonia Park Club hosts many company picnics throughout the year, so activities such as hayrides, a Trick-Or-Treat trail with costumed characters, and a hay maze are events it has hosted before and indeed provided for Under Armour's festivities—another way of saving money since additional outside vendors were not necessary. Decorations were also available through Padonia Park Club, and guests enjoyed an immersive environment. Most of the decorations were available through the club, and a balloon vendor offered the finishing touches.

Forming an event committee is important so that you can hear the ideas of others. It is vital to discuss the budget of the event so that everyone is conscious of the costs, but someone needs to exercise budgetary leadership. Committee members might have terrific ideas, but an event can have too much going on at once, which can escalate the budget. It is best to keep it simple. Many times, people working together can come up with inexpensive ways to make a good event great. Committee members might also have connections to local vendors they know or have worked with in the past, which can usually save money. Committee members can also help perform tasks in preparation for and during the event, which can save costs.

Branding an event creates a positive energy that gets guests excited to attend. In the case of Under Armour, the company worked with Padonia Park Club to create a logo using the event name *Fall Family Fun Day*, in conjunction with Padonia Park Club. This logo appeared on event invitations, eblasts, and signage. Under Armour even provided each of its guests with an athletic bag with the branded event logo for the trick-or-treat trail, which was a great takeaway from the event. These types of branded items leave a lasting impression for years to come.

In attendance were the mascots from the Baltimore Orioles and the Baltimore Ravens. Padonia Park's in-house DJ provided music and hosted a costume contest among the Under Armour employees. Activities like these create engagement among the guests and add little cost to the event. While the budget communicates the bottom line of an event, it must also communicate so much more than just the financial costs.

Contributed by Matt Musgrove. Copyright © Kendall Hunt Publishing Company.

CASE STUDY — Planning a Marketing Campaign for the Circus

Edie Brown, Principal, Edie Brown and Associates

© Diana Hlevnjak/Shutterstock.com

The world-famous Ringling Bros. and Barnum & Bailey Circus, produced by Feld Entertainment, comes to Baltimore annually. Year after year, the challenge has been to ensure that Ringling Bros. continues to succeed in spite of growing competition in the entertainment industry. Perhaps most difficult is keeping the image of the circus "cool" in an age of social media domination among those who in the past have populated the event. To achieve maximum reach to the core audience (youths ages 7–16), we have to plan and execute an annual integrated marketing communication campaign that includes research, grassroots media, social media and online campaigns, community relations, and general brand awareness. This means targeting a wide variety of audiences to fill the seats in the local arena where the circus sets up.

We have developed a keen understanding of how to communicate effectively to tweens, teens, and parents, and how to motivate them to act. This is, of course, in addition to the traditional forms of media. For example, in a newer means of outreach, we have been working closely with mom bloggers throughout the area to inform and educate them about the circus event and to obtain necessary buy-in (think "Kid Tested, Mother Approved"). With some research and educated appeals to this population, we are able to interest a new generation of youth in a visit to the Big Top. We also engage social media sites as a way to build buzz and inform area youth about what they will love during a visit to the circus.

To build media awareness, we drop off gifts to key media figures, host an opening night party for the media that includes food and photo opportunities for guests, arrange for phone and print interviews, and hold an early morning public relations event for the TV stations. This event consists of all four local TV stations either going live or taping an act, such as acrobats, from the show. Building and fostering a relationship with those in the media is perhaps one of the most essential tasks of public relations and promotions professionals. Being attentive to their needs, prepared for their questions, and eager to accommodate media requests will help the PR professional reap rewards—even if the results are not immediate. As its name suggests, public relations is about relationship building, which demands honesty, trust, availability, and reliability. These characteristics cannot be discounted in any relationship, but they are of utmost importance in a field where everyone wants a piece of the news.

Sometimes getting good public relations and promotional results means taking a new approach to a story or an event that occurs yearly. In order to respond to some of the public concerns about circus elephants, for instance, some publicity centered on the fact that the circus has set up its own research Center for Elephant Conservation in Florida, and will eventually move all of its elephants there within a few years. Instead of focusing on the elephants, the news media were treated to information about a new ringmaster from New York City—Ringling's first African-American ringmaster—who would be anchoring the new "Legends" show. A familiar story suddenly became fresh again and received a lot more notice than it might have. Good integrated marketing communication means thinking ahead to see obstacles, realize new angles, and develop effective strategies for reaching the public.

So You Think You Want To Be Your Own Boss?

Paul Wolman, Principal, WolmanEdge
(Feats was ranked an 8-time Top 50 Event Company World-Wide by
Special Events Magazine and a 2015 Future 50 Fast-Growth Company by Smart CEO)

If you are focused on building great wealth, business school is a good place to start. You will explore business models, think about scale, and profits, profits, profits.

If you are like me, you probably have a very different motivator. I learned I thrive on being acknowledged and appreciated for what I do for others, and I have a drive to achieve. Others have a passion for great design. I recommend identifying what drives you first.

After co-founding a 15-year entertainment business starting in junior high, I thought I would go to law school and "do something" with my life. Bored, after graduation I joined a 30-person ad agency. I worked with business owners, digging into what good marketing and communication could do for them. Equally important, I was fortunate to work directly with the agency owner. Without realizing it, I was observing leadership styles, management techniques, culture, and how to make money. I recommend working for someone else first. Learn all you can—build your perspective, experience challenges, and test solutions before taking that leap.

After four years at the agency, I was unhappy.

I had saved a little money and had access to borrow a little more. When an old, dying retail magic shop I had loved as a kid came up for sale, I jumped. Against the advice of a business advisor and accountant, off I went to prove them wrong. The business lost money in the first two years but would soon become the catalyst for our successful event strategy, design, and production business today.

If you are not a risk-taker, but you have a passion for the work, find a partner who is willing to take a second mortgage, or is able to get appropriate lines of credit. Have the ability to fund yourself for four to six months—with savings, with loans you can pay back, or perhaps with a second income while you are working to bring in an initial and ultimately sustainable client revenue base.

I had no road map. No one had prepared me for the retail business. If you cannot work without a road map or business plan, buy a franchise. Why? Because the world changes; disrupters come along, the economy will tank, and good people will leave you hanging. And there's always another person ready to do something faster, better, or for less. Keep one eye out for that next opportunity. We are in an ever-evolving global economy; there will always be someone ready to disrupt you.

Therefore, let no one out-network you. From day one, I spent lunches and evenings attending every networking event I could to build a strong network of support and promote what we do. After we had been in business for five or six years, a well-financed, brash young competitor marched into town. While we were continuing to focus on current customers, he went door-to-door, bad-mouthing us to each of them. He took out a two-page ad in the local paper that ran during the Summer Olympics. I will never forget the headline: The Thrill of Victory, The Agony of deFEATS (our company's name was P. W. FEATS). My heart sank. He was attacking the one vulnerable area in those days—we had grown quickly and were concerned about being too busy to give our clients the attention they each deserved. But, because we had built a solid company foundation with so many loyal fans, our good clients laughed him out of town.

Finally, and most importantly, recruit and grow great people. We are each only as good as those around us—full time, part time, or those we contract. This includes leveraging yourself. A successful real estate broker we know has three assistants who research, market, and schedule her. What is your highest priority and best use of time at the moment? Go do that. And find others to do the rest.

Contributed by Paul Wolman. Copyright © Kendall Hunt Publishing Company.

GLOSSARY

A

Accommodating: In conflict situations, a type of behavior that occurs when one is always willing to give in to the other person at any cost (Chapter 12).

Action-oriented listeners: Those who focus on the task during listening (Chapter 2).

Advertising: The controlled use of media ensuring that a message reaches the audience in exactly the form it was intended and at the time it was intended; it can be print, broadcast, or Web-based (Chapter 13).

Affective stage: In Social Penetration Theory, the inner core of social penetration that examines ideas such as value systems and beliefs (Chapter 2).

Ambiance: All of the background features of an environment (Chapter 9).

Americans with Disabilities Act (ADA): The federal law that prohibits discrimination and ensures equal opportunity for persons with disabilities in employment, State and local government services, public accommodations, commercial facilities, and transportation (Chapter 3).

Amount: In self-disclosure, the frequency and the duration of the disclosure (Chapter 2)

Appreciative listening: A type of listening that occurs when people attend for pleasure or enjoyment (Chapter 2).

ARFD: Apologize, Review, Fix and follow up, Document (Chapter 5).

Argument: A rhetorical approach that relies on a logical order that is grounded in reason, research and evidence (Chapter 12).

Artifacts: All of those pieces of the outward physical appearance, including clothing and other accessories, and most obviously one's facial features, hair and hair style, posture, and body type (Chapter 3).

Assessing: In the context of Emotional Intelligence, the ability to be able to produce emotions that help you make a decision (Chapter 14).

Atmosphere lighting: A kind of lighting used to highlight special features at an event (Chapter 9).

Attribution Theory: A theory that seeks to explain why people do the things they do (Chapter 2).

Attributions: Perceived causes that individuals select or construct for events in their lives (Chapter 2).

Authenticity: In the context of dialogue, being direct, honest and straightforward in communicating all information and feelings that are relevant and legitimate for the subject at hand (Chapter 1).

Autocratic leadership: A type of leadership style that focuses on one person holding all the power to make decisions (Chapter 14).

Availability: Accessibility for service or help (Chapter 4).

Avoiding: In conflict situations, a behavior that occurs when individuals intentionally remove themselves from the situation (Chapter 12).

B

Baby Boomers: Those born approximately between 1946 and 1964 (Chapter 5).

Back-of-house workers: Those in hospitality who deal with housekeeping, food, and engineering, and whom guests seldom see (Chapter 5)

Backlighting: A type of lighting used behind a performer or speaker to make them visually stand out from the backdrop (Chapter 9).

Ballyhoo: A way to get an audience excited by moving a spotlight in a fast, random fashion all around the room (Chapter 9).

BATNA: Best Alternative to Negotiated Agreement; a strategy that articulates a fall-back plan in an event (Chapter 8).

Behavioral uncertainty: In Social Penetration Theory, the belief that the actions of others is often unpredictable (Chapter 2).

Black hat: In the context of the Six Thinking Hats, the one who evaluates the negative aspects and plays devil's advocate toward decisions (Chapter 6).

Blanked Expressors: In facial displays, those who believe they are expressing emotions but actually show very little expression (Chapter 3).

Blue hat: In the context of the Six Thinking Hats, the one who creates summaries, conclusions and overviews of the decision-making process (Chapter 6).

Brainstorming: The process by which groups are able to create new ideas or solve problems (Chapters 5 and 6).

Brand: The "image" or personality of a product, service, or event (Chapter 13).

Branding: The process of distinguishing a product, service or person through quality delivery that adds incremental value to the client by anticipating, innovating, and excelling at execution (Chapter 15).

Breach of contract: An occurrence in which one of the contract signers fails to uphold his or her part of the agreement (Chapter 8).

Breadth: In self-disclosure, the amount of information disclosed (Chapter 2).

Budget: A formal statement by management of its plans for a given time period which will be used as a guide during that period (Chapter 7).

Budgetary risk prevention plan: A device that looks ahead of an event in order to reduce the likelihood or severity of a possible loss (Chapter 7).

Bureaucratic leadership: A type of leadership style in which the procedures and rules guide one's action (Chapter 14).

Business plan: A written framework that embraces the vision for the company or enterprise, including its goals for its niche market and market analysis (Chapter 15).

Business savvy: The ability to comprehend the social and economic systems and realities that affect one's success in the marketplace (Chapter 4).

C

Channel: The means by which a message is sent (Chapter 1).

Charismatic leadership: A type of leadership style that focuses on infusing energy and eagerness into a team's efforts (Chapter 14).

Chronemics: The study of time, focusing on the concepts and process of how people manage their formal and informal obligations in relation to time (Chapter 3).

Cognitive flexibility: The ability to create a mindset of continual change (Chapter 4).

Cognitive uncertainty: In Social Penetration Theory, insecurity about another's beliefs or attitudes (Chapter 2).

Collaborating: In conflict situations, the optimal method of creating positive alternatives for everyone involved; a constructive response to conflict (Chapter 12).

Communication: A complex process with many components involving the creation of a message through which the receiver interprets the sender's meaning (Chapter 1).

Communication apprehension: Fear associated with communicating with another person (Chapter 14).

Communication competence: A dyadic process that includes one's self-perceptions of social/communication skills and is contingent upon the other's perception of one's social/communication skills (Chapter 1).

Communication ethics: The philosophy of communication brought into engaged communicative application in the marketplace of ideas (Chapter 8).

Competing: In conflict situations, the act of striving to gain something, focusing on the struggle of who is going to win a conflict (Chapter 12).

Comprehensive listening: A type of listening that occurs when people are focusing on understanding the message of a speaker (Chapter 2).

Compromising: In conflict situations, behavior that requires both parties to make sacrifices to accommodate the other (Chapter 12).

Confirmation: In the context of dialogue, affirming and not merely tolerating a partner in dialogue, even though we oppose her or him on some specific matter (Chapter 1).

Conflict: A sizeable disagreement situated in perceptions, goals and values and involves heightened senses and emotions (Chapter 12).

Conflict management: A type of behavior that works from a dialogic approach that looks at the conflict from all sides, uncovering various assumptions of what is fair in a particular situation (Chapter 12).

Conflict map: A practical theory that frames the coordinates of a conflict (Chapter 12).

Conflict resolution: A strategy that focuses on examining the facts of the situation to solve the issue (Chapter 12).

Consumer-generated media: Another name for social media (Chapter 13).

Content-oriented listeners: Those who are more critical and evaluate what they hear during listening (Chapter 2).

Context: The historical, physical, social, psychological and cultural setting of the communication that helps people understand any distortions or miscommunications in the message (Chapters 1 and 3).

Context attribution: The belief that behavior is derived from a combination of one's own motives or behaviors combined with a task or situation (Chapter 2).

Contract: An agreement that stipulates what is expected of all parties and notes what will occur should a difficulty arise (Chapter 8).

Convention: a large, purposeful gathering of people with common interests or goals (Chapter 11).

Convention and Visitors Bureau (CVB): A not-for-profit organization that offers information and services to those from out of town (Chapter 9).

Costs: In Social Exchange Theory, the negative aspects of a relationship (Chapter 7).

Creative problem solving: A method of discovery that requires individuals to identify, construct, search, and acquire information, generate ideas, and then select, evaluate, and implement them (Chapter 6).

Creativity: The development of ideas explained by new combinations or regrouping and restructuring of elements that involve thinking (Chapter 6).

Crisis: A challenging event that includes unexpected, unique moments that can cause high levels of uncertainty and chaos (Chapter 12).

Critical listening: A type of listening that occurs when the goal is to evaluate a message for purposes of accepting or rejecting the argument (Chapter 2).

Critical path: The sequence of stages that indicate the minimum time needed for an event's duration (Chapter 4).

Critical Path Method: A plan in which all the connected jobs of a project are laid out in paths according to the order they must be performed, with a time listed for completion (Chapter 4).

Criticism: The analysis and/or judgment of a new or innovative idea with regard to creativity (Chapter 6).

Cross-promotion: A method of marketing that targets buyers of a product with an offer to purchase a related product (Chapter 13).

D

Decoding: The cognitive process of unpacking the meaning of a message (Chapter 1).

Delegation: The act of giving over work responsibilities in varying degrees to co-workers or helpers (Chapter 14).

Delphi Technique: A business process in which several cycles of questions are asked and re-asked in order to look at future possibilities (Chapter 5).

Democratic leadership: A type of leadership style in which there is a participatory factor in decision making process (Chapter 14).

Demographics: The composition of a certain group, often including statistical information (Chapter 9).

Depth: In self-disclosure, the intimacy of information disclosed (Chapter 2).

Design: The ability to envision how an event could be staged and executed with exceptional creativity (Chapter 4).

Design thinking: An approach to innovation that is powerful, effective, and broadly accessible, that can be integrated into all aspects of business and society, and that individuals and teams can use to generate breakthrough ideas (Chapter 4).

Detail-oriented: The ability to see the big picture and also have an eye for the particulars (Chapter 4).

Dialogue: The meaning made through words that implies more than a simple back-and-forth of messages in interaction; it points to a particular process and quality of communication in which the participants 'meet,' which allows for changing and being changed (Chapter 1).

Direct costs: Expenses incurred because of a consequence of producing a good or service and are not related to overhead or indirect costs (Chapter 7).

Discriminative listening: A type of listening that occurs when you distinguish among various sounds (Chapter 2).

Diversity: The ability to engage in various activities and work with various people (Chapter 1).

Direct Marketing Organization (DMO): A bureau or group whose job is to promote a specific locale as an interesting and viable place to visit

Drawing power: the distance people will travel to experience an event (Chapter 11)

Duration: In self-disclosure, the time spent by an individual describing each item of information (Chapter 2).

E

Emblems: Movements that have meaning and can be understood by all members of a particular culture or subculture (Chapter 3).

Emotional expressions (or affect displays): Involuntary signals that provide important information to others (Chapter 3).

Emotional Intelligence (EQ): The ability to be judicious about emotions, to have the ability to rely on one's own emotional resources during periods of stress, change, conflict, and even chaos, and to be able to create an emotional climate that encourages innovation, develops sustainable relationships, and increases performance (Chapter 14).

Empathic listening: A type of listening that demands looking at all conversations from the client's point of view, and which occurs when the goal is to provide emotional support for someone else (Chapter 2).

Empathy: The ability to understand others (Chapter 5).

Encoding: The cognitive process of creating a message (Chapter 1).

Entity attribution: The belief that behavior is derived from a task or situation (Chapter 2).

Entrepreneur: A person who starts a new business (Chapter 15).

Entrepreneurship: The act of starting and managing one's own business (Chapter 15).

Ethical issues: Problems that center on behaviors involving a conscious choice that can be judged by standards of right and wrong (Chapter 8).

Event planners: Individuals who work through all the details of an event (Chapter 1).

Event planning: A communicative process in which a person plans and coordinates the celebration of an occasion or forms a gathering at a specific location where attendees can learn, socialize, conduct business, and/or serve the community (Chapter 1).

Event schema: The picture that people register of how different social settings might play out (Chapter 10).

Event sponsorship: an investment, in cash or in kind, in return for access to exploitable business potential associated with an event or highly publicized entity (Chapter 11)

Event tourism: an all-inclusive approach to creating, planning, marketing and executing special events (Chapter 11).

Events: Common occurrences within various cultures and societies generating revenue and jobs in the economy (Chapter 1).

Ever-Ready Expressors: In facial displays, those who display the same emotion as a first response to various situations (Chapter 3).

Exploratory phase: A time of brainstorming and researching to ascertain if starting a business is the right career path (Chapter 15).

Exploratory affective stage: In Social Penetration Theory, an intermediate level in which people reveal more information around their preferences (Chapter 2).

External noise: Stimuli in the environment that distract you from the message (Chapter 1).

F

Fanfare: Any sense elements that play a part in the arrival atmosphere of an event (Chapter 10).

Feasibility study: a research project that examines new or untested ideas through best practices in research, design, budget planning, coordination, and evaluation (Chapter 5).

Feedback loop: A response to the message sent (Chapter 1).

Financial flexibility: The ability to move and shift numbers depending on the budget (Chapter 4).

Fixed costs: Costs that do not rely on the number of people attending an event (Chapter 7).

Flexibility: Willingness to yield in a certain circumstance; adaptability (Chapter 4).

Flooded-Affect Expressors: In facial displays, those who frequently show more than one emotion (Chapter 3).

Focus group : A small group of carefully chosen volunteers who participate in discussions for research about a new product (Chapter 5).

Food decisions: Choices that require event planners to examine the budget, catering, location, kitchen space, equipment, culture, presentation, and timing (Chapter 10).

Force Majeure: An occurrence beyond the control of the contractual parties that prevents one or both of them from fulfilling their obligations under the contract (Chapter 8).

Forethought: In the context of Emotional Intelligence, a means of anticipation for spontaneity (Chapter 14).

Framing: The way in which people identify with their own sets of beliefs about their own world around them (Chapter 15).

Framing [a message]: The way in which meaning is managed by actively choosing a set of words for a particular context; consists of language, thought, and forethought (Chapter 15).

Front-of-house workers: Hospitality workers who interact directly with guests on a regular basis (Chapter 5)

Frozen-Affect Expressors: In facial displays, those who constantly show one emotion even if they are not feeling that particular way (Chapter 3).

Functional flexibility: The ability to perform and move among a range of jobs (Chapter 4).

G

Gantt chart: An event management tool used to track the schedule of a project (Chapter 10).

Gatekeeper: Someone who controls access to a particular person or locale (Chapter 10).

Gen X: Those born approximately between 1965-1976 (Chapter 5).

Gen Z: Those born after 1997 (Chapter 5)

Geographical flexibility: The ability to understand the increased mobility of working groups (Chapter 4).

Gift giving: The action of giving a sentiment or token that allows for recognition, gratitude, community-building, motivation, and increasing sales in today's business and personal settings (Chapter 10).

Goal-directed behavior: A way of acting that is motivated by the desire to achieve an outcome (Chapter 4).

Gobos: Plates used to customize names or patterns through lighting on a wall or floor (Chapter 9).

Green economy: A system that tries to reduce environmental risks and that promotes sustainable development without harming the environment (Chapter 5).

Green hat: In the context of the Six Thinking Hats, the one who focuses on creativity by exploring alternatives or imagining new possibilities for ideas (Chapter 6).

Gross profits: Revenue minus the cost of goods sold, shown on the income statement (Chapter 7).

H

Haptics: The study of touch (Chapter 3).

Hallmark Events: major one-time or recurring events developed to enhance a tourist destination, and whose uniqueness attracts attention (Chapter 11).

Hashtag: The pound sign followed by a word or phrase, used on social media to identify messages on a specific topic (Chapter 13).

Hazardous Analysis Critical Control Point (HACCP): A food safety plan that addresses issues of contamination and risk (Chapter 10).

Hearing: A basic sensory system through which vibrations in the air are translated to sounds (Chapter 2).

HEART: Hear, Empathize, Apologize, Respond, Take Action and Follow Up (Chapter 5).

Hidden costs: Costs that occur every day in organizations and are usually expenses that do not normally include the purchase price of goods (Chapter 7).

High-context cultures: Cultures in which the message is communicated indirectly (Chapter 3).

Honesty: In self-disclosure, the truth of those revelations (Chapter 2)

Hospitality: The inherent value of making guests feel welcome away from their homes (Chapter 5 and 10).

Hybrid entry model: A career plan in which one remains in a salaried job in an existing organization while beginning a new venture part-time (Chapter 15).

I

Illustrators: Movements that help explain speech, usually augmenting it, but sometimes contradicting it (Chapter 3).

Immediacy: The perceptual availability of one person to another (Chapter 9).

Inclusion: In the context of dialogue, the attempt to experience another perspective and see the other's perspective as an important part of the conversation (Chapter 1).

Indemnification clause (Hold Harmless): A clause written into a contract that secures someone against any legal responsibility for their actions (Chapter 8).

Indirect costs: Expenses that pertain to the company doing business and not to the product that one is selling or producing (Chapter 7).

Influencers: Those individuals who have power over potential customers through postings on social media (Chapter 15)

Integrated Marketing Communication (IMC): A communication practice that connects public relations, marketing, promotions, advertising, and social media through the communication process whereby the essential characteristic is creating one consistent strategic message that reaches a target audience (Chapter 13).

Intelligence Quotient (IQ): A value that measures someone's ability to perceive and process information meaningfully (Chapter 14).

Intelligent lights: Lights at an event that can automatically change positions, colors and patterns (Chapter 9).

Intent: In self-disclosure, the willingness of the individual to disclose (Chapter 2)

Intercultural communication: Examines communication across cultures (Chapter 1)

Internal noise: Thoughts and feelings inside your head that distract you from the message (Chapter 1).

Interpersonal communication: Communication that takes place between a few—typically two—people (Chapters 1 and 2).

Interpersonal evaluation: The process by which others evaluate your ideas and you evaluate the ideas of others (Chapter 6).

Intrapersonal communication: A basic form of communication within oneself (Chapter 1).

Intrapersonal evaluation: The process by which you evaluate your own ideas (Chapter 6).

Intuition: The ability to understand something immediately, without the need for conscious reasoning (Chapter 4).

Invitations: Written or verbal requests that set the tone of an event before it even begins, and ensure that guests are properly notified so they can build the event into their schedules in order to attend (Chapter 10).

K

Kinesics: The study of body language as it relates to communication and is patterned by both social and cultural experiences (Chapter 3).

L

Laissez-faire leadership: A type of leadership style in which there is a hands-off approach to guiding people (Chapter 14).

Language: In connection with Emotional Intelligence, the set of skills that help people categorize and classify thoughts (Chapter 14).

Leadership: The capacity to influence others by unleashing their power and potential to impact the greater good. (Chapter 14).

LEARN: Listen, Empathize, Apologize, Respond, Notify (Chapter 5)

Listening: The process of receiving, constructing meaning from and responding to spoken and/or nonverbal messages (Chapter 5).

Logo: A recognizable symbol that represents a company's image (Chapter 15).

Low-context culture: A culture's communication in which the message is directly stated, often through facts and personal reports (Chapter 3).

M

Maker space: a designated location where creativity can occur (Chapter 6)

Manipulators: Movements whereby one part of the body or face manipulates in some fashion—stroking, pressing, scratching, licking, biting, sucking, etc.—another part of the body or face (Chapter 3).

Marketing: The science of combining the understanding of human psychology with deliberate and scientific analysis to promote or sell products or services (Chapter 13).

Mass communication: Communication with a geographically dispersed, large, diverse audience (Chapter 1).

Mega events: Events that yield extraordinarily high levels of tourism, media coverage, prestige, or economic impact (Chapter 11).

Mentor: An experienced or trusted advisor (Chapter 15).

Menu: A meal format that patterns dishes and items in time and space (Chapter 10).

Message: Verbal and nonverbal utterances used to convey meaning (Chapter 1).

Millennials (Gen Y): Those born approximately between 1977 and 1997 (Chapter 5).

Mind map: A trademarked system of representing ideas, with related concepts arranged around a core concept (Chapter 4).

Mindfulness: A mental state in which one waits to form judgments until information is completely collected (Chapter 2).

Mission statement: A formal summary of the goals and values of a company (Chapter 15).

Monochronic time: Time that is viewed as linear and is tangible, compartmentalized, and planned (Chapter 3).

Motivation: The reason a person acts or behaves in a particular way (Chapter 14).

Multitasking: The act of performing several tasks simultaneously (Chapter 4).

N

Narratives: Socially agreed-upon ideas that are accepted as true or representative of the way the world and human life is constituted (Chapter 8).

Negotiation: Communication process in which people work to reach an agreement (Chapter 8).

Negotiation storyboard: A script that allows the event planner to address the kinds of challenges that may arise during a negotiation (Chapter 8).

Net profits: The actual profit after working expenses not included in the calculation of gross profit have been paid (Chapter 7).

Networking: The process of developing and nurturing relationships with professional organizations, local chambers of commerce, educational institutions and service organizations, and practicing professionals (Chapter 15).

NICE: An acronym for *Neutralize* emotions, *Identify* the type, *Control* the encounter, and *Explore* options when dealing with people who enjoy creating conflict situations (Chapter 12).

Noble self: The concept that focuses on individuals who are not sensitive to others and context (Chapter 2).

Noise: Anything that interferes with a message (Chapter 1).

Non-compete clause: A term used in contract law by which an employee agrees not to start a similar profession or trade in competition against another (usually the employer) (Chapter 15).

Nonsocial perception (or "thing perception"): Awareness of inanimate objects (Chapter 2).

Nonverbal communication: All communication interactions that transcend the written and/or spoken word (Chapter 3).

Numerical flexibility: The ability to find the number of people needed to complete a task (Chapter 4).

O

Oculesics: The study of eye contact and pupil dilation in nonverbal communication (Chapter 3).

Olfactics: The study of communication through the sense of smell (Chapter 3).

Organization: A systematized approach to a task that focuses on process (Chapter 4).

Organizational communication: The study of communicative understandings of business processes and practices (Chapter 1).

Organizational crisis: A specific, unexpected, and non-routine event or series of events that create high levels of uncertainty and threaten or are perceived to threaten an Organization's high-priority goals (Chapter 12).

Organizational flexibility: The ability to allow for changes in the structure and system of how a company operates (Chapter 4).

Orientation stage: In Social Penetration Theory, the peripheral layer where information might be described as small talk (Chapter 2).

P

Paralanguage: The nonverbal vocal qualities and sounds that are produced by the throat, nasal cavity, tongue, lips, mouth, and jaw (Chapter 3).

Passion: A fervor or enthusiasm for an idea or plan (Chapter 4).

People-oriented listeners: Those who focus on the relationship during listening (Chapter 2).

Perceiving: In the context of Emotional Intelligence, the ability to be able to recognize and label the emotions that you or someone else is experiencing (Chapter 14).

Perception: Ways in which people come to understand the world around them (Chapter 2).

Perseverance: Persistence or determination to accomplish a task (Chapter 14).

Person attribution: The belief that behavior is derived from one's own motives or traits (Chapter 2).

Physical appearance: The qualities that characterize someone's outward form such as build, height, weight, and clothing (Chapter 3).

Polychronic time: Time that is viewed spatially where people are more important than planning (Chapter 3).

Positioning: Not what you do to a product, but what you do to the mind of the prospect; that is, you position the product in the mind of the prospect (Chapter 13).

Preliminary budget: A financial tool composed during the initial planning stage of an event that will be emended as the project gets underway (Chapter 7).

Presentness: In the context of dialogue, giving full concentration to bringing your total and authentic self to an encounter, willing and able to learn from others without the everyday distractions that can impede a conversation (Chapter 1).

Press kit: Items produced and used for a variety of public relations purposes, including items such as a press release, backgrounder, and brochure (Chapter 13).

Problem-focused approach: A rational way of responding to a challenge that involves taking control, seeking information, and evaluating choices (Chapter 4).

Program: A printed guide that lists the order of the events, through which guests can receive helpful information, as well as background notes (Chapter 10).

Proxemics: The study of messages sent in a spatial environment (Chapter 3).

Public communication: Communication that shapes civic engagement with others (Chapter 1).

Public Relations (PR): A strategic communication process that builds mutually beneficial relationships between organizations and their publics (Chapter 13).

R

RACE: A technique involving research, action, communication, evaluation used to understand the process of public relations (Chapter 13).

Receiver: The recipient of the message (Chapter 1).

Red hat: In the context of the Six Thinking Hats, the one who examines emotions and feelings; this person's goal is to figure out how people are feeling about a particular situation (Chapter 6).

Reflection: A method that allows people to turn their experiences into learning opportunities by thinking about what occurred (Chapter 10).

Registration: The first point of contact with your attendees and can serve as the command center for your event (Chapter 10).

Regulating: In the context of Emotional Intelligence, the ability to offer others evaluation and accept critique in a suitable way (Chapter 14).

Regulators: Actions that maintain and regulate the back-and-forth nature of speaking and listening between two or more interactants (Chapter 3).

Responsibility: The ability to perform a duty that is demanded of someone (Chapter 4).

Return on Investment (ROI): The benefit an investor derives that is the result of an investment of a resource (Chapter 7, 13).

Revealers: In facial displays, those who show all expressions with the face (Chapter 3).

Revenue: The amount of money that results from selling products or services to customers (Chapter 7).

Rewards: In Social Exchange Theory, the positive aspects of a relationship (Chapter 7).

Rhetorical reflection: Analysis that focuses on those constantly willing to alter their personal goals in order to adapt to others (Chapter 2).

Rhetorical sensitivity: The ways in which individuals effectively analyze interpersonal situations (Chapter 2).

Rider: A condition added to a contract that has already been signed (Chapter 8).

R.S.V.P.: From the French, *Répondez s'il vous plaît* (Respond if you please), this request allows the event planner to get an accurate representation of attendees (Chapter 10).

S

Scenario building: A practice that involves envisioning a future situation and then assessing its organizational repercussions based on the analysis of historic trends (Chapter 5).

Script: A coherent sequence of events expected by individuals, involving them either as a participant or as an observer (Chapter 10).

Self-confidence: The ability to believe that you can accomplish a specific series of tasks successfully (Chapter 14).

Self-control: Restraint regarding one's own actions in order to achieve a goal (Chapter 4).

Self-disclosure: Any unknown information individuals communicate verbally about themselves to others (Chapter 2).

Self-efficacy: The idea that people believe in their own ability to accomplish something (Chapters 4 and 14).

Semantic noise: Meaning that is derived from certain symbols and behaviors that distract you from the message (Chapter 1).

Sender: The person who creates the message (Chapter 1).

Seven Deadly Sins: Service errors including apathy, brush-off, coldness, condescension, robotics, rule book, and runaround (Chapter 5).

Service: The action of handling a welcoming task (Chapter 5).

Set the scene: The act of making a space ready for an event (Chapter 9).

Sharing economy: An economic system in which individuals share services, sometimes free, usually through the Internet (Chapter 5).

Six Thinking Hats: The process of stimulating creativity by examining the aspects of emotion, logic, wishful thinking, and both the negative and positive consequences of making a particular decision (Chapter 6).

Small group communication: Communication with at least three people who share a common purpose or goal (Chapter 1).

SMERF: Acronym for social, military, educational, religious, and fraternal (Chapter 5)

Social competence domain: The ways in which people manage relationships (Chapter 7).

Social Exchange Theory: A theory that says social behavior is the result of an exchange in which people want to maximize benefits and minimize costs, weighing the potential benefits and risks of social relationships (Chapter 7).

Social media: Anything that is promoted digitally that informs, markets goods and Services, shares opinions, and entertains (Chapters 13 and 14).

Social penetration: A theory that describes how a person's self-disclosure moves from Superficial topics to more intimate information (Chapter 2).

Social perception (or "person perception"): An awareness that occurs when speaking of the perception of another person (Chapter 2).

Spatial context: The space that is available at an event that influences guests' perception, cognition, and emotions (Chapter 9).

Special speakers, guests or invitees: Individuals who attend functions as keynote speakers, dignitaries, community and government leaders, or honored members of families (Chapter 10).

Spirit of Mutual Equality: In the context of dialogue, treating each other as persons rather than as objects, not as things to be exploited or manipulated (Chapter 1).

Sponsor sincerity: The belief that consumers link the level of authenticity to how much the event or sponsorship benefits and supports the community (Chapter 11)

Standing room only (SRO): A reference to an event where space is at a premium but such popularity will help increase profit and make the event even more desirable (Chapter 7).

Stable stage: In Social Penetration Theory, the most personal stage of identity (Chapter 2).

S-TLC: An acronym for Stop, Think, Listen, and Communicate that is a way to deal with various conflicts (Chapter 12).

Substitute Expressors: In facial displays, those who feel an emotion but do not necessarily express that emotion to others (Chapter 3).

Supportive climate: In the context of dialogue, allowing each other to communicate with free expression, limiting prejudgment and assumptions that may cause harm to others (Chapter 1).

Sustainability: Avoiding the exhaustion of natural resources to maintain an ecological balance (Chapter 5).

SWOT analysis: A process that includes analyzing the (S) strengths, (W) weaknesses, (O) opportunities, and (T) threats with the client as a starting point for the development of a marketing plan (Chapter 13).

T

Temporal flexibility: The ability to analyze the time patterns of when things get done at work (Chapter 4).

Territoriality: The space people claim and preserve as their own (Chapter 3).

Theory X: A theory of management that examines coercion, intimidation and regulation as factors that motivate workers (Chapter 14).

Theory Y: A theory of management that examines spaces in which people want to be creative, find new and different solutions to problems, and use their imagination to help the organization (Chapter 14).

Thought: In connection with Emotional Intelligence, a reflection process that allows people to strategically create an insightful message (Chapter 14).

Thought speed: The rate at which an individual can process words during communication (Chapter 2).

Time management: The ability to create behaviors that achieve an effective use of time while performing goal-directed activities (Chapter 4).

Time-oriented listeners: Those who are concerned with efficiency and prefer information that is clear and concise (Chapter 2).

Touch point: Each contact experience a hospitality employee has with a guest (Chapter 5).

Trained incapacity: The state of affairs whereby one's own abilities can function as blindness (Chapter 1).

Trade shows: industry-driven opportunities to showcase products or to promote awareness of a business or organization (Chapter 11).

Trend analysis: A study that attempts to find patterns in data that has been collected (Chapter 5).

U

Uncertainty reduction Theory: An interpersonal communication theory that looks at initial interactions of an interpersonal nature (Chapter 2).

Understanding: In the context of Emotional Intelligence, the ability to appreciate how emotions cause you to act in a certain way (Chapter 14).

Unwitting Expressors: In facial displays, those do not realize they express emotions with the face (Chapter 3).

V

Valence: In self-disclosure, positive and/or negative statements revealed by the individual (Chapter 2)

Variable costs: Costs of those items dependent on the number of people attending an event (Chapter 7).

Vision: The ability to see what the future may hold and plan accordingly (Chapters 4 and 14).

Vision board: A tool that helps clients visually construct their ideas for an event (Chapter 6)

Vision statement: A statement that defines a picture of what an organization wants to achieve over time (Chapter 15).

Vocalizations: A subset of paralanguage that includes specific nonverbal cues in speech, made up of vocal characterizers, vocal qualifiers and vocal segregates (Chapter 3).

Voice qualities: A subset of paralanguage that includes specific nonverbal cues in speech including pitch, range, and tempo (Chapter 3).

W

WAC'em: An acronym for *What* is really bothering you? *Ask* the other person to do something or change something. *Check in* with the other person to see what he or she thinks about the changes (Chapter 12).

WAG: Acronym for "Week-at-a-glance" meetings that occur before an event (Chapter 5)

White hat: In the context of the Six Thinking Hats, the one who analyzes information, facts, and figures that are known and needed (Chapter 6).

Withholders: In facial displays, those who show very little expressiveness (Chapter 3).

Working budget: A financial tool that grows from the preliminary budget for an event and that becomes more specific and detailed as the project develops (Chapter 7).

Y

Yellow hat: In the context of the Six Thinking Hats, the one who explores the positive aspects that can encompass one's values and beliefs about the potentially strong components of a decision (Chapter 6).

Z

Zero-based budgeting: A kind of budgeting plan that begins each event with a clean slate (Chapter 7).

INDEX